⊲ **W9-COZ-520**

Taking SIDES

Clashing Views on
Controversial Issues in
World Politics

Fifth Edition

Edited, Selected, and with Introductions by

John T. Rourke
University of Connecticut

The Dushkin Publishing Group, Inc.

For my son and friend—John Michael

Photo Acknowledgments

Part 1   UNHCR/Y. Müller
Part 2   Colorado Tourism Board
Part 3   Black Star/Christopher Morris
Part 4   UNITED NATIONS/John Isaac

Cover Art Acknowledgment

Charles Vitelli

Library of Congress Cataloging-in-Publication Data

Main entry under title:
   Taking sides: clashing views on controversial issues in world politics/edited, selected, and
with introductions by John T. Rourke.—5th ed.
   Includes bibliographical references and index.
   1. World politics—1989–. I. Rourke, John T., *comp.*
      D2009.T35   909.82′9—dc20
      ISBN: 1–56134–260–2   93–34760

 Printed on Recycled Paper

The Dushkin Publishing Group, Inc.
Sluice Dock, Guilford, CT 06437

PREFACE

In the first edition of *Taking Sides*, I wrote of my belief in informed argument:

> [A] book that debates vital issues is valuable and necessary.... [It is important] to recognize that world politics is usually not a subject of absolute rights and absolute wrongs and of easy policy choices. We all have a responsibility to study the issues thoughtfully, and we should be carefull to understand all sides of the debates.

It was gratifying to discover in the success of *Taking Sides* that so many of my colleagues share this belief in the value of a debate-format text.

The format of this edition is the same as the last. There are 20 issues on a wide range of topics in international relations. Each issue has two readings: one pro and one con. Each is also accompanied by an issue *introduction*, which sets the stage for the debate, provides some background information on each author, and generally puts the issue into its political context. Each issue concludes with a *postscript* that summarizes the debate, gives the reader paths for further investigation, and suggests additional readings that might be helpful.

I have continued to emphasize issues that are currently being debated in the policy sphere, and the authors of the selections are a mix of practitioners, scholars, and noted political commentators. In order to give the reader a truly international perspective on the issues of world politics, the authors of the selections represent many nations, including Canada, China, England, Japan, Mexico, and Russia, as well as the United States.

Changes to this edition   The dynamic, constantly changing nature of the world political system and the many helpful comments from reviewers have brought about significant changes to this edition. Twelve of the 20 issues are completely new; four other issues have been recast to reflect changing emphasis. Thirty-two of the 40 readings are new, and of the 40 readings, the majority are from publications dated 1992 or later.

For this edition I have redoubled my efforts to select lively articles and pair them in such a way as to show clearly the controversies of a given issue. (See, for example, Issue 14 on the military role of the United Nations.)

A word to the instructor   An *Instructor's Manual With Test Questions* (multiple-choice and essay) is available through the publisher for instructors using *Taking Sides* in the classroom. A general guidebook, *Using Taking Sides in the Classroom*, which discusses methods and techniques for integrating the pro-con approach into any classroom setting, is also available through The Dushkin Publishing Group.

A note especially for the student reader You will find that the debates in this book are not one-sided. Each author strongly believes in his or her position. And if you read the debates without prejudging them, you will see that each author makes cogent points. An author may not be "right," but the arguments made in an essay should not be dismissed out of hand, and you should work at remaining tolerant of those who hold beliefs that are different from your own.

There is an additional consideration to keep in mind as you pursue this debate approach to world politics: To consider objectively divergent views does not mean that you have to remain forever neutral. In fact, once you are informed, you ought to form convictions. More importantly, you should try to influence international policy to conform better with your beliefs. Write letters to policymakers; donate to causes you support; work for candidates who agree with your views; join an activist organization. *Do* something, whichever side of an issue you are on!

Acknowledgments I received many helpful comments and suggestions from colleagues and readers across the United States and Canada. Their suggestions have markedly enhanced the quality of this edition of *Taking Sides*. If as you read this book you are reminded of a selection or issue that could be included in a future edition, please write to me in care of The Dushkin Publishing Group with your recommendations.

My thanks go to those who responded with suggestions for the fifth edition:

Steve Alumbrush
Avila College

Agnes Bakhshi
Richard Bland College

Blaine D. Benedict
Houghton College

Robert B. Breckinridge
Lycoming College

Roger Crownover
Madonna University

Douglas M. Dent
Madonna University

Jonathan Gordon
University of North Carolina at
  Chapel Hill

Reinhard Heinisch
Michigan State University

Ole Holsti
Duke University

Cheng Tian Kuo
University of Wisconsin–
  Milwaukee

Susan MacFarland
Wesleyan College

Nelson Madore
Thomas College

Christian Maisch
American University

Kathleen H. Manzella
Lafayette College

Elizabeth S. Rogers
Case Western Reserve University

Abdoulaye Saine
Washington State University

J. David Singer
University of Michigan

Jorge Virchez
Laurentian University

Kristine Thompson
North Dakota State University

Jutta Weldes
Kent State University

I would also like to thank the program manager for the Taking Sides series, Mimi Egan, for her help in refining this edition.

John T. Rourke
University of Connecticut

CONTENTS IN BRIEF

CONTENTS

Falk contends that it is necessary and feasible to work toward a new world order, one based on cooperation and the development of a global community. Tucker argues that the standard of *national* interest remains the most reasonable one for the formulation of foreign policy.

Belyaeva maintains that although Russia will face crises in its governance, democracy will prevail. Laqueur maintains that the democratic tradition in Russia is weak and that, amid turmoil, an authoritarian system based on nationalist populism is likely to occur.

Tonelson argues that the level of strong internationalism exhibited by the United States during the cold war period is no longer politically required, nor is it economically viable. Abrams contends that the United States can best serve its own interests and contribute to world stability by maintaining a high level of international involvement.

to a regional, even global, superpower. Kim maintains that China is a weak state that will be hard pressed to survive the multiple threats from within.

Cohen characterizes the U.S. decision to join the UN military force sent to Somalia as based on humanitarian concerns. Pilger argues that intervention in Somalia was based on political motivations and is a symptom of a new age of imperialism.

Pikcunas argues that Japan has emerged as a determined and serious adversary to the United States in the economic field. Taira says that although Japan has been thrust into a leading world role it is not likely to economically dominate the world.

Head contends that the South's continued poverty constitutes a threat to developed countries. It is, therefore, in their interests to increase their efforts to help the South. Bauer maintains that foreign aid goes to the wrong recipients and that it usually does not help, and may in fact be detrimental to, economic development.

Hartung contends that controlling the proliferation of weapons throughout
the world by restricting arms sales should be a top foreign policy priority.
McDonnell argues that selling weapons to allies enhances the security of
both the seller and the buyer and promotes economic prosperity in the seller
country.

Sheehan charges that many ecological zealots want to use central planning to
create strict environmental restrictions, which will negatively affect economic
activity, causing national prosperity and individual standards of living to be
diminished. Browder contends that concerns about the economic costs of
protecting the environment are overdrawn and that creative planning can
drastically reduce the adverse effects of environmental protection.

Wiesner et al. maintain that U.S. defense expenditures can be reduced dramatically, while still ensuring the physical safety of the United States and
protecting its vital interests. Powell argues that drastic cuts will harm national security and are unacceptable.

Boutros-Ghali contends that both the scope of the United Nation's security mission and the extent of the UN's military capabilities should be expanded significantly in the interest of world peace. Gerlach criticizes the recommendations of Boutros-Ghali. He is concerned that such expansion would lead to the United Nations imposing its "international collectivist" will on others, especially small, Third World countries.

Horowitz maintains that there are many purposes behind the feminists' efforts to restructure the military, but national security is not one of them. Tunnicliffe contends that opposition to women in combat positions is *not* based on concerns about national security; rather, it is primarily an attempt to perpetuate male political domination.

Bork contends that trying criminal suspects kidnapped from other countries does not violate the law. Binns argues that bringing suspects to the United States for trial by kidnapping them, rather than through the legal process of extradition, is bad law and worse foreign policy.

INTRODUCTION

World Politics and the Voice of Justice

John T. Rourke

Some years ago, the Rolling Stones recorded "Sympathy With the Devil." If you have never heard it, go find a copy. It is worth listening to. That theme is echoed in a wonderful essay by Marshall Berman, "Have Sympathy for the Devil" (*New American Review*, 1973). The Stones and Berman's theme was based on Johann Goethe's *Faust*. In that classic drama, the protagonist, Dr. Faust, trades his soul to gain great power. He attempts to do good, but in the end he commits evil by, in contemporary paraphrase, "doing the wrong things for the right reasons." Does that make Faust evil, the personification of the devil Mephistopheles among us? Or is the good doctor merely misguided in his effort to make the world better as he saw it and imagined it might be? The point that the Stones and Berman make is that it is important to avoid falling prey to the trap of many zealots who are so convinced of the truth of their own views that they feel righteously at liberty to condemn those who disagree with them as stupid or even diabolical.

It is to the principle of rational discourse, of tolerant debate, that this reader is dedicated. There are many issues in this volume that appropriately excite passion—for example, Issue 6 on whether or not Islamic fundamentalism represents a threat to political stability or Issue 8 on the intervention in Somalia. Few would find fault with a commitment to end starvation in Somalia. How to get to that end is another matter, however, and we should take care not to confuse disagreement on means with disagreement on ends. In other cases, the debates you will read do diverge on goals. Jerome Wiesner and two other authors argue in Issue 13 that the United States can and should reduce military expenditures by a very great amount now that the cold war is over. General Colin Powell disagrees that this can be done without endangering U.S. security. Issue 2 deals in part with how the former opponents of the former Soviet Union should establish new relations with Russia. A key issue is whether or not democracy will survive there.

As you will see, each of the authors in all the debates strongly believes in his or her position. If you read these debates with an objective attitude, you will find that each side makes cogent points. They may or may not be right, but they should not be dismissed out of hand. It is also important to repeat that the debate format does not imply that you should remain forever neutral. In fact, once you are informed, you *ought* to form convictions, and you should try to act on those convictions and try to influence international policy to conform better with your beliefs. Write letters to policymakers, donate money to causes you support, work for candidates with whom you agree, or join an activist organization.

On the subject of lethargy and evil, Ethiopia's emperor Haile Selassie (1892–1975) told the United Nations in 1963:

> Throughout history it has been the inaction of those who could have acted, the indifference of those who should have known better, the silence of the voice of justice when it mattered most that made it possible for evil to triumph.

The point is: Become Informed. Then *do* something!

APPROACHES TO STUDYING INTERNATIONAL POLITICS

As will become evident as you read this volume, there are many approaches to the study of international politics. Some political scientists and most practitioners specialize in *substantive topics,* and this reader is organized along topical lines. Part 1 (Issues 1 through 8) begins with a question about the future of the international system, currently an emphasis of many scholars. Beginning with Issue 2, the focus of Part 1 shifts to regional issues and actors. Debates here deal with Russia, the United States, Europe, Asia, Latin America, Africa, and the Middle East. Part 2 (Issues 9 through 12) focuses on international economic issues, including Japan's international economic strength, North-South development, the wisdom of the global arms trade, and the conundrum of ecologically sustainable economic development. Part 3 (Issues 13 through 16) examines issues surrounding the use of force in international relations, including whether or not countries can drastically reduce defense expenditures and remain secure, the future of the United Nations' military activities, and how women serving in combat equally with men would impact national security. Part 4 (Issues 17 through 20) examines values and the future operation of the global system. Issues here concern whether or not morality should be a centerpiece of foreign policy formation, the possibility of establishing global human rights standards, population growth, and the justness of modern war.

Political scientists also approach their subject from differing *methodological perspectives.* We will see, for example, that world politics can be studied from different *levels of analysis.* The question is: What is the basic source of the forces that shape the conduct of politics? Possible answers are world forces, the individual political processes of the specific countries, or the personal attributes of a country's leaders and decisionmakers. Various readings will illustrate all three levels.

Another way for students and practitioners of world politics to approach their subject is to focus on what is called the realist versus the idealist debate. Realists tend to assume that the world is permanently flawed and therefore advocate following policies in their country's narrow self-interests. Idealists take the approach that the world condition can be improved substantially by following policies that, at least in the short term, call for some risk or self-sacrifice. This divergence is an element of many of these debates.

DYNAMICS OF WORLD POLITICS

The action on the global stage today is also vastly different from what it was a few decades ago or even a few years ago. *Technology* is one of the causes of this change. Technology has changed communications, manufacturing, health care, and many other aspects of the human condition. Technology has also led to the creation of nuclear weapons and other highly sophisticated and expensive conventional weapons. One debate (Issue 13) is over whether or not, having created and armed ourselves with these weapons, we can and should reverse the process and disarm. Similarly, there is controversy (Issue 11) over whether or not arms-producing countries should be selling their wares to other countries. Another dynamic aspect of world politics involves the *changing axes* of the world system. For about 40 years after World War II ended in 1945, a bipolar system existed, the primary axis of which was the *East-West* conflict, which pitted the United States and its allies against the Soviet Union and its allies. Now that the Warsaw Pact has collapsed as an axis of world politics, many new questions have surfaced, such as whether or not the primary successor state to the Soviet Union, Russia, may someday once again represent a threat to European countries, as well as other countries. One standard that is being used to estimate that possibility is whether or not Russia will remain democratic (see Issue 2). Insofar as containing communism and the Soviet Union were the mainstay of U.S. post–World War II policy, the end of the Soviet threat also brings the United States to a pivotal choice about future foreign involvement. As Issue 3 explains, there is a growing tide of isolationist sentiment in the United States, but there are also those who argue that abandoning internationalism would be foolhardy.

Technological changes and the shifting axes of international politics also highlight the *increased role of economics* in world politics. Economics have always played a role, but traditionally the main focus has been on strategic-political questions—especially military power. This concern still strongly exists, but it now shares the international spotlight with economic issues.

Another change in the world system has to do with the main *international* actors. At one time, states (countries) were practically the only international actors on the world stage. Now, and increasingly so, there are other actors. Some, such as the United Nations, are global actors, and Issue 14 debates one aspect of the UN's current and future role. Other actors are regional. Issue 4 explores the future of the world's most advanced regional actor, the European Community. Then Issue 5 takes up what may become another great regional actor, the North American Free Trade Association, which would come about if a free-trade agreement between Canada, the United States, and Mexico goes through.

PERCEPTIONS VERSUS REALITY

In addition to addressing the general changes in the world system outlined above, the debates in this reader explore the controversies that exist over many of the fundamental issues that face the world.

One key to these debates is the differing *perceptions* that protagonists bring to them. There may be a reality in world politics, but very often that reality is obscured. Many observers are, for example, alarmed by the seeming rise of radical actions by Islamic fundamentalists. As Issue 6 illustrates, the image of Islamic radicalism is not a fact but a perception; perhaps correct, perhaps not. In cases such as this, though, it is often the perception, not the reality, that is most important because policy is formulated on what decisionmakers *think*, not necessarily on what *is*. Thus, perception becomes the operating guide, or *operational reality*, whether it is true or not.

Perceptions result from many factors. One factor is the information that decisionmakers receive. For a variety of reasons, the facts and analyses that are given to leaders are often inaccurate or at least represent only part of the picture. Perceptions are also formed by the value system of a decisionmaker, which is based on his or her experiences and ideology. The way in which such an individual thinks and speaks about another leader, country, or the world in general is called his or her *operational code*. Issue 3, for example, explores the United States' role in the world. How U.S. presidents and other Americans define their country's role creates an operational code governing relations. Thus far, President Bill Clinton has shown himself to have more of an internationalist operational code than the public does. Clinton, for example, wanted to launch a military intervention into Bosnia-Herzegovina to assist the Muslims who were under attack by Serbian forces there. The American public was opposed to intervention in this civil war, showing much less willingness than the president to cast their country in the role of defender of democracy, of human rights, or of what President George Bush called the "new world order," as addressed in Issue 1.

Another aspect of perception is the tendency to see oneself as peacefully motivated and one's opponent as aggressive. This can lead to perceptual distortions such as an inability to understand that your actions, perceived by you as defensive, may be perceived as a threat by your opponent and, indeed, may cause your opponent to take defensive actions that, in turn, seem aggressive to you. Issue 9, for example, focuses on relations with Japan and how Japan's recent economic rise is perceived by some as a prelude to world domination. Such perceptions could lead to economic conflict.

Perceptions, then, are crucial to understanding international politics. It is important to understand objective reality, but it is also necessary to comprehend subjective reality in order to be able to predict and analyze another country's actions.

LEVELS OF ANALYSIS

Political scientists approach the study of international politics from differing levels of analysis. The most macroscopic view is *system-level analysis*. This is a top-down approach that maintains that world factors virtually compel countries to follow certain foreign policies. Governing factors include the number of powerful actors, geographic relationships, economic needs, and technology. System analysts hold that a country's internal political system and its leaders do not have a major impact on policy. As such, political scientists who work from this perspective are interested in exploring the governing factors, how they cause policy, and how and why systems change.

After World War II's end, the world was structured as a *bipolar* system, dominated by the United States and the Soviet Union. Furthermore, each superpower was supported by a tightly organized and dependent group of allies. For a variety of reasons, including changing economics and the nuclear standoff, the bipolar system faded. Some political scientists argue that it is now being replaced by a *multipolar* system. In such a configuration, those who favor *balance-of-power* politics maintain that it is unwise to ignore power considerations. The debate in Issue 7 about the future of China as a regional, perhaps global, power affects considerations of how to deal with China over trade disputes, the suppression of democracy by China's government (symbolized by the 1989 massacre at Tiananmen Square), and many other issues.

State-level analysis is the middle, and the most common, level of analysis. Social scientists who study world politics from this perspective focus on how countries, singly or comparatively, make foreign policy. In other words, this perspective is concerned with internal political dynamics such as the roles of and interactions between the executive and legislative branches of government, the impact of bureaucracy, the role of interest groups, and the effect of public opinion. There are a number of issues in this reader that are subject to strong domestic pressure on political leaders, such as Issue 11 on international arms sales.

A third level of analysis, which is the most microscopic, is *human-level analysis*. This approach focuses, in part, on the role of individual decisionmakers. Political scientists who take this approach contend that individuals make decisions and that the nature of those decisions is determined by the decisionmakers' perceptions, predilections, and strengths and weaknesses. Human-level analysis also focuses on the nature of humans. Issue 15 about women in combat is about much more than physical and emotional suitability; it is about whether or not equal participation by women in all aspects of politics—from leading countries to shouldering guns—will have a substantial impact on the way countries and the world operate.

REALISM VERSUS IDEALISM

Realism and idealism represent another division among political scientists and practitioners in their approaches to the study and conduct of international relations. *Realists* are usually skeptical about the nature of politics and, perhaps, the nature of humankind. They believe that countries have opposing interests and that these differences can lead to conflict. They further contend that states (countries) are by definition obligated to do what is beneficial for their own citizens (national interest). The amount of power that a state has will determine how successful it is in attaining these goals. Therefore, politics is, and ought to be, a process of gaining, maintaining, and using power. Realists believe that the best way to avoid conflict is to remain powerful and to avoid pursuing goals that are beyond one's power to achieve. "Peace through strength" is a phrase that most realists would agree with.

Idealists disagree about both the nature and conduct of international relations. They tend to be more optimistic that the global community is capable of finding ways to live in harmony and that it has a sense of collective, rather than national, interest. Idealists also claim that the pursuit of a narrow national interest is shortsighted. They argue that, in the long run, countries must learn to cooperate or face the prospect of a variety of evils, including possible nuclear warfare, environmental disaster, or continuing economic hardship. Idealists argue, for example, that armaments cause world tensions, whereas realists maintain that conflict requires states to have weapons. Idealists are especially concerned with conducting current world politics on a more moral or ethical plane and with searching for alternatives to the present pursuit of nationalist interests through power politics.

Several of the issues address the realist-idealist split. For example, in Issue 17, Cyrus Vance contends that human rights represent a fundamental principle and should strongly influence policy, while George Shultz contends that morality must be balanced with other factors to determine policy. There is also an idealist-realist element to Issue 15, based on the contention by some feminists and scholars that full participation of women in the political system would promote idealist, rather than realist, policies. The debate over intervention in Somalia (Issue 8), and by extension other troubled countries and places in which modern conflicts may arise (Issue 20), also involves realist-idealist considerations.

THE POLITICAL AND ECOLOGICAL FUTURE

Future *world alternatives* are discussed in many of the issues. Issue 1, for example, debates whether or not an idealist "new world order" is a reasonable goal. The Issue 10 debate on the North providing aid to the South is not just about humanitarian impulses; it is about whether or not the world can survive and be stable economically and politically if it is divided into a minority of wealthy nations and a majority of poor countries. Another, more far-reaching, alternative, is if an international organization were to take over some (or all) of the sovereign responsibilities of national governments. To explore this alternative, Issue 14 focuses on the authority of the UN Security Council to assume supranational (above countries) power in the area of peacekeeping. Another possibility for governance falls between current countries (each governed independently) and the possibility of a single global government, represented by the United Nations. Issue 4 on the European Community debates the possibility of such governments developing.

The global future also involves the availability of natural resources, the condition of the environment, and the level of world population, which are addressed in Issues 12 and 19.

THE AXES OF WORLD DIVISION

It is a truism that the world is politically dynamic and that the nature of the political system is undergoing profound change. As noted, the once primary axis of world politics, the East-West confrontation, has broken down. Yet, Issue 2 is related to the question of whether or not, in a nonideological context, this axis might be reconstituted by an ultranationalist, hostile Russia.

In contrast to the moribund East-West axis, the *North-South axis* has increased in importance and tension. The wealthy, industrialized countries (North) are on one end, and the poor, less developed countries (LDCs, South) are at the other extreme. Economic differences and disputes are the primary dimension of this axis, in contrast to the military nature of the East-West axis. Issue 10 explores these differences and debates whether or not the North should significantly increase economic aid to the South.

Then there is the question of what, if anything, will develop to divide the countries of the North and replace the East-West axis. The possibility for tension is represented in several issues. Some believe that the remnants of the USSR, especially Russia, will one day again pose a threat to Western Europe, as noted. There are also those who argue that the European Community (Issue 4), an Asia organized and dominated by Japan (Issue 9) or China (Issue 7), and a North American region that is based on the existing United States–Canada free trade agreement and the agreements both Washington and Ottawa are negotiating with Mexico City (Issue 5) could form the basis of a new split.

INCREASED ROLE OF ECONOMICS

As the growing importance of the North-South axis indicates, economics is playing an increased role in world politics. The economic reasons behind the decline of the East-West axis is further evidence. Economics has always played a part in international relations, but the traditional focus has been on strategic-political affairs, especially questions of military power.

However, political scientists are now focusing increasingly on the international political economy, or the economic dimensions of world politics. International trade, for instance, has increased dramatically, expanding from an annual world total of $20 billion in 1933 to $3.2 trillion in 1990. The impact has been profound. The domestic economic health of most countries is heavily affected by trade and other aspects of international economics. Since World War II, there has been an emphasis on expanding free trade by decreasing tariffs and other barriers to international commerce. In recent years, however, a downturn in the economies of many of the industrialized countries has increased calls for more protectionism. This is related to the Issue 9 debate on Japan's international trading practices.

Another economic issue is whether or not the environment can withstand current and increased economic activity. For people in industrialized countries, the issue is whether they can sustain current standards of living without continuing to consume unsustainable levels of energy and other resources and while lowering levels of pollution and other forms of environmental degradation. For people in less developed countries, the issue is whether they can develop their economies and reach the standard of living enjoyed by people in wealthy countries without creating vast new drains on resources and vast new amounts of pollution. This concern is the core of the debate in Issue 12.

CONCLUSION

Having discussed many of the various dimensions and approaches to the study of world politics, it is incumbent on this editor to advise against your becoming too structured by them. Issues of focus and methodology are important both to studying international relations and to understanding how others are analyzing global conduct. However, they are also partially pedagogical. In the final analysis, world politics is a highly interrelated, perhaps seamless, subject. No one level of analysis, for instance, can fully explain the events on the world stage. Instead, using each of the levels to analyze events and trends will bring the greatest understanding.

Similarly, the realist-idealist division is less precise in practice than it may appear. As some of the debates indicate, each side often stresses its own standards of morality. Which is more moral: defeating dictatorship or sparing the sword and saving lives that will almost inevitably be lost in the dictator's overthrow? Further, realists usually do not reject moral considerations. Rather, they contend that morality is but one of the factors that a country's decisionmakers must consider. Realists are also apt to argue that standards of morality differ when dealing with a country as opposed to an individual. By the same token, most idealists do not completely ignore the often dangerous nature of the world. Nor do they argue that a country must totally sacrifice its short-term interests to promote the betterment of the current and future world. Thus, realism and idealism can be seen most accurately as the ends of a continuum—with most political scientists and practitioners falling somewhere between, rather than at, the extremes. The best advice, then, is to think broadly about international politics. The subject is very complex, and the more creative and expansive you are in selecting your foci and methodologies, the more insight you will gain. To end where we began, with Dr. Faust, I offer his last words in Goethe's drama, *"Mehr licht,"* ... More light! That is the goal of this book.

PART 1

Regional Issues and Actors

The issues in this section deal with countries that are major regional powers. In this era of interdependence among nations, it is important to understand the concerns that these issues address and the actors involved because they will shape the world and will affect the lives of all people.

- Is a "New World Order" a Realistic Possibility for International Politics?

- Will Democracy Survive in Russia?

- Should the United States Abandon Its Superpower Role?

- Will the European Community Increase Its Level of Integration?

- Will the North American Free Trade Agreement Benefit All Its Member Countries?

- Is Islamic Fundamentalism a Threat to Political Stability?

- Will China Become an Asian Superpower?

- Was Intervention in Somalia Strictly for Humanitarian Purposes?

ISSUE 1

Is a "New World Order" a Realistic Possibility for International Politics?

YES: Richard Falk, from "In Search of a New World Model," *Current History* (April 1993)

NO: Robert W. Tucker, from "Realism and the New Consensus," *The National Interest* (Winter 1992/1993)

ISSUE SUMMARY

YES: Richard Falk, a professor of political science, contends that it is both necessary and feasible to work toward establishing a new world order, one based on cooperation and the development of a global community.

NO: Social critic Richard Tucker argues that fundamental changes in the way that international relations are conducted are not likely and that the standard of *national* interest remains the most reasonable one for the formulation of foreign policy.

It is not unusual for political leaders, scholars, and pundits to witness dramatic events occurring on the global stage and proclaim, "The world is at a turning point." Such pronouncements, which have been made throughout history, are often overstatements—understandable but overdrawn reactions to the immediacy of the moment. It just may be, however, that the world is now facing what will indeed prove to be a turning point.

In actuality, most changes in direction on the global political stage occur over an extended period of time, and so-called turning points are seldom fully revealed except through the lens of history. The period from the mid-1300s through the mid-1400s is one example of a turning point. The cultural and intellectual upsurge called the Renaissance began in this period, the Protestant Reformation was launched, and the Treaty of Westphalia (1648) was signed, which marked the origins of an international political system based on sovereign national states, the system that still exists today.

Another example occurred during the period from the late 1700s through World War I. Democratic revolutions exploded onto the scene, first in the United States and then in France. Monarchism came under increasing attack around the globe, and democracy slowly spread. The colonial empires in the Americas were almost entirely eradicated. (Many people around the world still had colonial masters, but that also would eventually end.) By 1919 and the end of World War I, the great monarchical dynasties in the Austro-Hungarian and Ottoman empires, China, France, Germany, Russia, and Turkey had all fallen. Indeed the idea of empire was on its last legs.

A rough beginning date for the modern political era is the end of World War II, in 1945, although several key elements of the international political system established in earlier historical eras are still present. The sovereign national state (independent countries with a people who identify themselves politically with the state) has been the basic building block of the international system, beginning in the seventeenth century. And democratic revolt, begun in the eighteenth century, has continued to spread—a greater percentage of the world's population now lives in democracies than ever before. The collapse of the Soviet Union in December of 1991 and the subsequent independence of its 15 constituent republics marked the end of the last great multiethnic empires.

The word *global* is a good one to use in order to begin to think about what characteristic of the current era might mark it as a true turning point in the international political system. Modern mass communications and transportation have increased the pace, nature, and amount of worldwide interaction. Real-time (instantaneous) telecommunications bring fighting in Sarajevo, economic summit meetings in Tokyo, and protest demonstrations in South Africa into our living rooms. World trade has risen rapidly since World War II. Now global trade strongly affects jobs, inflation, standards of living, and other aspects of daily life in every country, even the most economically powerful ones. This reality is the basis of what is called interdependence. Many other ties now bind the world together.

Former U.S. president George Bush popularized the phrase "new world order" during the crisis surrounding the invasion of Kuwait by Iraq and the global reaction to that aggression. As Bush put it at the time, "a new world order [is] struggling to be born.... [A world] where the rule of law supplants the rule of the jungle. A world in which nations recognize the shared responsibility for freedom and justice. A world where the strong respect the rights of the weak." "Struggling to be born" is the pivotal phrase in Bush's words. Clearly, a new world order has not emerged. Many of the factors mentioned above in our discussion of global interdependence may have furthered its gestation, but it still has not come to fruition.

The essential issue is: Is achieving a new world order desirable and possible? Richard Falk, in the first selection, shows himself to be among those who believe that it is possible to achieve a new world order based on the idea of global, rather than national, self-interest, on the rule of law rather than the law of the jungle, and on cooperation rather than conflict. Such people are commonly referred to as idealists. Robert Tucker is a proponent of the school of thought often termed realism. He contends that the idea of a new world order is illusory and that a safer and wiser standard is to follow the biblical maxim about God helping those who help themselves.

3

YES

Richard Falk

IN SEARCH OF A NEW
WORLD MODEL

The new director of the Central Intelligence Agency, James Woolsey, vividly described the present historical mood during his confirmation hearings in the United States Senate: "Yes, we have slain a large dragon, but we live now in a jungle filled with a bewildering variety of poisonous snakes. And in many ways, the dragon was easier to keep track of."

The Soviet Union, of course, is the slain dragon, and what was tracked were the familiar structures of conflict associated with the long period of the cold war. In the new global setting nothing seems altogether familiar or simple. There are many smaller dangers, not just one large one. But even the smaller ones—ethnic strife in the former Soviet Union, religious fundamentalism in the Arab world, and possible nuclear proliferation in North Korea, Iran, and Pakistan—are poisonous in character, threatening to United States interests, and of an ambiguous nature. And such dangers are "small" only by comparison with the imagery of a world war between superpowers relying on huge arsenals of nuclear weapons. Within their immediate geographic scope, these post–cold war problems threaten cataclysmic results with genocidal implications (as in Bosnia and Herzegovina).

THE SHORT-LIVED "NEW WORLD ORDER"

In the months after Iraq's invasion of Kuwait on August 2, 1990, President George Bush spoke in a different vein, suggesting the likelihood of "a new world order" premised on respect for international law and made secure by an effective United Nations. These uplifting sentiments expressed in part the lingering exhilaration over the end of the cold war, a feeling that with the collapse of the Soviet challenge the world was a safer place—and could be made safer still if the challenge posed by an evil, reckless Saddam Hussein were met.

In this sense, the Persian Gulf War appeared as a watershed between past and future, a test of whether the possibilities for peace and justice in international relations that had been created by the end of the cold war could be realized and even institutionalized. It now seemed feasible to establish a

From Richard Falk, "In Search of a New World Model," *Current History*, vol. 92, no. 573 (April 1993). Copyright © 1993 by Current History, Inc. Reprinted by permission of *Current History*.

global security system of the sort envisaged by President Woodrow Wilson at the end of World War I: a system based on norms, administered by international institutions, and resting on the commitment of leading states to the maintenance of peaceful international relations. What seemed to make such a project plausible was the absence of ideological rivalry or fundamental conflict among states.

In retrospect, the Gulf War was an ambiguous interlude in a wider process of restructuring that has been going on since the cold war's end. From some viewpoints Bush's efforts to rally a response to Iraqi aggression were a brilliant success, fully consistent with optimism about the setting up of a law-based global security system in place of the war-based geopolitical system resting on military capabilities and alliance relations. Broad diplomatic support was achieved for a strong riposte by the UN, including backing from several key countries in the region. The UN Security Council was able to reach agreement on an approach that was effect and consensual, authorizing first sanctions, then military force to reverse Iraq's occupation of Kuwait.

The countries spearheading the coalition opposed to Iraq, especially the United States, ensured UN effectiveness by making available sufficient military capabilities, along with an impressive resolve to provide diplomatic leadership. Iraq was compelled to withdraw from Kuwait and even to open its borders subsequently to UN inspection teams seeking to identify and destroy any sign of weapons of mass destruction. Collective security under UN auspices had carried out its basic mission, and had done so quickly, with surprisingly little loss of life on the prevailing side. The new world order, one would have thought, had been successfully established, and one might have expected Bush to continue celebrating it as the crowning achievement of his presidency, especially in light of the approval with which Americans greeted the war's outcome....

[Among other things,] the results of the fighting... reshaped the debate over power relations after the cold war. Most conservative commentators wrote glowingly about "the unipolar moment" of indisputable American ascendancy in the field of global security, which brought both the opportunity and responsibility to spread American values far and wide while upholding United States interests....

Yet even amid the patriotic fervor there were solid reasons to doubt that the mood would last and to question the whole episode's diplomatic implications....

[One] was the apparently cynical reversal, shortly after the cease-fire, by leading United States officials who now believed it was actually beneficial to keep Saddam in place in order to ensure the unity of Iraq and the containment of Iran and Islamic fundamentalism....

Additional disenchantment arose from White House behavior. At first, Bush basked in the sunshine of popularity.... [But people soon] began to feel that George Bush was acting more like the "President of the World" than of the United States, and this despite a serious recession at home that was causing growing social distress.

Also relevant was the grim realization that Saddam Hussein was not the only poisonous snake out there. The situation in Yugoslavia was heading toward the disaster of unbounded ethnic violence, given a criminal edge by genocidal Serbian actions....

Other troubling developments helped create a growing impression of disorder in the post–cold war world, and even a certain nostalgia for the order imposed on international relations by the all-encompassing superpower rivalry. Several former Soviet republics were already in the throes of large-scale civil strife.... There were humanitarian emergencies in several African countries.... The efforts to restore peace in Afghanistan and Cambodia were proving far more difficult than anticipated.... The Middle East peace process, initially treated as a diplomatic dividend of the Gulf War, seemed stalemated....

A SOUNDBITE STICKS

Given all this, it is not surprising that the White House quietly abandoned the phrase "the new world order." But, intriguingly, neither the media nor international dialogue followed suit. Frequent references to the new world order continue to be made, although the intentions behind them differ....

In the third world, because of the American authorship of the term, the new world order has been treated from the beginning as neither more nor less than a plan for Pax Americana, and this line of interpretation persists. No one in the third world seems to notice or care that United States leaders have stopped referring to the new world order.

Whether or not the words are used, the American project to control North-South relations is taken for granted. The only matters deemed worthy of consideration in third world circles are assessment of the specific effects of United States geopolitical ambitions on the various regions of the world, and analysis of whether America's financial weakness will significantly influence the country's political behavior in the years ahead, especially with respect to the interventionary diplomacy of the sort practiced during the cold war.

A more conservative line of discussion in the North, strongly represented in the mainstream media, retains the new world order as a normative yardstick by which to measure the adequacy of foreign policy and UN activity in any given setting. For instance, in relation to the atrocities in Bosnia, editorial writers lament the impotence of the United States response by noting the White House's refusal to uphold the promise of the new world order, and so on. The hidden premise behind such editorializing is that the United States has responsibilities of global scope, and that its leadership role requires a readiness to use its military capabilities and to intervene as necessary in the internal affairs of foreign countries for a range of goals, including preventing the spread of nuclear weaponry and promoting market-friendly democracy.

In other words, by ironic circumstance, despite the abandonment of the phrase by the United States and growing despair about the incidence of disorder in the world, the search for coherence has given "the new world order" a weird, almost ghostly, afterlife that has little to do with its triumphal origins in the Iraqi desert. Thus the backdrop for inquiry into the state of the world in 1993 is this conceptual tension between relying on an optic that stresses "order" and an impressionistic sensibility that transmits the salience of "disorder" or "entropy." In this respect the transition from new world order to new world disorder has been completed in a very short time.

WHY ENTROPY?

The excitement and hopefulness of 1989 already seem part of a distant past. At the time, the collapse of the Berlin Wall and the electrifyingly rapid process of German unification that dramatized the end of the cold war were both welcome and unexpected developments of such extraordinary magnitude as to generate a tidal wave of optimism about the future of international relations. And this hopeful pattern of course extended beyond Germany. The countries of eastern Europe recovered their political independence after decades of bureaucratic grayness and cruel domestic repression—arrangements that had appeared virtually permanent given the rigidity of the cold war blocs.

This high drama of emancipation was carried to new heights the following year, as the Soviet Union itself repudiated communism and shortly thereafter collapsed. The old Soviet internal empire was superseded by 15 independent states. These new political entities were all committed in some way to achieving transition at breakneck speed to a Western-style political order and market-based economy.

During this same period, democratizing movements were challenging established authoritarian political arrangements elsewhere in the world: civilian leadership reemerged in Brazil, Argentina, and Chile; multiparty democracy was introduced in several African countries; and impressive democratic challenges were mounted in China, Thailand, Burma, Nepal, and South Korea, although these were largely unsuccessful. Then there was the startling reversal of position by the white leadership in South Africa on the core matter of race relations, including its totally unexpected readiness to abandon apartheid and agree on a transition to black majority rule in a multiracial democracy.

Democracy seemed, despite the several Asian reversals, to be sweeping across the world. It was an exhilarating time. No wonder the temptation to draw momentously optimistic conclusions proved irresistible. Neoconservative writer Francis Fukuyama rode this wave of triumphalism proudly proclaiming the "end of History," insisting that the values of market-oriented constitutionalism had decisively proved their superiority over all rival approaches to the organization of political and economic life.

How can we come to understand what went wrong? Why the poisonous snakes? One easy explanation is connected with purely structural approaches to world order that regard the cold war world as a positive arrangement of power because of its bipolarity. Thus two adversary superpowers, each capable of destroying the other in retaliation for an attack, organized much of the world into opposing alliances; a reasonable strategic balance was achieved that created a state of mutual deterrence in relation to vital interests, and had the incidental effect of containing and suppressing lesser tensions. Such a balance did not preclude tests of will at the periphery, as in the third world, producing such costly and devastating wars as those that took place in Vietnam and Afghanistan. Concentrating on relations at the core, however, the historian John Lewis Gaddis, in a description that proved influential, termed the cold war "the long peace."

When bipolarity collapsed, the discipline of the bloc system also was lost. There was no longer an enemy to serve as a focus for a unified response. Without an enemy, there is less reason to ignore other social forces. The lack of correspondence between the territorial boundaries of states and the ethnic identification of people gave rise to intense new political conflicts, especially in settings of economic disparity and ideological tension. The eruption of these conflicts in areas long subject to Communist domination partly expressed the fury of impoverished peoples who had been denied the opportunity to act politically. In effect, the disorder manifest in the 1990s was earlier disguised by the repressive discipline of bipolarity and the related worry that instabilities in either bloc could spin out of control, leading to the worst-nightmare scenario—a nuclear war between the superpowers.

A complementary account of global disorder revolves around a critique of the initial triumphalism after the fall of communism. In reality, the defeat neither validated the claims of capitalism nor amounted to a health certificate for the West. True, the bankruptcy of Soviet-style socialist governance was revealed, but moving from its failed legacy to an alternative political and economic order was far more difficult than was at first appreciated. Also, the generalized suppression of the Soviet era had had the unappreciated benefit of sparing Europe and Asia the torment of unresolved ethnic rivalries. The breakdown of repressive authority brought these back to the surface of political relations, and the result was chaos.

The ideological point is more subtle and complex. It is now obvious that liberation from Communist repression does not lead easily to the sort of moderate and affluent political economies that exist in western Europe and North America. Whether such a goal is even partially attainable remains open to question. If no new and more preferable system emerges in formerly Communist countries, the appeal of new extremisms is almost certain to grow.

Beyond this, the internal realities of capitalist countries are producing some disturbing problems. A prolonged and deep economic recession has driven up chronic unemployment in affluent countries, exacerbating, for example, the scandal of homelessness in the United States. The globalization of the world economy, with its accompanying new divisions of labor and capital, continues to marginalize certain regions and industrial sectors, with little hope for their recovery. Such troubles are aggravated by the demographic and environmental pressures that are adding to the plight of the poor in the North and the South.

The conflict and civil strife, as well as the economic desperation, is inducing large-scale migrations of people from the poorer nonwhite countries to richer white countries. Given the economic challenges already confronting these societies, economic and racist resistance is growing with respect to foreigners and refugees. Indigenous political patterns are also discouraging, especially the spread of fundamentalist politics in Africa and Asia. The rise of Islamic and Hindu fundamentalism is in part a symptom of the failure of secularist politics to solve the basic problems of poverty in the third world while at the same time relinquishing cultural identity in the face of westernizing influences.

It is obvious, then, that the ending of the cold war gave political space to long-suppressed tensions and also coincided with frustrations in the third world related to a successful development process. Of course, overcoming the sterility and militarism of the cold war era remains beneficial in many respects, including the elimination of any threat of World War III. However, the post–cold war challenges are in certain respects more fundamental and pervasive, making it increasingly accurate to conceive of the new world order as the new world disorder.

RECOVERING HOPE BETWEEN THE EXTREMES

It is not desirable to adopt either the early post–cold war overoptimism or the more recent dark pessimism. Additional developments offer solid ground for constructive action, and even hope, although history shows there are no guarantees for happy endings.

Most interpretations of the end of the cold war and the widespread disorder that has ensued ignore the relevance of globalizing tendencies in international life. Increasingly, matters of economic and environmental policy raise challenges that are global in scope, or at least regional. The world is now linked in a manner that enables global communication, whether the concern is the news or popular culture. Market forces are also unifying the globe, embodied in the franchise outlets that range from the McDonald's arch to the Mickey Mouse T-shirt. Democratic social forces are also increasingly organized on a transnational basis.

The hundreds of grass-roots environmental groups that took part in the counter-conferences held during the 1992 "Earth Summit" in Rio de Janeiro attest to the growth of an environmentalism motivated by a human or global identity. This extension of an identity beyond traditional categories of nation, race, class, gender is even more evident in the context of human rights, underpinned by citizens associations with a transnational mandate. Amnesty International, the various Human Rights Watch groups, and the Helsinki Citizens Assembly are characteristic, each notable for concerns that are much wider than the boundaries on maps or the geopolitical cleavages between states.

Reinforcing these trends are the increasing destructiveness of large-scale war and the related danger of widely dispersed weapons of mass destruction and missile technology. The Gulf War was in part fought to deprive Iraq of nuclear weapons. Pressures are currently being brought to bear on North Korea, and Iran and Pakistan. The global reach and destructive magnitude of modern weaponry make it increasingly anachronistic to conceive of international security by reference to the sovereign rights of territorial states.

These various factors suggest that our conceptions of world order, whether new or old, are caught up in an unproductive either/or between the geopolitics of the cold war and the hyper-nationalism of the 1990s. Neither of these works from the perspective of the well-being of the peoples of the world, and both are oblivious to the two sets of globalizing tendencies—from above as conditioned by market forces in collaboration with leading states, or from below in the form of transnational, grass-roots democratic forces. This interpretation suggests that a geopolitically driven type of world order characteristic of the cold war is militarist and suppressive, whereas an ethnically and nationality driven world order, as is currently manifest, is fraught with extreme violence and anarchy.

At the same time, a market-driven alternative, as represented by the effort to constitute free trade regimes in Europe and North America, will accentuate the gaps between North and South and neglect the plight of the disadvantaged everywhere. Globalization-from-above, by way of market and state forces, is also antidemocratic in operation and spirit. However, if balanced by globlization-from-below—that is, by democratic social forces gradually organized in the shape of transnational networks that together comprise what might be described as an emergent "global civil society," the conditions exist for a future world order that benefits all the world's peoples.

The benefits can be assessed by looking at the promotion of human rights; the protection of the environment; the avoidance of warfare, militarism, and arms races; the strengthening of international institutions; the development of effective transnational democracy, including holding political leaders accountable and enabling participation on behalf of global civil society; and the muting of hyper-nationalism and religious fundamentalism through the wider distribution of political authority, especially through regional economic and political initiatives.

World order as traditionally conceived in terms of territorial states, their conflict patterns, and their particular internal tensions has reached a historical dead end of dangerous and tragic proportions. Only by conceiving of world order in its global dimension can we find grounds for hope and fruitful directions for struggle and effort. This is not a call for globalism as such. On the contrary. Another negative scenario for the future arises from the prospects for globalization-from-above: a world order shaped to suit the priorities of markets and finance capital, weighed down by antidemocratic manipulations, and tied to an antienvironmental endorsement of a consumerist ethos of human fulfillment.

But there is hope and political space for creative initiative. The endorsement of human rights and constitutionalism establishes a foundation on which globalization-from-below can evolve to balance and neutralize the negative features of globalization-from-above. It is from this interactive play of opposing forces that one can envision a new world order that serves the human interest, and yet is rooted in the realities of political trends. To envisage a future world order entirely shaped by transnational democratic forces would be naive and utopian. To conceive of a creative tension emerging out of various beneficial and detrimental globalizing tendencies seems sensible, although the outcome is by no means certain to be positive.

NO

Robert W. Tucker

REALISM AND THE NEW CONSENSUS

Political realism has seldom found much favor in American thinking on foreign policy. Historians may remind us that the Founding Fathers thought and acted in terms of interest and power, that it was this country's first president who cautioned that, "No nation is to be trusted farther than it is bound by its interests"—a statement that presumably applied to the new American nation as much as to others—and that Washington's Farewell Address, so long the nation's sacred text on foreign policy, was cast in classic realist terms.

Yet the realism that undoubtedly characterized so much of early American thinking about foreign policy was not unalloyed. There was from the outset another outlook that vied with realism, that contended the American nation stood for something new under the sun, and that saw our destiny as a nation to lead the world from an old and discredited international system to a new order of things. The principles and policies of republican government were considered to be the very antithesis of the principles and policies that marked the monarchies of Europe.

The logic of reason of state was the logic of monarchies, not of republics. It was the logic of those who found in war the principal outlet for their passions and energies, and who made the fundamental rule of governments the principle of extending their territories. "Why are not republics plunged into war," Thomas Paine had asked, "but because the nature of their government does not admit of an interest distinct from that of the nation?" Paine's answer might just as well have been given by Thomas Jefferson and by the party of Jefferson, the Republicans.

The view that republics were naturally peaceful, monarchies naturally aggressive, was rejected by Jefferson's great adversary, Alexander Hamilton. That the "genius of republics is pacific" seemed no more plausible to Hamilton than the equation of peace with commerce. "The causes of hostility among nations are innumerable," he argued in *The Federalist*, and they operated independently of forms of government. War was to Hamilton an inescapable fact of political life. It was to be avoided not through the absence of preparedness but through the moderation of diplomatic ambition. In this respect as well, Hamilton was at odds with Jefferson, whose diplomacy entertained grand objectives while shrinking from the means required for realizing those objectives.

It is often said that the nation's views on foreign policy are above all an amalgam of the view of Jefferson and Hamilton. But this gives to Hamilton a greater influence than the historical record warrants. Particularly in this century, it is Jefferson—or rather Jefferson's principal successor, Woodrow Wilson—who has dominated our thinking about foreign policy. Wilson articulated, as no other president has done in this century, the nation's ideals and aspirations. Wilson is the great expositor of America's distinctive reason of state, the expansion of freedom, just as he is the fount of the reformist impulse that has marked American diplomacy. It is true that America's post–World War II foreign policy embraced Hamiltonian means, the means of the old diplomacy. The essential feature of the policy of containment was the organization of power to counter power. In the pursuit of a favorable and stable balance of power, an alliance system was created and sustained over a period of four decades. The principal means employed in waging the Cold War can scarcely be seen as a vindication of either Jefferson or Wilson.

If, however, we consider the ends for which the great contest with the Soviet Union was ostensibly waged, the paramount influence of Wilson is clear. The ends held out by the Truman Doctrine—the prospect of a world in which free peoples might work out their own destinies in their own way, of a world that would make possible the

lasting freedom and independence of all nations—were vintage Wilson. The Truman Doctrine reflected Wilson's belief that only a democratic world would be a truly peaceful world, just as it reflected Wilson's belief that a peaceful world could only be achieved and maintained through America's leadership.

The world that has emerged after the Cold War appears to many a striking vindication of Wilson's vision. The promise of a new international order—an order in which the principles of the consent of the governed, equality of right, and freedom from aggression are joined with the idea of America's leadership—has never seemed brighter. America's leadership, it is maintained, will no longer be expressed through a balance of power but through a community of power (the United Nations) whose working will result from this nation's hegemonic position in a progressively capitalist and democratic world that is no longer dominated by the prospect of war between the great powers.

It is around this vision of a new order that a foreign policy consensus is now forming. That this consensus is unreceptive to the outlook and counsel of political realism is not surprising. Experience indicates that realism is likely to be given a serious hearing in times of adversity, not of good fortune; that its persuasiveness is the result of harsh necessity, not of benign freedom. The great spokesmen of realism—from Thucydides to Max Weber—have written against the background of conflicts and disaster. In our own history, the realism of the Founding Fathers was forged in a hostile and unforgiving world. More recently, the experience of the Second World War and of the early years of the Cold War gave to realism a currency and standing that it had not enjoyed for some time.

The circumstances of the passing of the Cold War, however, are not such as to evoke a realist outlook. The task of maintaining a balance of power no longer forms the overriding imperative of American policy. Without a great power adversary, the United States is released from the necessity that was for so long the principal, if not the sole determinant of its foreign policy. For the foreseeable future, at any rate, this nation has no major military competitor; for all intents and purposes, it is freed from the requirements of the balance. At the same time, it is more than ever before the dominant military power in the world. In the reach and effectiveness of its military forces, America compares favorably with some of the greatest empires known to history. If its military power nevertheless has limits, those limits reflect domestic political constraints more than those imposed by a resistant world.

* * *

It is in—and because of—these circumstances that a new foreign policy consensus is forming today, a consensus that in time may match the vaunted Cold War consensus of a generation ago. The consensus that fell apart over Vietnam was one of ends and means. Critics eventually attacked both. America had become, the argument ran, not simply the world's policeman but a reactionary policeman. From a progressive and liberating force it had become a repressive and counter-revolutionary power. The identification of American power with reaction persisted well into the 1980s. But the collapse of the Soviet Union and its socialist satellites, and the avidity with which the developing

world has embraced liberal-capitalist principles and institutions, have dealt a fatal blow to this criticism of yesterday. The skepticism with which the purposes of American policy were once viewed by the liberal left has all but disappeared. In its place, we have a Democratic president... who has urged that America "lead a global alliance for democracy as united and steadfast as the global alliance that defeated communism."

More significant still is the emergence of a consensus over means. The great division in foreign policy since Vietnam reflected more a disagreement over the means of policy than over ends. It was the issue of force, of the interests for which and the conditions in which military power should be employed, that formed the nerve root of controversy. The major fault line of the foreign policy debates of a generation, that issue separated an interventionist Republican Party from a non-interventionist Democratic Party. The Gulf War, in all likelihood, marked its last appearance. That conflict promises to be to the divisions of the past generation what the war in Vietnam was to the early Cold War consensus. Long-standing democratic opponents of intervention learned a lesson that has since led to a striking shift in attitude toward force and its uses. The causes of this shift, domestic political expediency apart, are apparent. It was in large measure due to an appreciation that with the Soviet Union's disappearance from the international scene, intervention no longer carried the risks and costs it once did. The Gulf War appeared to provide a persuasive demonstration of this lesson. But it was also seen to demonstrate that given sufficient technological superiority in arms, intervention might be undertaken quickly and almost painlessly.

And it indicated that in a world no longer driven by superpower conflict, intervention under the leadership of the remaining superpower could be endowed with the kind of international legitimacy seldom enjoyed in the past.

Clearly, these are not the circumstances in which realism might be expected to flourish and there are a few signs that a new foreign policy consensus arising from them will be so informed. In the prevailing contemporary temper, realism cannot but seem curiously irrelevant. Realism is above all a profoundly conservative outlook, a classically conservative outlook. Its temper is skeptical both of human nature and of the possibilities of political action. Its emphasis is on the limitations attending the conduct of statecraft. Its principal prescription is prudence.

In almost any period, these elements of a realist outlook have formed at best an uneasy fit with American views on foreign policy. If there seems little fit at all today it is because the extraordinary success and good fortune that in recent years have attended our encounter with the world have not surprisingly encouraged traits long resistant to the insights of realism. A reformist tradition in foreign policy, more exuberant today than it has been in many years, can have little use for a view that is as skeptical as realism over the prospects for anything resembling fundamental change in the international system. A nation so deeply committed to the belief that it is a great power unlike other great powers in history, that its power is only exercised on behalf of justice and freedom, must find it difficult to accept the realist admonition that hegemonic states have always called forth the counterbalancing efforts of others and that, sooner or later, these

efforts may be expected in the present instance as well. A diplomacy addicted to entertaining grand ends unmatched by adequate means may be expected to give little heed to the realist counsel of prudence in circumstances where it does clearly enjoy a vast superiority in military power over all other states. Where power is seen for all practical purposes as being virtually unlimited, what need is there for the discipline of realism?

* * *

Yet it is precisely in these circumstances that realism may be most needed, for it is in these circumstances that the limitations attending all statecraft—even the statecraft of a nation as powerful as this one—will be ignored or simply rejected. The utility of the insights afforded by realism have often been exaggerated. As a general disposition toward politics— above all, international politics—realism deals with the perennial conditions that define the activity of statecraft, not with the specific conditions that confront the statesman. It does not so much tell the political actor what he can do in a concrete situation as what he can not expect to do in almost any situation. Realism warns that successful policy can no more afford to ignore the contingent than it can the invariable. Still, it cannot deduce the specific requirements of a successful policy from necessities that are independent of time and place. This is one reason why realists, although sharing common assumptions about the nature of political reality, have often had marked disagreements over policy.

That realism cannot provide a ready "policy guide" to success for the statesman is a defect only from the perspective of those who impose this unreasonable requirement. A far more serious charge, however, is the failure of realists to live up to the essential commitment of realism, in Machiavelli's words, "to go to the real truth of the matter" when the real truth is far reaching, even transforming, change in the international system. At a time when the international system appears to be undergoing such change, this failure may be critical. An unwillingness today to acknowledge that among liberal democratic states war may well become all but precluded as a means for resolving conflicts of interest or that nuclear weapons may rule out the possibility of major war among states that possess them can only serve to discredit realism. Both propositions may be true; there is increasing evidence to support the conclusion that they are true. Their truth would not invalidate realism, only a version of realism that insists on making the structure of the international system— that is, its decentralized or "anarchic" character—the overriding determinant of war and its persistence. The case for doing so, however, has never gone unchallenged. Today, it appears more questionable than ever.

Nor can realism resolve the great moral dilemmas of statecraft. To be sure, realism prescribes prudence and insists that the political actor concern himself with the likely consequences of his actions. But prudence may otherwise set little limit to self-interest. After all, if Churchill was prudent, so was Stalin. Prudence is compatible with almost any purposes that hold out the solid prospect of success. Realists nevertheless have often contended that realism enjoins reciprocity, and that it does so not only by virtue of its emphasis on prudence but because of its preoccupation with the limits of statecraft. There is surely some merit to these claims. Even so, realism, while mitigating, still does not resolve the moral dilemmas the conduct of foreign policy so often raises.

These considerations no more than make the point, which should be obvious enough, that there are limits to the utility of political realism. But if realism does not explain the whole of international politics and foreign policy it still explains a great deal. Even more, it encourages an outlook toward foreign policy that is sorely needed in a time of triumphalism and unbounded optimism. Whether it will gain the hearing it deserves, though, remains very much in doubt.

POSTSCRIPT

Is a "New World Order" a Realistic Possibility for International Politics?

Is the world truly at a turning point? That depends on all of us, singly and collectively. There are two main questions for you to ponder and decide what your preferences are. One is whether a new world order, the kind that idealists like Richard Falk envision, is desirable. There would be clear advantages to international cooperation and control in areas such as conflict deterrence and resolution, protecting the environment, and furthering human rights. Yet there would also be costs, such as decreased national sovereignty, which Robert Tucker and many other realists would be loathe to see.

Do you lean toward the idealist or the realist camp? Furthermore, if you favor basic change, what specific things would you recommend? Would you, for instance, urge the establishment of a powerful and independent United Nations army? These questions and several other realist vs. idealist debates are addressed elsewhere in this book.

The second basic question is whether there is a reasonable prospect of establishing a new world order. Richard Falk thinks so, while Robert Tucker is skeptical. The views of the two authors can be explored more fully in Richard Falk, *Explorations at the Edge of Time: The Prospects for World Order* (Temple University Press, 1992) and Robert W. Tucker and David C. Hendrickson, *The Imperial Temptation: The New World Order and America's Purpose* (Council on Foreign Relations Press, 1992). To add perspective, in this case Canadian, see the symposium issue, "Canada & the New World Order," *International Journal* (Summer 1992).

There is little doubt that the new world order has not arrived. Brutal ethnic warfare in the Balkans has been met with the most tepid of responses by the major international powers. Some observers even argue that we will some day look back with nostalgia at the cold war as a period of relative stability. For an excellent exposition of this view, written in 1989 before the post–cold war turmoil became so obvious, see John J. Mearsheimer's "Why We Will Soon Miss the Cold War," *The Atlantic Monthly* (August 1990) and "Back to the Future: Instability in Europe After the Cold War" *International Security* (Summer 1990).

Realists would tend to argue that events like the contemporary tragedy of the Balkans are evidence that the world is a dangerous place, that countries' foreign policies should continue to be guided by self-interest, and that political leaders who pursue idealistic goals risk the interests of their own people. Idealists would reply that the events in the Balkans at least captured international attention and brought diplomatic and humanitarian aid. The threat of military intervention, they would continue, gave more relief to the battered Bosnian Muslims than they would otherwise have received, particularly in an earlier, less "global" era. Thus, an idealist might conclude, the events in Bosnia represented progress. Idealists would argue at the highest level that realism is an outmoded philosophy in today's interconnected world. This view is explained in Fareed Zakaria, "Is Realism Finished?" *The National Interest* (Winter 1992/93).

To explore the idea of the world system and the momentous forces that are now buffeting it, you might wish to read such works as James N. Rosenau, *Turbulence in World Politics: A Theory of Change and Continuity* (Princeton University Press, 1992) and Seyom Brown, *New Forces, Old Forces, and the Future of World Politics* (Scott, Foresman, 1988).

ISSUE 2

Will Democracy Survive in Russia?

YES: Nina Belyaeva, from "Russian Democracy: Crisis as Progress," *The Washington Quarterly* (Spring 1993)

NO: Walter Laqueur, from "Russian Nationalism," *Foreign Affairs* (Winter 1992/1993)

ISSUE SUMMARY

YES: Nina Belyaeva, president of the Moscow-based Interlegal Research Institute and a visiting fellow at the United States Institute of Peace, maintains that although Russia will face crises in its governance, democracy will prevail in that country.

NO: Walter Laqueur, chairman of the International Research Council at the Center for Strategic and International Studies in Washington, D.C., maintains that the democratic tradition in Russia is weak and that, amid turmoil, an authoritarian system based on nationalist populism is likely to occur.

Russia has experienced two momentous revolutions during the twentieth century. The overthrow of the czar in 1917 began the first. After a brief attempt at democratic rule, Lenin's Bolshevik Communists seized power in 1918 and established a totalitarian government, naming the remade Russian empire the Union of the Soviet Socialist Republics.

The seeds of the second revolution were sown with the elevation in 1985 of reform-minded Mikhail Gorbachev to the leadership of the Soviet Communist party. His reforms, including *perestroika* (restructuring) and *glasnost* (openness, including limited democracy) unleashed strong forces within the Soviet Union.

The revolution that Gorbachev's reforms promoted—or at least contributed to—reached a crisis stage in 1991. The old-guard Communist party leaders, whose positions of power were being threatened by both *perestroika* and the demands of many of the Soviet Union's constituent republics for greater autonomy, staged a coup against Gorbachev, by then the Soviet president, on August 18.

The coup collapsed within several days, however, in part because hundreds of thousands of Soviet citizens took to the streets to rally against it. Boris Yeltsin, the president of Russia (then a Soviet republic), was the most visible symbol of democratic defiance of the old guard.

In the aftermath of the crisis, the already weak Soviet state lapsed into a terminal coma. Central authority dissipated. Real power shifted rapidly to Yeltsin's office in the Russian White House and to the other 14 republics, which moved rapidly toward independence. On December 25, 1991, the red Soviet flag, with its yellow hammer and sickle, was lowered for the last time from atop the Kremlin and the red, white, and blue Russian flag was raised in its stead.

The collapse of the Soviet Union meant the independence of 15 new countries. Of these, Russia is by far the largest, has the largest population, and is the most powerful. The retention by the Russians of all of the Soviet Union's tactical nuclear weapons and the vast majority of its strategic-range nuclear weapons makes Russia's course a matter of great concern for the world.

Having a democratic revolution and securing democracy over the long term are very different propositions, as many countries—including Russia in 1917—have discovered. Democracy does not just happen. It requires commitment by all or most of a country's people to abide by decisions made through due democratic process. It requires practice by citizens and elected officials in order to master the complex processes by which democracies are governed. It requires, some say, underlying supports such as favorable social and economic conditions.

The absence of these qualities in Russia threatens the future of democracy there. First, there is no democratic tradition in Russia. Prior to its reestablishment in 1991, Russia's only democratically elected Parliament had been overthrown by the Bolsheviks after just six weeks of existence. Second, Russia has experienced difficult times since independence. Many forces, most importantly the shift from socialism to capitalism, have created hardships. Unemployment has risen as state support for inefficient economic enterprises ended. Hyperinflation ravaged the standard of living. Crime and other social ills have skyrocketed.

Numerous political conflicts have arisen. President Yeltsin and the Russian Parliament (composed of holdover legislators from the Russian delegation to the last Supreme Soviet) continue the struggle for power. Yeltsin occasionally has threatened to rule by decree; and at times the Parliament has tried to reduce him to a figurehead.

In the following articles, Nina Belyaeva and Walter Laqueur differ over the probable course of democracy in Russia. Belyaeva does not overlook the economic, social, and political difficulties that lie ahead for Russia. It will be a hard road, she concedes. Yet she believes that Russians will successfully make the transition from a long history of czarist monarchism and communist totalitarianism to democracy. Laqueur is skeptical of Russia's democratic future. The troubles that Russia is experiencing are powerful fuel for the right, he argues, and he concludes that democracy will probably succumb to nationalist authoritarian forces.

YES

Nina Belyaeva

RUSSIAN DEMOCRACY: CRISIS AS PROGRESS

Democracy in Russia—is it possible? Is it likely? Two years ago, as the old totalitarian structures were rapidly crumbling, the answer to both questions seemed obvious. Political change in Russia was moving rapidly from pre-democratic to democratic. Today, the answers are less obvious.

Most of the analysis available to Westerners on these questions comes from two sources. One is Western Sovietologists, many of whom seem completely unshaken by their wholesale failure to anticipate Soviet collapse. The other is the old *nomenklatura* [political power holders], many of whom are to be found on the pages of Western newspapers rewriting history to serve their personal interests. The result is a tendency to misread the Russian political dynamic. Analysis proceeds at a gross level of generalization about essentially irrelevant issues—with ready reference to abstract forces of the past and future, Communists and democrats, reformers and reform opponents.

This essay offers a different perspective on events in Russia. My own points of reference should be made clear. As the founder and president of a Moscow-based research institute focusing on nongovernmental forces, including political parties and movements, I believe that too little attention has been paid to underlying political forces in Russia. Some of these are significant but not as yet well formed. Others are quite well established, with firm institutional structures and political agendas, such as the Democratic Party of Russia chaired by Nikolai Travkin. There are more than 100 parties and political movements that are monitored regularly by the independent think tanks whose work, unfortunately, is generally overlooked by foreign researchers and journalists. These forces play an important role in channeling political developments.

I also note with frustration the mistake of many commentators in trying to apply models derived from other times and places to explain events in Russia, although I certainly believe that Russian democratization can and must be seen in contemporary historical perspective. Among the most frequently used clichés are the repeated inferences that Russia has no democratic tradition or

From Nina Belyaeva, "Russian Democracy: Crisis as Progress," *The Washington Quarterly* (Spring 1993). Copyright © 1993 by The Center for Strategic and International Studies. Reprinted by permission of The MIT Press, 55 Hayward Street, Cambridge, MA 02142. Notes omitted.

experience of any kind; that the political consciousness of Russians is so underdeveloped that they can only believe in strong leaders or czars; or that social economic, and political turmoil will necessarily lead to mass riots. It is remarkable that these arguments, heard so often during the Cold War, have survived the dramatic political events of recent years.

This essay begins with a review of the political forces that led to the collapse of the Soviet Union, for it is only with a proper reading of their role that one can appreciate the forces now at work. I go on to discuss the processes of political change evident in Russia today. Essential factors in the ongoing process are identified. The critical events at the Seventh Congress of People's Deputies in early December 1992 are reviewed and interpreted. I conclude with some speculations about the future of democracy in Russia.

SETTING THE STAGE

Before attempting to understand what is happening now, it is important to put recent experience in perspective. Indeed, a faulty interpretation of events after 1985 has led to a serious misunderstanding of contemporary affairs.

Because Western scholars of totalitarianism have generally believed that such systems depend on a superior leader, Sovietologists have concentrated on the leaders of the Soviet Union. This accounts for the tendency to impute such great importance to Mikhail Gorbachev, as direct heir to the totalitarian legacy of Stalin, Khrushchev, Brezhnev, etc. But of course a totalitarian system does not need a single, specific leader. It is a system and structure in itself that, once built by authoritarians like Stalin, no

longer needs a leader. The leader is not important, it is the function that matters. It is a system of authority and the leader is simply a representative of the system. The system guides the person much more than the person guides the system. This is why the "leader"—whether Brezhnev or Gorbachev—was not empowered to undertake initiatives of his own and could work only within the limits established by the system.

This outlook provides a perspective on what happened in the Soviet Union very different from the one in vogue in the West. It points to the fact that change was not brought about by the courage or influence of any specific person but by the collapse of the regime itself. That was the inevitable result of systemic exhaustion. The collapse was not merely economic, although corruption and the inefficiency of the administrative command economy certainly played a significant role in undermining public support for the regime. The collapse was also ideological. Communist systems are very much based on faith. The spread of information through the country alerted people to alternative ways the country could be governed, and this broke their faith in the system, and accordingly their support and respect for it. Thus the regime collapsed, and with it the ideology of lies and the repressive administrative apparatus that had been created to keep the regime alive. But the country, of course, was liberated....

I am frequently struck by how many Westerners cling to an image of Gorbachev as a courageous fellow who really wanted to create a market economy and to change socialism to capitalism....

Of course, Mikhail Gorbachev opened something of a Pandora's box. By opening the window a crack to partake of the democratic wind, he hoped only to show a bit of flexibility in the old totalitarian structure, permit some freer exchange of information to win the support of the intelligentsia, and prove the Party's leading role in the democratic transition.... He and his advisers simply miscalculated. Such a process is not easily stopped—if you admit that there is corruption at top levels sooner or later someone will think to ask why the system allowed bad people to be at the top in the first place....

Demonstrations began in full swing in 1987 as the repressive apparatus was slightly relaxed.... [P]eople no longer feared the state, and the partial relaxation of the repressive apparatus allowed the people to participate in social and political activities, although not yet in the business sphere. The result was a flourishing of civil society and an explosion of voluntary movements, citizens' fronts, independent newspapers, and civic groups of all kinds. Once unleashed, this process could not be stopped or even controlled from above. It was reinforced by the parallel relaxation of economic rules and the slow appearance of non-state actors in the economy who sought both independent action and legal protection....

The first elections to the Congress of People's Deputies of the USSR in 1989 gave some expression to these competing forces although, given the numerous violations of electoral laws, the Congress was a far from representative body....

The 1990 elections to the Congress of People's Deputies of the Russian Federation reflected a quite different political environment. They took place with the very active participation of political associations and citizen voters' clubs and a developed network of social organizations that had a lot of control over who was elected and how....

The coup attempt of August 1991 and the nationalist movement to which its failure gave such a boost saw to the final destruction of the old system. When Russia assumed its independent role and the Communist party was forbidden, a new period started in which the different republics began to develop in different directions. For Russia this new period has been dominated by the interplay between the new institutions of the Russian state and the elements of civil society that had been allowed to emerge in the Gorbachev years. It is to this area that Western Sovietologists have paid too little attention and where Western theories of and strategies for democratization offer little of help to Russian democrats. Yet the sudden energy of Russian civil society and its underappreciated political role also attest to the profoundly democratic pressure it exerts on developments.

The Russian democratic movement has been constructed along the way. It began with small political clubs that grew into movements, then united into popular fronts, and then in 1990 won the elections in the union republics....

Today, the ideology of democratic transition and the social forces necessary to support such a transition are being built even as the process goes on and have their roots in social groups. No general model under which Russia might develop has been created. This is why there are so many different concepts about the means and ends of the transition process. Different social groups argue for different models—Boris Yeltsin's government, for example, has pursued shock therapy as the best means of reform. But this hardly makes it the only force in favor of reform.

Indeed, much of the debate cast as anti-reform by Western observers is really about different notions of how to chart a course through a period of transition. Many different social forces have begun to become engaged in the political process.... Some of these groups welcomed shock therapy while others rejected it outright. Can they all be dismissed as "reactionaries" and anti-reform just because they have different visions of how reform should be carried out?

POLITICAL STRUCTURES

The point of this essentially historical discourse is to underscore the primary relevance of political forces ignored by the West. What does this tell us about the future? It should direct our attention to the ways in which political structures are being refashioned to suit new forces. There are two processes at work today.

Political dismantling still continues—which is to say that the vestiges of the old system are slowly being removed. Westerners frequently fail to understand that the old system is not yet entirely gone.... The people from the Party have found their way into new executive organs, business, lobbying efforts, and interest groups. Their control, particularly at the local level throughout the provinces, remains impressive....

Some building up of political structures is accompanying the efforts to eliminate old structures and their lingering influence. But the new structures are not generally the formal state ones that are the natural focus of Western political scientists.

Increasingly, authority is defined by control of resources....

Regionalism, not federalism, is growing. Moreover, these centers of power are located around resources rather than re-public institutions. Political groups concentrate wherever there is something to sell, divide, or consume. Usually, it is the old structures, like local executive councils, wearing a new hat that end up controlling the resources.

New formal structures are being created, especially for direct presidential power. These include political appointees serving as delegates to the provinces. But these representatives of executive power compete with the system of soviets and their local executive councils, which remains in place....

Legislative power does exist in great abundance throughout Russia. The major problem is that there is more legislative power than there should be. Every local soviet makes its own legislation, not paying attention to higher authority. A war of laws has developed....

In surveying this array of political forces it is logical to wonder whether Western journalists are not in fact right about the chaos of which so many of them are so fond. How can the country continue working without distinct and clear rules? Is it at all governable? Is the crisis manageable? The answer is paradoxical: it is manageable *because* it is ungovernable. The truth of the matter is that Russia does not yet have governors who are ready to govern. As the old team departs (or changes its colors), the new team is not always sure about what it wants and is casting about for new ideas and policies. Because this new team is not yet fully capable of managing the problems of the country, the less they govern the better. This leaves political, economic, and managerial "space" for those independent entities that are struggling to survive. As these entities use their common sense to exploit bureaucratic loopholes, and as their capacity to adjust and survive improves, the power of the center in Russian politics declines. In saving themselves they are also saving the country.

Of course, the balance between executive and legislative power is the very essence of a democracy. Legislative power is inherent to democracy because it is representative power. Executive power is a threat to democracy because the president becomes strong and authoritarian and imposes presidential rule. True in theory, this observation has its specifics in Russia. Again, it relates to the genesis of these organs and the elections of the Gorbachev era.... [T]he elections of the Gorbachev era were indeed different from what went before. But they were hardly democratic, given the restrictions that were placed on democratic [processes].... The legislature [therefore] reflected instead a mix of apparatchiks, local Party members, and a few interesting newcomers whose visibility and popular support gained them the endorsement of the old regime. They all became deputies in the parliament and acquired a great deal of power through the new laws on elections and parliament under the banner of "all power to the soviets." With time, it has become clear that their primary, indeed sole, role is to blindly and automatically oppose every initiative of the executive....

Yeltsin's threats to dissolve parliament and call new elections have been met with Western concern that this would be an abuse of presidential power inconsistent with the commitment to multiparty democracy and a balance of power. Yet the existing "balance" masks a deep conflict of power that results only in paralysis. The crisis has been deepening precisely because there is no such properly defined balance. This creates a dilemma for the friends of Russian democracy: Would it be more democratic to halt reform in the name of institutional balance or to stimulate reform by dissolving the parliamentary wing? My own view is that Yeltsin would long since have dissolved the parliament had he not feared being branded a coup maker by Westerners. In my view, dissolving the parliament would help nothing. Despite the presence of so many apparatchiks and hard-liners, it is the only political structure enjoying some legitimacy and also capable of controlling Yeltsin, who clearly has an authoritarian tendency.

Attention must also be given to the role of the military in Russian politics, especially given the widespread fear of another coup against the government in Moscow. It is very unlikely that the military will walk in, take over, and establish authoritarian rule. Why? The military has never played a separate role in Russian society. It has always been an instrument of the state guided by political forces in the government, and even the recent open expressions of disgruntlement give little evidence of a new theory or concept for military intervention. Moreover, on the ideological and cultural level, the army sees its basic role as protecting the people.... Thus it is reasonable to think that the military may actually serve as a bulwark of constitutional order in the new republic....

Within Russia itself there is... a process of regionalization and a growing autonomy among the confederation's many elements. Economic forces have carried particular weight in Russia as new power centers have come into clearer focus in the grain regions of the South and in Siberia.

We do a disservice to this review of political change by focusing solely on the structures of governance. After all, democracy is about both democratic practice and democratic culture. It is fair to say that public sentiment in favor of democracy is very high. Between 1985 and 1987, the basic impulse to democracy was understood, not by researchers but by the people in the street and the majority of the population, to be freedom of expression and action. In the current political climate, after all the movements and the coup attempt and the dismantling of the old system, democracy is not being abandoned, but it is understood in a slightly different way—as freedom of choice. Yet this is being leavened by an increasing appreciation of the importance of political stability, which is seen as the very basis for democracy.

THE CRISIS OF DECEMBER 1992

The crisis of the Seventh Congress of People's Deputies in December 1992 epitomized the issues of legislative and executive power in the new Russian democracy. As before, an understanding of these events in the West has been skewed by the type of coverage provided by the media and the opinions of experts who so often miss the underlying political forces, who have seen the tip of the iceberg but not the less visible but mammoth forces at work beneath the surface. The media were full of quotes from the speeches of the various protagonists, including so-called radical democrats and the hard-line opposition, as they blamed one another for destroying the country. But this hardly helped to explain the reasons for the sudden sharpening of relations between the power structures. And it obscured the underlying social demands and political forces that gave such energy to the unfolding crisis.

Rather than review the essential factual material, the focus of this analysis is on the implications for the future of Russian democracy of the division of executive and legislative power established at the Congress on December 14....

The basic results of the deal struck at the Congress include the following:

(1) A reasonable balance of forces was formally established between the powers of the legislature and the executive. The legislature won control over the key ministries by securing the right to vote on ministerial appointments, while the president retained the right to propose all members of his cabinet and to appoint an acting prime minister where legislative support cannot be secured. Moreover,... the Supreme Soviet will no longer consider amendments to the role of the legislature that could breach the established balance between legislative, executive, and judicial powers....

(2) Legal procedures for resolving conflicts won out over "revolutionary necessity" as proclaimed by the nation's leader. Russian leaders have been in the habit of abandoning existing institutions and norms in times of decisive social transformation, while appealing directly to the people's "revolutionary consciousness" and the hope—usually realized—that visions of a bright, ideal future might generate emotional and political support in their battles with the so-called enemies of reform.... Yeltsin was unsuccessful in his effort to appeal for public support over the heads of the legislature. Why? Perhaps because many of the so-called "people's enemies" had been his partners in building the institutions of Russian governance and statehood after the collapse of the USSR....

(3) The public refused to be provoked into participating actively in the disputes of their elected leaders. There was no enthusiasm for supporting either side in the escalating conflict among the masses—no desire to return to the streets. Each side accused the other of precipitating a civil war that, despite such irresponsible provocations, never occurred....

(4) The role and authority of the Constitutional Court was clearly and finally established. The creation of the Constitutional Court came rather late in the process of institution building, when it became clear that a strengthening of checks and balances was necessary.... Thus the Court has depended for its legitimacy on both the deputies in the Congress and on society at large. One of its primary functions is to resolve conflicts as they arise between the executive and legislative powers.

Despite the absence of historical precedents in Russia, the constitutional court... has managed to take strong positions on a number of issues. It [for example] protested the presidential ban on the Communist party after the 1991 coup attempt and handled the subsequent case with thoroughness, professionalism, and without political bias....

CONCLUSION

To return to the beginning, what is the future of Russia's democratic transition? To borrow the words of Lenin about the future of Russian democracy, made famous by Russian playwright Mikhail Shatrov, the answer is both a description and an injunction: "further... further... further!"

As the December 1992 crisis revealed, the democratization process is alive and well. No one should be surprised that it also encounters crises. Democracy can only emerge and develop through a series of crises and their peaceful resolution. The major winner in the Seventh Party Congress was not... any individual or separate political force, but democracy itself.... [T]he simple fact that existing institutions and practices weathered the crisis without resort to violence creates confidence in their growing capacity and strength. The perception that they are working effectively to resolve the many conflicts of Russian society and development adds substantially to the further development of democratic structures, institutions, practices, and values....

From the perspective of late 1992, and despite the panic and handwringing everywhere to be found in the Western press, Russia shows many signs of being able to manage this transition [to democracy] thoughtfully and carefully—so far. Instead of destroying the past—a primary goal of the Bolshevik revolution—there is now a clear tendency to take the past seriously by working and learning from it, as part of a vision of the future that builds on experience.

A close examination of the facts shows little evidence that... democratic structures are absent or meaningless, or that a Russian proclivity for the "strong hand" has prevented the development of democratic traditions and legal consciousness. Social and political developments since 1985 show clearly the development of new democratic structures, although they are slow-moving, clumsy, and controversial. They also show a certain democratic political consciousness, although it is extremely diverse and fraught with divisions. They also reflect the rapid emergence of a patient political will among Russians, one that appears relatively immune to violence.

To be sure, crises remain. There are many more to come. But so far each in turn has been surmounted. Is this not in itself proof that the process of democratic development in Russia is under way?

NO

Walter Laqueur

RUSSIAN NATIONALISM

A TIME OF TROUBLES FUELS THE RIGHT

Once again Russia is entering a *smuta*, a time of troubles the outcome of which cannot be predicted. Only one thing is certain: the reappearance of a nationalist movement, one firmly believing that Russia's rightful role as a great power can only be saved by a strong authoritarian government. For many years students of Russia focused on the left; having been decisively defeated in 1917, the right no longer counted politically, and ideologically it had nothing of interest to offer. Yet today the whole spectrum of Russian politics has moved to the right and become more nationalist.

This trend is a reaction to the breakup of the Soviet Union and is bound to continue. Much nationalist sentiment could be contained or assuaged if moderation and common sense prevailed. But those attributes are always in short supply in times of crisis. Millions of Russians still reside in the former republics of the empire, and separatist groups inside Russia itself insist on autonomy and even full independence. Allowed free rein such pressures threaten the survival of the Russian republic.

Given the strongly nationalist moods that also prevail among the non-Russian republics and ethnic groups, the stage is set for collision. The age of aggressive nationalism and nationalist conflict that ended in western Europe, by and large, in 1945 has returned with a vengeance in eastern Europe and the former Soviet Union. Thus present conditions in Russia are not conducive to consolidating democratic ideas and institutions. Nationalist forces, some of the extreme right, others moderate, have a reasonable chance in the struggle for Russia's soul and political future, at least in the short run.

COMPETING IDEAS OF NATIONALISM

For all its nuances and tendencies the supreme moral authority of Russian nationalism is academician Dmitri Likhachev, the grand old man of Russian historiography and letters. Neither a politician nor head of any party, he stands to many Russians, except those of the extreme right, as the conscience

From Walter Laqueur, "Russian Nationalism," *Foreign Affairs,* vol. 72, no. 5 (Winter 1992/1993). Copyright © 1992 by The Council on Foreign Relations, Inc. Reprinted by permission of *Foreign Affairs.* Notes omitted.

of the nation. With emphasis and eloquence he has argued that true patriotism spiritually enriches the individual, as it does the nation, and that patriotism is the noblest of feelings.

Members of the educated Russian public who constitute the national liberal camp share many of Likhachev's views. As moderate nationalists they are perhaps comparable to European conservatives, with an emphasis on patriotism and in many, but not all cases, a shared religious faith. They want a free Russia (not necessarily patterned on Western democracy) and are deeply saddened by the loss of large territories populated predominantly by Russians.... [Among these] are political leaders [such as] Boris Yeltsin,... who, following the downfall of the Soviet Union, insisted with increasing frequency and intensity on Russian concerns and interests.

It is probably easiest to define the national liberals if they are compared with the radical democrats, who exist by and large in... [a] tradition... comparable to the West's liberal democrats. For radical democrats the creation of democratic institutions is paramount; the absence of such institutions was the main cause of Russia's misfortunes, and they fear that individual freedom will not be secure until democratic institutions are firmly entrenched. The radical democrats have no wish slavishly to imitate the West, but nor do they feel any urge to follow a decidedly Russian social and economic policy. They see no specific Russian tradition that could now serve as a guide for the perplexed.

Most radical democrats... regard the loss of traditional Russian territories as a misfortune but see no way to undo it, at least not in the foreseeable future. They have no agreed program for Russia's

economic system.... They strongly insist on a multiparty system and regard the extreme right (as opposed to the more moderate national liberals) as the main danger that, if in power, would lead Russia back to tyranny, war and total disaster. They love the culture of their native land;... but they are pitiless in their criticism of the dark side of Russia's past. They are open to Western influences, and their feeling of nostalgia for old Russia is not as intense as that of the national liberals.

Given Russia's past and the enormous difficulties ahead, national liberals think that an (enlightened) authoritarian regime is more or less foreordained.

They hope that religion will play a crucial role in the future. They tend to idealize pre-1917 Russia and envisage a political and social regime not altogether unlike the one prevailing then—of course cleansed of its negative features but in line with old Russian traditions. Most believe that the price that had to be paid of late for freedom was probably too high. What future is there for a Russia deprived of the Ukraine, White Russia, the Crimea and predominantly Russian northern Kazakhstan?

This is the strongest point in their thinking, and it is shared to some extent by the radical democrats. The Balkanization of the former Soviet Union is a tragedy; it will certainly make democratization infinitely more difficult....

TRAUMA OF SOVIET BREAKUP

The breakup of the Soviet Union is the central event bound to shape the course of Russian nationalism and Russian politics as far ahead as one can see.... The new Russia... has no more than half the population of the old Soviet Union, and many millions of ethnic Russians now live outside Russia; they have become ethnic minorities at the mercy of new not-so-tolerant masters....

The Russian shock...is...severe. True, the loss of empire had not come as the result of military defeat. True, some Russian nationalists had argued for a long time that their country would be better off without the Central Asian republics and perhaps also the Caucasus. Russia, they claimed, had been exploited and in some ways subverted by the non-Russian republics. Russian nationalists... had suggested well before August 1991 that Russia should take the initiative and leave the union. But imperial ambitions and feelings of historical mission were still very much present and, in any case, no one had assumed that the Slavic republics would secede.

The full extent of the trauma is realized only as time goes by. As in Germany after 1918 there was much readiness to accept all kinds of "stab in the back" theories—the disaster had been caused by Russia's sworn enemies abroad and at home. There was growing resentment particularly against the ingrates in the Baltic countries, Ukraine, Moldova but also the Caucasus, who had after all benefited to no small extent from Russian help and protection. There is growing anger about the treatment of the Russians outside Russia. Is it not the duty of the Russian government to protect Russian interests outside the borders of the old Russian Federation? Had not all self-respecting countries throughout history been ready to protect the lives and interests of fellow citizens if these had been in jeopardy?

This mood is widespread and would have been suicidal if the radical democrats and national liberals had left patriotism and the defense of national

interests to the extreme right.... [I]t would have been tantamount to surrendering the country to extremists. The great danger is that the republics that seceded might prove increasingly recalcitrant in their nationalist intoxication, unwilling to accommodate legitimate Russian interests. This in turn would make the Russians even more resentful and hostile, prompting conflicts even less amenable to solution. Appeals to reason in such circumstances are bound to fall on deaf ears, and the state is set for an outburst of the worst instincts. This was the lesson of the new order established after Versailles.

Russia, it is sometimes said, has been condemned by history and geography to be a great power. But what if the forces of cohesion should be weaker than generally believed? What if the disintegration of the Soviet Union should be followed by the disintegration of Russia and the emergence of several smaller independent or semi-independent units, such as Tatarstan, Siberia Yakutia and others? This possibility had been discussed even before the Soviet Union ceased to exist, and it certainly cannot be ruled out at the present time....

The assumption that political conditions in Russia will become normal as the result of successful economic reform cannot be taken for granted. Quick improvement in the economic situation is unlikely and, in any case, man does not live by bread alone. People need spiritual beliefs, myths and symbols, and some countries such as Russia need them more than others. Human existence is not a financial balance sheet, a series of profits, losses, allocations and budgets.

In this respect postcommunist Russia is a desert. Both communism and nationalism are adrift; this is why they may find it easy to get together on some common ground. The churches seem to have neither the message nor the apostles that could generate the energy, enthusiasm and willingness for sacrifice that will be needed in the years to come. Such a vacuum opens the door to all kinds of madness.

After the Second World War Germany and Japan succeeded in rebuilding prosperous and civilized societies.... True, their defeat had been total, which made it easier to make a new start and shed outdated beliefs. It would have been suicidal for Germans, Italians or Japanese to refuse to accept their fate; they had to accept it to survive. The Russians, on the other hand, were not defeated in war. On the contrary successive generations were educated in the belief of their invincibility, military and otherwise. In these circumstances a truly new beginning is psychologically much more difficult.

WHO BELONGS TO THE NATION?

In a time of deep crisis the negative ugly aspects of Russia's past—tyranny, darkness and servitude—tend to overpower Russia's beautiful and harmonious features....

The greatness of Russia has never been in dispute, and the greater the achievements, the greater the pain felt at the end of seventy years of ruin and destruction....

Russian nationalists of the extreme right claim that patriotism, nationalism and chauvinism are synonyms. In their hearts and politics they differentiate little between patriotism and nationalism. As they see it, nationalism is the most sacred inspiration in life; only through belonging to a nation (or a folk) does the life of the individual gain spiritual meaning; differences between nations are fundamental and commitment to one's nation transcends all other obligations.

Who belongs to the nation? Only ethnic Russians who also belong to the Orthodox Church. Catholics, Muslims, Protestants or Jews can be Russian subjects, they can be tolerated and given freedom of religious practice, they even can be given certain civic rights. But since "Holy Russia" is meaningless for them, they cannot be true Russians. Some enlightened souls on the right are willing to make concessions; certain individuals of non-Russian blood can become true Russian patriots and identify themselves thoroughly through a great effort and their willingness to sacrifice for the motherland. But these will always be a very few. Others, more extreme, will not make exceptions whatsoever: a Jew baptized is a thief pardoned, as a Russian proverb says.

This kind of argument involves the extreme right in many problems and inconsistencies for which there might be no answers. The religious test for membership in the Russian nation is senseless in the postcommunist era. According to the most favorable polls less than half the Russian population are religious believers, let alone practicing members of the Orthodox church. To replace the religious with a racial test for belonging is not feasible, partly because as a result of Nazism this kind of doctrine has become impossible to accept by all but a few sectarians. Even if it were different, racial doctrine would not be applicable in a country with so much intermingling of peoples and races....

The basic differences between liberal western and authoritarian eastern nationalism have been noted for a long time. Nationalism in the West emerged in countries that were ethnically more or less homogenous or whose borders were at least well defined; they were economically and culturally highly developed. Nationalism in eastern Europe (and in the Third World) arose—or was invented—in conditions that were altogether different; hence its anti-liberal character, the suppression of minorities, the frequent conflicts and wars with neighbors and generally destructive character. True, not all western nationalism always behaved according to these high standards. But since the bitter lessons of two world wars, western nationalism has, by and large, lost its aggressive character.

In recent years... [t]he prospect that moderate [Western] nationalism will prevail over its more nasty [Eastern] alternative [in Russia] is uncertain.

There was a time when European rightists rejected freedom, their conversion to modern democracy came only gradually. In the ninety years since it first appeared, the Russian right has not made any significant progress... toward acceptance of democracy....

It is true that as communism is bankrupt and the Soviet Union has fallen apart, a political vacuum has come into being. But it seems unlikely that it will be filled by a native Russian fascism....

[Still, t]here are certain features specific to Russia's extreme right, at least with regard to emphasis [that are akin to fascism]. This refers above all to Satanism, the Judeo-Masonic plot and xenophobia. All fascist, para- and prefascist movements believed to some extent in conspiracies; none liked Jews, freemasons and detractors of their respective history and culture. But in no other country were the ultraright patriots so hypnotized by the intrigues and other hostile actions of enemies that

were almost entirely imaginary—and in any case of no great consequence. What could have been the reason—atavistic fear, a feeling of inadequacy and inferiority vis-à-vis the diabolical enemy or perhaps a specific Russian fanaticism? But if such fanaticism had existed, it would have shown itself in other ways, which it did not: there have elsewhere been cases of cultural ultranationalism comparable to present-day Russia. But nowhere has the belief in conspiracies been so pronounced....

As far as fascism is concerned, there is truly nothing new under the sun, except perhaps the fact that in Russia it is postcommunist in character. Only the future will show what this could mean in practice—that, despite all its opposition to communism, it may inherit certain of the same essential features.

AUTHORITARIANISM PROBABLE

... It is easy to think of reasons that seem to favor the growth of some extreme nationalist movement—the feeling of humiliation following the breakup of the Soviet Union; the need to pursue an assertive policy vis-à-vis the former republics in defense of Russian interests and the presence of many millions of Russians abroad; the bad economic situation and the need to engage in unpopular reforms; the frequent impotence of the authorities in face of a breakdown of law and order; the fact that democratic institutions are not deeply rooted in Russia; the traditional psychological need for a strong hand; the old Weimar dilemma of how to run a democracy in the absence of a sufficient number of democrats; the deep divisions on the left.

All these and other circumstances seem to bear out those on Russia's extreme right who have claimed all along that time works for them....

While full-fledged fascism still seems unlikely in Russia, an authoritarian system based on nationalist populism appears probable. The blueprints for a Russian version of national socialism have existed for a considerable time. They envisage "union between labor and capital," a broad political movement or, in its absence, the security forces assuming the necessary functions of control in society. Such a regime would be a regrettable step backward in Russia's political development, but it would be wrong to classify it as fascist.

To be a good Russian, it is said, one has to cast one's eyes back to the glorious deeds of the virtuous ancestors. This is how patriotic inspiration has been provided everywhere, especially in a time of spiritual as well as political crisis. Totalitarian revolution and liberal reform have failed. Neither the international proletariat nor the fellow Slavs, and certainly not the other nations of the former Soviet Union, have shown enthusiasm to link their fate with Russia's. In these circumstances a retreat to the nation seems the logical and indeed only possible response. Other nations have reacted in a similar way in times of crisis. The Russian slogan *nashe* (ours) is an equivalent of the Irish *sinn féin* (we alone); no phrase has been dearer to the hearts of the French nationalists than *la France seule*.

The reference to the glorious deeds of virtuous ancestors, of a golden age, a paradise lost and to be regained, are of course mere myths, for there was no golden age. But myths still have their use and, if all other bonds have broken down, why disparage the appeal to nationalism in order to mobilize a people to undertake the giant efforts that will be needed to extract it from the morass and to build a new base for its existence? The temptation is great, but the doubts whether such an appeal will achieve its aim are even greater.

POSTSCRIPT

Will Democracy Survive in Russia?

The future of Russia is an important question both to Russians and to the rest of the world. The country possesses a strong nuclear arsenal, although arms-control treaties with the United States are reducing the weapons held by Russia and the other former Soviet republics (Belarus, Kazakhistan, and Ukraine) that had nuclear capabilities.

Idealistically, many Americans, Canadians, and others who live in democratic countries believe that they should help promote democracy in Russia and elsewhere. This viewpoint is argued by Larry Diamond in "Promoting Democracy," *Foreign Policy* (Summer 1992).

More pragmatically, there is a strong assumption in the West that a democratic (and capitalist) Russia is more likely to be friendly in the future than would be an autocratic Russia. U.S. president Bill Clinton has said that "democracies are our partners. They don't go to war with each other." This perspective is supported by a great deal of academic research. A recent article discussing this research is David A. Lake's, "Powerful Pacifists: Democratic States and War," *American Political Science Review* (March 1992).

Another widely held assumption, as touched on in the Introduction to this issue, is that Russia's time of turmoil—its *smuta*, Laqueur calls it, using the Russian word—threatens its democracy. This assumption has the West galvanized to offer Russia considerable foreign aid, both bilaterally (country to country) and multilaterally (through international organizations). However, the Western economies have been slumping, and that has increased domestic opposition for foreign aid programs. In the United States, President Clinton has tried to counter this sentiment with the argument that, to a degree, U.S. "security and prosperity . . . lie with Russian reform and with Russian reformers like Boris Yeltsin." In "By a Thread: A Plan for Helping Boris Yeltsin," *The New Republic* (April 5, 1993), Michael Mandelbaum, a leading academic expert on Russia and its region, recommends aid.

Since Nina Belyaeva and Walter Laqueur wrote their articles, Russia has continued to teeter between democratic consolidation and potential chaos. Ethnic tensions, within Russia and other former Soviet republics and between them, have resulted in fighting, which threatens to dissolve into anarchy. By 1993 inflation had eased somewhat from its 1992 estimate of 1,000 percent, but it was still high and dangerous. Yeltsin forced a national referendum in early 1993 that backed his economic reforms, but the lasting power of that mandate seems unlikely. In mid-1993, for example, Yeltsin substituted a new ruble for the old one; but only limited conversions from old to new were allowed, which immediately set off further unrest. Yeltsin has also demanded that the

Parliament set a date for new parliamentary elections. So far the legislature has not responded. For a sense of how the issue looks from Parliament's perspective, see *The Struggle for Russia* (Routledge, 1993) by Speaker of the Russian Parliament Ruslan Khasbulatov.

Clearly, neither Russia's socioeconomic future nor its democratic future is secure. There are, understandably, many new works being published analyzing the Russia of today and tomorrow. One of the newest is Walter C. Clemens, *Can Russia Change?* (Routledge, 1993).

ISSUE 3

Should the United States Abandon Its Superpower Role?

YES: Alan Tonelson, from "Clinton's World," *The Atlantic Monthly* (February 1993)

NO: Elliott Abrams, from "Why America Must Lead," *The National Interest* (Summer 1992)

ISSUE SUMMARY

YES: Alan Tonelson, research director of the Economic Strategy Institute in Washington, D.C., argues that the level of strong internationalism exhibited by the United States during the cold war period is no longer politically required, nor is it economically viable. These realities mean that the United States should significantly reduce its international involvements and commitments.

NO: Elliott Abrams, former assistant secretary of state for Latin America, contends that the United States, as the world's leading power, can best serve its own interests and contribute to world stability by maintaining a high level of international involvement.

Isolationism was one of the earliest and most persistent characteristics of U.S. foreign policy. In his 1796 Farewell Address, President George Washington counseled: "Our detached and distant situation invites and enables us ... to steer clear of permanent alliance with any portion of the world, ... taking care always to keep ourselves ... in a respectable defensive posture."

Washington's view played a strong role in U.S. foreign policy-making until World War II. It is not true that the country was isolationist until that point and then became internationalist. History is considerably more complex than that, and it is more accurate to say that there has always been among Americans a tension or an ambiguity about isolationism and internationalism. Even during the 1700s and 1800s the world could not be ignored, as U.S. foreign trade, sporadic clashes with other countries, and other factors occasioned U.S. international involvement. In the late 1800s and increasingly in this century, U.S. global interaction increased as trade grew in volume and importance, as U.S. military and economic power gave the country world-class strength, and as the speed of communications, transportation, and military movement shrank the world operationally.

Still, isolationism remained both a strong and respectable policy through the 1930s. World War II brought an end to that. The emergence of the United States from that conflict as the world's richest and most militarily powerful country, and the perceived global threat from communism backed by Soviet military strength, combined to thrust the United States into virtually unchallenged internationalism. The very term *isolationism* became discredited.

Isolationism did not disappear, however. Although it was a distinctly minority view, isolationism did receive public support among Americans, as surveys throughout the cold war period showed. Gallup surveys from 1945 through 1986 indicate that the percentage of Americans surveyed who said the United States should "stay out" of world affairs averaged 27 percent. Over the years, an average 7 percent had no opinion, and 66 percent favored the United States playing an "active part" in world affairs.

Now, in the early 1990s, the isolationist-internationalist debate has been rejoined. Two factors have been the main (though not only) causes for this renewed debate. One is the end of the cold war and the perceived end of the threat from the Soviet Union. The containment doctrine that countered the communist and Soviet military threat was one of the main thrusts behind U.S. internationalism. That doctrine waned after the Vietnam War, and it has fallen into seeming irrelevance with the recent collapse of the USSR. Second, U.S. economic power has been in flux, and the country is experiencing troubling economic conditions. One could debate the source and gravity of these difficulties, but no matter what the objective truth is, many Americans are convinced that huge defense budgets, gaping trade imbalances, increasing foreign ownership of U.S. economic assets, and other symptoms demonstrate that internationalism has become too expensive a policy to pursue.

In the following articles, Alan Tonelson and Elliott Abrams debate the future of U.S. international involvement. Neither they nor anyone else of serious standing argue for the extremes of isolationism or internationalism. Tonelson does not argue for complete disengagement, or for a fortress-like American stand. Indeed, he is loath to label his position as isolationist. Instead, Tonelson calls for a new, "interest-based" approach that significantly reduces U.S. international involvement. Abrams counters that American global leadership is necessary to increase the chance of a peaceful world.

YES

Alan Tonelson

CLINTON'S WORLD

Although Bill Clinton was elected president on a platform of domestic reno-
vation, he knows that he will not be able to avoid foreign-policy challenges.
To judge by his major campaign addresses on foreign policy, he is less cog-
nizant of the constraints he will face in meeting them, which are both real and
intellectual. The chief real constraint is financial; the intellectual constraints
are assumptions left over from the Cold War—encrusted ways of thinking
about the world and about U.S. power which are prevalent not only among
conservatives and Republicans but also among Democrats like him. Here-
with a primer on the realities that will shape the first post–Cold War foreign
policy.

THE FISCAL CRUNCH

For much of the post–Second World War period American leaders have strug-
gled to fund history's most sweeping foreign-policy agenda while satisfying
the American public's entirely understandable desire for more government
benefits and guarantees—just like those enjoyed in most of the advanced
industrialized countries we have defended. Complicating the challenge have
been Americans' limited appetite for higher taxes, the economy's inability to grow as fast as the popular demand for social spending, and the
fact that the costs of our foreign-policy responsibilities and consequent defense burdens have not been borne by our protectorates. Rather than cut
domestic programs or significantly reduce defense spending, American Presidents from Lyndon Johnson to George Bush simply ran enormous budget or
international-payments deficits.

   With debt repayments now exceeding our military budgets each year, it's
clear that profligacy is no longer a workable fiscal policy. The demise of the
Soviet Union may have let us off the hook by permitting us to "do more with
less," as Clinton has argued. But the new President intends to cut defense
spending by only five percent more than President Bush would have, and
thus to leave our military budget significantly higher in real terms than it
was in 1981—shortly after the Soviets invaded Afghanistan.

From Alan Tonelson, "Clinton's World," *The Atlantic Monthly*, vol. 271, no. 2 (February 1993).
Copyright © 1993 by Alan Tonelson. Reprinted by permission.

These cuts will shrink military spending as a share of gross national product down to a level (3.5 percent) not seen since before Pearl Harbor. If we could afford defense budgets that ate up eight or nine percent of GNP thirty and forty years ago, some foreign-policy mandarins wonder, why can't we afford this relatively much smaller defense burden today?

There are two reasons. First, we had an even more parsimonious welfare state then than we have now, along with a much smaller deficit. Therefore it was easier to be fiscally responsible while accommodating heavy defense spending. Of course, in terms of raw numbers, the main culprits responsible for the big deficits have been greatly expanded and underfunded domestic programs—chiefly entitlements indexed to inflation. But as Clinton recognizes, a deficit-reduction plan that zeroes in on entitlements alone is a deficit-reduction plan going nowhere.

Second, optimism about funding our international agenda seems to assume that we're already meeting our domestic needs pretty well. Yet even if entitlements could be slashed, the new President favors spending vast new sums on infrastructure and education. His plans for addressing the health-care crisis, the drug crisis, and the urban crisis will surely cost a great deal as well. And his desire to give business tax incentives to encourage productive investment (not to mention giving tax relief to the middle class) will also strain the budget—at least in the short run.

Moreover, as the outgoing budget director, Richard Darman, warned, there are literally hundreds of billions of dollars in underfunded, off-budget federal liabilities—deposit insurance, mortgages, student loans, small and minority business loans—lying in wait, in his memorable phrase, like hidden Pac-Men, ready to gobble up lines of resource dots if economic conditions stay sluggish enough long enough.

Deep cuts in U.S. defense spending alone—which would inevitably mean a very different, less grandiose foreign policy—would not solve our budget crisis. But they could help break the fundamental budgetary impasse, which is not economic but political. By supporting a defense establishment that will consume nearly one of every five tax dollars for the indefinite future, the policies that Clinton espoused during the campaign practically guarantee a further weakening of the compact that must lie at the heart of successful tax policy in any reasonably democratic system: the taxpayer will pay only if he is persuaded that most of his money will be spent in a way that benefits him.

Because the United States is so secure geopolitically, it has always been difficult for American Presidents to persuade voters to make sacrifices for national-security objectives like anti-communist containment in far-off regions. That's why Lyndon Johnson and Richard Nixon tried to fight in Vietnam on a business-as-usual basis. Now that the Cold War is over, how will American leaders justify the "shared sacrifice" that all thinking people acknowledge is necessary to solve the budget crisis—and do so, moreover, while so much of our national wealth goes to defending rich economic rivals, such as Germany and Japan, against threats that no longer exist? Without a presidential confession that Washington's priorities have long neglected domestic needs, together with energetic efforts to right the balance, voters probably won't respond.

HOW MUCH WORLD ORDER?

The demise of the Soviet Union, rising ethnic and regional conflict around the globe, and George Bush's use of the term "new world order" set off a classic modern American foreign-policy debate about which of two utopian goals we should stake our national security and prosperity on: global stability or the worldwide triumph of democracy. Bush was seen—notably by Democrats—as having surrendered to prudence, siding with stability and kowtowing to tyrants who were doomed to fall. He countered by emphasizing the strategic importance of some dictatorships and the urgent need in a nuclear world to prevent complete international chaos.

Though loath to admit it, the two sides are promoting ideas rooted in the same venerable ground of American diplomatic thinking—namely, that the nation's welfare depends critically on a benign international environment. But American history has never borne this out. We have thrived even though we have been surrounded by dictatorships for most of our national life. Today, in a world greatly shrunken by technology, the international environment arguably affects us more than ever. At the same time, this environment is just as arguably becoming less controllable.

A more orderly, more democratic world would of course be wonderful. But both goals seem fanciful. Thus we need to stop thinking of foreign-policy planning as an exercise in creating wish lists and instead focus on questions that can actually provide useful guidance for policy-makers: How much interna-

tional order and democracy do we really need? Are there some regions where we don't need much at all? What is achieving our goals worth to us in the way of defense and aid resources and human lives? What will it take in the way of economic resources to advance these goals? How are budget planners to proceed? How will we know when we have succeeded? Most important, given the difficulty of promoting peace and democratic change, and given our budgetary constraints, how can we enhance our own security and prosperity if much of the world remains turbulent and oppressed? What are our fallback positions—in other words, how can we hedge?

Nowhere is this new approach needed more than in our relations with the former Soviet Union—too big and too badly broken down to fix anytime soon with any politically realistic amount of Western aid, and still armed to the teeth with nuclear weapons. Aid programs designed to give Russian democracy "a fighting chance," in Clinton's words, implicitly admit that the situation is already hopeless. A truly responsible President would start thinking a lot more about shielding America from the worst effects of anarchy in this huge region. One way to do this would be to withdraw the vast majority of our military forces from Europe, and not leave 75,000–100,000 soldiers, as Clinton has suggested doing. If disorder in the former communist world spreads, American soldiers should be as far away as possible. Moreover, if Clinton really is worried that a nuclear conflict among the former Soviet republics will endanger America, he'll devote a much larger share of defense spending to the task of developing conventional weapons that can find and destroy weapons of mass destruction held by any untrustworthy forces before they are used. In other words, in some instances the new international realities will force us to become more, not less, interventionist.

HOW MUCH INTERDEPENDENCE?

Many foreign-policy doers and thinkers view interdependence and its close relatives cooperation and globalization as America's salvation. These conditions are supposed to make great-power conflict obsolete—much as it was supposed, by Sir Norman Angell at least, on the eve of the First World War that the dense web of commerce connecting the great European powers made peace too profitable to jeopardize, at any rate for very long. Moreover, they are supposed to be the key to solving a series of new "transnational" problems, such as drug abuse, AIDS, and environmental destruction.

The idea seems to be that once mankind understands just how widespread interdependence *et al.* have become and what their true implications are, international relations will become an essentially harmonious enterprise. Power will no longer be important, and the struggle for advantage and for relative position will end. Regarding transnational problems, all countries will recognize that they have a stake in the solutions, and will promptly identify those responses that reason says are in every country's true best interests. It's the dream world of America's early-twentieth-century Progressives and other "good government" types revived and writ large. In the realm of economics, governments and special interest will finally recognize that nation-states have become anachronisms, step out of the way, and let capital flow to wherever in the world it will reap the highest return. The resulting international division of labor, based on nothing but considerations of efficiency, will bring the greatest good for the greatest number. It is hard to find a major official American speech on foreign economic policy which fails to endorse these goals wholeheartedly.

Of course, interdependence, cooperation, and globalization are extremely important and becoming more so. But they hardly eliminate the need to think in terms of power and advantage. What the mainstream forgets is that they are inevitably complex. As long as we live in a world of multiple sovereign political units (and economic integration in Europe and elsewhere doesn't alter this reality; it simply changes the size of the units), these conditions will have structure, and particular content. And their structure and content are going to be determined by someone or something. If we assume that states will all have the same preferences as to how to solve problems, then power may indeed be unimportant. Similarly, we need not worry about power if we assume that whose preferences prevail is unimportant. But all those who assume that the different sizes, locations, strengths, cultures, and histories of states and other units will regularly produce different preferences, some of them more desirable than others, will care deeply about power. They will care because in all negotiations not refereed by a commonly accepted authority, power will decide which preferences prevail. Only an academic political scientist could seriously argue that success at international negotiations is a matter of convincing one's interlocutor that one's ideas have everyone's best interests at heart. Winners are determined not primarily by merit but by how much material wherewithal they bring to the table—the better to bribe or coerce others or to create realities that others must accommodate.

Hence the growing importance of interdependence *et al.* demands that the United States pay much more attention than it has so far to accumulating and preserving national military and economic strength. This shift, in turn, requires us to rethink our determination to put America's economic fate entirely in the hands of free-market forces, an objective that makes it all too easy to rationalize the loss of key industries and technologies to other countries. In an age of interdependence, intelligent economic nationalism—striking a balance between efficiency and self-reliance—becomes more important than ever.

THE ROMANIZATION OF AMERICAN LIFE

The very prominence of national security in American life for the past forty years has seriously warped American politics, society, and culture. During the Cold War this Romanization of American life was probably unavoidable. But we need to rethink it now that we are no longer maintaining a state of national emergency.

America's defining political system, which consists in a limited government resting on the principle of the separation of powers, was never meant to help exercise the kind of active world leadership that we have pursued since 1945. Decades of an outsized foreign policy have put it under considerable strain. That foreign policy has produced excessive secrecy in government. It has helped to imbue our leadership classes inside and outside government with a contempt for the man in the street which has been growing since the 1930s—when the public ostensibly was determined to ignore the fascist threat—and contributed to the alienation from these leaders that Americans have developed in return.

The Romanization of American life has also generated some troubling theories about America's national identity and purpose which have become all too uncontroversial. Specifically, many of us have come to believe that America will never be true to its best traditions unless it is engaged in some kind of world mission, that creating a more perfect United States is not a noble or an ambitious enough goal for a truly great people, that we will be morally and spiritually deficient unless we continue to be the kind of globe-girdling power we have been for the past half century.

One important strain of the conventional wisdom has seen the lack of connection between national-security imperatives and America's eighteenth-century political institutions as evidence that the institutions should be brought up-to-date. Yet the end of the Cold War reveals another possibility: that we should work harder to put national security in its proper place. We need, for example, to move away from viewing public opinion as an impediment to an effective foreign policy. To the contrary, public opinion in this geopolitically secure and economically strong country has been serving as a desperately needed commonsense check on the utopian security and economic designs of the foreign-policy industry. The more democratic foreign-policy decision-making in America becomes, the more effective it may well be. Consequently, the new

President should start thinking about ways to open up the process, perhaps using some variant of Ross Perot's electronic town hall to permit the public to make the kinds of foreign-policy decisions in which the national-security stakes are low but the risks to certain groups of Americans are potentially great—for example, military intervention in a strategically marginal hot spot like Bosnia.

Above all, Bill Clinton needs to understand that foreign policy is not an end in itself but a means to a highly specific end: enhancing the safety and prosperity of the American people. A domestic focus is imperative not in order to rebuild the foundation for American world leadership but to prepare America for a world that cannot be led or stabilized or organized or managed in any meaningful sense of those words.

Tying foreign-policy initiatives tightly to domestic needs will unquestionably carry risks. Third World conflicts we ignore might spread, regions in which we reduce our military presence might become less stable, opportunities to bolster international law and institutions might be lost for years or forever, and one day America might indeed rue a decision to retrench.

But the risks of continuing to neglect domestic problems or of seeking their solutions in promoting millennial global change are much greater—and they are not conjectural. Recognizing these risks is not a matter of being a declinist or a protectionist or an isolationist. It is not a matter of sticking our heads in the sand. It is not a matter of being selfish or parochial. It is a matter of drawing axiomatic distinctions—between needs and wants, between the likely and the unlikely, between present realities and future hopes. It is a matter, that is, of governing.

NO

Elliott Abrams

WHY AMERICA MUST LEAD

The struggle for mastery in Europe engaged the United States for nearly three-quarters of a century. It was a struggle that exacted enormous sacrifices. In the two world wars over half a million Americans lost their lives, and another 100,000 were killed in a global Cold War that was not always cold. The question arises: With the Cold War won, should the American definition of security now begin to contract? Are the great tasks and sacrifices of the last seventy-five years finally behind us?

The temptation to withdraw from leadership in international politics is great. A variety of sophisticated and plausible arguments is on offer to justify such a course. As the year 2000 approaches, some take a millenarian position that non-violence and democracy have already triumphed, leaving little reason for American activity. Some argue that the collapse of communism and Soviet power has eliminated any serious physical or ideological threats to American interests. Others maintain that while threats remain, a collective security system will emerge to protect us. Perhaps most important is the assertion that, however real the need for American leadership, our own social and economic weaknesses are so deep as to prevent us, now or in the near future, from continuing to carry the burdens involved.

Whether reflecting optimism about the international system or pessimism about America, these views have a common thread: they manifest a desire to declare an end not only to the Cold War but also to the period of American leadership. Arguments that the world's problems are solved, or irrelevant to U.S. security, or likely to regulate themselves in a new and interdependent world political system, or beyond the range of current American influence, all excuse (and often celebrate) the reduction of American activity, influence, and power. But before accepting such arguments and joining in the celebration, we should subject them to close scrutiny; and when we do, they appear seriously flawed.

HAS DEMOCRACY TRIUMPHED?

The expansion of democracy in the 1980s, first in Latin America and Asia and then, triumphantly, in Eastern Europe, is a stunning phenomenon. Given the insight, familiar since Kant [the 18th-century German philosopher], that democracies are more likely to pursue peaceful foreign policies, and given the shifting balance of power in Europe after the disintegration of the Soviet Union, the prospect of war among the major powers continues to diminish.

Starting with the region I know best, as recently as 1980 the vast majority of Latin Americans lived under military dictatorships. When these juntas began to fall, it was often said (not without justification, in light of past experience) that this merely constituted a familiar pendulum swing which would soon be followed by movement back to autocracy. Remarkably, however, in spite of the region's deep economic difficulties and the fragility of new political structures, as the 1980s ended not a single new democracy in Latin America had fallen to a coup. There has also been real movement toward democracy in both Africa and Asia, while the transformation of Eastern Europe and the former Soviet Union has been the most spectacular and important event of the epoch.

The impressive consensus on democracy and the peaceful resolution of disputes, however, is incomplete. For one thing, it is missing some key adherents among the Islamic countries, as Iraq reminded the world in August 1990. Among these countries the most common political patterns are monarchy and tyranny, with rare examples of more modern democratic systems in Turkey and Egypt (but, sadly, no longer Pakistan). Can it be accidental that the most democratic country in the region, Turkey, is the most secular one?

The problem is not the imperfect translation of Islamic political ideals into reality, but the incompatibility of some of those ideals with democracy as the term is used in the West. Moreover, under current conditions and contrary to prevailing doctrine, the introduction of free elections in these countries might well increase, rather than decrease, the propensity toward violence, and might—as in Algeria recently—produce results that bode ill for Western-style democracy. In some Arab states, where the anti-Western strain is deepest in the Islamic world, greater popular participation in foreign policy decision-making might actually be conducive to war and state-sponsored terrorism. Who can say how a referendum on war with Israel, or with other Arab countries for that matter, would fare in each Arab state?

At the same time, from Central Europe eastward to the Islamic regions of the former Soviet Union, innumerable boundary, nationality, ethnic, and religious disputes remain unresolved. It is not inevitable, or even probable, that all these disputes will be resolved democratically through peaceful political processes. In the excitement of victory it was easy to equate the collapse of communism with the success of democracy, but clearly this is a false equation. Given the polarized state in which these societies were left by the totalitarian experiment, whether democracy can take hold is uncertain. Even if it does, the equation of democracy with peace and harmony is questionable. In Asia, democracy seems to be a distant goal for Vietnam, North Korea, and the world's most populous nation, China. And to return to Latin America for a moment, recent events in Peru make it clear that even in the Western Hemisphere the triumph of democracy is neither universal nor permanent.

The point need not be labored further. Democracy has expanded spectacularly and the gains continue. And it is true that hitherto democracies have a good record of avoiding war with each other. Still, the international political system is very far from becoming an exclusively democratic society living under a rule of law that eliminates the use of violence to settle arguments. Vast portions of the world's population do not live in democratic countries, and it seems unlikely that they will soon have this privilege.

A SELF-REGULATING SYSTEM?

The sense of relief at the end of the Cold War was both enormous and understandable. Understandable, too, was the initial, euphoric belief that, with its conclusion, international stability was almost assured. If the danger to us and our allies, and more generally to world peace, had come from immensely powerful and aggressive dictatorships and their totalitarian ideology, it seemed reasonable to conclude that the demise of those regimes and their ideology would deliver us from problems of security and stability. The new interdependent, multipolar world would surely lend itself to a stable balance of power, replacing the prolonged superpower confrontation.

This view, however attractive, lacks both logical and historical foundation. Two centuries ago, [the French philosopher Jean-Jacques] Rousseau observed of the states of Europe that they "touch each other at so many points that no one of them can move without giving a jar to the rest; their variances are all the more deadly, as their ties are more closely woven." More recently Robert W. Tucker pointed out in the Fall 1991 *Foreign Affairs* that "interdependence itself is not constitutive of order.... [but] creates the need for greater order because it is as much a source of conflict as of consensus."

Peace is not the normal state of affairs. Equilibrium in the international system is not a natural or automatically realized phenomenon. History establishes that the international system can be peaceful only if determined, sustained, and intelligent efforts are made to keep it so....

Determinism is the enemy of resolution. As Robert W. Tucker and David Hendrickson observe in *Empire of Liberty*, the balance of power "may be most endangered precisely when men persuade themselves that the tendency toward equilibrium is an iron law, for in this way they free themselves from the onus of maintaining it." In Hans Morgenthau's terms, some nation must act as "holder of the balance" or "arbiter" of the system, bestowing "restraint and pacification" upon it. Many of the conditions prevailing in the European state system during the eighteenth and nineteenth centuries no longer exist. The system has expanded to embrace the world. Communication, transport, weaponry, and many other things have been revolutionized. But if the terms have changed, the basic requirement remains: one nation, deeply committed to the rules of international conduct and strong enough to enforce them, must assume the role of "holder of the balance." The only country capable of this in today's world is the United States.

The role is particularly important when circumstances call for coalition-building. The participation of the most powerful nation helps other, weaker states to reach agreements or to undertake actions that they might otherwise be reluctant to. The latter are aware that the absence of the most powerful nation can render their decision tentative and frustrate their efforts. They can be undone by its opposition. The American-led coalition against Iraq could not have been assembled by the Soviet Union, or Japan, or France, or Great Britain, without the engagement of the United States. Why should states with fewer resources risk committing them if the greater nation hangs back? Its reluctance to act will reduce the chance that a coalition will be formed at all, let alone succeed, and it will raise the cost enormously for those who proceed without it.

The most critical role for the arbiter lies in its capacity to enforce the rules of international behavior. The invoking of collective security mechanisms all too often fails to achieve this, for collective security is little more than a system of mutual promises among peacefully inclined states. "A system of general collective security," Henry Kissinger observes, "has historically proved useless against the biggest threat to peace—a major rogue country. How would the 'peaceloving' states respond? What sanctions would be at their disposal?" (*Washington Post*, March 15, 1990). With the disappearance of Cold War constraints on rule-breaking, some other form of enforcement—and its crux, military force—must be found if rogue countries are to be restrained.

Neither Germany nor Japan is a convincing candidate to succeed the United States as world leader. Within living memory, both these countries made unsuccessful efforts to achieve dominance and, as a result, suffered the trauma of utter defeat, disgrace, and occupation. In both cases the experience has left deep scars that make it difficult for the two countries to carry their full weight as

major powers. Both are inhibited about possessing or projecting military force. Both are aware that they are viewed with suspicion by other countries in their regions. Even more important, behavior in which timidity and assertiveness tend to alternate in an unpredictable manner suggests that, even in their own eyes, the two countries lack legitimacy as world leaders. In the case of Japan, in particular, its attempt to accumulate and exert political influence has been purposely circumscribed by the Japanese themselves, precisely to protect them from involvement in divisive and dangerous crises.

In addition to all this, Japan and Germany are not quite today the economic superpowers they appeared to be yesterday. Japan's export of capital is slowing markedly, and Germany is both suffering under the great economic burden of absorbing the East and showing signs of entering a period of political turmoil. Moreover, they are among the most rapidly aging countries in the world. The impact of an aging population is evident in a contracting labor force, a rising dependency ratio (defined as population aged sixty-five and over as a percentage of population aged fifteen to sixty-five), a decline in the savings rate, and an ever larger welfare bill. These are not historical and economic conditions conducive to strong international leadership. Except in rare and usually minor regional crises, the central actor in the enforcement of standards of international behavior must remain the United States.

THE END OF VIOLENCE?

For a brief moment in the late 1980s, the end of the Cold War was thought to mean an end to the threat and use of force in international politics. Many mistook the declining likelihood of world war for an increasing chance for world peace, as if these are the only alternatives. They are not, of course.

It is true that among the current major powers the areas of conflict will usually not be political and military, but economic. But the avoidance of violence by the most advanced nations in their conflicts with one another will not be emulated by others. It is also wrong to assume that the major powers will always be able to stand aside from the conflicts started by those other actors.

... In place of the Cold War's translation of every regional problem into a world crisis, we have what Geoffrey Kemp has called "the regionalization of regional conflicts." But the dangers that originate in regional conflicts can spread, as the Iraq-Kuwait crisis of 1990–91 demonstrated. The possibility of violence is highest in two areas: the Middle East and the formerly communist regimes of the old Soviet bloc.

Today's political map of the region made up of those two contiguous areas is scarred by dozens of fault lines, most of which cut across official borders. As Soviet power dissolved and Eastern Europe was liberated, politics returned to the region with a vengeance, and in forms not confined to the ballot box. It is far too soon to know how many national, religious, or ethnic groups will use violence to seek rights or privileges they think they deserve. But some have already done so and it will be surprising if others do not.... Intrinsic to the specific problems of the Middle East—the Kurdish search for independence, the Arab-Israeli struggle, or even the interstate conflicts among Arab nations—is a widespread rejection of the very sys-tem from which the code of Western international behavior springs, "a rejection," in the words of historian Bernard Lewis, "of Western civilization as such, not only what it does but what it is, and the principles and values that it practices and professes." This is not a problem that can be solved by adroit diplomacy. Human rights, democratic politics, and, most critically, an aversion to violence, remain alien—and alien-ating—concepts to many Islamic leaders. Within these states, among them, and against any enemy they identify, vi-olence can be expected and is often practiced.

The Islamic world and the newly liberated areas of Europe are far from the only places where force may be used. Though the world's most pop-ulous nations, China and India, differ enormously in their internal structures and in their relations with the interna-tional system, they have these common traits: each sees itself as a dominant power in its own region, each has an enormous military establishment, and each has demonstrated a willingness to use force to protect its interests. The troubled internal situation in China, as well as the currently declining levels of tension along the Sino-Soviet border and between China and Taiwan, Indochina, Korea, and even Vietnam, make it dif-ficult today to imagine circumstances in which China's rulers would send troops abroad. But China's foreign policy since 1949 has been marked by violent discontinuities, and it is far from incon-ceivable that China may seek to play a greater military role in the region as its economic power grows. Should the communist regime collapse, the ensu-ing struggle for power and national unity will most likely include violent episodes.

The immediate risks are greater in the case of India, which spent the 1980s in a steady build-up of its military. In its neighborhood, India has used force time after time. Tensions with Pakistan and within Sri Lanka are unresolved. Internal discord within India—much of it reflecting religious differences—may spill over to affect its neighbors. Among democracies in the Third World, India's resort to the non-defensive use of force and its large military build-up are exceptional, and given its size and weight the exception is very significant.

Nor is the use of violence restricted to nation-states. During the last decade Americans have been subject to repeated terrorist attacks, from airport and airplane bombings to the mass slaughter at the U.S. Marine barracks in Beirut in 1983. While we have recently confirmed that Soviet bloc states assisted not only ideological allies but anti-Western terrorists, the collapse of communism will deprive terrorist organizations of that support. True, too, the PLO's sponsors among the Gulf monarchies have shown reduced enthusiasm for it after Palestinian support for Iraq's invasion of Kuwait.

Nevertheless, the rich mix of ethnic, nationalist, and religious divisions in the former Soviet Union and Eastern Europe is likely to lead to the use of violence by groups unable to attain their goals peacefully. And familiar terrorist groups continue to exist and draw support from states including Iraq, Cuba, North Korea, Syria, Iran, and Libya. Several of these regimes can fairly be considered "terrorist states" themselves—not only do they train, arm, bankroll, and house terrorists, but they accept the use of violence and terror toward their own people as a normal activity of the state. What is good enough for fellow countrymen is certainly good enough for foreigners, when the occasion arises.

Violence, then, will not vanish with the Soviet-American rivalry. There is even worse news: the technology of violence is becoming more dangerous and destructive than ever before.

IS AMERICA INVULNERABLE?

It is comforting to believe that whatever the world's troubles, their salience for the United States has dropped dramatically now that the bipolar struggle has ended. The physical and ideological threat of Soviet communism has been removed, and America is unquestionably the world's greatest military power. While the fate of Nicaragua, Cuba, or Vietnam is of surpassing interest to their citizens and perhaps their neighbors, it is of little import to Americans. The United States no longer needs to dedicate nearly so much time, personnel, and money to safeguarding European security. Instability in the Balkans is unfortunate, fighting between Armenians and Azeris is tragic, but these are not matters seriously affecting the security of the United States.

All true. But if many issues have faded in importance, others continue to grow. The argument that if during the Cold War everything mattered, after it nothing does, cannot be sustained. Even at its height, the Cold War did not define the sum of American interests in the world. Indeed, the disintegration of the Soviet Union and the end of its control of the countries of Eastern Europe, combined with advances in military technology, have created a new peril for the United States: the ready availability of weapons of mass destruction to dozens of states and terrorist organizations, along with the incentive to acquire them.

A more fluid international order, even as it leaves some nations safer, will leave others feeling more vulnerable. As security guarantees by superpowers to friends and client states weaken or end, these states are most likely to seek security not in new alliances or new superpower guarantees, but in new weaponry.

The spread of sophisticated military technology has given many lesser nations, including terrorist states, unprecedented capabilities and potential in chemical, biological, and nuclear warfare, as well as delivery systems for their new arsenals. Long-range missile technology is already available in some of the world's most volatile regions, and the number of countries with ballistic missiles has doubled to eighteen in the last decade. Efforts to limit proliferation have failed in part because purchasers have been able to modify short-range missiles to reach longer-range targets and to adapt space-launch vehicles for military use; in part because the most advanced nations no longer maintain a monopoly on production. Many countries hostile to the U.S., including Iran, Iraq, and North Korea, are developing biological or chemical weapons. Many developing countries are also investing heavily in conventional forces (India, for example, now has the world's third-largest army and seventh-largest navy).

There is a painful irony for the United States in all this. After seventy-five years of costly conflicts, we are now finally at peace with all of the most powerful nations, only to find that developments in, and the dissemination of, military technology threaten to make America vulnerable once again.

The end of the Cold War, then, has produced a number of perceptions which, although superficially plausible, are mistaken. It is a mistake to believe that democracy's triumph worldwide is assured; that the international system will regulate itself in the absence of a leading power; that violence will wane; and that the United States is now militarily invulnerable.

The post–Cold War order is characterized not only by opportunity but by uncertainty. One thing, however, is certain: American leadership, far from being a casualty of the peace, remains a precondition for a peaceful world.

POSTSCRIPT

Should the United States Abandon Its Superpower Role?

The past five years have radically altered the previous four decades of world politics and the accompanying assumptions about U.S. foreign policy. Not only have the bipolar era and the cold war ended, so has the Soviet Union. The anticommunist foreign policy consensus has been replaced with discord. What role should the United States play in the world? What are the country's vital interests, and how much internationalism can Americans afford? For further debate on the issues, valuable insights are provided by two articles in *International Security* (Spring 1993): Robert Jervis, "International Primacy: Is the Game Worth the Candle?" and Samuel P. Huntington, "Why International Primacy Matters."

There are several dimensions to opinions about what the U.S. world role should be. A recent source that explains the various ideological divisions within the U.S. population, and many other aspects of foreign policy opinion, is Ole R. Holsti, "Public Opinion and Foreign Policy: Challengers to the Almond-Lippman Consensus," *International Studies Quarterly* (December 1992). There can be little doubt, however, that recent world changes have had an impact on isolationist opinion. Surveys show that a majority of Americans still favor an active, global role for the United States, but there are limits to how active a role Americans will support. A 1991 survey found that only 21 percent of Americans polled wanted their country to play the role of world policeman, or globocop as it has become known popularly. A survey taken in 1993 that asked respondents whether the United States should "take a leading role" in world affairs or "reduce its involvement" found that 70 percent favored the less involved option. One recent article that explores public sentiments of both American leaders and the public is John Rielly, "Public Opinion: The Pulse of the '90s," *Foreign Policy* (Spring 1991).

Yet it is uncontestable that "fortress America" is not a viable option. The United States has global political and economic interests, and in a world that has not forsaken force, those interests may sometimes require military defense. Furthermore, there are vast and pressing environmental and human needs that can only be addressed through global cooperation. Can the United States abandon its role as an international leader?

51

ISSUE 4

Will the European Community Increase Its Level of Integration?

YES: Walter Goldstein, from "Europe After Maastricht," *Foreign Affairs* (Winter 1992/1993)

NO: Angelo M. Codevilla, from "The Euromess," *Commentary* (February 1993)

ISSUE SUMMARY

YES: Walter Goldstein, a professor of international relations, contends that the European Community's setbacks, which were caused by trying to do too much too soon, can be overcome and that the EC can move toward integration if it follows a more gradual, realistic path.

NO: Angelo M. Codevilla, a fellow at the Hoover Institution, argues that a crescendo of disapproval has been building along the path toward European integration. The EC framework and the future of integration are doubtful.

Regionalism is not a topic that has traditionally occupied the center of discussions about international politics. It may well be, though, that regionalism will be one of the most powerful components of the international system in the twenty-first century. There is the potential for a North American region, the heart of which is now being founded by way of free-trade agreements among the United States, Canada, and Mexico. There are also indications that Japan and other Pacific Rim countries may be drawing together. Much more advanced than either of these two nascent regions, however, is Europe.

The European Community (EC) stands at the heart of the European region. In the 1950s two Frenchmen, Robert Schuman and Jean Monnet, figured prominently in the move toward European cooperation. Schuman, the French foreign minister, proposed in 1950 that European countries cooperate in the production of coal and steel, a suggestion that soon led to the establishment of the European Coal and Steel Community (ECSC). Monnet, a respected economist, diplomat, and the first president of the ECSC, argued that economic prosperity required an eventual European economic union. These ideas led first to the European Atomic Energy Community (EURATOM), designed to coordinate peaceful atomic energy production, and later to the European Economic Community (EEC, also known as the Common Market), which was established by the 1957 Treaty of Rome. The EEC began with six member countries, and has since expanded to 12 members. In 1967 the three communities (ECSC, EURATOM, and EEC) joined together to form the EC. Monnet's vision took another step forward in 1985 when the leaders of the EC countries pledged to completely eliminate most economic barriers to the flow of goods and services by 1992. This goal was simply called "Europe 1992," and it was largely, though not totally, met.

However, the Europe 1992 goal was not the final step in integration according to the vision held by many European leaders. They think even more expansively. One move they have continued to pursue is to expand membership in the EC. In 1991 the seven-member European Free Trade Association (EFTA) and the EEC signed a pact establishing a new common market, the European Economic Area (EEA). Furthermore, several EFTA members have applied for or are likely to apply for EC membership and will probably be admitted at some point. Still other countries, including former communist nations such as Poland and Hungary, have concluded association agreements with the EC. Even at the current membership level, the EC is an economic superpower. Its population (328 million) is almost a third larger than the U.S. population (251 million), and the EC's 1990 GNP ($6.0 trillion) is almost 20 percent larger than the U.S. GNP ($5.1 trillion).

A second EC trend is toward an even higher level of economic integration. At the December 1991 EC summit meeting in Maastricht, the Netherlands, the leaders of the EC members agreed to several advances in such cooperation, the most important of which were the associated goals of creating a common currency (the European Currency Unit, ECU) by January 1, 1997, and establishing a common bank to issue and control the ECU.

A third EC direction, toward political integration, is much trickier. The EC leaders have generally supported exploring such a move. The Maastricht Treaty, for example, introduced the idea of "European citizenship," a concept which would mean that a citizen of any EC member country would have nearly equal legal rights to those of a country's citizens. This would even include voting and holding office. The Maastricht Treaty further called for a common defense policy among EC members and raised the possibility of a common defense force.

When the Maastricht Treaty was signed, many European leaders were optimistic that the groundwork for a true European union had been firmly established and that the future of integration was secure, but it remains unclear if the EC will ever reach full economic and political integration.

What will happen? William Goldstein and Angelo Codevilla debate the future of the EC in the following selections. No one, including these two authors, are rash enough to predict outright what that future will be. But Goldstein is relatively optimistic that the EC will progress toward further integration. Codevilla thinks that there is a great "Europmess," one that leaves the future of European integration in grave doubt.

YES

Walter Goldstein

EUROPE AFTER MAASTRICHT

A PREMATURE TREATY

It was inevitable that the Maastricht treaty on European union would run into difficulty. The pact was premature in conception and too ambitious to survive intact. It had been signed in December 1991 when a mood of "Europhoria" held sway. With spirits boosted by a surge of economic growth the 12-nation European Community (EC) pledged to build a lasting union.... The historic Maastricht treaty was to take the next step: to create a far-reaching economic and political union that might one day become the United States of Europe.

European leaders realized nine months later that their conception was ill-timed. The EC-12 proved too divided to commit to a revolutionary compact on monetary integration by decade's end or to surrender a major portion of power to federal authorities in Brussels [the administrative capital of the EC]. A failed referendum in Denmark, and later a marginally successful plebiscite in France, revealed unexpectedly low support across Europe for unification....

RESISTANCE ON THE ROAD TO UNION

Why did the treaty meet such stiff resistance? Three explanations have been offered. First, the EC lost its balance in the temporary breakdown of the ERM; it could not restore cohesion among the 12 stalled economies. Second, the ratification debates in Denmark and France exposed a lack of popular understanding and sympathy. Third, the union treaty fell victim to the financial and trade wars waged between the strong and weak currencies of Europe, Japan and the United States.

The strength of each explanation will be tested over time. For the moment it must be noted that the Maastricht treaty had a time bomb ticking amid its turgid legal prose. It had to be ratified by all 12 member nations before further progress could begin. Most states preferred to ratify through cautious parliamentary action rather than popular referendum, allowing them to evade popular scrutiny. But in June Denmark rejected the treaty by a 0.5

From Walter Goldstein, "Europe After Maastricht," *Foreign Affairs*, vol. 72, no. 5 (Winter 1992/1993). Copyright © 1992 by The Council on Foreign Relations, Inc. Reprinted by permission of *Foreign Affairs*.

percent margin in a plebiscite, and Britain held up progress until the government led by Prime Minister John Major regained voters' confidence.... In a late-October emergency summit meeting in Birmingham, the EC leaders pledged to continue the drive for closer political and monetary union. They tried to win over the opposition among European voters by offering greater concessions to the "interests and diversity of member-states."

It would be wrong to assume that the momentum of European union is exhausted. The treaty might fail, but the Community will remain as a functioning body, and its goal of union will be preserved. The next stage of union will begin operating on schedule in January 1993. Most internal border controls will be suspended. The EC's national markets will become closely knit in a barrier-free system that will serve an affluent population larger than the U.S. and Japanese markets combined. European leaders hope that integration will elevate the EC-12 out of a prolonged recession by joining their industrial strengths together. The EC's ambition to build a federal union might be salvaged in years to come if a business recovery gains momentum.

The aim of the Maastricht treaty was to unify key elements of Europe's strength. First, the economic and monetary union (EMU) was to develop [in] stages.... [It was to] promote the "convergence" of monetary and fiscal policy among the EC-12, so that... by 1999 a central bank and a joint currency [would be established]. By century's end each of the 12 nations would submit to conservative economic priorities; pledged to suppress inflation and deficit financing, each would restrict exchange-rate fluctuations and fiscal policy.

Equally as ambitious as the EMU is the design for the second agency, the European Political Union (EPU). It aims to harmonize the foreign policy interests of the 12 member nations and to "give the Community a voice in international affairs by establishing a common foreign and security policy." An ambiguous addendum to the Maastricht treaty noted that this might "include the eventual framing of a common defense policy... and in time lead to a common defense." It left open the question whether NATO was to remain the essential military alliance in a new Europe.

Third, ambitious policy objectives were designated under the treaty. Broad authority to regulate public health, education, agriculture and the environment was to be assumed by the European Commission, the EC's executive.... In addition a Social Charter was adopted to standardize health and workers' safety conditions. And a separate protocol committed the Community to narrow the gap between the poor states of the south and the rich in the north by channeling aid to the poorest regions.

The principal intent at Maastricht was to construct a federal union and to transfer portions of national power to the EC'S centralized agencies.... Britain and the smaller but richer countries in northern Europe dissented, fearing excessive German hegemony in Europe's financial affairs. No one suspected that the monetary proposal would implode when trading (at a trillion dollars a day) in currency futures was rocked by speculative frenzy.

Provision was also made at Maastricht for revisions in the EC's five-year budget and for the eventual admission of a dozen new nations. The first six to enter, perhaps as early as 1996, might include the wealthy Austrian, Swiss and Scandinavian members of the European Free Trade Association (EFTA). After a long delay the remaining six could consist of three poor nations in the Mediterranean (Turkey, Malta and Cyprus), and three struggling economies in eastern Europe (Hungary, Poland and the Czech state) that have aligned themselves together as the Visegrad group. It is unlikely that the latter six will be admitted in this century.

LOWERING EXPECTATIONS ON UNION

The EC is now trying to shake off a malaise of false expectations. It had come to take success for granted in the halcyon days of the late 1980s [which were marked by economic prosperity and political stability]. The enthusiasm generated ... was supposed to lead to the decisive and rapid integration of western Europe. Project '92 aimed to prepare the single market for a dramatic industrial and political blastoff.

The euphoria turned sour before 1992. An economic downturn simultaneously took hold in all three of the world's regional trading blocs: North America, the EC and the Pacific rim. A wave of immigration from Africa and eastern Europe gathered force, and riots tore apart several European cities. Unemployment stalled at a painful ten percent, and violent turmoil in the former Yugoslav republics rattled Europe's politicians. Fearing that the malaise would impair each nation's authority, the EC governments questioned whether so much power should be ceded to the Council of Ministers and the Commission. It became popular to denounce the Eurocrats who issue imperious directives and hold midnight conclaves in the labyrinths of Brussels.

The first doubts emerged after Denmark's referendum in June 1992. The stunning refusal to ratify the EC treaty suggested that, while government elites were committed to unification, a majority of voters harbored severe misgivings. Doubts increased during the bitterly argued debates in France.... Poll experts claimed that millions of French voters disliked the treaty but voted in favor of it simply to bind Germany closer to the Community. Others claimed they voted against it, not because they were opposed to European federalism but because they feared that France and its currency would be held in thrall to a united Germany.

The second set of doubts came from Germany itself. Opposition had mounted across Germany to the proposal for a single currency and a central bank. Seventy percent of Germans said they refused to trade off their national crown jewel, the strong deutschemark, for a dubious new unit, the ECU. Many spoke of a compelling national interest: to curb the alarming surge of the money supply and an inflation rate rising toward four percent.... If the remaining ERM members chose to follow the Bundesbank's tight money policy it was not Germany's fault; Bonn's priority was to stabilize prices, not to assist the futile attempts of its neighbors to fend off inflation and currency devaluation.

Naturally Germany's EC partners turned against the Bonn government and the Bundesbank.... Germany's partners felt they had been pushed toward a forcible deflation at a time when they needed to expand their own money supply and deficit financing. It was neither just nor reasonable, they insisted, that Germany had stifled their economic recovery by hiking interest rates to placate its voters' anxieties. If the EMU was to follow inexorably the edicts of the Bundesbank, Germany's neighbors wanted to change the rules: the EMU had to serve a democratically governed union, not a national bank.

Germany emphatically disagreed. If the EMU was to discipline its members it could not allow them to realign their exchange rates whenever they ran into trouble. Germany set the ERM parity limits because it had the strongest economy and the hardest currency. If EC states could not reform their flagging economies, they could not stay in the ERM. Britain and Italy chose to drop out and devalue their money by 10 percent against the deutschemark. France managed to stay in, after drawing down half its reserves and receiving massive German assistance to prop up the franc. The forced march to monetary convergence and to a strong EMU was exhausted for the time being.

SUMMITS FAIL TO RESOLVE TENSIONS

It would have been timely if a wave of optimism had crested as Europe entered a second stage of political and economic integration after Maastricht. The year 1992 was supposed to mark a mystical turning point in Europe's glory.... A new era of history was to create a colossal superstate, anchoring Germany into the EC, fixing the troubled frontiers in the East and matching the global power of the United States and Japan.

The European union treaty envisaged the first transnational state of the nuclear era. Ancient frictions between Germany and France, between the industrial north and the Mediterranean south, were to be contained within the federal institutions of the union: a European parliament, a court of law and a powerful executive Commission. For all their objections the weaker EC nations would profit handsomely. An insular Britain, a fast developing Spain and Italy, as well as other Mediterranean states, would stabilize their shaky finances and share in the accelerated growth capacity of the continental union. Subsequently, the theory held, the federalists would publish their final constitutional draft for a United States of Europe. When completed the union would rank among the legends of world history.

Initially the accomplishments of the Maastricht negotiators were widely hailed. Twelve rival tribes of politicians had managed to broker constitutional differences and to reaffirm that the single market would start on time in January 1993. A raft of powerful laws assured the unrestricted flow of goods, capital, services and people within the EC. In the meantime two critical questions were left unresolved at Maastricht: whether to "widen" the Community and admit new members; and whether to "deepen" the Community, first by putting more federal power in the Brussels agencies, and second by extending judicial safeguards for wronged citizens and for democratic controls held by parliament. The omissions were to be fixed after the treaty was ratified. Unfortunately the move to ratification was overtaken by strange events.

It had been widely predicted that the removal of the EC's internal barriers would unleash a great surge of business and confidence. Those expectations were not fulfilled. First, the Danes' vote against the Maastricht treaty came as a shock....

The confusion doubled after France ratified the treaty with a minuscule majority. It was evident that voters resented discretionary power passing to the Commission in Brussels. A monster of a treaty had been drafted, and it defied popular understanding. European public opinion turned against the "federal dream" of Chancellor Kohl and the crafty technocrats reporting to the EC President, Jacques Delors....

A second setback appeared in the drifting, futile sessions of the two summit meetings that convened in 1992. The EC summit in Lisbon failed to move forward from the positions staked out in Maastricht. Nothing was done to promote the widening or deepening of the Community. The entry of new members was put on hold. The five-year budget was once again delayed; so too was the integration of monetary and foreign policy arrangements. Worse, Europe's recession dragged on, and the Yugoslav bloodletting intensified....

A TWO-SPEED EUROPE?

One beneficial trend lingered after the euphoria of the 1980s had evaporated. The seven members of EFTA chose to join forces with the EC-12 and establish a grand European Economic Area (EEA) by 1996. Some also promised to apply for associate status in the Community. The timing of the EFTA merger has not been settled, but the trade consequences are potentially significant.

As a 19-nation economic bloc the EEA would comprise a population base of 360 million people, generate a collective GNP of $6 trillion and account for 46 percent of world trade. Its industrial clout and its economies of scale would balance against the North American and the Pacific trade blocs. And if the dollar continues to lose value the ECU could become the major transaction and reserve currency of world trade.

It had been assumed that the EFTA entrants would link their currencies into the ERM and bind their monetary policy to its parity zones. At a later stage they would have to meet the convergence requirements set by the EMU, and their financial independence would disappear. That had been the formal plan until the ERM exploded and the pound and the lira were driven through the floor of the permitted exchange values.

It is possible that the exchange-rate mechanism linking the key EC currencies could split in two. A core of hard currency states could bring Germany, France and the Benelux countries into a single currency unit, while the remainder of the Community and the new entrants from EFTA would be condemned to float their currencies—at least until they reformed their inflation-prone and faltering economies. The ECU might be adopted as the inner-core denominator, but it would not achieve the global leverage to which the ERM had once aspired—since six of the EC-12 might be excluded from the EMU bloc. This resort to a two-speed system would leave urgent matters unresolved. Britain, Italy and other possible outsiders could enjoy a 12–15 percent price advantage if they traded freely in the single market while rejecting its rate-setting discipline. But if the insiders objected, the economic foundations of the Community could be imperiled.

The Community needs to cope with other forms of competition—internal and external—if it is to achieve a tighter union. The EC posts a growing deficit in its high-tech commerce and in its trade and capital flows with the United States and Japan. It has lost its lead in several strategic industries: computers, software, semiconductors, automobiles, air transport and financial services. Though the G-7 summit leaders invite President Delors to join them as an observer, he cannot speak for the EC with any forceful mandate. Once the EMU and EPU are established, it is argued, he could powerfully represent the union and its single-currency clout. But for now he only speaks for the 17 [EC] commissioners in Brussels.

COMMON FOREIGN POLICY ELUSIVE

It was tentatively agreed at Maastricht that foreign policy and defense matters would eventually pass to the jurisdiction of the EPU. No one is quite sure what that means. For now there is little evidence of a cohesive foreign policy within the Community. Indeed it was obvious that discord during the Gulf War had been acute. Many EC members had distanced themselves from the American-led buildup for Desert Shield, and they had split from the NATO camp on other issues as well.

When it came to moving against Yugoslavia's murderous strife and "ethnic cleansing" the EC again proved ineffective. Germany urged Slovenia and Croatia to declare independence. Britain and France were loath to move against Serbia. Britain argued that greater responsibility should be taken by NATO and the United Nations, but France disagreed. As a result, the EC'S cease-fire agreements and peace conferences collapsed, and the combatants ignored the good offices of the EC Commission. Matters were not helped when the Bush administration said the Balkans were "Europe's area of responsibility."

As far as "collective security" hopes go for a new Europe, the concept of a European "defense identity" remains an empty phrase. France and Germany planned to raise a joint army corps to serve as a defense nucleus for a European army—or at least for the nine EC nations belonging to the Western European Union. But as the Yugoslav chaos intensified it was clear that neither the corps nor the WEU could ever replace NATO as the bedrock of European security. Germany, Britain and the "neutral" EFTA states agreed that a continuing U.S. presence in Europe was vital and that the NATO structure be left intact. France maintained its historical thrust of opposition, holding that Europe must eventually discard the familiar "umbrella" provided by U.S. nuclear hegemony.

Three further obstacles threaten to block movement toward European unity in 1992. The poorer nations in the Community, relapsing into economic stagnation, demand more money for regional aid and structural assistance from the richer north and from the new applicants in EFTA. That is their price to negotiate an enlargement of the EC. Spain, Greece, Portugal and Ireland report a GNP per capita less than half that of the northern members of the Community. They are in no hurry to admit the poorer countries of eastern Europe and the Mediterranean, or to sacrifice their slice of the perennially contested EC budget.

The budget has been the cause of determined infighting for twenty years, and there is little prospect for peace. Currently limited to 1.3 percent of the Community GNP (a sum of 66 billion ECUs or $85 billion), it is due to rise to 1.4

percent if GNP growth resumes. Half the budget goes to the CAP, especially to the richest farms in the north, and a quarter goes to regional assistance. But radical changes will have to be made. The EC cannot borrow or run a deficit, and its revenues largely come from value-added taxes and customs duties. The problem remains: wealthy states in the north are unwilling to hike Community-wide taxes and spending, while the poor states demand increased aid as the price for straightening out the budget mess and admitting new members.

A third obstacle appears in the form of mounting distrust of EC bureaucracy. To counter it President Delors announced a novel principle: "subsidiarity." His aim was to answer objections raised by Britain, Denmark and others. They claimed that ceding power to Brussels would lead to a dangerous centralization. Delors offered a timely compromise: to preserve national diversity and the widest local autonomy, the EC would limit executive jurisdiction only to "appropriate levels" where states cannot act alone.

"Subsidiarity" became the weapon of choice for governments fighting off the Commission's power drive. The EC had asserted the right to issue regulations that could unify financial services and professional standards, environmental protection guidelines and public health requirements, and to guarantee access to national markets. But the Brussels bureaucracy was too zealous in rule-making and triggered costly litigation before the European Court. First it tried to harmonize the "Euro-sausage" and then to limit the noise level of lawn mowers. Germany was censured for shutting out French beer and bottled water with absurd medieval laws; France was told to modify its best cheeses and Italy to close its beaches.

It was a shrewd move by President Delors to restore the principle of local power, but it is not at all certain that he can counter the growing hostility to a Brussels-led Europe. Public opinion polls in the EC indicate mounting disenchantment with the pan-European treaty. More than two-thirds of Britons polled recently were opposed to the Maastricht pact, and former Prime Minister Margaret Thatcher continues to provide a powerful voice of criticism from the House of Lords. Prime Minister Major has resisted the call for a referendum from his own party, insisting that parliament will eventually ratify the treaty. His political fortunes are closely tied to the European cause and his economic strategy to the ERM. Both stand in considerable danger.

ADMISSION OF NEW MEMBERS DELAYED

The impasse over the EMU and EPU is not as shattering as it might seem. A spirit of cooperation has survived among EC governments, and progress could be made at forthcoming summit sessions to liberalize the operations of the single market. Decisions to widen or deepen the Community will clearly have to be put on hold, and timetables to implement EMU phases II and III will most likely have to be scrapped. The deadlock over the GATT Uruguay Round and CAP will stretch into a sixth year unless the G-7 leaders can spur the world credit markets into action. No member state, however, is likely to reject the statement of principles that holds the Community together. It would be a pointless gesture at a time when economic recovery is desperately awaited.

The admission of new members will be delayed until the five-year budget is resolved and possibly until the treaty is revised in 1996. Most of the states that have or will request admission will not be considered until the year 2000. In the meantime discrepancies between the rich applicants from EFTA and the rest of the EC aspirants are embarrassingly visible. Per capita GDP ranges from $33,000 a year in Switzerland and $23,000 in Scandinavia, to a low of $1,600 in both Poland and Turkey. The present EC average is almost $17,000, though Portugal and Greece earn far less. More important, the EC population of 325 million would grow by only ten percent if the EFTA states joined, but it would swell immensely if the others entered: 65 million would be added by the Visegrad trio, and 50 million more by the Baltic and Balkan nations. And then there is Turkey, a loyal NATO member, with 56 million people now, but with 85 million in the next generation.

The impact on the EC economy could be equally drastic. If classic laws of comparative advantage were to hold, the non-EFTA applicants would undercut most of the farm prices and the low value-added manufacturing costs of the union. Eastern Europe could ship cheaper textiles and steel than any of the import-protected and state-run sectors of the west. To stress the contrast of factor costs: EC citizens pay roughly $400 per capita each year in farm supports, through tax transfers and rigged consumer prices; but those in EFTA pay $1,000 each, and the east Europeans zero. By comparison the United States subsidizes food by $300 per capita and Japan by $500.

The issues of subsidies and protectionism go to the core of the EC's problem. If it ever rationalizes its economic resources a large number of unskilled workers in western coal mines, steel mills and farms would be displaced from declining industries and channeled into welfare or low-paid service jobs.

EC farmers would become park keepers, and the unsubsidized economies of the east would overwhelm their high-cost Community competitors. Workers in the east would accelerate low-cost production at home rather than migrate to the west. These eastern European workers might well hope that the EC would bolster their fledgling democracies and free-market regimes—as the Community had done so effectively in Spain in the 1980s. For now they stand as outsiders hungrily tapping at the EC's well-stocked windows.

Protectionist forces will surely challenge the EC's future progress. They will influence decisions on enlargement and the thrust to extend environmental or industrial policy. EC states spend $100 billion a year on industrial subsidies, especially for coal, railways and labor-intensive industries. Public subsidies average 6 percent of GDP in Italy, 3.5 percent in France and 2.5 percent in Germany. In Greece the figure is nearly 15 percent. With millions of jobs funded by these subventions no state will surrender them just to liberalize the European economy. Nor will the EC admit a flood of unsubsidized food and goods coming from low-wage exporters in eastern Europe or the Mediterranean.

A MORE REALISTIC UNION

It is impossible to forecast which way the EC will move in the 1990s. The Maastricht treaty left member-states intact as sovereign agencies, but it forced unity on their economic life. Their material destiny was cast into an integrated economic mold while political conflicts kept them angrily apart. This might prove to be the treaty's undoing. The EC could possibly rectify the current impasse by splitting itself into a two-speed entity. Some of the EC-12 could, theoretically, join together at the core and later entrants could circle in outer orbits of power. Or the Community could simply resign itself to its current status as a common market and customs union—remaining a loose association of states, free of internal tariff barriers. None of these options is appealing. Each would involve the scrapping of the popular aspiration to unify Europe in this century.

Arguably the dictates of European economics will weigh more heavily than political concerns. The EC cannot move to the next stage of political evolution until it improves on growth and productivity. It would be pointless to develop the EPU, the commission or the parliament or to admit new members if the Community fell behind in the scramble for world trade and industrial technology. The compelling need is not to curb national sovereignty but to improve industrial productivity and living standards across the Community.

Europe's gift for pragmatism and compromise will surely help as it experiments with new forms of organization. It has served well in the past. It may be that proposals for a two-speed Europe will be tried. That would probably lead to the development of a deutschemark currency bloc. But Germany would be troubled if it ever succeeded. Its alliance with France and the Benelux countries is of critical importance: both Chancellor Kohl and President Mitterrand insist that Europe should not succumb to political paralysis or division, and both aim to keep the Community intact. Moreover Germany needs to preserve its ties to Britain and Italy, and, no less, to the Atlantic world. It is not ready to sever its close relations in order to build a two-speed Europe with a minority rump at the core. It will strive aggressively to block the changes that a bifurcated, two-speed union would entail.

Whatever happens, appeals within the EC for public sector intervention and for trade protection will tax the patience of industrial and political leaders as unification proceeds. Practical choices will have to [be made]. Welfare policy, as well, will require closer attention as the population ages and the availability of resources declines. Ultimately Europe cannot afford to ignore market pressures: it has an uncomfortable surplus of labor and farm products and an inadequate purchasing power to fuel its drive for prosperity.

The political forecast is more troubling. The EPU will not easily cope with the security and diplomatic threats that Europe faces. If the union can be gradually widened or deepened it may survive. But it will remain divided by ethnic and nationalist tensions. Eastern Europe is no longer sealed off by an iron curtain. The broad continent cannot ignore turbulence in Yugoslavia, in central Europe and in Russia, or in the world's industrial markets. A self-limiting enterprise, to build an inner club or a multi-speed political union, will be futile if economic dynamism lags or security fears escalate.

No matter what course the movement to union takes it is unlikely that the United States will be excluded from an emerging Europe. If economic and political uncertainty intensifies the EC will have to strengthen its global links. It may not become a harmoniously united Europe; but at a minimum it will have to mobilize its scarce resources with greater efficiency. The North American Free Trade Agreement [among Canada, Mexico, and the United States] will offer vital opportunities to extend the EC's trading reach and economies of scale. Similarly, a resurgent and unified Europe will repudiate fortress-like barriers to foreign competition as it strives for export expansion. Liberalizing of trade, moreover, will present major opportunities for U.S. exporters and, hence, better prospects for U.S. recovery.

The cause of European union is not dead but it has experienced a severe setback. If the Maastricht treaty is not ratified or revised it may need another surge of economic growth before the constitution writers revive their former mood of enthusiasm. Itwould be better if the revival came quickly. Nationalism too often fires enthusiasms among groups who seek prosperity by beggaring their neighbors, and its containment in Europe is long overdue.

One of the founding fathers of a united Europe, Jean Monnet, wrote a thoughtful warning in his memoirs nearly forty years ago. It is highly pertinent today: "The construction of Europe, like all peaceful revolutions, needs time—time to convince, time to adapt people's thinking and time to adjust to great transformations."

The Maastricht treaty attempted to do too much too soon. A renewed effort toward the cause of European unity could succeed if it were to follow a more realistic path in the next few years.

NO

Angelo M. Codevilla

THE EUROMESS

Just a year ago [December 1991], as representatives of the twelve governments making up the European Community (EC) met in the Dutch city of Maastricht to sign the latest in a series of pan-European agreements, polite opinion was unanimous that a united Europe would challenge the United States economically, that it would take charge of reordering the formerly Communist world, and that its "advanced" approach to economic, social, and environmental matters had a lot to teach us. Indeed, polite opinion strongly backed the prospective Clinton administration's desire to imitate Europe's approach to industrial policy, medical and child care, and much more. Today, however, it is evident that Europe will not unite according to the vision of the Maastricht treaty, that its economic policies are a drag on us, that Western Europe is being contaminated by the Communist compost pile, and that its approach to socioeconomic matters has mostly cautionary tales to tell. In 1992 Eurotopia was supposed to emerge. Instead, 1992 became the year of the Euromess.

The Danish people's narrow rejection [by referendum] of the Maastricht treaty; the French people's equally narrow acceptance; Britain's, Italy's, Portugal's, and Spain's abandonment of attempts to maintain the value of their currencies against the Deutschmark; anti-foreigner riots as well as various Eurosummits rife with talk of "saving Europe"—all these are only symptoms. The Euromess itself consists of nothing less than the bankruptcy of the postwar political order. Within each European country people are searching for ways of saying "no" to politicians of all parties, whom they perceive as really belonging to a single party, that of the ruling bureaucracy—a bureaucracy that takes about half a worker's income and no longer seems able to justify doing it.

Contrary to a common perception, the explanation for the opposition to the Maastricht treaty is not nationalism. Rather, it is that people who are growing surlier about national governments which they can control only theoretically are understandably wary of approving a level of government which they cannot control at all.

I

The modern European state is so familiar to us that we rarely realize how historically anomalous it is. Yet the high level of taxation in today's Europe—a bit over 50 percent in Scandinavia, a bit less on the continent—is comparable only to what the most rapacious empires of antiquity exacted from slaves. Among all the governments of human history, only the recently deceased Communist regimes have exceeded the modern European states in taking over the family's responsibilities for raising the young and caring for the old, in assuming society's role as arbiter of taste and religion's role as arbiter of truth....

This is all the more remarkable given that the bedrock of European civilization is inhospitable to governmental regimentation of ordinary life. Western civilization is built on the distinction—going back to Aristotle and then Augustine—between families and civil society on the one hand and the political realm on the other. On this basis there grew during the Middle Ages a set of restraints on the power of the king to demand one's property, one's military service, entry into one's home, etc. Moreover, no king would have dreamed of setting standards for exercising a profession, let alone for raising children. Sovereignty belonged to God alone.

In the 16th and 17th centuries, however, the theorists of sovereignty, Jean Bodin and Thomas Hobbes, made into a principle the growing preference of noblemen for subjection to a king as the only way to put an end to continued feudal and religious war. But while Europeans first agreed to sacrifice ancient freedoms primarily to secure internal peace, the state's claim to sovereignty quickly shifted to the necessities of international war.

Indeed, it is no exaggeration to say that the 19th-century European state was built from the ground up for war. It was in order to administer conscription that Napoleon and then the rest of Europe numbered houses. He first and then others also established schools of engineering and mines and fostered certain industries for the same reasons that they adopted national anthems and that, later, they required universal education: to prepare citizens morally, intellectually, and materially to fight for the state....

Yet just as all this began for the sake of war, so it all came to an end as a result of war. The very senselessness of World War I—the mutual slaughter of peoples who differed from one another much less than they thought—dealt a grievous blow to nationalism, and World War II further weakened its legitimacy. Today, it is almost impossible to imagine the frame of mind of the millions who not so long ago were cheerfully ready to die for the state.

II

But the discrediting of nationalism did not also delegitimize the state, since an alternative justification for the state's power had been gaining currency even before World War I: the state, as the agent of modern science, would ensure material progress, while state schools would spread expertise, culture, and morality.

The origins of this view were threefold: utopian socialism, with its dream of establishing happiness through governmental schemes; the... tradition of public administration,... which saw impartial bureaucrats as the embodiment of Reason itself; and the Christian rejection of the 18th-century liberal notion that individuals should be left to themselves to sink or swim. Hence, by the end of the 19th century, [there began] the idea of what came to be called the welfare state.

The unprecedented domestic regimentation that accompanied World War I also taught the disastrous lesson that government rationalization of the economy could boost production dramatically.... The result was that, while fratricidal war was discrediting the state as a vehicle for glory, a growing fascination with socioeconomic engineering was providing the state with a warrant for expanding its powers farther than even the most rabid nationalist would have dreamed. Just when people became less and less willing to give their lives for the state, they became more and more willing to give it more and more power *over* those very same lives.

By now, however, this alternative justification for state power has, like nationalism before it, just about run its course. For if nationalism turned out to mean senseless slaughter, the welfare state turned out to mean economic stagnation, social corruption, and above all bureaucracy.

The story of Europe's economic performance over the past generation is essentially that as soon as the goose began to lay golden eggs, the state smothered her. In the 1950's governments took about 25 percent of Europeans' incomes through various kinds of taxes. This was already close to twice the level of taxation in the interwar years, and some three times the pre-World War I level. But few noticed, because postwar rebuilding was roughly doubling standards of living.

By the early 1990's, everyone noticed, since growth in personal income had virtually stopped, while the growth of the public sector and of its "bite"—by now roughly 50 percent of gross domestic product (GDP)—continued apace.... Government was reducing hope to a counterintuitive proposition: the less you get to keep, the better off you will be.

Today, high taxes are only a part of Europe's economic troubles. Starting and running a business involves more red tape and officious officials than most Americans can imagine. "Social" laws that make it difficult to shed employees also make businesses think twice before hiring them. Generous unemployment benefits reduce the pressure to take available jobs. Substantial percentages of the workforce are employed in inefficient nationalized industries, from railroads to coal mining to broadcasting, as well as in subsidized private industries, from agriculture to computers to aircraft.

The bottom line is that a mid-level bureaucrat in Europe now takes home the equivalent of $30,000 per year. But given that prices in Europe are almost twice as high as in the U.S., this average European's lot is not too far above the official U.S. poverty line. A two-earner professional couple in Copenhagen or Milan can afford to own a modest apartment or a car, but not both. Understandably, then, Europeans no longer regard the state as a creator of wealth.

* * *

So, too, with major social problems, which until recently Europeans turned to the state to solve. The first and still the biggest European uplift project—Italy's 40-year attempt to bring its southern regions up to socioeconomic parity with the north—has corrupted both recipients and donors, and is now fueling a serious movement in the north to secede from the south. Then there is Germany's attempt to uplift the former Soviet zone of occupation by artificially raising wages and unemployment and other social benefits to West German levels while forestalling the collapse of East German companies. Whether these methods, comparable to methadone maintenance for heroin addicts, will ever wean the East Germans from socialist habits, they surely are increasing the weight of government in the West....

It is not surprising that Germans, accustomed to lining up for state privileges, should strike out against those they perceive as alien competitors for the largest handouts they have ever seen (especially since the German asylum law, written for another time, invites foreigners to line up)....

The immigration of millions of people from the third world adds to this process.... Europe's planned, bureaucratized, welfarized economies already have trouble generating enough jobs for the (decreasing) number of young people that they produce.

But giving the new immigrants a chance at economic integration would be child's play in comparison with the problem of cultural integration....

* * *

On top of all this, the European state has lost its former reputation for administrative efficiency. The non-poor increasingly avoid national health-care systems, while the poor and lower middle classes are stuck with worsening service and ever higher charges. European parents, who once considered state schools to be the very standard of high culture, now notice that their children are learning less than they themselves were taught, and that they are bringing home the opposites of culture and morality. Pension systems vary, but everywhere the impression has spread that tomorrow's retiree will receive only so much as tomorrow's workers may be willing to give them. More importantly, today's retirees are receiving less than they thought they would, and fear further austerity.

Europeans have also lost their old faith in the state's impartiality. While it had never crossed the minds of Italians that government might be impartial, many other Europeans seem to have been genuinely shocked in recent years at revelations that officials high and low were dispensing preferential treatment in connection with jobs, contracts, credit—in other words, that bureaucrats have friends and that the state is not a family but a giant patronage machine.

The harsh truth is that impartiality was possible in grandfather's time because the tasks of government were smaller and better defined, whereas spending half a nation's income—whether it is done by socialists or by conservatives—involves making the fortunes of some at the expense of others. That is why Europeans do not believe they can throw the rascals out without putting in a set who are just as bad....

* * *

In contrast to domestic affairs, real differences did persist in European politics until only yesterday over policy toward the Communist world. Indeed, from the late 1970's until the fall of the Berlin Wall, these differences even widened, as many in the European Left seemed bent on returning to the openly pro-Soviet, anti-American attitudes of the late 1940's....

Hence during the 1980's, elections were dominated more often than not by the question: do you want to stand with the Americans or do you want to accommodate the Soviets? ... But that is all gone.

Gone with it is the last vestige of the European state's original basis for legitimacy—war-making. Much as Europeans detested war, a substantial percentage of them supported the Atlantic alliance that was keeping the Communist monster at bay. Polls throughout the cold war showed consistently that the bulk of voters, even for leftist parties, opposed unilateral disarmament and wanted American troops to stay in Europe. Today the polls show that while the proportion of Europeans who want American armies on their continent has actually risen, so (except in France) has the proportion of those willing to make radical cuts in their own armed forces. What this means is that Europeans no longer look to their own governments to protect them. And the reason is that these governments are run by a generation of leaders who do not inspire trust.

The elder statesman, France's François Mitterrand, represents a party that has been receiving only about one-fifth of the popular vote. Germany's Helmut Kohl bet everything on trying to introduce capitalism in the East through socialist methods, and has nothing to offer but more taxes as far as the eye can see. Britain's Prime Minister, John Major, is a colorless man who drifts with the wind. In Italy, where there is no real distinction between government and opposition, the entire political class is widely regarded as a bunch of thieves.

Contemporary Europeans are not revolutionaries. They express their disaffection with the state in protest votes for regional and local parties as well as in referenda. But mostly they are turning their backs on government. One gets the impression that few if any Europeans would put themselves in harm's way to stop extremist mobs from rushing parliament buildings, and that perhaps even news of a foreign invasion would not prevent anyone from sitting down to dinner.

In short, European welfare states are as weak as they are big.

III

The movement for European unity that began in the 1920's with the writings of Jean Monnet was supposed to be something of a cure for a political culture mortally wounded by World War I. Monnet's immediate aim in proposing functional economic integration was to restore some of the interdependence and human contact that had existed prior to the Great War. But since passportless travel and easy trade had not prevented that war, they could not ensure future peace. That is why Monnet hoped that in the long run a new, vital European identity would transcend the now-discredited nationalisms. In Monnet's view, it was economic technocracy that would serve primarily to foster the growth of pan-European sentiment.

Monnet's plans did not get serious attention until after World War II had discredited nationalism even further. Yet the statesmen who championed Monnet's approach—Konrad Adenauer, Robert Schuman, Alcide de Gasperi, and Charles de Gaulle—did not wait for a common market to tackle the task of uniting Europe psychologically. The culmination of their work was the de Gaulle-Adenauer treaty of 1963, celebrated by a solemn Mass over Charlemagne's tomb, which American observers ridiculed as the old men's wedding. Nevertheless, Franco-German concord has been the primary blessing of European life since World War II.

In 1992 the outlines of a pan-European consensus remain as clear and firm as they were 40 years ago: never again a war among us; free movement of people and goods; stand together to safeguard and promote our common civilization. The EC has enjoyed broad support because of the misconception that it has been working on the basis of this consensus. But now the Maastricht treaty has for the first time brought home to the average European the fact that the EC is on a path very different from that of Adenauer and de Gaulle.

The old men's approach amounted, on the one hand, to the dropping of barriers to common economic and social life, and, on the other hand, to greater coordination of government policy. Instituting a common market was to be easy: simply drop trade restrictions and free enterprise would do the rest. The governments were also freely to adopt increasingly similar policies in order to pursue similar objectives, and technocratic arrangements were to support this growing agreement.

But even before Adenauer and de Gaulle left office a generation ago, the pan-European movement began diverging from this set of prescriptions. The EC's ancestor, the Coal and Steel Community (1952), brought together the thoroughly cartelized German coal and French iron industries under the auspices of an international High Authority—in other words, a super-cartel. It resulted in more people and goods crossing borders, but it was not free trade. The Common Market's Common Agricultural Policy of 1962, which set a common (high) tariff on agricultural products in order to ensure uneconomically high incomes for French, German, and Italian farmers at the expense of all European consumers, was the very denial of the free market.

All this was intended to be temporary, transitional. Instead it provided both the financing and the model for the EC.

Thus the EC's approach to economic integration is the very opposite of the free market. In any given sector (agriculture, cars, computers, condoms), the EC Commission begins with an external tariff. Then it sits the leading producers in each of the member countries down with labor and government regulators from those countries, and works out standards for production, prices, and trade. These are implicit market-sharing arrangements. Big businesses love the EC Commission because it virtually assures that they will stay alive. The lucky ones can be picked as champions to be built up by subsidies, and then to go out and conquer global markets. (In fact, however, the major recipients of government aid—computers and aircraft—are losing money.)

EC regulations have been justly ridiculed for banning all but six kinds of apples from commerce and for setting the length of Eurocondoms at precisely 15.2 cm., while at the same time failing to touch the monopolies owned by the member states, from tobacco to telecommunications. But the EC has been unjustly credited with breaking down borders. To be sure, truck traffic now flows from the Baltic to the Mediterranean without stopping at borders. But that is because the product and its destination were regulated beforehand.

Obviously the regulators are aiming at an enterprise other than mere European integration. That enterprise is the corporate nanny-state. It is no coincidence that as socialism has acquired a bad name in national governments, it has found a home in the EC Commission under the stewardship of Jacques Delors, an unreconstructed French socialist out of the *Ecole Nationale d'Administration.*

But the most important effect of the EC's single-market regulations has been to diminish the public's fervor for European unity. For years now, national bureaucrats have answered the public's inquiries about new regulations by explaining that it was something required by the EC. That meant the matter was out of the government's hands, out of the citizen's hands: it might as well have come down from heaven, and objecting to it was not only futile but something akin to disturbing the peace of Europe. Indeed, the EC has become the perfect source for intrusive, picayune socialist legislation that national parliaments would be loath to pass for fear of public retribution.

IV

The Maastricht treaty was supposed to carry the current approach to its logical conclusion. The heart of the treaty is a set of procedures for adopting a common currency and a common independent central bank on the model of Germany's Bundesbank. Never mind that Germany itself did not meet the inflation and deficit criteria for admission to the club; only two out of twelve signatories did. More important, divergence in actual economic policies had already undermined the thirteen-year-old system of exchange-value coordination.

Quite simply, in 1991 the German government did not ask permission from other EC governments (and disregarded the advice of its own central bank) when it traded real Deutschmarks for worthless East German marks, undertook to subsidize the East, and decided to pay for it all by borrowing rather than taxing. This drove German interest rates up to 10 percent, forced other EC governments to follow, and placed the EC's more vulnerable currencies (British and Italian) in a squeeze between low growth and high interest rates. The result was that in September 1992, Britain and Italy (and then Spain and Portugal in November) had to devalue their currencies after paying billions of dollars to fight speculators in futile attempts to maintain the integrity of the system.

The lesson was lost on nobody that everyone would have been better off if Europe's leaders had made more competent economic policy decisions, and coordinated actual policy better, rather than working on abstract plans for a new currency. The turmoil also raised the question: do we want to put the economic future of the whole continent into the hands of these people?

The treaty's second most important feature is the social chapter. This consists of a lengthy list of subjects, like worker safety, rules for hiring and firing, medical care for women, sexual discrimination, the rights of labor unions, and practically everything else that might come to the mind of a social engineer. The treaty empowers the Commission to issue directives on these subjects which every government in the Community would be obliged to adopt. The British government, recently having won major battles against labor-union power and not wanting to refight them with its opponents backed by Europe, opted out of the social chapter. In so doing it raised for all Europeans another question: do we really want to give the Eurocrats a blank check over the most intimate details of our lives?

With regard to foreign policy, the Maastricht procedures for arriving at decisions are complex—obviously the fruit of long, hard bargaining. But there is scarcely a word about objectives and none at all about the problems of the day: what to do about war in the former Yugoslavia; how to avoid a war in the former USSR, and how to respond if one breaks out; whether or not to build all-European forces for expeditions off the continent; what sort of relations to have with NATO; etc., etc.

Still, if the EC is so unsatisfying, why are governments lining up all the way to Kiev to get in? Because the EC offers a tempting bargain, the very bargain that led to the accession of Ireland, Spain, Portugal, and Greece. The poor country coming in gets a lot of money up front. Ireland, for example, gets over $1,400 for every man, woman, and child. The money pays compensation for damages suffered through competition, and to support the welfare state. The country's big businesses get to sell to the big EC market, and at prices higher than those they had at home. They also get protection from Japanese and American imports.

In exchange, the new member gradually accepts all the EC's regulations. This tends to raise labor costs and to drive out of business and into government dependency those firms that are too small or not well enough connected to play by the new rules. In the long run this is a bad bargain for the recipients, who are deprived of the opportunity to undercut the continent's high-cost countries, as well as for countries like France and Germany, who pay the bill. But in the short run it looks good to the outs.

As for the ins, the reaction to the Maastricht treaty has been a crescendo of disapproval. The more people from Denmark to Crete have learned about Maastricht, the less they have liked it. So it is a safe bet that the treaty has already been overtaken by events.

V

Nevertheless, the Euromess remains. To get some perspective on it, imagine how different Europe would be if Konrad Adenauer were alive today and chairman of the EC Commission. Anyone proposing that the Commission issue fine-print Euroregulations would have received an Adenauer lecture on how inspiration builds allegiance while meddling in details destroys it. And just imagine what that austere old Rhinelander would have said to the Eurocrat who placed on his desk a proposed standardization of Eurocondoms. *What? Is this what 3,000 years of civilization have led to? Don't you have anything better to do with your life?*

Imagine, too, how different German unification would have been if it had been run by Adenauer. Drawing on his miracle of 1948, he would have allowed the rotten system in the East to disintegrate, permitting Westerners to make real investments at bargain prices. Instead of raising taxes to pay for welfare, he would have cut both taxes and regulations to smooth the way for Easterners into the economy.

And imagine, finally, his response if an aide had pointed out to him that support for military action to stop the war in Bosnia was shaky. Adenauer would probably have answered as he did in 1954, when he confronted opposition to the establishment of the West German army: *Let's set to work and build up that support.*

The worst news about the Euromess is that politicians who have grown up as amoral brokers of favor are not about to become Adenauers. True, these Europoliticians have begun to perceive that promising, taxing, and spending more will not make them more secure in their jobs. Hence there is now a lot of talk about privatization, decentralization, or, in Eurospeak, subsidiarity. Even socialists are campaigning on the need to lower taxes, and Sweden itself is in the third year of a much ballyhooed process of backing away from statism. Even so, no one has begun to wean the vast patronage networks—rich companies, middle-class intellectuals, or poor welfare recipients—off the state.

New politicians are thus needed, but as in the formerly Communist countries, they will arise only to the extent that the old ones default. Two phenomena already mentioned bear watching: the growing use of referenda, and the growing importance of local and regional government. Both enable new politicians to build direct relationships with the electorate and to strike a decent balance between their usefulness to society and their cost. But in Western Europe, the decay and the default are slow and statism is not yet completely discredited. That is why the Euromess will get worse before it gets better.

POSTSCRIPT

Will the European Community Increase Its Level of Integration?

The years that followed the optimistic signing of the Maastricht Treaty in December 1991 have been a time of mixed signals for Europe. Resistance to the treaty has been based on many factors. Some Europeans fear that they and their heritage could be swallowed up by a greater Europe dominated by one of the more powerful EC countries, especially Germany. The continuing role of nationalism in Europe and its impact on the EC can be explored further in Anthony D. Smith, "National Identity and the Idea of European Unity," *International Affairs* (Winter 1992). There is also hostility toward the burgeoning EC bureaucracy, headquartered in Brussels. There are now some 17,000 so-called Eurocrats working for the EC; they currently issue over 600 regulations and directives a year, and they manage an annual EC budget of approximately $84 billion. The budget is raised through tariffs and through a value-added tax (a type of sales tax) on goods sold in EC countries. "We don't want a centralized executive in Brussels which tries to insert its tentacles into the nooks and crannies of national life," one British politician said, expressing a common view. The Danish referendum is discussed by Karen Siune and Palle Svensson in "The Danes and the Maastricht Treaty: The Danish Referendum of June 1992," *Electoral Studies* (June 1993). For an analysis of the French vote, consult Michel Brulé, "France After Maastricht," *The Public Perspective* (November/December 1992).

The 1990s have thus far been a time of advances and reversals for European integration. The final agreement of all 12 EC countries to the Maastricht Treaty is the latest step forward. Many obstacles remain, however. There are differences in political philosophy among the countries. Great Britain, for example, is more conservative than is France. Nationalism is one the rise. For a pessimistic view of this phenomenon, see William Echikson, "Europe's New Face of Fear," *World Monitor* (November 1992). There are also significant economic problems plaguing integration. The difficulty of merging currencies, especially when countries have different economic strategies, remains one. There is also a wide disparity between the economic circumstances of EC countries. Germany, France, and some other countries are relatively wealthy, while others, especially Greece, Ireland, Portugal, and Spain—the so-called poor four—lag economically. All that is certain then, is that a great experiment in political integration is underway and yet hangs in the balance.

ISSUE 5

Will the North American Free Trade Agreement Benefit All Its Member Countries?

YES: Jaime Jose Serra Puche, from "The North American Free Trade Agreement: A Source of Competitiveness," *Vital Speeches of the Day* (April 15, 1993)

NO: Sheldon Friedman, from "NAFTA as Social Dumping," *Challenge* (September/October 1992)

ISSUE SUMMARY

YES: Jaime Jose Serra Puche, Mexico's secretary of commerce and industrial promotion, maintains that the North American Free Trade Agreement will be mutually beneficial to Americans, Canadians, and Mexicans.

NO: Sheldon Friedman, a union man and an analyst with the Department of Economic Research for the AFL-CIO, charges that NAFTA will work to the disadvantage of all workers, particularly those at the lowest end of the wage scale. Its benefits will flow only to business owners, corporations, and other similar interests.

During the period between World War I and World War II, the countries of the world moved toward protecting their domestic economies by dramatically increasing tariff rates and other barriers to foreign trade. These steps led to further retaliation by other countries, which caused an upward spiral of protectionism and a downward spiral of trade. The Great Depression that occurred in the 1930s and the resulting economic chaos made for fertile ground for the rise of dictators such as Adolf Hitler and Benito Mussolini and the cataclysm of World War II that ensued. After the war, and as a consequence of what they saw as lessons learned, international leaders, especially those in the United States, favored breaking down barriers to international trade, monetary exchange, and investment. Organizations such as the General Agreement on Tariffs and Trade (GATT) and the International Monetary Fund (IMF) were established, and international trade rose rapidly. World exports soared from $53 billion in 1948 to approximately $4 trillion in 1993.

A major issue today is whether this move toward free trade will continue. The latest rounds of GATT talks have foundered over a variety of issues among the industrialized countries and the less developed countries. Also complicating the issue is a concern that the growth and solidification of the

European Community will create a regional economic giant that will try to exclude others and dominate world economic interchange.

It is in light of these trends that the value of NAFTA is being considered. In part, the thrust toward signing an agreement comes from the post-Depression idea that good fences do, in fact, make bad neighbors. And in part it results from reaction to the establishment of the European Community. In 1988 Canada and the United States agreed to eliminate virtually all trade barriers, and many other economic restrictions, between their two countries by 1999. After a close vote in Canada's Parliament, the treaty was ratified and took effect on January 1, 1989. Then the United States and Mexico and Canada and Mexico undertook simultaneous free trade negotiations. These negotiations were concluded successfully in late 1992, and a NAFTA treaty was signed by the heads of state of the three countries. Ratification was assented to by the federal legislatures in Mexico City and in Ottawa. Whether the U.S. Congress would agree to the ratification of the treaty was another issue. Many legislators, especially those with strong ties to blue-collar workers and their unions, worried that NAFTA would mean that jobs would flow to Mexican factories and their lower-wage workers. Environmentalists also objected to the treaty. They were concerned with what they charged was a lack of environmental safeguards, which would mean that U.S manufactures would go to Mexico to take advantage of less stringent, thus less costly, environmental laws.

Candidate Bill Clinton argued during the 1992 U.S. presidential campaign that NAFTA was not acceptable without stronger protections for displaced U.S. workers and stronger environmental safeguards. He proposed renegotiating the U.S.–Mexico part of the treaty. President Clinton announced in August 1993 that the renegotiation had been completed and that he would send the treaty to Congress for its approval. The Administration said that significant improvements had been made. Opponents claimed that Clinton's efforts had been a sham, mostly designed to conceal the fact that in supporting NAFTA as president he was abandoning a campaign stand he took as a candidate.

The regional trading bloc envisioned by NAFTA will have a population of more than 360 million and combined gross national products of approximately $6 trillion. The three countries are already closely tied economically. More than 70 percent of Canada's trade is with the United States; two-thirds of Mexico's trade is with the United States; Canada is by far the largest U.S. trading partner; and Mexico is the third-largest single U.S. trading partner, accounting for about 6 percent of both U.S. exports and imports. Beyond this, there is an immense amount of investment interchange among the three countries. A trilateral NAFTA would expand these figures even more.

What is debatable about NAFTA is who the "winners" and "losers" will be. In the following selections, Jaime Jose Serra Puche argues that all three countries will benefit. Sheldon Friedman replies that some wealthy interests will benefit, but the impact on workers makes NAFTA a bad bargain for the people of North America.

YES

Jaime Jose Serra Puche

THE NORTH AMERICAN FREE TRADE AGREEMENT: A SOURCE OF COMPETITIVENESS

First of all, let me thank The Economic Club of Detroit and the Engineering Society for the invitation to this lunch because, in my view, it grants an opportunity to share with you a few thoughts about the North American Free Trade Agreement and the issue of competitiveness....

I would like to share with you a few thoughts about the North American Free Trade Agreement, and from now on I'll call it NAFTA.

I think that the debate on NAFTA has been missing some of the major points, some of the main issues, because the debate has been concentrated mostly on issues related to labor impact, jobs and environment. And I refer to those issues, as well, that we have been calling parallel issues. But before I do so, I would like to talk to you about what I think is the core of NAFTA, which is how NAFTA can help the North American region to become more competitive.

And when one looks at countries or regions that have become more competitive, one sees at least five elements, five features. And I would like today to prove to you that those features that usually are so observed and present in those more competitive regions will be brought about by NAFTA as an instrument to the region.

First, to be competitive, you have to operate in an environment that gives you full certainty, where things are permanent over time, where you know that you will be facing continuity in the policy design. Where you know probably that making a major investment decision today under a set of rules, and not knowing but expecting that in years from then or even months, those rules could change. And even though you make your decision under the present rules and it's the right decision, it could be the wrong decision two or three years down the road if the rules and the policies change.

So, the point is that we have to find us a region, a tool, an instrument that will help the continuity or the permanence of the policies with the certainty that investors need. And NAFTA does that. NAFTA is an international commitment made by three countries which defines from the outset the rules

From Jaime Jose Serra Puche, "The North American Free Trade Agreement: A Source of Competitiveness," *Vital Speeches of the Day,* vol. 59, no. 13 (April 15, 1993). Copyright © 1993 by Jaime Jose Serra Puche. Reprinted by permission.

of the game to trade, to invest, and to provide services. Rules, that is, for the years to come, rules for the decades to come, which would allow investors and firms in the region to allocate resources over the long term with full certainty that those rules would be permanent over time, and that things won't change and they will not face any surprise down the road that would make an originally profitable decision an unprofitable decision. The continuity, the permanence, the certainty that NAFTA provides will help us to allocate our resources optimally in the region, and therefore the region will gain competitiveness.

The second issue is that the North American Free Trade Agreement would put together a very large market with 360 million consumers and with $6 trillion of regional production, the largest free trade area in the world, including the European area. That would allow firms in the region to take advantage of economies of scale by serving large markets and through access into this huge market, lowering average costs and therefore gaining competitiveness through a lower average cost scheme.

Now that would happen because we are putting together a large market, but also because the potential of the Mexican market, above all, in consumption goods and in some particular technologies, like environmentally-related technologies, the mass of those products would increase dramatically in Mexico in the years to come. Therefore, the opportunities in terms of using economies of scale within this market would open opportunities to the firms in the region to lower average costs and therefore gaining extra margins of competitiveness. So, NAFTA will contribute to competitiveness through large markets.

The third element that I think is present in markets that have been competitive is the so-called economies of scope; that is, the ability to specialize in certain market regions, in certain economic sectors. And I think that one typical example of that is something that I'm sure is going to be a little bit of a surprise for this audience. And that is that Mexico is today the Number One supplier of refrigerators to the United States. We are the country that sells the most refrigerators to the United States, which is something we are very proud of.

Mexican producers of refrigerators did not establish their plants in order to compete head to head with the huge producers of refrigerators in the United States, but rather they chose a market niche. The market niche for small refrigerators for offices, for hotels, for small apartments in big cities, for university campuses, etc. And by becoming a specialist in that market of small refrigerators, they gained a tremendous margin of competitiveness because being smaller in relative terms than the U.S. producers, they have a great deal of flexibility to adapt to the market changes and to the market requirements. And through that we gained competitiveness by using the so-called economies of scope and becoming specialists in a given sector or in a given market region.

What is going to happen with NAFTA is that you will see a number of market niches developing because a typical Mexican consumer is quite different from a typical American or a typical Canadian consumer. Both because of different income levels, different cultures, different tastes, and so on.

So, in NAFTA the number of market niches are going to be multiplied in the years to come and this will allow firms in the region to become specialists in certain market niches and to take advantage of economies of scope, gaining through that an additional margin of competitiveness. There you have a third element why NAFTA would create more competitiveness in the region as a whole.

The fourth very important element of competitiveness in my view is to allow firms to choose the right technology. If a firm thinks that very labor-intensive technology is the right one, a firm should be able to choose a very labor-intensive technology. If a firm thinks that a very capital-intensive technology is the right one, a firm should be able to choose capital-intensive technology. And what NAFTA is going to do is going to make wider the choices of technology in the region. And I think this is essential for competitiveness in today's world.

Let me refer to one topic that I know in this city [Detroit] is particularly important—the whole discussion and debate on Japanese competitiveness. And I have seen many books about how the Japanese industry is very competitive, and most of the argument boils down to the philosophical approach: the attitude of Japanese workers, the attitude of Japanese management. And I think there is something to this. But very seldom do I see reference to the following facts or figures. Thirty-five percent of Japanese exports come from the so-called production-sharing mechanisms, which is nothing more than if this microphone is Japanese, part of this microphone is not produced in Japan. Assume that putting the head to the microphone is something that requires lots of labor, they don't do that in Tokyo or in Africa, they do it in Indonesia or Malaysia. And through production-sharing, which the Japanese industry is doing, it widens the choice of technology. And using labor-

intensive technology in countries where labor in relative terms is less expensive, and through that they have the ability to choose or to use very labor-intensive technologies for the whole production through production-sharing, or very high tech technology in their own land.

Thirty-five percent of their exports come from production-sharing. Less than five percent of U.S. exports come from production-sharing, which means that producers in the U.S. are limited to the endowment of factors of production, labor and capital, and so on, that you have in your own territory. With NAFTA, those endowments will change. And with NAFTA in the decades to come you have in the region plenty of labor, plenty of capital and plenty of possibilities to use high tech. So, by NAFTA bringing the three countries together will widen the choices of technology that the firms can make in the years to come, and therefore will allow firms to choose the most appropriate technology to thereby minimize costs and to gain an extra margin of competitiveness. To me that is an essential argument related to NAFTA.

My final point related to competitiveness is to try to minimize costs. And through NAFTA we will be able to lower costs in most services—transportation, value-added telecommunications, financial services—because NAFTA includes chapters related to services. And by opening up the total region to those services, we will be able to lower costs and therefore allow firms in the whole region to become more competitive because they will have access to more competitive service and therefore lower costs, better quality.

So, if you look at NAFTA from this point of view, you see that NAFTA offers you these five conditions to increase competitiveness in the region. First, certainty through permanence of quality and continuance of quality; second, economies of scale through a very large market with tremendous potential in some specific elements; third, economies of scope through an endless number of market regions that are going to be developed in the whole region; fourth, a very wide technological choice for firms in the region; and, finally, a cost structure that is much more competitive and therefore gives you an extra margin of competitiveness as a firm, as a user of services.

This is why I have said publicly that NAFTA is a win, win, win situation is not only rhetoric, the point here is that NAFTA can make us more competitive and by making us more competitive means that it will be a possibly sound gain, and not an ill-found gain. Because the competitiveness that NAFTA will bring about in the region will allow us to get a bigger share of world markets and therefore will create jobs on both sides of the border, and actually in our three countries.

Now I would like to refer to the so-called parallel issues—one, the labor one; and the other one, the environmental one. On the labor one, I think that there are several mistakes when you look at the concerns that the unions have regarding the job effect of NAFTA. The first one is that their approach to NAFTA in my view is the wrong one because the approach is that NAFTA is an ill-found gain, which means that if the U.S. gains, Mexico loses; or if Mexico gains, the U.S. loses. On the point I have just made is that this is not an ill-found gain. But, for the sake of the argument, I will accept the assumption that this will be an ill-found gain. The first argument.

The second assumption that this position has is that low wages drive exports, which in my view is the wrong assumption as well. The reason being that if indeed a country with low wages would by that sheer fact become very competitive, a power to export, we would have countries with low wages in the world. Because a country with low wages would start exporting, by exporting growing, demanding more labor, increasing wages. Therefore, you cannot believe that only low wages drive exports. That is not what evidence in the world shows.

But let me assume for the sake of the argument that I accept that assumption as well. So, I'm accepting now two assumptions. One, that it is an ill-found gain and that NAFTA wouldn't have any effect on competitiveness—but that is fully against my intuition. And two, that low wages drive exports. Now in that world that I think is ill conceived, let me give you the following facts.

Mexico is the third trade partner to the U.S. after Canada and Japan. But Mexican exports only represent 5.7 percent of U.S. imports. Of the total import bill of the U.S., Mexico only has a share of 5.7 percent. At the same time, total imports in the U.S. are around 10 percent of total GDP in the U.S. Therefore, Mexican exports only represent .57 percent—less than 1 percentage point of total GDP in the U.S. Less than one percentage point.

Now, assume that through NAFTA Mexico becomes extremely successful in exporting to the U.S. and we double our share, but this is a very aggressive assumption because it would mean that Mexican exports into the U.S. would have to grow twice as much as exports from all parts of the world into the U.S. But let us look at that, if it happened. It means that our total exports into the U.S. would represent 1 percentage point of total GDP in the U.S. It is impossible to think that that would create massive job dislocation.

So, even accepting that this is an ill-found gain, that lower wages drive exports—both assumptions wrong from my point of view—even accepting those two assumptions, the numbers just don't match. We are not large enough to create such a dislocation in the U.S. economy.

Now the argument could be that the dislocation would happen in some regions and in some industries. But that would be an issue that is not related to NAFTA. It is an issue that I think is being discussed in this country that has to do with the industrial transformation that the U.S. is going through that has nothing to do with NAFTA. NAFTA will not change that dramatically because of the sheer size of our smaller exports on a very different scenario in smaller businesses than in the U.S. Therefore, I think that the issue of job losses has been overgrown in the discussion and debate of NAFTA....

[E]ven accepting that negative approach, the numbers just don't quite match. They don't click. They cannot create a massive job dislocation as this has been argued in the past few months in the debate related to NAFTA.

The second issue has to do with the environment. And the full discussion of the environment and its relationship with NAFTA has been sort of paradoxical, and I say this with all due respect because it sounds like sheer legitimate concerns about the environment in the U.S. would be overriding concerns about the environment in Mexico for Mexicans. That is, sometimes the discussion and the debate makes it sound like an environmentalist

in the U.S. is more concerned about the quality of air in Mexico City than myself. And I live in Mexico City. My family lives in Mexico City. My children live in Mexico City. And we want clean air. And I know of no Mexican that doesn't want to have a better environment.... But it takes a great deal of effort. And the point I want to make is that Mexico and President Salinas have had a very strong leadership in terms of our environmental care, not only because he believes in that, but also because the society demands that.

I will give you one example that I find very interesting. In Mexico City today we have a phone service that tells you the quality of the air. So, if you want to go out jogging, you can call that phone—it's 658-1111—and I do jog, so I know it by heart. You call and you find out the quality of the air in certain regions of the city. That gives you the sense, an idea, of the awareness of the Mexican population about the environment. People want clean air, clean water, clean environment in their city. So, we want to put more resources into the environment and we will. But we need to have the resources.

And let me make a point in the relationship between NAFTA and the environment. There is a recent study that came out from Princeton University, and please look now at the handout at your table. It's a handout that describes the relationship between per capita income and environmental degradation. It basically describes by sort of an inverted U-shaped curve, a bell curve, that shows that very poor countries with very low per capita income have very little environmental degradation, naturally. And as countries develop, the environmental degradation gets worse and worse, and there is a turning point that if countries have more resources undeveloped, the environmental degradation goes down. So, that inverted view bell curve shows you that there is a clear relationship between NAFTA and the environment, and it makes a lot of sense. These countries do not pollute. As they industrialize, they pollute more and more. And once they are rich enough they have resources to avoid pollution through the use of new technologies and so on.

Well, Mexico happens to be right at the peak of this curve. Between $3,700 and $4,000 per capita income. Now, if NAFTA will start to increase the per capita income of Mexicans, it means that NAFTA will put us in the lower part of the curve, to the righthand side of the peak, and therefore NAFTA will help us improve our environment. NAFTA won't hurt the environment. NAFTA will help the environment because it will give Mexico more resources to invest in the care of the environment and therefore to improve it. And I think this is the point that we have to make, that NAFTA indeed could be a very important instrument to clean the environment. And this is why NAFTA is the first trade agreement in the world that has environmental provisions. And it has two very strong environmental provisions. One of them is that the three countries— Canada, the U.S. and Mexico—belong to multinational, multilateral or regional environmental organizations and we have agreed on NAFTA that all of the features that come out of these negotiations override NAFTA provisions, are dominant over NAFTA provisions. Point Number One.

And Point Number Two. If any of the three countries intend to attract investment by having a loose policy on the environment, that is forbidden by NAFTA.

So, if tomorrow a governor of a state in Mexico tells you,

"You come to me, you put your plants here, and I will ask you to [use] this filter, or I will let you dump the water in the river. But do that in Mexico, because if you do that in the U.S., you will have higher costs and you couldn't do it.

That is not allowed by NAFTA. That would be stopped by NAFTA. No investment can be promoted, no investment incentive can be given with a loose environmental policy.

Those two provisions are very strong, very strong, and they are right in the NAFTA pact.

And the third point is between Mexico and the U.S. Here there is a very important problem that is environmentally related on our borders. And we have put our money where our mouth is. Even though we are a poor country, we are allocating $460 million to take care of problems on our borders. And the same amount of money is being allocated by the U.S. Government on the U.S. side. I think we distributed some sort of green pamphlet that explains the Mexican public works orders for the border regions, which describes how we are allocating that $460 million to take care of environmental problems on our border.

So, really the environmental issue could be tackled properly with NAFTA. NAFTA could be an instrument that actually helps environmental care, instead of hurting the environment due to the sheer relationship between the wealth of a country, the per capita income of a country, and environmental issues.

So, this is why I say that NAFTA makes a great deal of sense. That is, NAFTA will help us to create more jobs, it will help us become more competitive, and NAFTA will help us improve the environment as well.

Let me conclude by sharing with you a final thought that I wrote on the plane. Over the years your city of Detroit has a bigger and bigger challenge by the changing business climate, by evolution in consumer tastes, and by other shifts that require a restructuring of the priorities and the practices of the Detroit business community. No one could deny that there have been periods of adjustment. And yet you have adjusted and continue to adjust. Detroit, and indeed the state of Michigan, remain a great industrial center producing not only some of the world's finest automobiles but thousands of other products and services that are recognized around the world for their quality. We Mexicans certainly are familiar with the products of Detroit and Michigan. Some of you may be surprised to learn that Mexico is your state's second largest export market, exceeded only by Canada. In 1991, Michigan's exports to Mexico totaled $1.6 billion, an increase of more than one-third just since 1987. Our share of your exports has risen over the past five years up to 7 percent.

What does Mexico purchase from Michigan? Well, we are a cross-section of your output—transportation equipment, industrial machinery and computers, fabricated metal products, electric and electronics equipment, rubber and plastic products, and others. Mexican purchases support thousands of jobs here in Michigan. For example, Michigan-made components account for three-fourths of the value of the small cars and trucks produced in Mexico by Ford Motor Company. Brakes, fuel tanks, electronic components, interior trim—all that comes from the U.S. and from Michigan specif-

ically. Production sharing of this sort sustains about 72,000 jobs in Michigan.

Here is an example with which I would like to conclude. By increasing trade between Michigan and Mexico, we have been able to create jobs both in Michigan and in Mexico, as these figures show. And this is why I promote the idea of NAFTA. The NAFTA negotiations are over. The text took us three years to negotiate with a very intensive process of consultation in which the automobile industry from Detroit had a major participation, particularly people like Bob Lutz who participated very actively in that negotiation. There we have an instrument that is really an opportunity to improve the relationship between our two countries. It is an opportunity from which we can both win. It is an opportunity which will help us to become more competitive, create more jobs and clean our environment. This is why I truly believe that NAFTA makes sense. But if I may say with a non-economic argument, with more of a human argument, NAFTA is an instrument to help two neighbors live better. And the fact is that Mexico and the U.S. will be neighbors forever. Thank you.

NO

Sheldon Friedman

NAFTA AS SOCIAL DUMPING

The conventional wisdom that the North American Free Trade Agreement (NAFTA) will be unambiguously good for North American incomes and jobs may be comforting, but it is almost certainly wrong.... NAFTA is more likely to harm than help the overwhelming majority of participants in the U.S. economy. Its benefits even for many, if not most Mexicans, are doubtful as well.

Much is at stake.... NAFTA will accelerate the division of the world into rival trading blocs, and will do much to define the terms on which the North American/Western Hemispheric bloc seeks to compete.

Quite unlike the approach being followed in the European Economic Community (EC), the Bush-Salinas blueprint for economic integration will likely be silent or at best, ineffective by design, on the critical issues of labor standards, workers' rights, and health, safety and environmental protections. [This selection was written toward the end of President Bush's term of office. President Clinton also favors NAFTA, with some limited modifications.— Ed.] There is even a serious risk that the agreement will undermine existing federal and state protections in these and other areas. In contrast to the care which has been taken in the EC to undertake economic integration in a manner which avoids "social dumping," the Bush-Salinas NAFTA will be an open invitation to continue and intensify this already-rampant practice.

Closer integration between the United States and Mexican economies is likely, with or without a NAFTA. What is neither inevitable nor desirable is economic integration based on an international division of labor in which Mexico supplies cheap labor and lax enforcement of health, safety, and environmental standards, the United States supplies the consumer market, multinational corporations derive the profit, and U.S. workers face further wage cuts and the loss of their jobs.

For Mexican workers, the benefits are doubtful. Any attempt to raise their abysmal wages will lead to complaints by multinational employers, threats of capital flight to even lower-wage countries and, if recent history is any guide, a repressive Mexican government reaction. The Mexican and border environments will continue to be despoiled by corporate polluters; Mexican workers will continue to be subjected to toxic exposures which would be illegal in the United States. It is also likely that control over oil and other natural resources, which under Article 27 of the Mexican constitution have been reserved for the Mexican people since the turbulent 1930s, will be ceded slowly but surely to the big U.S. oil companies. The number of jobs which will be destroyed in agriculture and small business raises serious doubts about whether NAFTA will lead to net job creation even in Mexico.

In a word, NAFTA will accelerate the *maquilazation* of Mexico [locating factories in Mexico just south of the U.S. border]. Under the *maquiladora* program, which was initiated in 1965, equipment and parts can be imported duty-free into Mexico, provided the products into which they are manufactured or assembled are exported from Mexico. The United States then permits goods finished in Mexico and exported from there to the United States to be charged duty only on the low-wage value added in Mexico. Yet, until Mexican wages began to tumble in the early 1980s to below the level of East Asian developing countries, the scale of foreign investment in the *maquilas* remained relatively modest. Since 1982, the number of *maquiladora* plants and workers has more than tripled. Over the last eight years, the number of *maquilas* and *maquila* workers has increased 16 percent per year. By the end of 1991, more than 2,000 *maquilas* were employing over 600,000 Mexican workers. More than half of all *maquiladora* employment is concentrated in the auto parts and electronics industries, key industries in which employment has fallen sharply in the United States. Though precise figures are not available, most if not all of the growth in *maquilas* represents the relocation of plants and the shift of jobs from the United States.

What the rapid shift of jobs to the *maquilas* in the 1980s and now NAFTA represent, first and foremost, is a joint effort by the U.S. and Mexican governments, Mexico's creditors and multinational corporations to replace Mexico's greatly diminished oil export earnings with manufactured exports generated by Mexico's abundant low wage workforce. With the collapse in value of oil exports, Mexico desperately needs foreign exchange from manufacturing exports to pay foreign debts.

Citibank and certain other of Mexico's biggest creditors are not in the best financial health; despite the "Brady Plan" Mexico still must pay $10 billion per year to service its debt to U.S. and Canadian banks, funds which are desperately needed in Mexico for economic development purposes.

LOW WAGES AND REPRESSION

Low wages, often only one tenth of U.S. wage levels, are the centerpiece of this strategy, which depends on attracting foreign investment to Mexico. In this respect, the Mexican government under Salinas and his predecessor have succeeded admirably. Real wages of Mexican workers, none too high to begin with, have plunged 40 percent since 1982. Back then workers received nearly 40 percent of Mexico's GDP; their share fell to just 24 percent last year.

When Mexican workers attempt to resist such exploitation, the repression visited upon them by their own government is severe and swift. In January 1992, while in the midst of negotiations with thirty-three primarily U.S.-owned *maquiladora* employers, two days before a strike deadline, Mexican trade union leader Agapito Gonzales was arrested.

Gonzales had been unusually effective by *maquiladora* standards, in raising the wages of some of the lowest-paid industrial workers in the world. That effectiveness did not sit well with the employers. They took their case directly to President Salinas. His response to this perceived threat to the Mexican low-wage economic development strategy was decisive and immediate: Agapito Gonzales was seized in the dead of night—on a tax evasion charge.

How did the Bush Administration react? NAFTA negotiations did not miss a beat. On the contrary, President Bush announced with great fanfare that the timetable for completing a tentative agreement had been accelerated. What about Agapito Gonzales? Though a court threw out the government's original charge against him, he remains under detention, more than six months after his arrest. The workers at the thirty-three plants in negotiations at the time of Gonzales' arrest settled for wage increases well below Mexico's recent rate of inflation—in sharp contrast to the substantial real wage gains won several weeks earlier, after short strikes under Gonzales' leadership, by their co-workers at twenty-five other *maquila* plants.

Suppression of Mexican wages may benefit the profit margins of multinational corporations, but it runs directly counter to the alleged benefit from NAFTA associated with improved access by U.S. exporters to the Mexican market. Transfer of production from the United States to Mexico under such circumstances, moreover, contributes to the kind of economic stagnation which the United States is experiencing and which Walter Russell Mead has written about so perceptively.

Contrary to claims by Administration spokespersons, increased U.S. exports to Mexico in recent years do not primarily reflect the growth of Mexico's internal consumer market. Rather, they largely reflect the increase in shipments of machinery, components, and materials from U.S.-based plants in Mexico, typically from U.S. parent companies that have relocated production facilities to Mexico, thereby simply transfering North American production from the United States to Mexico. Of all countries' exports to Mexico in 1991, capital goods (manufacturing plants and equipment) accounted for 22.5 percent, intermediate goods (parts used to make final products sent back to the U.S. market) accounted for 62.7 percent, and consumer goods only 14.8 percent. In other words, the touted "export boom" was not targeted to Mexico's internal consumer market; rather, it provided logistical support for the U.S. *import* boom of Mexican-assembled products. NAFTA will accelerate these trends.

ENVIRONMENTAL DISASTER

Low wages are not the only benefit accruing to multinational corporations that transfer operations to Mexico. Additional savings can also be realized by avoiding the cost of complying with U.S. health, safety, and environmental regulations. The U.S.-Mexico border area, astride the longest boundary on the planet between first and third world nations, and the areas where three fourths of all *maquila* plants are located, is generally regarded as an environmental disaster. Air and water pollution, hazardous waste and pesticides, are among the area's many festering environmental problems. Severe birth defects and other serious air and water pollution-related public health problems have been painstakingly documented, despite obstacles imposed by official indifference or worse, on both sides of the border.

Figure 1
The Resource Gap:
Per Capita Spending on
Environmental Protection in
the United States and Mexico

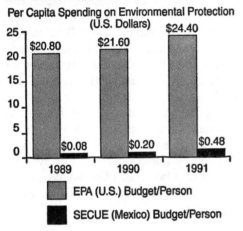

Per Capita Spending on Environmental Protection (U.S. Dollars)

Source: Data provided by Congressional Research Service, based on information obtained from EPA.

The problem is not so much that Mexico lacks regulations, though in at least three important areas subject to regulation in the United States, it does: underground storage tanks, land disposal of hazardous wastes, and clean-up of abandoned hazardous waste sites. The greater problem, typical for an impoverished developing country, is Mexico's lack of resources to enforce the environmental regulations that it has. SEDUE, Mexico's EPA, had a 1991 budget of $38 million; EPA's 1991 budget was $5 *billion*, 132 times as large.

Equally serious, public input to the process of environmental standard-setting and enforcement is virtually nonexistent in Mexico. Mexicans who complain to their government about serious adverse public health consequences for themselves and their families of toxic emissions caused by foreign-owned factories are labeled unpatriotic and placed under investigation. In the absence of U.S. trade sanctions which could be used to support their efforts, Mexican workers and the Mexican public are in an extremely weak position to face down environmental blackmail and force foreign corporations to adhere to health, safety, and environmental standards.

HARD HIT U.S. WORKERS

For U.S. workers, the consequences of NAFTA will be job loss, downward pressure on wages and benefits, and downward pressure on health, safety, and environmental standards. Hispanic workers in the United States, together with other blue-collar workers with a high school education or less, will be disproportionately represented in the ranks of those who are most adversely affected.

Hispanic workers were almost 30 percent more likely than non-Hispanics to suffer dislocation in the form of permanent job loss between 1985 and 1989. Already in recent years, relocations to Mexico by companies such as Farah and Green Giant have had grossly disproportionate adverse impact on Hispanic and other minority workers in the United States.

U.S. workers will also face increased environmental blackmail, as weak standards and lax enforcement in Mexico cost more U.S. workers their jobs. The wood furniture in the Los Angeles area is an example of how serious this problem has become. Already by 1988 more than 150 U.S.-owned furniture plants were operating in Mexico's border area under the *maquiladora* program. Most if not all of them had relocated from the United States in search of low wages and less costly environmental and safety regulations. When California adopted tougher standards to control emissions of paint and solvents, up to 10 percent of the wood furniture manufacturers still remaining in the Los Angeles area in 1989 fled to Mexico rather than comply, thereby eliminating as many as 2,500 additional jobs.

The victims of NAFTA will be many of the same workers who have already been devastated over the last decade or more by plant closings, permanent layoffs, and real earnings declines. For these workers and their families, NAFTA will become one more cause of great hardship and suffering, as they cope with economic dislocation beyond their control, triggered by U.S. government policy.

U.S. workers displaced by NAFTA or other causes have one of the weakest safety nets in the industrialized world. They have no national health insurance; inadequate unemployment benefits; limited help with training or job search assistance; and no public job creation programs. The proportion of our GDP devoted to public labor market programs of *all* kinds, unemployment insurance, job training, job search assistance and job creation combined, is less than one-third as high as Canada's, and only one-fourth as high as Western Europe's (0.6 percent of GDP for the United States, versus 2 percent for Canada and 2.5 percent for Western Europe).

Trade Adjustment Assistance (TAA), the only U.S. program which comes close to meeting international standards in terms of duration of assistance and provision of training for dislocated workers, requires major improvements in benefits, eligibility rules, and funding in order to provide meaningful help for workers who will be injured as a result of NAFTA. TAA is the federal government's often-reaffirmed but never fulfilled commitment to help workers who are injured by trade. The program currently provides extended unemployment benefits (known as trade readjustment allowances, or TRA), training, job search assistance, and relocation allowances for workers who qualify.

When workers are injured as a result of deliberate national policy such as trade liberalization or a Free Trade Agreement, as a matter of basic fairness they should be entitled to compensation. Property owners who are dispossessed as a result of government action often are entitled to compensation; workers who lose their jobs as a result of government action can sustain far more serious damage and should have no lesser claim. To achieve this goal, major improvements are needed in TAA benefits, eligibility rules and funding.

... Funding is kept to such a bare minimum, and is dispersed so tightfistedly, that only 25,000 workers received benefits under the program last year [1991] despite a trade deficit of $65 billion and unemployed workers numbering nearly ten million (with nearly three million experiencing joblessness for over six months). [President Clinton favors TAA benefits for workers displaced by NAFTA, but he has not yet asked for specific funding levels.—Ed.] ...

ALTERNATIVE, POSITIVE
INTEGRATION

Under "fast track" procedures which the Bush Administration insisted upon and which the Congress narrowly approved in May 1991, it will be very difficult to amend the agreement. Thus, unless the Congress rejects it, [U.S.] trade negotiators will have succeeded in drafting a blueprint for economic integration with far reaching and profoundly damaging consequences.

It is possible, however, to conceive of a far more positive model of economic integration than the NAFTA of Salinas and Bush, one in which harmonization of workers' rights and labor, health, safety and environmental standards would be upward, not downward.

The model for this is the European Community, where economic integration has been accompanied by massive "social funds" and a social charter that intends to provide a framework for upward harmonization, and guard against the kind of "social dumping" that NAFTA will exacerbate.

In the North American context, upward harmonization would require the agreement to include specific provisions that allow each signatory country to invoke trade sanctions, in order to prevent unfair competition from imports which derive a competitive advantage based upon violations of workers' rights, or of labor, health, safety and environmental standards. These provisions are essential not only to protect U.S. workers and the environment, but also to support the efforts of workers and others to raise labor standards and protect the environment in Mexico. Bush Administration negotiators have completely rejected this approach.

Additional debt relief for Mexico would also be needed to assure an equitable NAFTA which takes us on a more positive road to economic integration.

A more equitable NAFTA would also require comprehensive improvements in the Trade Adjustment Assistance (TAA) program, to help compensate U.S. workers who will be among NAFTA's victims.

Most of all, there must be a democratic negotiating process which assures a seat at the NAFTA table for workers, farmers, environmentalists and others on both sides of the border who will be affected by the agreement, not just for the economic elites and multinational corporations who currently stand to profit from it.

The... NAFTA agreement ignores almost completely the interests of workers, farmers, and environmentalists on both sides of the border. The Congress should reject it decisively. Based on everything that is known about it, a NAFTA that bad will be much worse than no NAFTA at all.

POSTSCRIPT

Will the North American Free Trade Agreement Benefit All Its Member Countries?

What is certain is that NAFTA is a portentous and controversial issue in all three countries that negotiated the agreement. For more background and other viewpoints, see the February 1993 edition of *The Annals of the American Academy of Political and Social Science*, which contains 15 excellent articles. The articles examine NAFTA and also explore the idea of a free trade zone that might include *all* of North America, including the Caribbean and Central America, and perhaps even all of the Western Hemisphere! A view similar to Freidman's negative position can be found in Noam Chomsky, "The Masters of Mankind," *The Nation* (March 29, 1993). A more positive view of the impact of NAFTA can be found in Linda M. Aguilar, "NAFTA: A Review of the Issues," *Economic Perspective*, the journal of the Federal Reserve Bank of Chicago (Fall 1992).

In Canada, Audrey McLaughlin, leader of the New Democratic Party, argued against ratification during a debate in Canada's House of Commons in May 1993. The treaty should be rejected, she said, because "[t]his is not another commercial agreement; this is a sellout of Canada." Because of the physical separation between Mexico and Canada, Canadian concerns about job losses to Mexican factory workers and transborder pollution have been less acute than they are among some people in the United States. As Canadian pollster Angus Reid put it, "Because Mexico is a long way from Canada, worry about eroding standards is just not so relevant here."

There is also opposition in Mexico, although it is less obvious because the political system there has been dominated by one party, the *Partí Institucional Revolucionario* (PRI), since 1929. Some Mexicans worry that Mexico will become something of a satellite to its much more powerful neighbor. Writer Homero Aridjis believes that Mexico's economy and culture are "becoming Americanized," and that "many Mexicans are becoming aliens in their own country." However, Mexico's president, Carlos Salinas de Gortari, has made NAFTA a central part of his plan to reform and open up the Mexican economy to trade. Some critics charge that if NAFTA fails in Washington, Salinas's modernization program will suffer a severe setback.

ISSUE 6

Is Islamic Fundamentalism a Threat to Political Stability?

YES: Judith Miller, from "The Challenge of Radical Islam," *Foreign Affairs* (Spring 1993)

NO: Leon T. Hadar, from "What Green Peril?" *Foreign Affairs* (Spring 1993)

ISSUE SUMMARY

YES: Political researcher and writer Judith Miller argues that the radical Islamic movement in the greater Middle East region has created a combustible mixture that threatens domestic and international political stability.

NO: Leon Hadar, a professor of political science, maintains that Islam is neither unified nor a threat to political stability. The West's interests and ideals would best be served by staying out of the contest for power among Islamic governments and dissident groups.

Islam was founded by the prophet Muhammad late in the sixth century. The word *Islam* means submission to God (Allah), and Muslims (ones who submit) believe that Muhammad received Allah's teachings, which make up the Koran. There are several Islamic political concepts that are important to this issue. Some tend to bring Muslims together; others work to divide them.

One of the forces that serve to promote Muslim unity is the idea of *ummah*, the spiritual, cultural, and political community of Muslims. In part, this means that Muslims are less likely than people from the Western cultural tradition to draw distinct lines between the state, religion, and the individual. Instead, some Muslims believe that the conduct of government and of individuals should be governed by *shari'ah*, that is, Koranic law. *Ummah* implies that faithful believers of Islam should join spiritually and politically into one, great Muslim community. A related unifying element of Islam is that Muslims distinguish between Muslim-held lands ("the house of Islam") and non-Muslim lands ("the house of unbelief"). One of the fundamental tenets of Islam is the jihad, meaning struggle in the name of Allah. A jihad can be peaceful or violent; a jihad can defend Islam against nonbelievers or against individual Muslims or sects deemed to be heretical or disloyal to the true faith. Those who struggle to defend or promote Islam are sometimes called *mujahedin*.

A sense of common history is another factor that works to bring Muslims together. After a triumphant and powerful beginning, which included the spread of Islamic religion and culture into Europe and beyond from its Middle Eastern origins, the political fortunes of Muslims declined slowly after about the year 1500. Part of this decline was due to military losses during the Crusades (1095–1291). The Crusades were military expeditions undertaken by Christian, European powers in the 11th, 12th, and 13th centuries to win the Holy Land from the Muslims. By the start of the modern era, almost all Muslim lands were under the direct or indirect control of colonial—mostly European, mostly Christian—powers. Muslim history, therefore, includes conflict with Christian powers (especially those of Europe) and domination of Muslims by others.

There are also strong forces that tend to divide Muslims. One of these is the frequent rivalry between the majority Sunni sect and the minority Shi'ite sect. The origins of this division are not important to our political discussion here, except to point out that the minority Shi'ites tend to be more militant, and they tend to reject the legitimacy of Sunni control of such important Islamic places as Mecca, in Saudi Arabia.

Muslims are also divided over the degree to which they believe in strict adherence to *shari'ah* to govern both religious and civil conduct. Muslim traditionalists (or fundamentalists, according to common usage) want to establish legal systems based on *shari'ah* and reinstitute practices such as banning alcohol and having women cover their faces, which declined under the influence of Western culture.

Other Muslims, who are often called secularists (or less accurately, modernists) believe that religious and civil law should be kept relatively separate. For them, Koranic law is flexible enough to allow changes in tradition. The secularists reject the argument that they are not good Muslims.

Nationalism (primary political loyalty to a national state) is a third factor that divides Muslims. Individual Muslim countries are fiercely nationalistic. Achieving full Muslim political unity would necessarily entail giving up patriotism and other manifestations of nationalism.

Why are the forces of unity and division among Muslims a global concern? Since its low point after World War I, the Muslim world's role on the world stage has been enlarged. There are now many more independent Muslim countries. Moreover, Muslim countries are becoming stronger—a strength based in part on the wealth that petroleum has brought them. And Muslims everywhere have begun to reclaim their heritage in what might be called a Muslim pride movement.

The issue debated here is whether resurgent Islam, especially its traditional, fundamental aspects, represent a threat to political stability. Judith Miller argues that the answer is yes, that the traditionalists are fundamentally antithetical to stability. Leon Hadar disagrees, arguing that the traditionalists are neither an inherently destabilizing force nor likely to succeed in uniting and militarizing the house of Islam.

YES

Judith Miller

THE CHALLENGE OF
RADICAL ISLAM

In April 1991 an unusual meeting was held in the Sudanese capital of Khartoum. For four days, leading Islamic politicians and intellectuals from 55 countries and three continents met to draft a common strategy to establish Muslim states in their respective lands. It was an Islamic star-studded event....

The group ultimately approved a six-point manifesto intended to demonstrate that "whatever the strength of America and the West" in the aftermath of the Gulf War, "God is greater." The manifesto paid lip service to liberalism and democracy, asserting that they were "not incompatible" with *shura* [ruling Muslim council], or Islamic government through consultation. Political pluralism was fine, provided it was not "unlimited" and was subordinate to the need for "unity and the *shura*." Cooperation with the West and existing non-Islamic governments was permissible, if such exchanges were based on new and more equitable principles. "Good regimes," the document states, "will benefit from popular will; bad regimes will be fought." Read in its entirety, the manifesto's underlying message was clear: in Islam's war against the West and the struggle to build Islamic states at home, the ends justified the means.

The gathering received almost no attention in the Western press. But many regard the Islamic Arab Popular Conference, as it was called, as an important event. It marked the first serious effort by an avowedly Islamic state to define with other leading figures of the movement their own vision of a new world order and a strategy for achieving it. The conference also made progress toward Turabi's long-stated goal of overcoming the historic rift between Sunni Muslim states, like Sudan, and a Shiite state, like Iran—that is, toward ending the bitter historic enmity that has separated these two wings of Islam since the seventh century. In addition, the gathering helped fuse formerly secular Arab nationalist movements, which have dominated Arab politics in the anticolonial struggles for independence and statehood for nearly 50 years, with the increasingly more seductive and influential groups espousing the new Islamic rhetoric.

From Judith Miller, "The Challenge of Radical Islam," *Foreign Affairs*, vol. 72, no. 2 (Spring 1993). Copyright © 1993 by The Council on Foreign Relations, Inc. Reprinted by permission of *Foreign Affairs*.

WHAT IS TO BE DONE?

How should the United States and its new administration view the rise of militant Islam in the Middle East? How should Americans react? What, if anything, can be done about the trend?

The Khartoum conference is merely one example of the growing power of militant Islam. Since Islamic revolutionaries led by the Ayatollah Ruhollah Khomeini toppled the shah of Iran in 1979 and swept Islamic militants to power, an avowedly Islamic government has emerged only in impoverished, isolated Sudan. But everywhere, Arab governments are struggling to contain Islamic pressures and respond to a widespread desire among their citizens for more "Islamic" government and society. ...

Few serious analysts of militant Islam, or Islamic fundamentalism (an inappropriate but widely used term borrowed from American Protestantism to describe the phenomenon), argue that Islamic militant groups constitute a monolith. Fewer still see Islam... as the "Green Menace." ... Most sophisticated analysts know that militant Islam is as diverse as the Arabs themselves and the countries in which it is taking hold. They recognize that Islam is not inherently at odds with modernity; the two co-exist comfortably in Muslim societies from Indonesia to Bosnia. Nor do most foes of fundamentalism maintain that the Khartoum conference and other efforts by Islamists to enhance cooperation should be regarded as a new "Khomeintern"—a vast conspiracy led by Iran and Sudan.

However, radical political Islam placed atop the societies of the Middle East has created a combustible mixture. And those who believe in universal human rights (and women's rights in particu-

lar), democratic government, political tolerance and pluralism and in peace between the Arabs and Israelis cannot be complacent about the growing strength of militant Islamic movements in most Middle Eastern countries, or about the numerous and increasing ties among such movements and between Iran and Sudan. Western governments should be concerned about these movements and, more important, should oppose them. For despite their rhetorical commitment to democracy and pluralism, virtually all militant Islamists oppose both. They are, and are likely to remain, anti-Western, anti-American and anti-Israeli.

The Bush administration seemed to understand this point, but this recognition was never fully apparent in its policy. The administration tried to draw a distinction between good and bad Islamists, and it wound up fudging a response to the challenge posed by radical Islam. ...

[The] distinction was politically useful for the administration. It enabled Washington, on the one hand, to oppose any Islamic group that espoused violence and challenged regimes that the United States either liked or needed to do business with, such as Egypt and Saudi Arabia, and on the other, to resist the anti-American Islamic governments in power in Sudan and Iran, which met his criteria of being violent, intolerant and coercive. The doctrine, by extension, also justified American support for "good" Islamic groups—those seeking to overturn communist or tyrannical states (such as the Mujahedeen rebels in Afghanistan and the Mujahedeen-e Khalq, a militant Islamic group that is fighting Iran not only from inside Iraq but also from Washington).

A few analysts challenged the wisdom of America's support for these good Islamic groups. They warned ineffectively, but with keen foresight, that those Islamic factions supported by the West in their fight against Kabul would ultimately make Afghans nostalgic for the good old days of President Najibullah. And others labeled the American-tolerated, if not openly supported, Mujahedeen the "Khmer Rouge of Islamists."

Despite such reservations, the Bush administration's policy seemed fairly straightforward. Of course, the United States would oppose groups such as the violent wing of the Islamic Resistance Movement (Hamas), the Iranian-supported Hezbollah in Lebanon and the four—and still splitting—factions of the Islamic Jihad [holy war], all of which champion violence, terrorism and "holy war" to rid Muslims of the "un-Islamic" governments that oppress Arabs in Israel, Jordan, Lebanon and Egypt. But how would Washington view Islamic groups that pledged to create democratic rule, to respect human rights and pluralism?...

What the United States wanted, he explained, was for Middle Eastern nations to broaden political participation in their societies. At the same time... Washington would oppose those seeking to use the democratic process to come to power, only to destroy that very process in order to retain power and political dominance....

But how would Washington know which Islamic groups were genuinely committed to democratic principles and peaceful coexistence with its own minorities, women and the West? Here, the statement was diplomatically silent. "We'll know 'em when we see 'em," quipped one American diplomat. But Washington's reluctance to spell out its criteria was a deliberate evasion....

CLERICS IN CIVILIAN CLOTHES?

Why should one suspect the sincerity of the Islamists' commitment to truth, justice and the democratic way? In short, because of Arab and Islamic history and the nature and evolution of these groups. Consider, for one, the FIS [Islamic Salvation Front, an Islamic fundamentalist movement]. In Algeria the FIS won a plurality of the electoral votes in national elections in December 1991, but the group was denied victory by a military coup and the installation of an emergency government that has banned the FIS and ruthlessly hunted down its members ever since.

During parliamentary elections, FIS leaders led a double linguistic life. They offered Algeria's poor and disenfranchised vague slogans of spiritual and, more important, economic salvation through Islam, and to Western journalists and its more Frenchified but politically frustrated middle class, they gave reassurances of their belief in democracy and human rights. Before the first round of voting, in sum, FIS leaders were careful to stress their democratic intentions.

But their tone and message changed abruptly after the FIS scored so well in the first round and seemed destined to secure an overwhelming parliamentary majority in the second voting round. Only then did the supposedly moderate FIS leaders begin emphasizing the party's earlier slogan: "No law. No constitution. Only the laws of God and the Koran." While this linguistic double-talk may not justify the cancellation of elections and surely not the subsequent repression, it raises questions about what the FIS would have done had it been permitted to assume power.

A similar pattern of events occurred in the Sudan. Islam was brought to power there not by the ballot box, but by a military coup. Sudan's leaders now parrot the Islamic values and principles enunciated by the Svengali of the Islamic movement—Hassan Turabi, a Western-trained jurist who is spellbinding in at least three languages. On paper, it was hard to find fault with Turabi. He favored "Islamic" emancipation of women and respect for individual dignity and property. Islam, he said, did not believe in coercion. But the reality of life in his new Islamic state belies these sentiments and reassurances. Since coming to power, the military government has canceled freedom of assembly and the press, banned all non-Islamic parties, forced women to wear Islamic dress or lose their jobs and, according to Amnesty International and other human rights groups, tortured suspected heretics and other political dissidents in what the Sudanese call "ghost houses," which are sprinkled throughout the capital.

Minorities have fared even worse. Catholic bishops have accused the Sudanese government of waging a holy war against the state's Christians (almost ten percent of the population) and those who follow African religions. *Sharia*, or Islamic law, has been reimposed with new vigor: lashings of women for inappropriate dress are now common; so are other corporal punishments, such as amputations for repeated theft, stoning for adultery; the law even allows crucifixion.

Iran is often cited as another example of Islamic "pragmatism" and growing "moderation." While Tehran allows greater freedom of debate and political participation than was permitted under the shah,... no individual or group that questions the basic tenets of the Islamic revolution and theocratic rule is permitted to participate. Iran... remains nonetheless rhetorically and to some extent genuinely hostile to the West, the United States in particular. Finally, its refusal to retract the disgraceful religious ruling—or the bounty on his head—against Salman Rushdie for writing an allegedly blasphemous book, *The Satanic Verses*, reflects more vividly than any other single action Iran's total disregard for basic human rights and international law....

A new, more moderate political Islam may evolve and take root in the region. But many believe that this is unlikely. "Islam is today the language of opposition," says A. Abu Zayd, a Sudanese educator. "To attract the young, Islam must be fierce and militant, opposed to the existing order. So to speak of a moderate political Islam is a contradiction in terms."

Other analysts, such as Martin Kramer, associate director of the Moshe Dayan Center at Tel Aviv University, argue that militant Islamic groups, by nature, cannot be democratic, pluralistic, egalitarian or pro-Western. In a recent *Commentary* article, Kramer notes that Islamic law is not legislated but divinely revealed. It is, therefore, perfect law, which as such is beyond reform, abrogation or alteration. "While it is not above some reinterpretation," Kramer observes, "neither is it infinitely elastic." That law, he continues, stands in stark opposition to the Universal Declaration of Human Rights, which guarantees the freedom to choose, among other things, one's religion and spouse, both of which are restricted in Islamic law. While Islam over the centuries has proven far more tolerant toward minorities and diversity than Christianity (sectarian strife and religious persecution having been atypical and hardly ever as intense as the great persecutions that occurred under Christianity), minorities under Islamic law are given protected, not equal, status.

Bernard Lewis, a noted historian of the Middle East, argues in a recent article in *The Atlantic Monthly* that the nature and history of Islam and the relationship between Islam and temporal power do not make liberal democracy and Islam natural bedfellows. Islam, he explains, has been characterized throughout history by the absence of any legal recognition of corporate persons or the legal person, which is at the heart of the representative institutions embodied in Roman law. The Islamic state was in principle a theocracy, Lewis argues, "not in the Western sense of a state ruled by church and the clergy, since neither existed in the Islamic world, but in the more literal sense of a polity ruled by God." Therefore, devout Muslims believe that legitimate authority comes from God alone. And since the ruler derives his power from God and the holy law, and not from the people, defying authority has been tantamount to defying God. "Disobedience was a sin as well as a crime," Lewis concludes. Against such a backdrop, autocracy has been the norm, and the notions of plurality, self-criticism and disagreement—all essential features of liberal democracy—face an uphill, though not impossible, battle in winning widespread cultural acceptance.

PROMOTE HUMAN RIGHTS, NOT ELECTIONS

... American officials formulating new policies toward Islam and the Arabs should be skeptical of those who seek to liberate Arabs through Islam. First, they should understand that no matter how often and fervently Islamic groups assert their commitment to democracy and pluralism, their basic ideological covenants and tracts, published declarations and interviews (especially in Arabic) appear to make these pledges incompatible with their stated goals of establishing societies under Islamic laws and according to Islamic values. Far too many Middle Easterners, and Islamists in particular, have learned how to mollify the West (and deceive their own potential adherents, many of whom genuinely crave democracy, greater political expression and an end to political repression) by manipulating the words of democracy.

Moreover, to most Islamists, and to many Arabs today, democracy translates as majority rule. There is an almost total disregard for minority rights, an essential component of liberal democracy. If the majority want an Islamic state, Islamists maintain, then the minority or minorities—be they religious, ethnic or female—who do not will have to put up or shut up, or accept a far worse fate.

As it begins to chart its course in foreign policy, the new Clinton administration is likely to feel obliged to promote democracy in the Middle East. It must recognize, however, that the promotion of free elections immediately is likely to lead to the triumph of Islamic groups that have no commitment to democracy in any recognizable, meaningful form. In other words, there seems to be a paradox in America's relentless rhetorical (if not actual) promotion of democracy and pluralism in the Middle East. Because Islamic groups ... are currently the best organized opposition and, in some countries, the only organized opposition, given Arab reluctance to openly oppose associations that call themselves Islamic, free elections seem more likely than any other route to produce militant Islamic regimes that are, in fact, inherently anti-democratic....

What the Clinton administration should say is that the establishment of avowedly "Islamic states" risks jeopardizing the principles espoused in the Universal Declaration of Human Rights and codified in the International Covenant on Civil and Political Rights. The ICCPR declaration is not a new form of cultural imperialism, as Islamists argue, but rather a code of values that constitutes the basis of decent and humane government and has been approved by 117 countries. The fact that leading Islamic militants felt obliged to meet in Paris in 1981 to draft an Islamic Declaration of Human Rights, which omitted all freedoms that contradicted *sharia*, should give any policymaker pause about what can be expected from the Islamic radicals, should they come to power.

Consider women. While Islamists speak of the need to honor women and prevent their degradation, the governments most Islamists are promoting would, in accordance with their interpretation of *sharia*, deny women work in many sectors of the economy and deny them equal rights and equal legal standing. In Iran, the government in the name of Islam restored polygamy and child marriage, which the shah had earlier outlawed. This is not simply a different, and hence morally acceptable, way of organizing society. Rather, the systematic denial of women's rights is like binding female children's feet in China—a barbaric practice impeding economic and social development that should be denounced by any self-confident American government. No one is recommending that the United States invade Sudan or Saudi Arabia to liberate women. But neither should the alternative be official

American silence about such practices. While there will always be a difficult balance between realpolitik and idealistic values in foreign policy, American administrators should strive toward the latter.

The Bush administration should have said that America would promote elections tomorrow and civil society today—increased participation in public life by a growing number of individuals, groups and associations who genuinely crave liberal democracy—so that the concepts and traditions upon which democracy depends have time to take root, and so that countries that have known little else but one-party authoritarian rule will stand a better chance of developing truly democratic governments. It should have articulated openly the conundrum that is whispered about in the corridors of Foggy Bottom: that America's mindless, relentless promotion of elections immediately is likely for now to bring to power through the ballot box those who would extinguish democracy in the name of Allah. It should have stressed instead more modest goals: increased political participation in government and the need for a freer press and freer public debate in all countries in the region.

Any American policy is likely to be only marginal in affecting developments in the Middle East, given the enormity of economic and political problems facing most Arab governments (though this argument is rarely made when the Arab-Israeli conflict is discussed). But influencing events at the margin is better than not attempting to influence them at all. It is surely better than despairing and saying that nothing can or should be done about the trend toward fundamentalism. Ultimately, the triumph of militant Islam in the Middle East may say as much about the West as about the Arabs and the failure of their existing systems. Islamists, by and large, have come to power when no one is willing to oppose them at home and abroad. In any new world order, Americans should not be ashamed to say that they favor pluralism, tolerance and diversity, and that they reject the notion that God is on anyone's side.

FIGHTING RADICAL ISLAM WITH WORDS

The Clinton administration has an opportunity to speak in direct terms about the prospects for democracy and Islamic government. It can say what is suggested by so many specialists but rarely articulated—that the United States supports as a matter of principle the separation of temporal from spiritual power in government. It should seize the moment not to draw a line in the sand, as Bush did, but to make a firm commitment to democratic, pluralistic values.

Washington, under President Bush, did not take this position. It never said that the West believes that Islam is a great religion, which produced an inspired culture from which the West learned much, but that in the 21st century in the Middle East, in nation states that are ethnically, tribally and religiously heterogeneous, an Islamic state as espoused by most of its proponents is simply incompatible with values and truths that Americans and most Westerners today hold to be self-evident. Perhaps an American government that defines its interest along narrow strategic lines—that is, along access to oil at a steady and acceptable price—cannot afford to say such things. Such statements would surely antagonize

American allies such as Saudi Arabia, an avowedly Islamic state that denies basic human rights to half its population and all religious minorities but is dependably pro-Western, considerably less harsh and repressive than many of the states that surround it, and also America's major source of foreign oil.

While the American government cannot and perhaps, from a strict definition of national interest, should not say such things, there are individual Americans who can speak out. In the past decade, human rights activists have addressed many of these concerns. In the Arab world itself, human rights groups and activists are beginning to find their own voices, despite great risks and staunch government opposition.

Islamic militancy presents the West with a paradox. While liberals speak of the need for diversity with equality, Islamists see this as a sign of weakness. Liberalism tends not to teach its proponents to fight effectively. What is needed, rather, is almost a contradiction in terms: a liberal militancy, or a militant liberalism that is unapologetic and unabashed.

The administration can signal its commitment to these principles in many symbolic and practical ways. It can, for example, welcome at the State Department not the Turabis of the region, as the Bush administration did, but rather those who share a commitment to the dignity of individuals and their inherent right to speak out and disagree, such as the Sudanese scholar-in-exile in Washington, Mohammed Khalil, who practically wept when he learned that Turabi was being welcomed on Capitol Hill and at the State Department.

It should reject the assumption that seemed to underlie President Bush's policy toward Islamic forces—namely that such groups are destined to come to power in the region anyway, so the United States should have a dialogue with them now to avoid a repetition of what occurred in Iran in the future.

Washington can also say that the governments of Egypt, Jordan and Saudi Arabia are, for all their many, well-publicized failings, still more tolerant and less repressive than those that the Islamists would most probably establish in their stead. If Washington said this openly, those same governments might well be more receptive to American criticism of practices that Washington finds unacceptable—such as torture in Egypt and the repression of minorities and women in Saudi Arabia.

The Clinton administration should not seek to wage an American or Western secular war against the Islamists. But it should not be embarrassed to call attention to America's accomplishments, or afraid to discuss candidly the failings of an Islamic theocracy. Too often, American administrations, fearful of being accused of cultural imperialism, have remained silent about denials of basic human freedom in the Middle East.

It has been argued that America will not be strategically affected by the triumph of militant Islamic governments in the region. Given America's military might, Islamic governments would probably be reluctant to attack this country openly and directly. And Middle Eastern oil producers, no matter what their political orientation, will always need to sell oil.

But the proliferation of state-sponsored or assisted terrorist groups and of weapons of mass destruction in the region threatens the United States, as well as Israel, Egypt, and other allies. The United States would be hard pressed, given American domestic politics and its long-standing commitment to Israel, to remain aloof from a conflict that endangered the Jewish state. Moreover, a nuclearized Iran might prove to be more than simply a strategic nuisance to the United States. Even without nuclear weapons, Tehran managed to affect an election in this country through its ruthless manipulation of U.S. hostages. Moreover, in the aftermath of the bombing of the World Trade Center in New York City, the United States must acknowledge now that Islamic fervor nurtured overseas is bound to come home.

Finally, even what might be little more than a nuisance for Americans would be a catastrophe for democrats and Western-minded Arabs in the region. How sad it would be for a world emerging from the shackles of communism and a debilitating Cold War to accept a new era of darkness and autocratic rule for the Arabs, who have enjoyed far too little freedom and security.

NO   Leon T. Hadar

WHAT GREEN PERIL?

From home and abroad voices have begun to counsel the Clinton administration that with communism's death, America must prepare for a new global threat—radical Islam. This specter is symbolized by the Middle Eastern Muslim fundamentalist, a Khomeini-like creature armed with a radical ideology and nuclear weapons, intent on launching a jihad [holy war] against Western civilization.

In the search for new doctrines for a new world, this image of a worldwide threat from militant Islam could filter deep into the policymaking processes of the new administration. In the way that the perception of danger from Soviet communism helped to define U.S. foreign policy for more than four decades, the fear of Islam could embroil Washington in a second Cold War.

This policy, however, would rest on utterly fallacious assumptions: Islam is neither unified nor a threat to the United States. Were America to let these phobias drive its foreign policy it would be forced into long and costly battles with various, unrelated regional phenomena. In the Middle East, the principal battleground of this struggle, it would place America in the position of maintaining a corrupt, reactionary and unstable status quo. In short, such a policy would run against the long-term interests of the peoples of America and the Middle East.

CONJURING UP A NEW MENACE

Like the Red Menace of the Cold War era, the Green Peril—green being the color of Islam—is described as a cancer spreading around the globe, undermining the legitimacy of Western values and threatening the national security of the United States. Tehran [Iran] is the center of this ideological subversion.... The goal... is said to be support for anti-Western regimes stretching from North Africa across the Near East and the Persian Gulf to Central Asia. Tehran's aim is to control the oil-rich gulf, destroy Israel and threaten areas on the periphery of a new "arc of crisis"—the Horn of Africa, southern Europe, the Balkans and the Indian subcontinent.

The Islamic conspiracy theory ties together isolated events and trends: the recent bombing of the World Trade Center in New York City, the civil

From Leon T. Hadar, "What Green Peril?" *Foreign Affairs*, vol. 72, no. 2 (Spring 1993). Copyright © 1993 by The Council on Foreign Relations, Inc. Reprinted by permission of *Foreign Affairs*.

war between the Muslim government in Khartoum and the Christians and Animists in southern Sudan; terrorist attacks by radical Muslim groups in Egypt; the popularity of Islamic parties in Algeria and Tunisia; Arab support for the Bosnian Muslims; the instability in the newly independent Central Asian [former Soviet] republics; the Lebanese Shiites' struggle for political power; the continuing Palestinian uprising; and Iran's pursuit of economic power and political influence in the Persian Gulf and Central Asia. In short, all the changes and instability in the post–Cold War Middle East and its peripheries are described as part of a grand scheme perpetrated by "Islam International."

Apart from some frustrated Cold Warriors in Washington, this campaign has been eagerly joined by a strange group of foreign governments including Egypt, Saudi Arabia, Israel, Turkey, Pakistan, India and the old communist regimes in Central Asia. Some of these have repressive governments that need a new enemy to preserve eroding public support. All are concerned about their weakening strategic value to America, now that the superpowers have made peace....

These [countries'] strategies recall the way Third World countries exploited the U.S. obsession with the Red Menace during the Cold War.... Even Uganda has been requesting military aid from Washington to combat the Islamic threat from Sudan....

These governments and their lobby organizations use leaks, misinformation and media spins to help construct the new Middle Eastern danger. "Government sources" and "intelligence reports," sometimes using questionable evidence and exaggerating credible information, warn of Iranian subversion in Central Asia, the export of terrorism to North Africa and Egypt, and a Khartoum-Tehran connection.

Journalists, who have become the transmission belt for such reports, so reminiscent of Cold War propaganda campaigns, add drama to the mix. They impose the term "Islamic fundamentalism" to describe diverse and unrelated movements that range from CIA-trained Islamic guerrillas in Afghanistan to the anti-American clerics in Iran.... Think-tank studies, op-ed pieces and congressional hearings add color to this image of a unified and monolithic Islam.

THE MUSLIMS ARE NOT COMING

Before leading America into a war against Islam, President Clinton would be well advised to take a bird's-eye view of the so-called Islamic crescent. Instead of a monolithic Islamistan, he would uncover a mosaic of many national, ethnic and religious groups competing for power and influence; a multinational phenomenon ranging from Malaysia to France, in which Islam, like Christianity and Judaism, is less a transnational political force and more a vital religion that provides spiritual support for a broad spectrum of people, some liberal, some orthodox. It is a kaleidoscope producing shifting balances of power and overlapping ideological configurations that neither Tehran—nor Washington—can control.

Far from being a unified power... Islam is, in fact, currently on the defensive against militant anti-Muslim fundamentalists. In the former Yugoslavia, the Westernized and secular Muslim population of Bosnia and Kosovo is threatened with extinction by Serbian nationalists, who have a strong connection to the Eastern Orthodox Church.... In India, the Bharatiya Janata party, an anti-Muslim Hindu nationalist group, and the even more militant Shiv Sena are gaining power. In the West Bank, Gush Emmunim, the Jewish fundamentalist settlement movement, [is] suppressing the Palestinian nationalist movement, which includes many secular Muslims and Christians. And in France and Germany, racist and neo-Nazi groups are trying to violently eject large Muslim immigrant populations....

Ironically, the most militant and successful Islamic fundamentalist offensive has been led and financed by the United States. The broad coalition of Mujahedeen freedom fighters, trained by Washington and the Pakistani government, successfully ousted the Moscow-backed regime in Afghanistan in April 1992. Currently, the remnants of the Mujahedeen [rebels; holy warriors], which comprises various ethnic, religious and linguistic groups, are engaged in a bloody war for control of Afghanistan. The governments in Central Asia consider these warriors—not Tehran—the greatest threat to regional stability. These Mujahedeen veterans are also playing a key role in the Islamic rebel movements in Algeria and Egypt.

BALANCE OF POWER GAMES, NOT HOLY WARS

The disintegration of Afghanistan into mini-states ruled by different tribal leaders with complex ties to outside powers reflects the return of the nineteenth-century Great Game in Central Asia. Iran, Turkey, Pakistan, Russia, China and even Saudi Arabia and Israel are trying to establish spheres of influence in the area. But the new balance of power

constellations in Central Asia and the Middle East are not pitting a unified pro-Iranian coalition against a unified pro-Western axis. They are producing strange bedfellows whose moves are driven by a complicated set of interests and ideologies, Islam being only one part of the mix....

Iran's role in these developments, far from being revolutionary, leans toward maintaining the status quo. It has joined Turkey and Syria to discuss ways to prevent the rise of Kurdish nationalism. Worried over the secession of its own Azeri minority and the instability in its southern Caucasian backyard, Tehran has tried unsuccessfully to bring a peaceful end to the dispute between [former Soviet republics] Armenia and Azerbaijan over Nagorno-Karabakh....

Like other players in the region—the Arab states, Turkey, Israel—Iran projects a mixture of defensive and aggressive strategies that are motivated less by Islamic ideology than by its perceived national interests in Central Asia and the Persian Gulf, and in particular by the need to prevent the rise of unsympathetic players in these regions. On one hand, Tehran has promoted economic cooperation and trade through the formation of regional groups.... On the other hand, not unlike pan-Arabism, pan-Turkism and pan-Islamism, Iran has tried to export its own version of Islam, as well as the Persian language, as a way of advancing its interest in the Middle East and Central Asia....

The nightmare scenario of a new Iranian-led Islamic empire is a result of misguided Western fears. Even Egypt during the heyday of pan-Arabism [30 years ago] was unable to lay the groundwork for the unification of Arabs, who share a common language and culture. Iran's

Shiite religion, its historical animosity toward the Arab world, its struggles with Iraq over influence in the Persian Gulf and with Turkey over influence in Central Asia, and its limited economic and military power place severe constraints on its ability to become a magnet for the mostly Sunni Muslim world....

Turkey, Israel, Egypt, Pakistan and other states are self-interested and well equipped to contain Iranian expansionism even without American prodding. At the same time, Iran could find itself sharing interests with some of these rivals. Tehran supported the American-led Arab coalition against Saddam Hussein and, like Israel, is against the creation of a united Arab bloc in the region.... [S]trategic considerations and not religious beliefs have been the driving force. In fact, most of Iran's recent moves on the foreign policy front, including the reported attempts to acquire nuclear weapons, would probably have been applauded by the secular and pro-Western shah. In the anarchic environment of the Middle East, where Israel, Iraq, Pakistan and [former Soviet republic] Kazakhstan possess or could possibly possess nuclear weapons, Iran's interest in acquiring similar capability is hardly surprising....

THE MOSQUE AND THE AUDIOCASSETTE

If a crusade against Iran and Islam makes little sense from a realpolitik perspective, as an idealistic [Woodrow] Wilsonian project it lacks credibility. Unlike communism in its heyday, the Islamic movement is not a powerful global ideology competing with democracy. Rather, as an umbrella for diverse and disorganized political ideologies,

political Islam is only one of the many and multifaceted elements in the colorful Middle Eastern tapestry that the end of the Cold War is unfolding.

The Islamic resurgence is a response to the confusion and anxiety of modernity and a challenge to repressive and corrupt regimes. Like Christians during the Reformation, the Islamists attempt to reach directly the literal word of God and provide legitimacy to popular demands to transform their societies. Indeed, the political clout the Islamists now have is due not to the desire of Arabs and others to live under strict Islamic rule, but to the perceived failure of Western models of political and economic order, including nationalism and socialism, to solve the Middle East's problems.

As in other parts of the world, the political order in the Middle East is under challenge. With the end of superpower rivalry, Arab governments are finding it more difficult to extract economic and military support from external powers in return for their strategic services. That situation is exacerbated by the global economic recession and the fall in oil prices, which have reduced the amount of capital available for aid and investment in the region. The result is growing public disenchantment with and opposition to [many current regimes in Muslim countries]....

The Islamic groups that operate in opposition to the different autocratic regimes represent a diversity of players and organizations. They are populists who do not fit into a left-right dichotomy and combine a strange mix of atavism, romanticism, and a respect for certain free-market ideas and for Western technology. The mosque and the audiocassette have become their two major propaganda tools, reflecting the love-hate prism through which they view the West....

Many Islamic leaders do not fit the image of radicals and terrorists. Working together with secular parties and using the language of political liberalization, they have pressed for political reforms that have led to elections in Egypt, Tunisia, Algeria, Jordan and Kuwait and to the establishment of a consultative assembly in Saudi Arabia. Most Islamic groups that operate more or less freely in the relatively open systems of Egypt and Jordan or in the more democratic systems of Turkey and Pakistan have successfully adapted to the democratic game—running candidates in local and national elections, forming alliances with secular groups and holding cabinet positions....

Moreover, contrary to Western stereotypes, many Islamic leaders are not medieval figures. As in the case of the Islamic Salvation Front (FIS) in Algeria, they are educated professionals, such as engineers, physicians, lawyers and academics, who control modern institutions like hospitals, schools and businesses. They are not interested in returning their societies to the past as much as transforming their political and economic structures. Even Iran's theocrats utilize Western concepts of government—"republic," "democracy" and "constitution"—to legitimize their rule.

That does not turn the Islamists into Jeffersonian democrats.... The most extreme among them will try to rigidly enforce the *sharia*, or Islamic law, in their societies, which would require the complete segregation of the sexes outside the home and the introduction of stoning, flogging and amputation as legal punishments. Westerners who believe in the universal application of such ideas as in-

dividual rights and freedom of religion should not accept an argument, smacking of cultural relativism, that their values only apply to the secular West and that Muslims, unlike Christians or Jews, are more inclined to live under repressive religious systems. By the same token, however, neither should analysts and policymakers adopt a mirror image of this argument, suggesting that for some reason Muslim societies, unlike their counterparts in Eastern Europe or the former Soviet Union, are inherently resistant to democratic rule....

In fact, when it comes to free elections in Algeria or Egypt, Washington suddenly begins to lament over the "dilemmas," the "difficult choices," and the danger that democracy in those countries would bring anti-democratic forces to power and produce messy problems for the United States. Similarly, the media and Congress, which have constantly denounced human rights violations in countries like China, do not seem to express a similar sense of sorrow when the regimes in Algeria and Tunisia repress their own citizens.

This attitude is based partly on the genuine concern that if Islamic parties come into power through democratic elections, they will impose an intolerant, undemocratic order on society and usher in a new dark age of fundamentalist rule. But it is doubtful that any serious voice in Europe and the United States, using this same logic, would suggest that because of the real danger of rising nationalist-authoritarian regimes in Eastern Europe, the West in retrospect would have been better off with the communist governments remaining in power.

The inevitable rise of Islamic regimes in countries like Algeria or Egypt is a transitional phase in the process of political and economic transformation of the old order in the Middle East. Once in power, Islamic groups like the FIS, who have thrived on the martyrdom of political oppression, will have to deal with the mundane social and economic problems of their country....

Like other political parties, Islamic groups will be judged by their ability to "deliver the goods," mainly economic opportunities. Religion, as King Hassan of Morocco once said, is not enough to run a country. Iran's clerics, facing public discontent, including food riots, over their handling of the economy, have had to move toward major changes in domestic and foreign policy aimed at stimulating the economy....

Washington should not be surprised if, when [fundamentalist] groups come to power, they have a hostile attitude toward the West, which has, after all, applauded their repression and encouraged the stifling of democracy in their countries. The crusade against political Islam is in danger of becoming a self-fulfilling prophecy.

WASHINGTON: THE GUARANTOR OF THE STATUS QUO

The greatest hypocrisy in the debate over political Islam is the fact that Americans have fought a war and committed their military and diplomatic power to secure the survival of the most fundamentalist state of all—Saudi Arabia.

The Saudi regime's own legitimacy is based on an alliance with the Wahhabi movement, an extremely conservative Sunni sect. The Saudi government is actually more rigid in its application of Islamic law and more repressive in many respects than the one in Tehran. Saudi Arabia has no form of popular representation, political rights are totally denied to women and non-Muslims, and the regime has consistently applied *sharia* to criminal justice. It has financed a variety of [radical] Islamic groups worldwide.... Indeed, Saudi Arabia, like all other other Arab oil-exporting states of the Persian Gulf, is an absolute monarchy that does not recognize the concepts of civil rights or civil liberties....

Indeed, the language of Wilsonian idealism with which the current criticism of political Islam is being framed masks clear political interests and has little to do with concerns over the status of liberty in the Middle East. Such rhetoric is used to mobilize support for the pro-Western autocratic regimes and by extension to secure U.S. hegemony in the region, and in particular its access to oil.

There is a major contradiction between America's global democracy project and its pax-Americana program in the Middle East. U.S. policymakers know that democratically elected and popularly based governments—Islamic or otherwise—would be less inclined to bow to American wishes. It is not a coincidence that the governments in Jordan, Yemen and Algeria (before the military takeover) were the most critical of U.S. policy during the Persian Gulf crisis, reflecting the general public mood in those countries. Hence the vicious circle: continued support for repressive regimes, exacerbated by America's alliance with Israel, only fans resentment toward the United States. And the existence of that resentment makes it more difficult for Washington to tolerate the idea of democratization and reforms in the region.

CONSTRUCTIVE DISENGAGEMENT

The end of the Cold War has provided the United States with an opportunity to begin disengaging from trouble spots around the world, shifting security responsibilities to regional powers.... At the same time, the end of the superpower rivalry has also permitted Washington to decouple itself from Third World tyrants and despots who lost their job of serving as regional anti-Soviet policemen....

No similar post–Cold War reexamination of U.S. policies has taken place in the Middle East, with the exception that the Bush administration proved unwilling to sponsor then Prime Minister Yitzhak Shamir's Greater Israel policies. That shift in policy led indirectly to the defeat of the Likud government in June 1992 and helped revive the peace process, thus improving America's position in the region....

President Clinton should take a cue from one of his predecessors at the White House, John Quincy Adams, and resist the pressures from interested political parties and foreign clients to go "abroad in search of monsters to destroy." Indeed, searching for imaginary Muslim monsters will involve major costs for the United States....

A policy of constructive disengagement from the Middle East would permit the United States to encourage Europe and Japan to start taking care of their interests there. Such a policy will also help create new and independent balance of power systems and security arrangements. Washington will not need anymore to play the role of balancer in the Middle East and to use Israel, Egypt, Turkey or Saudi Arabia as regional cops, while Iran could play a role in the region that is commensurate with its political and military power.

... Realpolitik considerations suggest that the Clinton administration adopt a similar strategy vis-à-vis Tehran that could lead to the restoration of diplomatic relations and the expansion of trade relations with Iran. A policy that rejects the idea of a grand Western crusade against Iran fits with U.S. interest in having a diplomatically responsible and economically prosperous Iran in the Persian Gulf. It will, in turn, strengthen the Iranian nationalists interested in attracting Western aid and investment and integrating Tehran with the world community.

The new administrations's neo-Wilsonian orientation with its emphasis on defending democracy, human rights, self-determination and arms control worldwide clearly runs contrary to the interest of maintaining alliances with Middle Eastern despots and arming them to the teeth....

President Clinton should use American diplomatic influence in the region to be an honest broker and to help Israel make peace with its neighbors, including Palestinians.... An Arab-Israeli peace could be a nucleus for the economic renaissance of the region, which, in turn, would strengthen the hands of the more Westernized and modernizing forces there. An America whose ties with Israel have ceased to be a burden in its relations with Muslims and that has left its Cold War legacy behind will not have to chase any more monsters or saints.

America should not lead a crusade for democracy in the Middle East. But neither should it continue, through aid and military support, to provide incentives for maintaining autocratic rule.... Disengaging from the Saudis and the other

Middle Eastern despots will ensure that when new regimes come to power, they will not direct their wrath against Washington but against those external powers, like France, who might find it in their interest to maintain in power groups like Algeria's National Liberation Front. The interest of America lies not in isolating but maintaining friendly relations with the new Islamic governments and in playing into the hands of the liberal and democratic elements in their countries through trade and communication. By doing this America will best serve both its own interests and the interests of the people of the Middle East.

POSTSCRIPT

Is Islamic Fundamentalism a Threat to Political Stability?

The connections between politics and Islam are important because there are nearly 1 billion Muslims. They are a majority among Arab peoples, and in several non-Arab countries, including Algeria, Indonesia, Iran, Morocco, Pakistan, the Sudan, Turkey, and several former Soviet republics (FSRs), they are a majority as well. There are other countries, such as Nigeria and the Philippines, in which Muslims constitute an important political force. Indeed, only about one of every four Muslims lives in the Middle East. The history and beliefs of Muslims are complex and rich, and finding out more about them is not only rewarding, it also counteracts the tendency to stereotype things about which one knows little. To learn more about Islamic history and tenets, read Arthur Goldschmidt, Jr.'s *A Concise History of the Middle East* (Westview Press, 1983). A more recent publication is the symposium issue of *The Annals of the American Academy of Political and Social Science* (November 1993), edited by Charles E. Butterworth and I. William Zartman. It contains 15 articles about Islam and how it interacts with political ideas and practices.

There can be little doubt that the interplay between Islam and politics remains an important issue in world affairs. From a Western point of view, the images are mixed, future ramifications uncertain. Muslim countries, like most Third World countries, face many difficulties when resolving the tension between preserving their traditional values and adopting so-called modern practices, which are mostly those promoted by the dominant European and North American powers. Indeed, the rush of technological advancement associated with modernity, the loss of cultural identity, and a rate of change unparalleled in world history are troubling for many people in all types of countries around the world. As Hamad Alturki, a professor of political science at King Saud University in Riyadh, Saudi Arabia, puts it, "People are tackling previously unheard questions like: How do we deal with concepts of the state and region? How should we cope with the age we live in? And what should our relationship be with the 'other,' be that other persons, other creeds, other states, or other thoughts?"

Amid the turmoil, there are many signs that Muslim countries are adjusting to what is arguably a spreading homogenization (Western or not) of global culture. As elsewhere, democracy has taken hold in some Muslim countries and struggles to survive, and to be born in others. Should North American powers support, as in Algeria, traditionalists when they win democratic majorities or secularists who hold or seize power by dint of force? Some aspects of Muslim culture, such as the status of women, that bother many Westerners are also undergoing change. One symbol of that change is Tansu Ciller, a Muslim woman who not only has a doctorate in economics from the University of Connecticut, she is also Turkey's first woman prime minister.

Other aspects of Muslim politics are disturbing. There is a strong element of violence. For example, five (Iraq, Iran, Libya, Sudan, Syria) of the seven countries (also Cuba and North Korea) designated by the U.S. State Department as officially supporting terrorism (state terrorism) are predominantly Muslim. Another well-known symbol of what worries the West is the *fatwa* placed on Salman Rushdie, author of *Satanic Verses*, a book considered to be blasphemous by Islamic fundamentalists. Iran's President Hashemi Rafsanjani says the *fatwa*, a death sentence, with a reward for carrying it out, "is prescribed by an Islamic law that has been in existence for a thousand years."

ISSUE 7

Will China Become an Asian Superpower?

YES: Zhao Xiaowei, from "The Threat of a New Arms Race Dominates Asian Geopolitics," *Global Affairs* (Summer 1992)

NO: Samuel S. Kim, from "China as a Regional Power," *Current History* (September 1992)

ISSUE SUMMARY

YES: Zhao Xiaowei, a prominent member of the Democratic Liberal Party, a mainland China political party in exile, predicts that as China modernizes and becomes more stable domestically, it is likely to engage in an arms race designed to build itself up to a regional, even global, superpower.

NO: Political science professor Samuel S. Kim maintains that China is a weak state that will be hard pressed to survive the multiple threats from within. Thus distracted, China is not likely in the foreseeable future to become a regional, much less global, superpower.

China has a history as one of the oldest, most sophisticated, and most powerful countries in the world. Protohuman tool makers (Peking man, *Sinanthropus pekinensis*) inhabited north China a half million years ago. Four thousand years ago, under the semilegendary Emperor Yu of the Hsia dynasty, the Chinese built irrigation channels, domesticated animals, engaged in cultivation, and established a written language. Through fourteen Chinese dynasties China built a civilization marked by great cultural and engineering feats. The Great Wall of China, the only human creation visible from space, was begun in about 210 B.C. The great philosophy of Confucianism was soon thereafter established. China also exercised wide political influence, holding sway over a considerable regional area.

As is the way with empires, China's political fortunes waxed and waned and eventually declined. By the 1800s, increasingly ascendant outside powers came to dominate an ever more decaying China. The British provoked the Opium War (1839–42) over their instance on the right to sell drugs to the Chinese. China was easily defeated. Hong Kong was seized by the British and leased to them until 1997. British traders grew rich on the desperation of the patrons of Chinese opium dens. Over approximately the next eight decades, China underwent what was to the Chinese a period of humiliation.

Huge tracts of their territory were seized by the Russians, the island of Formosa (Taiwan, or Nationalist China) was taken by Japan in 1945, and various
European countries and Japan came close to making China a colony by dividing it up into zones of interest that they dominated. During the so-called
Boxer Rebellion (1900), Chinese nationalists tried to expel the foreigners, but
the Chinese forces were defeated by an international coalition that included
American troops. The moribund Manchu dynasty fell in 1911 and was replaced by a republic headed by Sun Yat-sen.

Sun died in 1916 and a struggle for power among various factions led to
the establishment in 1926 of a central government under Nationalist Chinese
leader Chiang Kai-shek. Although Chiang's government proved corrupt and
ineffective in many ways, it did largely consolidate power and moved to edge
foreign influences out of China. That trend became even stronger in 1949
when Chiang's government fell to the communists of Mao Zedong. Chiang's
government fled to the island of Formosa, now Taiwan, and established a
rump Nationalist Chinese government.

For two decades, many in the West were caught up in the psychology of
the cold war and perceived China to be part of the communist monolith
headed by the Soviet Union. That was never true, but in any case, by the late
1960s, China had gained enough strength and showed enough independence
(including sharp clashes with the USSR over border areas) that even the
coldest warrior had to see that China was a rising power in its own right. An
important symbol of that shift was President Richard Nixon's visit to China
in 1972. Relations between the United States and China improved even more
after Chairman Mao Zedong died in 1976 and Deng Xiaoping came to power.

By many standards, China is already a major power. It has the world's
largest population (over a billion) and a gross domestic product (GDP) approaching a half trillion dollars. Its territory is enormous. Officially, China's
defense spending for 1993 is only about $7.3 billion, but many analysts believe
the real figure could be two or three times higher. China's 3 million personnel
in uniform give it the largest standing military force in the world by that
measure. China's conventional forces have not achieved the same level of
technological sophistication as Western countries, but the country does possess strategic-range nuclear weapons. China is also a permanent member of
the UN Security Council, thus possessing a veto in that organization.

The issue is what the future of China will be. There are some, including
Zhao Xiaowei in the first issue, who contend that China will become a regional superpower. Others, including former president Richard Nixon, have
predicted that China will be a global superpower, perhaps the leading superpower, in the twenty-first century. Others focus on China's many problems,
including the political infighting that may occur when the aged Deng dies.
They forecast that internal travails will prevent China from becoming a superpower and could even lead it into decline. Samuel Kim, in the second
selection, is among those who take this latter view.

YES

Zhao Xiaowei

THE THREAT OF A NEW ARMS RACE DOMINATES ASIAN GEOPOLITICS

Asia has been largely eclipsed by the drama played out in Europe where the former Soviet Union, at least in its current incarnations, can no longer support the costs of the vast military machine built by its prior rulers. As a consequence, there has been talk of "the forgotten Far East."

This euphoria is understandable: Since the collapse of Marxism-Leninism in Europe, humankind seemingly has freed itself from the nightmare of a general nuclear conflict that would render the planet uninhabitable. Most of the industrial democracies are now caught up in a scramble to find ways to spend anticipated "peace dividends." The United States defense budget has been significantly reduced—and barring unanticipated changes in the international security environment, further reductions will be forthcoming. "Peace activists" have argued that the absence of adversaries has made the U.S. military obsolete. Many of those charged with the responsibilities of forming public opinion apparently share these convictions about the advent of universal peace—or at least enough peace to allow the United States to pursue some sort of disarmed detachment from the world.

ASIA BY YEAR 2000

Most of this, of course, has been a by-product of changes in Europe. But those who focus on Asia remind Americans that by the year 2000, the nations on the Pacific rim will be peopled by 70 percent of the world's population, will produce more than 50 percent of the world's commodities, will consume 40 percent of the world's production and are expected to account for 70 percent of the world's trade. Neglecting Asia could be fatal to the West's security and prosperity as well as for the masses of Asia.

Where Asia has not suffered from the benign neglect of most Western geopoliticians, the concerns expressed have largely been the result of selective trade tensions. There has been a body of reportage colored by the notion that

From Zhao Xiaowei, "The Threat of a New Arms Race Dominates Asian Geopolitics," *Global Affairs* (Summer 1992). Copyright © 1992 by The International Security Council. Reprinted by permission of *Global Affairs*. Notes omitted.

Japan might emerge as a security threat—as "the only runner in the arms race." From this perspective Japan not only threatened the economy of the United States, it was seen as an "invisible military giant"—a "strong samurai" prepared to overwhelm the world with its arms as it already had with its exports.

While there is little doubt that Japan's defense allocations make it one of the world's major military spenders, few military strategists consider it a current or future security threat. For the foreseeable future Japan's military will serve only as an element of the forward defense policies of the United States.

Furthermore, recently, the declining Japanese defense budget has largely allayed concerns. By the beginning of 1990, there were clear signs of a decreasing commitment to defense expenditures. That Tokyo has reduced its defense outlays appears to confirm what some observers have argued are the determinants of Japan's defense budgets.

Japan's budgets are a result of a process shaped by influences having very little to do with military purposes. Japan's military budget reflects the influence of macroeconomic policy objectives and the management of relations with the United States. For the determinate future, Japan's ties with the United States preclude its emergence as an independent actor in any Asian arms race.

More persuasive in the role of spoilers of the peace of East Asia are the antagonists on the Korean peninsula. The Democratic People's Republic of Korea—North Korea—continues to allocate almost 25 percent of its gross domestic product to maintaining an aggressive force structure that threatens not only the Republic of Korea—South Korea—but the peace of the entire region. South Korea, in turn, apparently will marginally reduce its current and future defense budgets to produce slower growth rather than significant reductions. The reduction in regional threats have reduced domestic arms orders.

The disintegration of the Soviet Union has diminished the overall threat in Northeast Asia—and has complicated the risk assessments of the leadership in Pyongyang. In and of itself, the regime in North Korea could hardly provoke a major change in the threat environment. Best evidence indicates that the economy of the North has been in negative growth for several years; there have been reports of North Koreans fleeing to Communist China to escape the all-pervasive poverty that dominates the countryside. Therefore, it would appear that North Korea could hardly underwrite an increased threat.

There is one aspect of North Korea military developments that is potentially destabilizing and merits attention: its nuclear program. It is an issue that "could have serious implications for the U.S. military/security role in Korea and Northeast Asia, and could threaten peace and stability there."

North Korea has a substantial nuclear program involving a major plant site at Yongbyon about 60 miles north of Pyongyang. One component is a small reactor (about 30-megawatt capability) able to produce about seven kilograms of plutonium annually. This reactor is supplemented by a larger reactor with a capacity to produce enough weapons grade plutonium to arm as many as five nuclear weapons a year. There is some evidence that North Korea may have hidden nuclear weapons sites, similar to those recently exposed in Iraq.

BEIJING'S ROLE AS PROVOCATEUR

It is uncertain how the communist leadership of an impoverished North Korea managed the cost, and developed the technological expertise, to put together the capacity now expected to manufacture its first atomic device in 1992. It is generally accepted that the Soviet Union provided North Korea a small research reactor in the 1960s and may have supplied technological assistance and training into the late 1980s. While there is no direct evidence, many analysts are convinced that Communist China has supplied North Korea major assistance. In the 1950s and 1960s, many North Koreans received training in nuclear technology in China, and the House Republican Research Committee's "Task Force on Terrorism and Unconventional Warfare" has recently reported that an agreement between the PRC and North Korea in October and November 1991 afforded Pyongyang the technological assistance necessary to expedite its program of nuclear arms development.

Should that prove to be the case, it is not North Korea, in and of itself, that threatens the peace and stability of Northeast Asia. It is the regime on China's mainland, the People's Republic of China (PRC), that has not only supplied critical components to North Korea's nuclear arms program, but has provided Pyongyang substantial political and moral support.

This suggests that whatever Beijing's role in the development of North Korea's nuclear arms program might prove to be, attention should be concentrated on Communist China's practices, security doctrine, and international concerns. Even if Beijing has provided no material assistance to Pyongyang, the arms sales practices of the PRC has reinforced North Korea's destabilizing undertakings.

Whether or not Beijing has assisted North Korea with its nuclear program in the past, or continues to do so in the present, it has been confirmed that the PRC has aided, or intends to aid, Iran and Iraq in their pursuit of nuclear arms capabilities. Presently, an agreement between the PRC and Algeria will supply the latter a nuclear reactor large enough to make weapons grade plutonium. Beijing is also prepared to provide Syria a small research reactor. The PRC has not only supplied a design for a reliable nuclear weapon to Pakistan, but has transferred enough enriched uranium for production of at least two atomic devices as well.

More recently, Beijing has assisted Pakistan in its effort to enrich uranium domestically, and sold the tritium gas commonly employed to enhance the yield of fission bombs. There have also been credible reports of an intended sale and transfer of a turnkey 300 megawatt nuclear power facility to Islamabad. Thus, whether or not Beijing is directly involved in the North Korean nuclear arms program, it is certainly a party to the proliferation of nuclear weapons capabilities that make up a substantial part of an emerging arms race in South and Southwest Asia.

CONCERN BY BEIJING'S NEIGHBORS

One result of China's readiness to assist in the development of nuclear weapons capabilities in Northeast, South and Southwest Asia has been to precipitate renewed concern among its neighbors. Early in 1992, [Pakistani] Foreign Secretary Shahryar Khan announced that, thanks to the assistance of the PRC, Pakistan can now assemble its own nuclear device. Involved in a long and volatile boundary dispute with India, Pakistan's announcement has increased tensions throughout South Asia.

All of this has obvious implications for the world power balance and for U.S. policymakers. What is not as obvious is why Beijing would wish to involve itself in such activities. In general, commentators allude to mainland China's preoccupation with domestic concerns—preoccupations that would seem to exclude controversial arms sales that might compromise its internal programs of economic growth and modernization.

Actually, for all its talk of "opening to the industrial democracies" in order to access their import markets and attract capital investments as well as technology transfers, Beijing still conceives the fundamental relationship between a socialist China and market-based democracy as adversarial. At the end of 1991, the Hong Kong publication Cheng Ming reported that the Chinese Communist Party, in a confidential document entitled "Fundamental Policies Toward the United States," identified Washington as China's "principal enemy." As a consequence, Beijing has regularly flouted Western attempts to halt the proliferation of nuclear weapons capabilities.

Together with its sale of nuclear arms components, the PRC has also sold systems suitable for nuclear and chemical weapons delivery. By the end of the 1980s, there were reports that Beijing was negotiating the sale and transfer to both Syria and Pakistan of short-range missiles designed to carry nuclear and chemical warheads. Protests from the United States did nothing to deter the negotiations.

WHAT MOTIVATES BEIJING'S POLICIES

Since that time, the Director of the [U.S.] Central Intelligence Agency has reported that China has been supplying Iran with "battlefield missiles, cruise missiles, ballistic-missile technologies and components, and nuclear technology."

> Beijing has supplied destabilizing technologies to real and potential enemies of the industrialized democracies. Even when Beijing's sales have been with allies of those democracies, the sales have nonetheless been destabilizing. They have involved either nuclear weapons technology or ballistic systems that increase security risks wherever they appear.

Whatever assurances Beijing offers the democracies, Gary Milhollin, director of the Wisconsin Project, a Washington-based organization tracing nuclear proliferation, stated that the "past conduct [of the Beijing leadership] indicates that they are very likely to go ahead and break their word." "China," he went on, "is definitely a renegade supplier."

While Chinese arms sales, both conventional and nonconventional, have heightened tensions throughout Asia and the Middle East, there are analysts who have argued that such sales are not strategically motivated. They represent, according to this line of reasoning, a simple search for profit on the part of a capital-poor actor on the world stage. It is certainly true that arms sales are profitable and the Chinese are desperate for foreign exchange. Others have suggested that the pervasive nepotism and corruption that characterize the export sector of the mainland Chinese economy make it impossible for the authorities to halt the flow of arms. The proof that is offered is that arms sales are pursued "aggressively" by "well-connected people, including Deng's son-in-law, He Ping." Chinese arms vending, however offensive and dangerous, it is argued, is simply the result of Chinese greed and corruption.

None of this is convincing when the evidence is examined. It is probable that there will be some "leakage" in any nation's arms sales, but it is equally clear that potentially controversial arms sales would have to be cleared by the highest authorities in Beijing before they could be undertaken. There are few who have studied the details of these transactions who believe that Chinese arms traffic is entirely explained by an inordinate desire for material gain. Chinese sales, in large measure, are an expression of Chinese foreign policy imperatives.

Since the mid-1980s, the People's Republic of China has been guided by a strategy policy that conceives the world divided into progressive and "reactionary" states. Those intrinsically hostile states can "coexist," even "cooperate" with "socialist China"—so long as the "imperatives of history" are recognized and defended. Within such a theoretical perspective, the leadership in Beijing dismisses any real possibility of a general nuclear conflict. In Beijing's judgment, the "imperialist" powers have learned that nuclear conflict is no longer a real policy alternate. Given that reality, China's "international class enemies" are left with only a few tactics to defeat "Chinese socialism." Among those tactics, "peaceful evolution"—the subtle introduction of "bourgeois spiritual values" and "capitalist" modalities into China's "progressive" economy—is currently the most prominent. But, the leadership in Beijing warns, the "hegemonists" might make an appeal to a certain acceptable level of violence to resist the "inevitable march of socialism."

In this context, Chinese arms sales, particularly those involving nuclear and missile technology, are calculated to undermine the remaining "hostile policies" left to "world imperialism." Thus Chinese arms sales must be seen as inspired by a defense of Chinese ultimate and long-term interests. Beijing sees nuclear proliferation as complicating the "new world order" the democracies hope to see emerge from the collapse of European Marxism-Leninism.

PART OF A BROAD STRATEGY

The sale of missiles and nuclear technology is part of a broad program that would not only make the People's Republic of China a major global power in the twenty-first century, but assure its ultimate victory. Thus the Chinese military budget is among the few in East Asia that has significantly increased in the immediate past. More than that, Western intelligence agencies estimate that the actual budget is 100–150 percent greater than that supplied by official Chinese figures.

In 1991, Beijing negotiated for the purchase of expensive high performance Soviet combat aircraft. The PRC sought to obtain the Sukhoi Su-27 and the Mikoyan MiG-29 air superiority aircraft together with the Sukhoi Su-24 ground attack fighter-bomber. At the same time, Beijing increased the power projection capabilities of its navy. Long considered a coastal defense force, the PRC navy is now capable of undertaking blue water missions far from China's ports. With firepower and firecontrol capabilities enhanced by purchases from Western inventories, Beijing has extended its influence throughout Asia.

Beijing's nuclear and missile technology sales and its extensive force structure modernization destabilize all of Asia and raise legitimate security concerns. In November and December 1991, both the Director of the Central Intelligence Agency and Secretary of Defense Dick Cheney identified the PRC as a long-term potential threat to the security of Asia as well as that of the United States.

None of this has been lost on the nations of Southeast Asia. Until recently, the defense strategies of the Association of South East Asian Nations (ASEAN) were largely devoted to the control of domestic insurgencies. By the end of the 1980s, however, the armed forces of the Southeast Asian nations began to focus on external threats, developing long-range maritime strike and air defense potential, together with some degree of airborne early warning, command and control capability as well. Defense analysts in the region have pointed to long-standing disputes in the South China Sea that threaten regional conflict and to the fact that with the threat of a new arms race, the Chinese Communist military has developed the capabilities that would permit it to pursue a military option should circumstances permit. Beijing has succeeded in arming itself with capabilities superior to those it would face in any regional conflict on its periphery.

The acquisition of new equipment has provided the People's Liberation Army [PLA] with significant increases in power projection and firepower. "Long range bombers, in-flight refuelling, long-distance naval replenishment, amphibious tanks and armored vehicles and a marine corps have all been de-

veloped in recent years—all of which suggests that Beijing is not just interested in defending China. The range of PLA operations is steadily being extended outward from China, and to that end the PLA has been mapping all its territory, including those islands and neighbors with which China is in dispute."

The nations of the ASEAN community have responded with a recognition of the objective threat to their national interests. The "recent build-up of Chinese... forces in the South China Sea [is] seen as Peking's signal that it intends, at a future date, to assert its claims in the area."

The emerging arms race in East Asia is being driven by a strategic policy informed by traditional Marxist-Leninist principles of "international class warfare." Beijing's current military doctrine is predicated on the probability of "small wars" breaking out along its periphery—conflicts of short duration for limited objectives. Convinced that the "internal contradictions of capitalism" will ultimately resolve the historic rivalry between Marxism-Leninism and "imperialism," China's current arms sales policies and military doctrine have increased the magnitude of threat with which the nations of the region, as well as the international community, must contend.

"THE OTHER RING OF FIRE"

These circumstances have led the editors of the *Economist* to speak of Asia, extending from the Northeast to the Southwest, as "the other ring of fire" that threatens the peace and stability of the "new world order." Others have simply recognized that "An arms race in Asia is not just a threat, it is already under way."

That Asia may be compelled to endure yet another arms race is a consequence of the anachronistic views still entertained by the superannuated leadership in Beijing. They have not only aided and abetted the nuclear program that now threatens Northeast Asia, but they have apparently enlisted the collaboration of Pyongyang in their enterprise to unsettle the Middle East and Southwest Asia with a flood of tactical range missiles and nuclear weapons technology.

Beijing persists in its maritime claims in the East China and South China Seas. Not only does that fuel the arms buildup among the nations of Southeast Asia, but on Taiwan [Nationalist China, Formosa] as well. Ultimately, Beijing's territorial pretensions may directly engage the Japanese. Not only does the leadership in Communist China advance claims against Japanese holdings in the East China Sea, it threatens the integrity of Southeast Asia—a region that has been identified as "the key to Japan's prosperity."

Tokyo has reported the fact that "China has strengthened its military presence in the Spratly Islands and Paracel Islands [claimed by several countries] while improving the bases for operation in these islands. As these developments indicate," the Japanese White Paper on Defense continues, "China's moves are seen as expanding its operational area on the ocean." Together with the naval and air threat to the sealines of communication, the long-term strategy of mainland China poses an evolving threat to the security and economic viability of Japan.

Not long ago, Gerald Segal warned the industrial democracies that "while in the short term it may appear that a modernized China is a more stable China, there are disturbing signs that in the medium term China is likely to pose a challenge to international stability—especially in the ever more important Pacific." As the United States is compelled to draw down its forces in East and Southeast Asia as a consequence of domestic priorities and budgetary constraints, the People's Republic of China will probably emerge as a major threat to Asia, and ultimately, to the international community. Barring major changes in the regime that the [former] U.S. Secretary of State James Baker characterizes as "anachronistic," the new arms race that has already commenced will probably accelerate.

NO

CHINA AS A REGIONAL POWER

What can we say about China's status as a regional power in the post–cold war era? The question seems elementary yet defies an easy answer since, in international relations, the perception of power matters as much as the reality of it. In the Chinese case there persists the belief that China, by dint of its demographic weight or the greatness of its civilization, has a natural and inalienable right to great power status. The country's erratic shifts in foreign policy behavior over the years have been based on the conviction that China's strategic value can never be taken for granted by any external power, for it is both willing and able to play a decisive role in reshaping the structure of global high politics.

Yet while the cold war helped China project power well beyond the Asia-Pacific region, its end stripped away the veil of the China mystique and the semblance of Chinese influence in international life. The ending of the cold war has also shattered the illusion of a consensus on what constitutes a "superpower," made evident by the rise of Japan as a global power of a different kind (a one-dimensional global power), the sudden "third worldization" of the former Soviet Union, and America's heroic but ineffective claim of global leadership without bearing the costs and responsibilities.

Just as Japan is seen as a wallet in search of a global role, China has become an empty seat on the United Nations Security Council searching for a new national identity. Suddenly, Beijing is unsure of its place in a world no longer dominated by superpower rivalry and the country is in the grip of an unprecedented legitimacy—identity crisis. Not since the founding of the People's Republic in 1949 have the questions of internal and external legitimacy-catalyzed by the Tiananmen carnage and the collapse of global communism—been as conflated as in the past three years.

CHINA'S ASIAN IDENTITY

The China threat—the image of a dragon rampant—looms large in the security calculus of every Asian state. Yet China's identity as a regional power is deeply problematic. Although most of the country's external relations pivot

From Samuel S. Kim, "China as a Regional Power," *Current History*, vol. 91, no. 566 (September 1992). Copyright © 1992 by Current History, Inc. Reprinted by permission of *Current History*. Notes omitted.

around the Asia-Pacific region, Beijing has yet to come up with any coherent definition of its place in Asian international relations.

The starting point for understanding China's awkward regional identity—and its inability to maintain any deep and enduring friendship with any Asian state, including North Korea—is to recognize that since the collapse of the traditional Sinocentric world order in the late nineteenth century, this proud and frustrated Asian giant has had enormous difficulty finding a comfortable place as an equal member state in the family of nation-states. During the cold war years the People's Republic succumbed to wild swings of identity, rotating through a series of roles: self-sacrificing junior partner in the Soviet-led socialist world; self-reliant hermit completely divorced from and fighting both superpowers; the revolutionary vanguard of an alternative United Nations; self-styled third world champion of a New International Economic Order; status quo-maintaining "partner" of NATO and favored recipient of largesse at the World Bank; and now, lone socialist global power in a postcommunist world.

None of these identities has much to do with Asian regional identity. The vast gap between being and becoming in the drive for status—and the contradiction between being a regional power and having global aspirations—have introduced a fundamental paradox in the prioritization of China's multiple identities: China as a socialist country; China as an anti-imperialist actor taking a radical system-transforming approach to world order; China as a poor developing country entitled to maximum preferential treatment in trade, investment, aid, and technology transfers;

China as an irredentist power flexing its military muscle power to defend its extensive territorial claims; China as a deft practitioner of zhoubian (goodneighbor) diplomacy; and China as a nuclear power, breaking the superpower nuclear duopoly. . . .

REASSESSING CHINESE POWER

The Chinese concept of power is broad, dynamic, and shifting, fed by historical traditions and experiences. Reacting to the growth of the "decline" school in American studies of international relations, the new game nations now play is said to be a multidimensional notion of "comprehensive national strength" based on population, resources, economic power, science and technology, military affairs, culture, education, and diplomacy.

Of this list, science and technology have become the master key for China in its intense drive toward the promised land of modernity. If China is to become a global power, it must beef up its national power, especially in high-technology industries. There is no escape from this high-tech rat race if China is ever to regain its proper place—"global citizenship" (qiuji)—in the emerging world order.

The government claims that science and technology do not have a class character; indeed, they are rationalized as a kind of global collective goods. Such a realpolitik—nationalistic technocracy dressed in hard globalism—is what is meant by "global citizenship." It also bespeaks the persistence of the nineteenth-century "ti-yong" dilemma— how to strengthen Chinese essence by using foreign technology.

Whether or not the party-state controls the guns, such technocratic realism gives the military a comparative advantage in shaping national policy. Without sufficient military power, according to China's strategic analysts, it will be impossible to preserve and enhance the country's status as a world power or play a decisive role in global politics. In the wake of America's high-tech military victory in the 1991 Persian Gulf war, Beijing decided to reorder its vaunted four modernizations, making science and technology a top priority before agriculture, industry, and defense. At the same time the PLA [China's People's Liberation Army] has been called on to take up a new mission at variance with the Maoist doctrine of protracted struggle: limited war to achieve a quick, decisive high-tech military victory in only a few days.

IS CHINA A GLOBAL POWER?

The sudden diminution of China's global status and influence threatens to take away the party-state's last remaining source of and claim to legitimacy: restoring China's great-power status in the post–cold war and postcommunist world.

Of course, there is no "scientific" way of assessing Chinese national power. In a rapidly changing international environment the very notion of "regional power" or "global power" is subject to continuing redefinition and reassessment. Elsewhere I have constructed a typology of Chinese power, comparing it against Japan, Germany, the United States, and the former Soviet Union and giving China's global ranking in 15 specific categories. Since the United States, the Soviet Union/Russia, Japan, Germany, and China are gener-

ally regarded as the world's great powers, China would have to be included in the top five global rankings to be regarded as a great power.

Not surprisingly, China easily ranks among the top five in population, strategic nuclear warheads, and global arms trade. The Chinese would be first to admit that the burgeoning population (now at 1.2 billion) is a liability rather than an asset in the enhancement of comprehensive national strength. Since 1978, China's population has grown by nearly 200 million people, and in the 1990s at least another 150 million to 180 million will be added. The implications of these enormous numbers wanting to become rich, and the accompanying social, political, and economic pressures, are staggering, especially when placed in the context of industrial modernization and shrinking ecological capacity. China has already become an environmental giant of sorts, contributing to global warming faster than any other major country (China now releases 9.3 percent of global greenhouse-gas emissions, following the United States and the former Soviet Union but ahead of Japan, India, and Brazil).

When Chinese military power is measured quantitatively in terms of the number of strategic nuclear warheads, global arms trade (including global nuclear technology proliferation), and military manpower, China comes out as one of the world's five-largest military powers. However, mere numbers say little about the quality of the PLA or its performance in armed conflict.

China's economic power is mixed. In aggregate gross national product China ranks ninth in the world, but it is projected to become the world's fifth-largest economy by the year 2000. Sheer demographic size left China's per capita GNP at only $350 in 1989 (104th in the world), and it is projected to reach about $800–$1,000 by 2000. Post-Mao China is a global economic power only in the sense of being a major source of cheap labor and a tempting cost-effective site for foreign toxic wastes and heavily polluting industries; indeed these are the defining features of China's place in the global economy. Although exports as a percentage of GNP increased from 4 percent to about 20 percent in the long Deng decade, China still has a long way to go to achieve the status of an important trading power.

Another category needs to be added in determining a country's global power position. East Asia emerged in the 1980s as the most dynamic region in the global economy with seemingly ever-expanding waves of regional economic integration. As the most important investor, trader, aid donor, and development model, Japan easily dominates the East Asian political economy. Japan's economic miracle demonstrates that a country's competitiveness in the global marketplace depends less and less on natural resource power and more and more on the brainpower needed for microelectronics, biotechnology, civilian aviation, telecommunications, robotics, computer hardware and software, and so forth.

China is extremely weak in this area. For example, China is not even included in the top fifteen in the category of issuing important patents. Revealingly, Chinese Foreign Economic Relations and Trade Minister Li Lanqing is reported to have proposed to Japanese Minister of International Trade and Industry Eiichi Nakao on March 22, 1991, a Sino-Japanese collaboration for the establishment of an "East Asian Economic-Cooperation Sphere." The prospect of China emerging as the world's second- or third-largest economy by 2010, which was prognosticated in 1988 by the Commission on Integrated Long-Term Strategy, is rather dubious.

Where does China rank among states when its international reputation, cultural and ideological appeal, development model, and diplomatic leadership in the shaping of international decisions, norms, and treaties in international organizations are considered? Advertised or not, Maoist China commanded such appeal as an anti-hegemonic third world champion of the establishment of the New International Economic Order, which led many *dependencia* theorists to embrace Beijing as a model of self-reliant development. Mao's China stood out as the only third world country that gave but never received any bilateral and multilateral aid. This alone vested Beijing with a measure of moral authority.

In 1978, all this changed when post-Mao China suddenly switched its national identity from a model of self-reliant socialist development to a poor global power actively seeking most-favored-nation trade treatment from the capitalist world. That same year also saw China's abrupt termination of its aid programs to Albania and Vietnam. The 1979 invasion of Vietnam was another reminder of the extent to which the post-Mao leadership was willing to bend the pledge never to act like a hegemonic power. These geopolitical and geoeconomic reversals, coupled with the harsh repression of the first wave of post-Mao democracy movements, began the decaying process of China's moral regime in global politics.

More than any event in modern Chinese history, the Tiananmen massacre, in a single stroke, dealt a severe blow to whatever credibility that was still retained by the make-believe moral regime. Almost overnight the People's Republic acquired a new national identity as an antipeople gerontocracy propped up by sheer repression. The worst was avoided because of a variety of geopolitical and geoeconomic reasons. Taking advantage of its permanent seat on the Security Council, Beijing once again demonstrated its negative power—and the Nixon/Kissinger/Haig/Bush line—that an engaged China is an irreducible prerequisite to any approach to world order. Beijing's bottom line seems clear enough: Ask not what China can do for a new world order; ask instead what every country, especially the lone superpower, can do to make China stable and strong in a sovereignty-centered international order.

The power China had as a "model" for the developing world has vanished in the post-Mao era. Not a single state in Asia or elsewhere looks up to Beijing as a development model. Nobody, not even the Chinese, knows what is meant by socialism with Chinese characteristics. That India and so many developing countries are now looking to Taiwan, not Russia, let alone China, as a model—or that this breakaway island country has recently surpassed Japan as the world's largest holder of foreign exchange reserves ($83 billion) must surely come as another blow to Beijing's national identity crisis. The born-again third world identity in the post-Tiananmen period seems hardly relevant to reestablishing a fit between tradition and modernity or for formulating the best strategies to make China the rich and powerful country that virtually all Chinese think is their due.

PERFORATED SOVEREIGNTY

Revolutionary power may grow from the barrels of guns, but no state—certainly not a huge multinational state—can be held together for long without a legitimizing value system, as was dramatically shown by the collapse of what was widely and wrongly perceived to be a strong state in the former Soviet Union. In at least one respect China is beyond compare. No country in our times has talked as much, launched as many ideological campaigns, succumbed to so many ideological mood swings, and accomplished so little in getting its ideological act together. Herein lies the ultimate tragedy of the Chinese Revolution.

To a startling degree, the post-Tiananmen government is paralyzed by a megacrisis—multiple and interlocking crises of authority, identity, motivation, and ideology. These have converged at a time when the center is fractured by another round of a deadly intraelite power struggle and is also facing challenges from an assertive civil society, peripheral but booming southern coastal provinces, and ethnonationalistic movements of non-Han minority peoples in the strategic borderlands of Tibet, Xinjiang, and Mongolia.

The extent to which China's legitimizing ideology has progressively decayed is captured in the common saying: "In the 1950s people helped people; in the 1960s people hurt people; in the 1970s people used people; in the 1980s and 1990s people eat people." For the majority of politically engaged intellectuals it is the Han Chinese nation, not the party-state, that has become the most significant referent for their individual and collective loyalty and identification, as found in the slogan, "We love our country, but we hate our government."

Viewed against the longstanding state-society and state-nation concordance and the Chinese intellectual tradition of dedication to serving the state, this represents a radical change in the conceptual evolution of China's intellectual community. The defining and differentiating feature of a weak state such as China today is the high level of internal threats to the government's security. External events are seen primarily in terms of how they affect the state's internal stability. The idea of national security, which refers to the defense of core national values against external threats, becomes subverted to the extent that the Chinese government is itself insecure.

China no longer has a legitimizing and unifying ideology of sufficient strength to do away with the large-scale repressive use of force in domestic life. As noted earlier, the post-Tiananmen government increased its defense budget by 52 percent in the last three years while China enjoys the best external environment in history and when outside security threats seem to have all but vanished. A renewed emphasis on political indoctrination of PLA members is reported to have taken up 60 to 70 percent of training time. More tellingly, the People's Armed Police has experienced unprecedented growth in personnel and equipment as a way of coping with growing internal security threats.

The great irony is that the center no longer fully controls the peripheries; Chinese state sovereignty is highly perforated. Well over half of China's economy has already escaped the control of central planners in Beijing. The center has lost control of tax collection, and even profit remittances from many of the state enterprises it owns. Virtually all the gains China has enjoyed since the early 1980s have come from nonstate industries with their share of industrial output zooming from less than 15 percent to a little over half today.

At the same time, the contemporary global information revolution has broken down the exclusive control over information that the center once enjoyed. This revolution has facilitated the rapid mobilization of people's demands, frustrations, and intolerance—indeed, it is the second "revolution of people power." Although its actual speed and magnitude in post-Tiananmen China are difficult to assess, the information revolution nonetheless undergirds the critical social forces and movements for change that are weighed down by the full repressive force of the weak and insecure state.

State sovereignty thus no longer provides the center with security or control, since it is constantly perforated by the forces of supranational globalization and local and regional fragmentation. Against such trends and pressures Chinese state sovereignty is a paper tiger. China is a weak, if not yet disintegrating, state. How can the wobbly edifice of the Chinese state survive the multiple threats from within? Can a weak, oppressive state be expected to act as a responsible and peace-loving regional power? The once widely shared image of a China in disintegration and of a dragon rampant in Japan and Southeast Asia seems to be moving perilously close to reality.

POSTSCRIPT

Will China Become an Asian Superpower?

The next few years are apt to be pivotal ones in China's history. One issue in China is who will take charge after Deng Xiaoping, born on August 22, 1904, dies or become so infirm that his behind-the-scenes control ends. He is almost certainly the last leader whose political lineage dates back to Mao Zedong and the pre-1949 struggle to overthrow Chiang Kai-shek and establish a communist government. Deng has played a strong role in bringing economic reform to China, but political reform has lagged badly. This was symbolized by the government's massacre of pro-democracy demonstrators in Tiananmen Square in Beijing in 1989. For a fascinating look at the Chinese leadership, read Harrison E. Salisbury, *The New Emperors: China in the Era of Mao and Deng* (Little, Brown, 1992).

Who takes power after Deng, and whether that will occur peacefully or amid great turmoil—even fighting—is unknown. The new leadership will decide what road China's economic and political systems will take, a crucial choice for China and the world. Further reading on the internal changes in China is available in Jeffrey W. Wasserstrom and Elizabeth J. Perry, eds., *Popular Protest and Political Culture in Modern China* (Westview, 1991).

There are also important questions over how assertive China is likely to be in making claims to regain lost territory, to reincorporate Taiwan, or to secure a regional sphere of influence. The Spratly Islands are especially significant. They lie in the South China Sea and are located in the middle of one of the world busiest shipping lanes. Furthermore, there is a strong possibility that the islands and their offshore zones may contain major petroleum deposits. The islands are claimed by China, Taiwan, Vietnam, the Philippines, Brunei, and Malaysia. There is also a dispute with Vietnam over the Paracel Islands and a dispute with Japan over the Japanese-controlled Senkaku Islands, lying just to the northeast of Taiwan.

China has also shown strong interest in developing its military capabilities. These capabilities include efforts to enhance in-flight refueling capabilities for its warplanes and to purchase high-performance bombers and aircraft carriers. In November 1992 the Beijing-based *China Business Times* quoted a senior officer of the Peoples Liberation Army (PLA) as saying that, "If we had an aircraft carrier, warfare in the South China Sea would be more lively, and many situations would be easier to handle." All this makes many Asians very nervous.

ISSUE 8

Was Intervention in Somalia Strictly for Humanitarian Purposes?

YES: Herman J. Cohen, from Statement Before the Committee on Foreign Affairs, U.S. House of Representatives (December 17, 1992)

NO: John Pilger, from "The US Fraud in Africa: Operation Restore Hope Is Part of New Age Imperialism," *New Statesman* (September 18, 1992)

ISSUE SUMMARY

YES: Herman J. Cohen, assistant secretary of state for African affairs, characterizes the U.S. decision to join the UN military force sent to Somalia as based on humanitarian concerns.

NO: John Pilger, an essayist for the British publication *New Statesman,* argues that the intervention in Somalia was based more on political than humanitarian motivations and is a symptom of a new age of imperialism.

The images were horrifyingly graphic. During much of 1992 and into 1993, television, newspapers, and magazines carried a seemingly unending torrent of pictures of hollow-eyed, scarecrow-like adults, of children with the withered limbs and the distended bellies that mark starvation, of abandoned buildings pockmarked by shell fire. Representatives from private charitable organizations also appeared on our television sets, bring more pictures of death and destruction, along with pleas for relief donations. In this case, the macabre reality that assaulted our vision and consciences were from Somalia. But they could have been from many places: Bosnia-Herzegovina was experiencing similar trauma; death and suffering were befalling the Armenians and Azerbaijanis fighting in Nagorno-Karabakh; Georgians and Abkhazians were clashing along the eastern shore of the Black Sea; Cambodians were caught between various warring factions in their country; and Liberians were terrorized by assorted brutal rebel groups. All bore terrible testimony to the thinness of just how thin the veneer of civilization can be.

What to do? In the past, such suffering mostly went unnoticed or unknown by most of the world. Often nothing was done. Or if it suited a nation's self-interest, an outside power might step in to end the fighting.

Now things are beginning to change. It is harder to ignore what is happening around the world, or to be unaware of it. Television and satellite transmissions bring pictures almost instantaneously into our living rooms from everywhere in the world. Another change is that there is now a much greater emphasis on collective action. Big powers still act independently, especially in what they consider to be their spheres of influence. The U.S. invasion of Panama in 1989 is an example. Increasingly, though, unilateral action is the exception, where it was once the rule. Countries are more apt to seek to act collectively through the United Nations or other international organizations, in part because international values now frown on acting alone and in part because of the high costs of trying to police or save the world, whichever the case may be.

In Somalia, the UN Security Council authorized an armed intervention against various warring Somali clans to ensure that relief supplies reached starving Somalis. It is worth noting that the UN now claims the right to intervene in a country even without the consent of the country's government.

In Somalia that claim was beside the point; there was no functioning, widely accepted government. In September 1992 the first UN troops, 500 Pakistanis, arrived. It soon became obvious that their numbers were too few to do the job. A more massive operation began in December. Soon some 30,000 blue-helmeted UN troops, including a large contingent of Americans, were deployed to the Somali capital of Mogadishu and to other cities and refugee camps.

At first the arrival of the UN troops went peacefully, and they seemed to be greeted warmly by most Somalis. Over time the mood began to change. Attempting to make both themselves and most Somalis more secure, the UN troops moved to disarm the clans, especially in Mogadishu. The clans resisted. In June 1993 forces reportedly under the control of clan leader Mohammed Farrah Aidid clashed with UN forces and killed 24 Pakistani troops. The UN put a price on Aidid's head. U.S. forces launched retaliatory raids on positions and facilities held by Aidid's followers, and Somali civilians as well as clan fighters were killed. Some Somalis began to claim that the UN troops were more military occupiers than humanitarian relief providers.

In August 1993, twenty-six private relief organizations sent a letter to UN secretary general Boutros Boutros-Ghali charging that the UN operations had killed dozens of civilians, had hampered humanitarian relief efforts, and had created a moral and legal cloud over the peacekeeping operation. "Decisions to use military force need to take into account the consequences such actions will have on humanitarian efforts," the letter said.

Was intervention in Somalia justified, and was it carried out for humanitarian reasons? In the first selection, Herman Cohen, an American assistant secretary of state serving President George Bush, answers yes. He argues that the suffering in Somalia could not be ignored and that the UN's motives for intervening were good. British commentator John Pilger disagrees. Pilger claims that the UN action was a thinly disguised imperialistic move prompted by U.S. desire to gain a strategic advantage, an argument he applies to more than just the situation in Somalia.

YES

Herman J. Cohen

INTERVENTION IN SOMALIA

*Statement by Assistant Secretary of State for African Affairs Herman J. Cohen,
December 17, 1992.*

We have all seen the horrific images from Somalia. The figures are numbing. Perhaps more than 250,000 have starved to death. Another 30,000 may have died in the fighting. The Center for Disease Control estimates that some 3,000 Somalis could be dying every day. More than 25 percent of children under age 5 have already died. One and a half million people are at risk.

To address this crisis, the United States is leading a coalition of forces under U.N. auspices to establish a secure environment for the delivery of food and other humanitarian aid in Somalia.

Our mission is clear; it is defined, and it is doable. But it is not without risk. Once sufficient order is established, we will hand the task back to an expanded U.N. peacekeeping operation.

PRELUDE TO OPERATION RESTORE HOPE

Why did we come to this decision? Simply put, the relief system was not working. It was broken. Someone had to fix it or tens of thousands more would die. Only we could do it.

The United States and other international donors had made massive quantities of food available to end famine in Somalia. The United States alone has already committed more than $240 million in assistance to Somalia over the past 20 months. But widespread looting, fighting, and anarchy prevented food from reaching at least half the population.

In August, at the President's [Bush's] direction, we began a major food airlift from Kenya, which has delivered nearly 19,000 metric tons to the neediest areas in the Somali interior. This was to be an interim

From U.S. House of Representatives. Committee on Foreign Affairs. *The Crisis in Somalia.* Hearing, December 17, 1992. Washington, DC: Government Printing Office, 1993. (H.Hrg. 63-884.)

measure until a high-volume road convoy system could be developed.

At the same time, the United Nations conceived a plan to deploy 3,500 peacekeeping troops to Somalia to serve as food and convoy guards. We airlifted the first 500 troops from Pakistan in September, but they were quickly pinned down by local groups and were unable to carry out their mission. As the situation in the country continued to deteriorate, the remaining 3,000 troops, which were to be drawn from several nations, could not be deployed.

THE DECISION TO SEND U.S. FORCES

Given the worsening humanitarian catastrophe, the President decided to propose to the United Nations the sending of a much larger military force to Somalia. He reached his decision at almost the same moment as U.N. Secretary-General Boutros Boutros-Ghali came to the same conclusion. Since the United States was clearly the only nation that could launch the sort of effort needed, the President offered to have the United States lead a military coalition of concerned nations under U.N. auspices to provide desperately needed humanitarian assistance. The United Nations subsequently accepted the proposal of a U.S.-led coalition.

... [T]he deployment of coalition forces for Operation Restore Hope in Somalia is proceeding smoothly. Within the next few days, we expect to have approximately 17,000 U.S. soldiers, sailors, airmen, and marines deployed for coalition operations in Somalia. We intend to send a total U.S. force of approximately 28,000 troops into Somalia.

OUR COALITION PARTNERS

We would also like to express our satisfaction with the response of countries from around the world who are committed to joining or providing assistance to the coalition.

So far, approximately 44 countries have pledged or expressed an interest in making military, logistical, and financial contributions for humanitarian operations in Somalia. This includes 18 nations which have offered to send forces to participate in the coalition and/or in the follow-on U.N. Peacekeeping Force. The total number of troops involved may exceed 16,000. At present, U.S. forces in Somalia have been joined by contingents from France, Saudi Arabia, Belgium, Italy, Canada, and Botswana.

Other countries, such as Turkey, have already sent liaison officers to coordinate the integration of their forces into the coalition.

THE SITUATION ON THE GROUND

Let me turn now to what coalition forces are actually doing in Somalia. The coalition has been largely successful in restoring security in the capital of Mogadishu. The city is relatively quiet, and there have been no major encounters involving coalition forces and armed Somali factions or lawless elements. The Marines have secured the airport and port in Mogadishu, permitting aircraft and ships to come in and unload vital shipments of humanitarian assistance.

This is a significant accomplishment. The International Committee of the Red Cross estimates that approximately 52,000 metric tons (MT) of food are needed each month to feed those at risk in Somalia. This amount was not being provided because factional violence and the looting of relief supplies by gangs of thugs had made it nearly impossible to move large quantities of food in convoys.

THE FOOD IS MOVING AGAIN

Now that the security situation is improving, the food is moving again. Convoys have already moved a sizable quantity of the 12,000 MT of food that was stockpiled in Mogadishu. A cargo vessel with 3,000 MT of humanitarian assistance for the Work Food Program is now being unloaded at Mogadishu's port. This is the first relief vessel to dock at the port in two months. Another 32,000 MT of food is moving through the pipeline from storage sites in Mombasa, Kenya. Between this month and next, approximately 73,000 MT of food aid from the United States will arrive in Somalia. An additional 20,000 MT provided by the European Community is also on the way. Future deliveries from the United States and the European Community in 1993 will total 350,000 MT.

COALITION FORCES MOVING INTO THE INTERIOR

Securing the airport and seaport in Mogadishu was also essential to speeding the deployment of coalition forces.

Besides Mogadishu, the city of Kismayo has the only airport and port facilities large enough to accommodate the type of aircraft and ocean-going vessels being used to transport troops and their equipment to Somalia. General Johnston and his Marines have done a remarkable job in readying the facilities at Mogadishu to receive coalition forces.

Now that this has been done, the coalition is beginning to push out into those areas of the Somali interior where the security situation has been unstable. A joint contingent of Marines and French Legionnaires arrived in Baidoa yesterday. Baidoa has been the scene of intense factional fighting and wanton looting by gangs of armed thugs.

The Marines and Legionnaires have secured Baidoa's airport and established a security cordon around the town. U.S. military and civilian relief flights have delivered much needed relief supplies to Baidoa, and the city is now relatively calm.

PREPARING FOR PHASE II: U.N. PEACEKEEPING

... [W]hat we are seeing now is merely the first phase of U.N.-mandated operations in Somalia. Coalition forces are, indeed, creating an environment for the safe delivery of humanitarian assistance.

As soon as this has been done, our intention is to turn the function of protecting food convoys over to the regular U.N. UNOSOM [United Nations Operation, Somalia] Peacekeeping Force. This transition from peacemaking to peacekeeping force is clearly foreseen in U.N. Security Council Resolution 794.

Although we cannot give you any firm timetable, we are confident this transition can be accomplished fairly rapidly. Certainly, success in beginning the long term reconstitution of Somali society and government is absolutely dependent on it.

UNOSOM II

For the plan to work, however, we need to put together a follow-on UNOSOM peacekeeping force of sufficient size to ensure the continued delivery of humanitarian aid. The United Nations is currently working on putting together this follow-on force. We are working actively with the United Nations to attract participants. As I noted earlier, at least 18 nations have already offered to participate in both the peacemaking and peacekeeping phases of U.N. operations in Somalia. This suggests that it may not be too difficult to organize the follow-on force.

NATIONAL RECONCILIATION

We also support U.N. efforts to broker political stability. All our good works could go for naught if we do not follow through on the long and difficult process of reconstituting Somali civil society and government. We strongly endorse the work of U.N. Special Representative Kittani, and President Bush has sent Ambassador Bob Oakley to Somalia to work with Kittani to gain the cooperation of Somali factions on security, relief operations, and rehabilitation.

The United Nations will convene a reconciliation conference in Addis Ababa in early January which we hope will set the process of political reconciliation firmly in motion.

COSTS AND FUNDING

Let me talk a bit about money. I know the Congress is concerned about the costs of Operation Restore Hope. It is fairly certain that this will be an expensive undertaking. We have all agreed to meet all the costs associated with our own force contribution. Rough estimates are that this could reach $500 million over a two-month period. This is a lot of money, but we believe it is a small price to pay for saving hundreds of thousands of lives.

I want to assure you that we will pay for our own costs. Other developed countries contributing troops to the operation will be required to pay their own way.

Nor will we pay for the many poorer nations who would like to join the coalition. Their incremental costs—those necessary to transport troops to Somalia and maintain them there—will be met by a special fund that is being established and managed by the United Nations.

... [W]e recognize that there are no easy solutions for the problems of Somalia and that our present efforts there will not be cheap. We cannot see into the future with crystal clarity, although we are confident of our course. We acted to save lives—hundreds of thousands of lives—and nothing can be more important than that.

NO

John Pilger

THE US FRAUD IN AFRICA: OPERATION RESTORE HOPE IS PART OF NEW AGE IMPERIALISM

On Christmas Eve, BBC television news announced that America's "only purpose" in Somalia was to ensure that hungry people were fed. This was generally agreed throughout the media on both sides of the Atlantic. Congratulations were offered to President Bush for his "bold" decision to "send the cavalry to the rescue". *Time* magazine published a two-page colour photograph showing Somali children reaching out to a marine for "the gift of hope". A marine corporal was asked about the danger he faced. "In a way," he said wistfully, "I'm sort of hoping for a little combat."

Within days of their arrival, two US helicopter gunships fired their missiles at three armed vehicles, killing all nine Somalis in them. The justification for this "little combat" was that the helicopters had been attacked. In fact, the Somalis were engaged in a private fight, and, according to witnesses, no one fired at the helicopters.

The nine dead equals the number of British soldiers killed by US aircraft during the Gulf war. The difference is that, while the British incident became a much-publicised scandal, the Somali incident barely rated a mention. Last week, on the eve of Bush's triumphant arrival in Somalia, US helicopters dropped leaflets warning people that if they were found merely carrying a weapon they would be shot. Many of the weapons were supplied originally by Washington; no irony was noted.

Operation Restore Hope, as this model of media manipulation is called, is not just a public relations stunt staged by a beaten and discredited president who, in the wake of his "bold" decision on Somalia, pardoned those who almost certainly would have blown the whistle on his role in the Iran-Contra crimes. Bush is not engaged in a humanitarian mission to restore hope to the starving. He has sent guns and bombs to skeletal children to restore order: the New World Order. It took a lone letter writer to the [British newspaper] *Guardian*, Andy Abel, to state the obvious, which professional commentators

From John Pilger, "The US Fraud in Africa: Operation Restore Hope Is Part of New Age Imperialism," *New Statesman* (September 18, 1992). Copyright © 1992 by Statesman and Nation Publishing Company, London, England. Reprinted by permission.

apparently could not. "We are invited," he added, "to believe that there is starvation in Somalia because armed gangs loot food stocks. There is looting because there is not enough food."

The severity of the drought in Somalia was known to the US and other western governments as long ago as mid-1991, when satellite evidence left no doubt about what was coming. They, and the international organisations they effectively control, did nothing until, as with Ethiopia in the 1980s, horrific television images exposed their culpable inaction. Until then, according to the US Congressional watchdog, the General Accounting Office, the US government had allowed its client regime in Somalia, the murderous dictatorship of Mohammed Siad Barre, to steal American-donated food and divert it from the starving to the army and profiteers. Once Barre had fled Mogadishu, the US, according to the last American ambassador, "turned out the light, closed the door and forgot about Somalia".

Not quite. The Bush administration ran a "rat line" for the war criminals of Siad Barre's regime. According to a Canadian Broadcasting Corporation report..., Washington dispensed tourist visas and easy passages to Canada for Somali officers who had trained at Fort Leavenworth in the mid-1980s, including one who allegedly ordered the execution of 120 villagers.

At the same time, Bush administration officials vigorously discouraged donors from helping Somalia, regardless of reports that up to 2,000 Somalis were dying every day. [In 1991]... Bush withheld American food aid for two straight months—right to 13 August when, as the underdog in a presidential election campaign, he mounted the podium at the Republican Party convention and announced to his prime-time audience that "starvation in Somalia is a major human tragedy" and he, George Bush, would ensure that the US "overcame the obstacles" of getting food to "those who desperately need it".

Within weeks of a US food airlift getting underway, most of its cargo planes were grounded after the wing of one of them was hit by a bullet: a relatively minor occupational hazard that did not deter private donors. In any case, it was now 18 September; the last phase of the presidential campaign was underway and, to no one's surprise, the "major human tragedy" in Somalia was no longer an issue. Somalis could go on starving until it was time to use them again.

When the time came, just before Christmas, the media images of Operation Restore Hope were almost perfect. The marines were greeted by massed TV cameras and satellite dishes and looked every bit like the cavalry coming to the rescue. They were, as one American TV commentator put it, "a sight for sore eyes back home". This was also true in this country, notably among liberal opinion. The American intervention, argued an editorial in NSS (18 December 1992), had "proved remarkably successful... for once, the US did not permit either free-market prejudices or 'strategic' interests to determine its foreign policy." Thus, the "good guys" and their New World Order were back on the road to redemption, regardless of the historical truth of every American intervention in the developing world this century.

In Somalia, the marines and the media have an ideal enemy. Like the British in pith helmets, they are facing amorphous "gangs" of natives led by "warlords". On the TV screen, Somalis are dehumanised.

There are no good Somalis, no wise Somalis, no professional and organised Somalis. There are only those "warlords" and their "gunmen" and, of course, their pathetic victims.

There have been few serious attempts to explain that the divisions and hatred between Somalis are largely the product of European colonialism and of the cold-war battlefield imposed on Somalia by the superpowers. Somalis share a common language and religion and have much more in common than most peoples of Africa. In the 19th century, they were divided between British Somaliland, Italian Somalia, French Djibouti and Ethiopian Ogaden. Others were incorporated into the British colony of Kenya. Tens of thousands of people were handed from one power to another. "They may be made," wrote a British colonial official, "to hate each other and thereby good governance is ensured." Siad Barre was the beneficiary of this, playing one group against another with the backing first of the Soviet Union, then of the United States, which flooded the country with modern weapons.

Rakiya Omaar and Alex de Waal, formerly of the human rights organisation, Africa Watch, wrote recently in the *Guardian*: "US military intervention in Somalia has followed a gross misrepresentation of the situation in the country." They reported that "three-quarters of the country is relatively peaceful, with civil structures in place", and the famine confined to scattered rural pockets. "Most of the food is not looted," they wrote. "Save the Children Fund has distributed 4,000 tons in Mogadishu without losing a single bag. Other agencies that work closely with Somalia suffer rates of 2–10 per cent, because they consult closely with Somali elders and humanitarian workers."

Omaar and de Waal say that where there is a major problem with starvation is Bardera, which the forces of General Mohammed Siad Hersi Morgan control. Morgan is the son-in-law of Siad Barre. His forces are armed and trained by Kenya, another US client. Had Bush been serious about getting supplies through, he had only to intervene with Daniel Arap Moi in Nairobi. "There has been nothing in the way of attempts to negotiate settlements in comparison with, say, Yugoslavia," wrote Omaar and de Waal. "The one serious attempt—by the former UN special envoy Mohammed Sahnoun—was meeting with remarkable success. Sahnoun was forced to resign in October because of his outspoken criticism of the UN's dismal failure in Somalia."

Bush's "humanitarian intervention" has a significance that goes far beyond a media stunt and is in keeping with radical policy and organisational changes at the United Nations that have seen the Security Council become an instrument of US power since the end of the cold war. The term "humanitarian intervention" is merely the latest, preferred euphemism for foreign intervention, with or without the consent of the invaded country. Of course, the UN charter specifically forbids any violation of national sovereignty; but in these days of Secretary General Boutros Boutros-Ghali, who has allowed the White House to dictate the reorganisation of the world body down to the appointment of its most senior executives, it matters not what the Charter says, but what Augustus in Washington wants.

*   *   *

The bloody coup ending democracy in Haiti in 1991 demonstrated this. In the

Security Council, the French argued that Haiti deserved "humanitarian intervention" by the UN. They won considerable support, though not from the US. "The nature of the discussion," wrote the UN specialist Phyllis Bennis, "made clear that potential targets were more likely to be those already demonised by the west: Gaddafi's Libya, Saddam Hussein's Iraq, Kim Il Sung's North Korea, Fidel Castro's Cuba, etc. The coup in Haiti was not on the agenda." In other words, the US would decide.

The French later proposed a multinational command for the UN's Military Staff Committee, which would carry out future "humanitarian interventions". They were told firmly that US forces, when playing a major part, would be answerable only to the Pentagon. The point had been made dramatically at the start of the Gulf war. When the bombing of Baghdad began on 16 January 1991, members of the Security Council emerged from the chamber unaware of what had been unleashed in their name.

Elsewhere in the developing world, there is an unmistakable pattern of US intervention, legitimised by the UN. In Cambodia, the UN's biggest operation, described as a "model for the world", the US has reimposed its will on Indochina, using the Khmer Rouge and its US-funded allies as a means of continuing to destabilise Vietnam.

In Angola, UN-monitored elections unfortunately produced the "wrong" winner in the [government]..., which is not forgiven for its ties with the former communist bloc. The [government] won in spite of American and tacit UN support for Jonas Savimbi, Washington's oldest cold-war client in Africa, who lost the election. Now, Washington is withholding diplomatic recognition, while

Boutros-Ghali pressures the democratically elected former rebel leader José Eduardo dos Santos to accommodate Savimbi and [his] Unita [rebels] in his government. Described by US officials as "power sharing" and an "acceptable solution", this is the equivalent of Clinton being forced to bring Bush into his cabinet....

Europe is quite a different matter. The US has minimal interest in a small, weak Balkan state like Bosnia, whose birth it did not attend or approve. Secretary of State Eagleburger's call for a UN tribunal to punish Serbia's "war criminals" should be set against its silence on the punishment of Pol Pot and his fellow [Khmer Rouge] genocidists, who have enjoyed UN (and US) protection. The Serbian proposal is hot air; collusion with Pol Pot is part of a policy that, since 1989, has seen the United States reassert itself in its traditional and most profitable arena: the third world.

The cold war was a superpower struggle on the surface only. The "Soviet threat" was most useful to Washington in allowing the US to maintain a degree of influence over its real, *economic* rivals—Japan and Germany. It also provided a rationale for intervention in poor countries whose resources or strategic position Washington regarded as essential to its dominance of the global system of imperialism that has operated during the past century and is now known as the "world economy".

But America is a declining economic power, and its future economic supremacy will be dependent on its ability to secure strategic and economic advantage by the implicit threat of military might. For example, the speed and scale of the American response to Iraq's invasion of Kuwait was entirely out of proportion to Washington's concern about the significance of the sheikhdom and its oil. The Bush administration chose dramatically to elevate the crisis for purposes other than oil, perhaps principally as a demonstration of America's continued world leadership over its more economically successful Japanese and European adversaries.

In March 1992, a Pentagon report, leaked to the *New York Times*, made this quite clear. Setting the "nation's destiny for the next century", American military planners visualised a global empire whose "first objective" was to "prevent the emergence of a new rival". Although the Pentagon later issued a "final report", with more cautious language, the veiled warning to friends and foes alike was unmistakable.

* * *

There is every reason to believe that President Clinton will pursue this policy and make full use of the Americanised United Nations that Bush has left him. Clinton has left no doubt that he will continue to support Israel, by any standards a terrorist state, whose "ethnic cleansing" policies are in defiance of a host of UN resolutions. He also wants to "institutionalise" the UN's success in the Gulf war. He says he likes the idea, for example, of a "UN rapid deployment force, that could be used for purposes beyond traditional peacekeeping, such as standing guard at the borders of countries threatened by aggression, preventing attacks on civilians, providing humanitarian relief".

It was this last category of "humanitarian relief" that moved Henry Kissinger to write some remarkable words recently, which the *Guardian* published. The "objective" in Somalia is "noble", he began.

"In fact, moral purpose has motivated every American war this century... The new approach [in Somalia] claims an extension in the reach of morality... 'Humanitarian intervention' asserts that moral and humane concerns are so much a part of American life that not only treasure but lives must be risked to vindicate them; in their absence, American life would have lost some meaning. No other nation has ever put forward such a set of propositions..."

The author of this tripe was also one of the authors of the "secret bombing" of Cambodia during which American pilots falsified their logs in order to fly B52 bombers in defiance of Congress over a small, neutral peasant country and drop the greatest tonnage of bombs in the history of modern bombardment. Between 1969 and 1975, three-quarters of a million people were killed. Kissinger was also deeply involved in the overthrow of the democratically elected Allende government in Chile.

That Kissinger's views should have been sought at all demonstrates the extent to which the hagiographers of the old imperialism and the apologists of the new retain credibility, using and twisting the words of life, words like "morality" and "humanitarianism". Just as there is now virtually no mainstream debate of difference between "democracy" and the "free market", there may be soon no debate of difference between "intervention", whatever its semantic mask, and imperialism; a non-word in today's Orwellian lexicon of control.

In the [British newspaper] *Observer* last week, Michael Ignatieff introduced his readers to what he called "liberal intervention". "We are moving towards a new world," he wrote, "in which the international community engages itself to protect minorities from majorities, to feed the starving and to enforce peace in case of civil strife." This is the same American-driven and bribed "international community" that oversaw the slaughter of some 200,000 people in Iraq, of whom many, if not most, were the very minorities the interventionists claimed they were "helping". That aside, the "we" is important here, for it assumes and emphasises the artificial division in humanity that was always and remains the essence of imperialism, and the antithesis of true internationalism.

POSTSCRIPT

Was Intervention in Somalia Strictly for Humanitarian Purposes?

The clash of views between Herman Cohen and John Pilger and the shifting circumstances in Somalia raise many troubling questions. These are surely questions about the specific actions taken in Somalia. But there are also larger ones that extend to all interventions, everywhere. What right does an outside power have, even acting collectively through the UN, to intervene in another country? The question is even harder if the country's government does not ask for intervention. If unrequested intervention is sometimes justifiable, under what circumstances? What should be done when the circumstances surrounding the intervention change? This happened in Somalia, where the primary thrust of UN troop activity shifted from safeguarding the delivery of humanitarian aid to suppressing clan fighting, and also to attempting to restore a civil, unified government to Somalia .

The workings of the United Nations add to the conundrum. The Security Council, which authorizes and sets the rules for the dispatch of UN forces, is dominated by its five permanent members (China, France, Great Britain, Russia, and the United States). Each exercises a veto. To some in the Third World, unilateral imperialism by individual countries seems to have given way to a form of collective imperialism under the auspices of the United Nations, dominated by many of the former colonial powers, especially the United States. (This concern is discussed further in Issue 14.) Based on its power and its world leadership role, the United States certainly has more diplomatic clout in the Security Council and the full UN than any other country. Whether or not the United States dominates the UN, as Pilger and others claim, is an arguable but not indisputable fact. Still, Pilger's charge that the Security Council is a surrogate for U.S. imperialism is worth debating.

There can be little doubt that the real, if unannounced, primary goal of the UN forces in Somalia shifted from ensuring the delivery of humanitarian aid to disarming, even subduing, the various armed Somali clans. For interesting reading on whether or not the UN should be in the business of "saving failed states," see Gerald B. Helman and Steven R. Ratner, "Saving Failed States," *Foreign Policy* (Winter 1992). They are prone to answer yes, as is Paul Johnson in "Wanted: A New Imperialism," *National Review* (December 14, 1992). Johnson's article is more benign than its title suggests, and he argues that "it's time to stop singing those twentieth-century blues and start considering ways to secure global stability and extend prosperity. The first step: re-establish Western imperialism." American columnist Charles Krauthammer has written that Somalia "is the humanitarian's ultimate nightmare. Famine relief turns into counterinsurgency. From Red Cross to Green Beret in six months." It might be better, Krauthammer suggests, if fragmented states such as Somalia were "given over in trusteeship to some great power willing and able to seize and rule it." This, he admits, "smacks of colonialism," but, he argues, "no one has come up with a better idea for saving countries like Somalia from themselves."

One of the reasons for the seeming upsurge of badly divided countries without the political or economic ability to survive, according to some scholars, is the overapplication of the idea of self-determination. For this view, which carries with it the idea that such states should not be either promoted nor saved, see Amitai Etzioni, "The Evils of Self-Determination," *Foreign Policy* (Winter 1992). Also commenting on this issue is Canadian scholar Robert H. Jackson in *Quasi-States: Sovereignty, International Relations and the Third World* (Cambridge University Press, 1991). Jackson says that many newer countries are but quasi-states that survive more by "negative sovereignty," that is because of international support than by "positive sovereignty," that is, the support and loyalty of a country's own people.

PART 2

Economics and International Affairs

International economic and trade issues have an immediate and personal effect on individuals in ways that few other international issues do. They influence the jobs we hold and the prices of the products we buy—in short, our life-styles. In the worldwide competition for resources and markets, tensions arise between allies and adversaries alike, and, in this section, we examine some of the prevailing economic tensions.

■ Does Japan Represent a Worldwide Economic Threat?

■ Should the Developed North Increase Aid to the Less Developed South?

■ Should the Global Arms Trade Be Severely Restricted?

■ Does the Global Environmental Movement Threaten Economic Prosperity?

ISSUE 9

Does Japan Represent a Worldwide Economic Threat?

YES: Diane D. Pikcunas, from "Japan's Economic 'Pearl Harbor' Threatens the United States," *Conservative Review* (November 1990)

NO: Koji Taira, from "Japan, an Imminent Hegemon?" *The Annals of the American Academy of Political and Social Science* (January 1991)

ISSUE SUMMARY

YES: Diane D. Pikcunas, an adjunct professor and a student of Asian affairs, argues that Japan has emerged as a determined and serious adversary to the United States in the economic field and is waging and winning the economic struggle to the detriment of others.

NO: Professor of economics and industrial relations Koji Taira says that although Japan has been thrust into a leading world role due to its economic success, the end of the cold war, and the relative decline of the United States, it is not likely to economically dominate the world.

Former Soviet foreign ministry spokesman Gennadi Gerasimov visited Washington in 1990 and acknowledged his country's decline and another great power's victory. "The cold war is over," Gerasimov declared, "and Japan won."

Since the end of World War II, Japan has become an economic superpower. Meanwhile the United States has experienced a relative decline in its global economic position since the years immediately after 1945. The United States remains the world's largest economy, with a gross national product (GNP) that is more than twice as large as Japan's. Similarly, the combined GNP of the member countries of the European Community is much larger than that of Japan. Still, an image has grown up in the United States, Europe, and elsewhere that Japan's economic tactics are predatory, and that the country may aspire to use its economic power to threaten other countries. In the United States and Europe, this idea has gained hold in part because of the troubled economies of these countries over the past few years.

Some view these trends as indications that the Japanese will rise to world dominance. There are political scientists who theorize that there are cycles in history marked by the regular rise and decline of dominant world powers (hegemonic powers, or hegemons). Especially in terms of a dominant sea power and international trading power, the argument goes that Britain declined and was replaced by the United States, which (in turn) is now declining and will be replaced by Japan. The hegemon, in part, establishes the international rules of conduct and, if necessary, enforces them.

There is concern that Japan will be able to dominate the world financially and technologically. Some international relations theorists contend that the nature of world power is changing and that soft (economic, leadership) power is replacing hard (coercive, military) power in importance. If that is true, Japan seems to be in a strong position. During the two decades beginning in 1974, the U.S. gross domestic product (GDP) increased an annual average of 2.26 percent; the EC's GDP rose an average 2.25 percent annually; and Japan's GDP annual average increase was 3.9 percent.

During 1993, based on International Monetary Fund projections, the United States had a balance of payments (a figure including almost all inflows and outflows of capital) deficit of $69.3 billion. The European Community's deficit was $55.6 billion. Japan had a balance of payments surplus of $88.1 billion. Other countries are especially critical of what they charge is Japan's unwillingness to open itself to foreign goods, investment, and contracting opportunities. Again for 1993, U.S. imports increased 7.8 percent; the EC's imports went up 5.0 percent. Japan's export increase lagged, up only 4.3 percent. Japan has also run up large trade supluses with almost every country.

The United States is particularly disadvantaged in its current financial relations with Japan. The 1991 U.S. trade deficit with Japan was $43.4 billion, of which about 40 percent was due to automobile imports. The deficit with Japan equaled two-thirds of the overall U.S. trade deficit. In addition to this financial outflow, there is concern about the pattern of trade. Japan sends high technology (computers) and heavy industry (automobiles) to the United States. By contrast, the United States exports less important products to the Japanese. For example, Coca-Cola has 60 percent of Japan's soft drink market, and 60 percent of Japanese men use Schick razors.

Those who do not see Japan achieving true superpower status point out that Japan has limited its military expenditures to 1 percent of GNP, and the country's defense budget amounts to only 10 percent of the U.S. defense budget. Furthermore, Japanese law prevents its forces from being deployed abroad. Perhaps ironically, Japan was criticized for following this law and not sending forces to the Persian Gulf during the 1990–1991 war. Reacting to the criticisms, the Japanese government introduced legislation in its parliament that would have allowed Japanese troops to serve with UN peacekeeping forces, but the measure was defeated in December 1991. Explained one legislator, "Some people... fear that sending troops overseas, even with the United Nations, means the revival of militarism."

Thus the question is the future of Japanese power. In the following readings, Diane D. Pikcunas argues that a mighty Japan is poised to inflict an economic Pearl Harbor on the United States. Koji Taira disagrees and argues that Japan is not an imminent hegemon.

YES

Diane D. Pikcunas

JAPAN'S ECONOMIC "PEARL HARBOR" THREATENS THE UNITED STATES

In 1942, Japan bombed Pearl Harbor; in 1990, Japan is buying up Hawaiian real estate at prices Americans find impossible to rival. As long ago as 1953 a retired Japanese real estate investor bought no less than 150 houses in Hawaii in a single year. Today much of Honolulu and the Hawaiian islands belongs to Japanese owners, with prestigious Kahala Avenue and Aukai Avenue being almost exclusively owned by Japanese. In those two prestigious streets, homes that previously sold at two or three hundred thousand dollars are now Japanese-owned and are priced from three to twenty-five million dollars. How did all this come about? How did Japan, a defeated and penniless nation in 1945, with tremendous war losses, emerge as the economic victor in the post-World War II world?

In the 1950s, Japan's products were the butt of jokes, representing something equivalent to shoddy, imitative junk. But since then, Japan has emerged as a major economic power, with manufacturers in other countries even giving Japanese-sounding names to their products to convey an aura of quality. Manufacturers such as Sony and Mitsubishi surpass American products, and the reader knows how many Americans buy Japanese automobiles due to their conviction that these are better value for the money. By the time American industrialists began to wake up to the reality, the Japanese invasion had eviscerated America's auto, steel, electronics and machine-tool industries. "Buy American" became more than just a slogan; it became a cry for help and survival for domestic industries and jobs of workers in face of the seemingly unbeatable Japanese onslaught.

Granted, Japan's invasion of the American automobile market with small, efficient, gas-saving automobiles such as Toyotas did force American automobile manufacturers to rethink and retool their priorities. These automobile giants began catering to the energy-efficient desire of American buyers for small cars—but not before Japan had captured a significant segment of the market. The mass wave of Toyotas helped to produce better Fords and Chryslers, but they cut deeply into U.S. auto-makers' markets, and have

From Diane D. Pikcunas, "Japan's Economic 'Pearl Harbor' Threatens the United States," *Conservative Review*, vol. 1, no. 7 (November 1990). Copyright © 1990 by The Council for Social and Economic Studies. Reprinted by permission.

earned billions of U.S. dollars which the Japanese understandably use to buy up U.S. property and U.S. businesses. Indeed, out of fear of possible American protective tariffs, the Japanese started to build automobiles in America, and many journalists are now beginning to predict an era when most U.S. graduates have no better hope for advancement than to become an under-manager in a Japanese-owned and managed industrial, commercial or financial institution in the U.S.A.

However, a greater fear has taken hold of American economic and political experts. Japan's great push may overshadow the United States in high tech industries which promise to dominate economic growth in the next century—such fields as biotechnology, superconductors, and industrial robots. IBM, which in 1980 accounted for 55.5% of the total value of installed mainframe computers around the world (and with other U.S. firms represented 80% of the world total), is now struggling against Japanese competition. The United States, once a dominant leader in industrial technology, may slip to a poor second or third place in the economic competition game. Japan stands as a foremost challenger to the U.S. in both power and influence.

AMERICA—THE WORLD'S LARGEST DEBTOR NATION

Meantime, the U.S. had declined from the largest creditor nation to the world's largest debtor nation. Japan's trade surpluses with the U.S. have piled up rapidly. And the vast mountain of Japanese dollars being poured into the U.S. is being used to buy controlling interests in such American corporations as Columbia Pictures.

America, while still giving away money generously around the world and canceling Third World debts (notably African), is surviving only by selling its homeland, and by running up mammoth international debts which will eventually erupt into a financial crisis of volcanic dimensions. At stake is not only the question as to who will control U.S. business, but the very livelihood of American workers. Action can be swift. The American-owned Goodyear Tire and Rubber Company has suffered a decline in sales and is being hard pressed in the tire market by France's Michelin Group and a rapidly moving Japan's Bridgestone Corporation which bought up Firestone Tire and Rubber (formerly an American-owned company). The Japanese have won a worldwide share of the tire market which trails only Goodyear and Michelin.

The close diplomatic and economic relations forged between the U.S. and Japan in the post-World War II era are crumbling, with Japan using the excuse of the treaties imposed upon it after World War II to escape sending troops to the Persian Gulf. True, the U.S. economy is still strong. Yet, Japan's growing economic strength is sure to lead to more independent action and less willingness to follow the U.S. lead in a global equation. As international corporations in the Western world seek to build an international New World Order—as so frequently mentioned by President Bush—in which nationalism will become anathema, and all the peoples of the world will become part of a common international labor force, moving to wherever the demand for labor exists, and industry will be free to cross national boundaries, to invest and operate wherever it chooses to operate, Japan stands out as a nation-conscious competitor, that despite its defeat in World War II does not wish to lose its ethnic identity, and whose industrialists and populace are united in their desire to survive as an independent nation. And the way things are working out, it looks as though they may succeed in doing this, while the international dream collapses in debt.

Because Japan's economic success is largely dependent on its ability to sell to the U.S. and Western Europe, its government has made token concessions to internationalism to avoid a tariff war, and also to increase its influence within the existing supra-national organizations. Japan has eagerly joined multinational institutions such as the World Bank and the International Monetary Fund, but by contributing to these it has also earned influence within them. Japan moves into the international arena offering foreign aid on its own terms. Its claim for more influence is direct: it has more money to give away! Demands that it reduce its own protective tariffs to allow American goods to sell in Japan have been met, on the face of things, by some easing of its protective stance, but in reality these concessions are in areas which either benefit Japanese industry or else present no threat to the Japanese economy. Besides, as Western Europe has demonstrated, protection against foreign imports does not have to take the form of tariffs; it can be equally effected by governmental regulations of product standards which favor the home industries.

In relations with the U.S., a trade war between the two giants remains a real and stark possibility. Previously, mutual interests in defense and economic cooperation have submerged the sharp edges of such a conflict. But as U.S. pressures on Japan have grown, so Japan has evidenced a new aggressiveness in trade talks and less willingness to reach an accommodation. The devastation of the American textile industry through Oriental competition is already a well-documented disaster for America. The U.S. appears a loser even in the battle for determination of the terms for reducing its annual $50 billion trade deficit with Japan.

Technology and market access are the keys to power. The current figures are making American policy-makers somber. Japan's consumers are already better off than American consumers and—as estimated by Japan's Nomura Research Institute in Tokyo—in ten years time, Japan's per capita gross national product will be 50 percent higher than that of the U.S. (i.e., by the year 2000). The shift is the same in other Newly Industrialized Nations which have imitated Japan, such as the ROC (Taiwan), the Republic of Korea (South Korea), and even Singapore. As U.S. governmental policy continues to stress "free trade" for the good of the Third World,... it refuses to protect basic U.S. industries from foreign competition, permits foreign nations to buy control of key U.S. industries and facilities, taxes its citizens and runs up unrepayable debts to provide largesse to nations which either cannot or will not support themselves. Japan and the other newly industrialized nations of the Orient do none of these things, and have not been slow to exploit U.S. folly. The U.S. is losing its control over global trade issues.

A turning point may have occurred in the battle over joint U.S.-Japanese coproduction of the FSX [military] jet. The U.S. appeared to come out ahead in denying Japan important U.S. technology, but Japan is moving toward a more independent stance—a more autonomous technological role. The growing power of Japanese companies, freed from dependence on the Japanese government, indicates more independence to pursue research and development free from any consideration of the impact on U.S.-Japanese relations. Some argue that the U.S. may need a stronger push to gain access to Japanese technology, rather than simply reducing the access of Japan to U.S. technology.

Defense issues remain another important stumbling block between the U.S. and Japan. The U.S. has provided Japan with a "nuclear umbrella" and for years saved the Japanese from the burden of heavy defense expenditures. The U.S.-dictated Japanese Constitution prohibited Japan from possessing nuclear weapons but allowed it a Self-Defense Force. Today, in its prosperity, Japan possesses the second largest defense budget in the Free World, with more destroyers in the Pacific than the U.S. Seventh Fleet as well as a significant investment in F-15 fighter planes. Japan is gaining a greater voice in the U.S.-Japan defense partnership as the U.S. Pentagon finds itself with less funding and the Japanese defense forces receive increasingly generous support from their government.

Even the once-dreaded USSR now seeks Japanese investment in Siberia, but although the Japanese see the Siberian potential, they seem determined to withhold financial investment until such time as a weakened USSR is prepared to return the southern portion of Sakhalin Island, which it annexed after World War II.

GROWING JAPANESE ASSERTIVENESS

The growing sense of assertiveness in Japan came to the forefront with the publication of an anti-U.S. book *The Japan That Can Say "NO"; The New U.S.-Japan Card*, written by two important Japanese—Sony Corporation Chairman Akio Morita and Liberal-Democratic Party Diet (Japan's legislature) member Shintaro Ishihara. The book reflects an assertive Japan, no longer responsive to U.S. needs and viewpoints. The theme is that Japan can now assume an international role independent of U.S. interests. It argues that Japan should inform the U.S. that it will protect itself, and that Japan should henceforth go forward on its own. Japan, the book emphasizes, must not hesitate to say "no" to the U.S. when it disagrees with U.S. actions.

The assertion that the book does not represent a majority view of the Japanese falls on deaf ears. The book appears to be a true reflection of Japanese feeling toward the Americans. Notably, it has sold over one million copies!

Americans, on the other hand, feel a growing resentment as they see Japan extending its influence over American industry with the profits it has made on its sales to America. The U.S. helped Japan to rebuild from wartime devastation; now, Japan appears to use its economic muscle to humble its mentor, bringing U.S. industries to their knees and throwing American workers out of jobs. At the same time, American specialists recall that in 1960 a large American firm filed a patent in Japan for the basic integrated circuit—a patent not granted until 1989. This represented a delay of three crucial decades, sufficient to allow Japan to move into a powerful position in that industry.

Japan's economic power exerts increasing influence in the everyday lives of Americans—and the future economic prospects of Americans. Its "closed market" makes it difficult for U.S. advancement. *Newsweek* magazine recently pointed out that Japan's imports of manufactured goods reach only slightly above 3 per cent of its gross national product while imports of manufactured goods are 7 per cent for the U.S. More importantly, perhaps, foreign direct investment in Japan amounts to 1 per cent of corporate assets, compared to 9 per cent in the United States!

JAPAN PLANS SATELLITE-BASED SOLAR-POWER STATIONS

Masanori Moritani, formerly of the prestigious Nomura Research Institute and a specialist in technology forecasting, has shown how Japan's surge ahead in nonmilitary technology has enhanced Japan's role in a wide variety of fields. While the U.S. government has abandoned research into the development of satellite-based solar power stations, collecting free energy from the sun's rays for transmission to earth (a project which is now technically feasible and which will eventually replace the use of solar and nuclear fuels), Japan is working hard on this project. Indeed, Japan is particularly involved in space technology research, at a time when the U.S. is cutting financial support for NASA and preventing private companies from entering into space.

JAPAN'S ECONOMIC TENTACLES NOW REACH AROUND THE WORLD

At Euston Railway Station in London, England, the town of Milton Keynes advertises that it has over 30 Japanese industries—a sign intended to imply that the town is on the cutting edge of economic progress. Japan has invested heavily in Britain and numerous other countries, including the People's Republic of China. Hong Kong is a large recipient of Japanese money, and in countries such as Thailand, Japan pours in aid accompanied by investment—and is steadily winning control. Many Thais have complained that joint ventures benefit only the Japanese, that the Japanese avoid hiring Thai managers, and that there is a low level of technology transfer from Japan to Thailand. They also protest that the Japanese are buying up their real estate as a result of their growing trade deficit with Japan. Japanese exports sell throughout South Asia, the Middle East, and Central and South America. Japan's influence even reaches into American territories far out in the Pacific, where it already exercises dominant economic power in Guam and the Commonwealth of the Northern Mariana Islands.

THE SECRET OF JAPANESE SUCCESS

When the U.S. was economically supreme after World War II, it hitched its economic philosophy to the concept of free trade. There was a twofold reason behind this move. First there was a confidence that U.S. technology and "work ethic" could out-compete that of indigenous industries in virtually any nation in the world if only the U.S. could persuade those nations to lower protective tariff and other import barriers and compete on equal grounds with U.S. industrial potential. But there was a second factor, which has become more dominant, especially as the major U.S. corporations have become increasingly international in their financial background—that is the ideal of creating and controlling a single global economy. In such a global economy, the major international corporations, controlling budgets far greater than those of any but the largest nations, would operate free from political interference by governments and local interests. Small countries like white-controlled Rhodesia and South Africa resisted that philosophy, and sought to retain their autonomy, but were beaten down not so much because of their racial philosophy (although this was much touted), as they sought to control their own resources rather than bend to the major international mining and financial corporations. Today, as the U.S. becomes increasingly internationalized both in the scope of its larger financial, commercial and industrial corporations (and through them its governmental policies) and in the composition of its population, it remains supportive of the idea that national interest should be subordinate to international trade rather than the reverse, and that national boundaries should present no barrier to the free movement of capital or labor. Unfortunately for the U.S., Japan and the Newly Industrialized Nations of the Orient have not accepted this ideal. They have put loyalty to the concept of nationhood ahead of loyalty to the idea of internationalism, and have demonstrated the fallacies inherent in the internationalist arguments.

JAPAN'S PROTECTIVE POLICIES

Japan has a clearly protective philosophy. Lacking any substantial natural resources such as enrich the U.S., and also lacking the large internal market that the U.S. possesses, Japan knows that young industries must be protected from competition from abroad if they are to survive. After its defeat in World War II, Japan was in total economic collapse. Its first steps towards economic recovery were supported by American aid and American investment, and American industrialists sought to obtain a foothold in Japan. But Japanese governmental policy chose the nationalist route, and developed protectionist policies. Japan has ever since remained a protectionist nation, guarding nascent industries against foreign competition and protecting its farmers so that it will not become dependent on imported food.

During the early phase of the post-War recovery, Japanese government controls tended to be bureaucratic, but as its economy expanded rapidly in the 1970s the governmental authorities realized that industrial vitality could not thrive under bureauratic control. Government could best help industry by studying export markets, identifying the best markets for different kinds of exports and providing data about competitors' products to Japanese industry, and also by encouraging private research through tax incentives. In this way they could help Japanese entrepreneurs without tying them down with red tape or distorting the market by subsidies. Furthermore, Japanese industry consciously decided to target not only the non-industrialized nations for its exports (permitting its exporters to bribe local officials while the U.S. prosecuted its own exporters who adopted such practices), but also U.S. and West European markets, since these were relatively unprotected against foreign competition.

The Japanese government knows that its prosperity lies in exports, and has consciously "dumped" excess stocks on U.S. and foreign markets at below cost prices, not only to earn foreign exchange but to gain recognition for its products and to beat down indigenous competitors. But Japan also has other advantages. Japanese culture further discourages conflict between employees and management, promoting good employee-employer relations by quasi-familial policies that build loyalty....

CAN AMERICA COMPETE AGAINST JAPAN?

How effective are the U.S. Administration and Congress in responding to the Japanese threat to the American market place? Japan is protectionist—which it has every right to be—while the U.S. remains committed to free trade, thereby attempting to compete with Japan with one hand tied behind its back. The principle of free trade is theoretically splendid, so long as all other nations abide by the same principle and open their markets to American products just as America opens its market to theirs. Furthermore, American government could help industry, not by subsidies that distort the market and promote inefficiency, but by the same supportive but non-interfering policies the Japanese government has extended toward its own private enterprise economy. In particular, the American government should stop imposing costly and inefficient "civil rights" legislation upon American industry, and allow employers the basic and fundamental right to hire the right employee for the job they need to get done.

Whether America will be able politically to effect these necessary remedies is questionable. American government is already a hostage to its minority lobbies, and its financiers would seem to be more ready to sell out to Japanese investors than to adopt protectionist policies. Many also complain that America does not have a government that responds to the interest or wishes of the majority, but only a collection of individual career politicians most of whom respond readily to the demands of organized lobbies and pressure groups. Furthermore, Japan itself has not overlooked the gentle art of lobbying in the "free" American political scene, pouring in money to universities, think-tanks and other institutions to foster viewpoints favorable to Japan's economic interest. Japan is reported to have spent more than $300 million in publicity efforts in the U.S. in 1989.

The Commission on U.S.-Japan Relations for the 21st Century, an American business group, has urged Japanese and American political leaders to stop blaming each other for trade friction and get ready to solve their problems at home. While the U.S. badly needs to take steps to make itself more competitive, Japan continues to work to ensure its own economic prosperity. Japan's military defeat forty-five years ago has become history in light of the new, dynamic economic war that nationally-minded Japan is waging—and winning—while too many of America's leaders seek only to keep themselves in office by any means, even if that means supporting policies that would internationalize America beyond recognition.

NO

Koji Taira

JAPAN, AN IMMINENT HEGEMON?

Today, two powerful historical trends appear to be converging on Japan. Trend 1 has to do with changes in international relations within the framework of hegemonic cycles, more commonly known as the rise and fall of great powers. The last cycle under the hegemony of the United States has apparently passed its peak, and a new cycle is on the rise. Trend 2 refers to the Hegelian dialectic that brings history to an end. This means that the world has finished its various systemic experiments and has settled down with one well-known design of world order. Conceptually, the completion of trend 2 should suppress trend 1. It is in this unique context of world history that Japan has become a great economic power.

These key concepts are briefly explained as a leadoff for this article. Then, Japan's great-power qualifications are examined. Finally, Japan's ability and will to lead the world are evaluated in light of Japanese opinions. A stabilization of U.S.-Japanese relations emerges as a conclusion.

HEGEMONIC CYCLES

[Scholar] Immanuel Wallerstein offers a useful, if simplified, historical perspective with implications for Japan. Since the dawn of the modern age, which is also the age of nation-states and capitalism, there have been three hegemons each with its own cycle of rise and fall. The hegemons are the United Provinces (1450–1739), the United Kingdom (1730–1897), and the United States (1897–).

During the declining phase of a hegemon, two contesters for succession emerge—England and France after Dutch hegemony; the United States and Germany after British; and now Japan and Western Europe after American. The victor then reduces the former hegemon to its "junior partner"—Great Britain vis-à-vis Holland, and the United States vis-à-vis Great Britain. If Japan is to be the next hegemon, the United States will be Japan's "junior partner" under a Pax Nipponica.

From Koji Taira, "Japan, an Imminent Hegemon?" *The Annals of the American Academy of Political and Social Science*, vol. 513 (January 1991). Copyright © 1991 by The American Academy of Political and Social Science. Reprinted by permission of Sage Publications, Inc. Notes omitted.

Paul Kennedy elaborates on the nature of hegemonic cycles. One of his contributions is in the analysis of decline: why a hegemon falls from grace. The simple formula he offers is "imperial overstretch" in the attempt to keep an ungovernable empire.

Recent events in the United States and the USSR are a partial validation of Kennedy's "overstretch" hypothesis. The Cold War hegemons have finally admitted that they can no longer bear the burden of the arms race....

Economics offers a different kind of explanation about the decline of a hegemon. It views the hegemon as a producer of international public goods, of which peace is primary. But the public goods are subject to opportunistic abuses by other countries—the free-rider problem. The hegemon then suffers from cost overruns and declines. In the absence of a world government, a hegemonic country is needed for international law and order. The great economic question today is what to do with peace dividends when peace, which has been the most costly international public good, suddenly becomes a free good.

THE END OF HISTORY

The second key concept of this article is the "end of History." This has a special significance for the evaluation of Japan's hegemonic qualifications. Japan's strengths are almost entirely economic. It is widely felt that a great economic power simply cannot remain a military midget forever. The "end of History," however, may put an end to the need for armed forces.

According to [Francis] Fukuyama [in his 1989 article on the subject], all the requisite ideas that would put an end to

history were produced during the Age of Enlightenment. These were the ideas of freedom, equality, and democracy supported by market forces and free enterprise. When democratic policy and market economy pervade the world, history comes to an end in the sense that all thoughts and experiments in search of a better world are exhausted and that history-making clashes of ideals and ideologies, often accompanied by armed struggles, no longer take place....

Fukuyama describes the state of the world after the end of history as follows:

> The struggle for recognition, the willingness to risk one's life for a purely abstract goal, the worldwide ideological struggle that called forth daring, courage, imagination and idealism, will be replaced by economic calculation, the endless solving of technical problems, environmental concerns, and the satisfaction of sophisticated consumer demands.

Military heroism dies with the end of history, and much less glamorous economics becomes the centerpiece of post-history life. Japan appears to be well suited for a leading role in this state of affairs.

To paraphrase Fukuyama further, as all regions and countries are peacefully integrated by global market forces, the nation-states, with their conventional "sovereign" rights to go to war and to make or break peace at will, become grotesque anachronisms. When war ceases to be an admired prerogative of state, the states submit to the rules and procedures of negotiation for the adjustment of differing interests or conflicting rights. The Japanese state, which has constitutionally abandoned war as a sovereign act of state, has long been a post-history state.

CHANCES FOR JAPANESE HEGEMONY

Japan has become a hegemonic candidate during a time when a major hegemonic function, production of peace, is no longer needed, because the end of history has made peace a sort of free good rather than a costly public good that has to be produced by the hegemon.

There are, however, other important hegemonic functions. These are largely economic. They have to do with leadership for the maintenance of international institutions embodying principles, norms, rules, and procedures consistent with market forces. The cost of global leadership consists, in part, in taking up a major share in the financing of these institutions. The hegemon must also efficiently respond to emergencies arising from imbalances in the balance of payments, shortages of development capital, misalignments of exchange rates, conflicting economic policies of various countries, and so on. The list of hegemonic functions, even after peace has become a free good, is fairly long. Is Japan ready for these tasks and responsibilities for world economic management?

The question of readiness breaks down into two parts. One part is about the availability of economic resources that a country can devote to world economic management. The other part concerns a country's ability and strategy to lead the world under normal as well as emergency conditions.

Resource Availability

The current level of Japan's economic impact on the world equals that of the United States. Japan is the largest donor of aid to less developed countries, surpassing the United States. In addition, Japan is the largest net creditor nation, while the United States is the largest net debtor nation. Net credit is the difference between assets held abroad by Japanese nationals and corporations and assets held in Japan by foreign nationals and corporations. A preponderant part of Japan's international net credit is held in developed countries, especially the United States.

What is remarkable about Japan's hegemonic impact on the world economy is how painlessly—hence without much thought, almost absent-mindedly—Japan has achieved it. The current status as one of the largest aid donors has been attained by devoting a minuscule three-tenths of 1 percent of gross national product (GNP) to economic cooperation. Thus Japan can increase foreign aid substantially without much harm to itself.

The status of largest net creditor has been attained by devoting 2 or 3 percent of GNP every year to foreign investment, especially foreign direct investment. These figures may be compared with national savings and domestic capital formation, which use more than 25 percent of GNP. At present, the multinationalization of Japanese companies is still at a low level by international standards. This implies that Japan's impact on the world economy can be expected to increase dramatically in the near future with Japanese companies' increased globalization and foreign direct investment.

The growth of the Japanese economy has been greatly helped by a very low level of defense expenditure, less than 1 percent of GNP in most years. The allocation of a larger proportion of GNP to defense would have slowed down economic growth. It is the public goods of peace and free markets maintained by the

United States that have enabled Japan to minimize its own defense spending.

While the United States as a hegemon had to sacrifice a fraction of its economic growth for hegemonic responsibilities, Japan obtained its high economic growth by the use of the U.S.-provided international public goods. To call Japan a free rider is one way of looking at the conventional U.S.-Japanese relations. How Japan should have paid for the ride is a difficult question, however. In recent years, Japan has been assuming an increasing share of the direct costs of the U.S. bases in Japan.

Japan's Ability and Strategy to Lead the World

It is clear that Japan has resources on a hegemonic scale. Does it know how to use them for the maximization of world economic welfare together with its own domestic well-being? In the history of the Pax Americana, there was a model period, from 1945 to 1970, when the United States as the hegemon based its domestic policy and world strategy on a world welfare function even at the expense of domestic needs. In the 1970s, however, the United States became a "predatory hegemon," trying to reap domestic advantages at the expense of the rest of the world. Thus there can be a good hegemon and a bad hegemon.

What objectives the hegemon has and what strategies it employs for attaining them must therefore be closely scrutinized. Foreign economic aid and foreign direct investment are instruments of hegemony. Studies are available about the motives, processes, and outcomes of Japan's use of these hegemonic instruments. Some of the Japanese practices can be faulted on grounds of suspicious motives, such as using aid for export promotion or for the relocation of polluting industries; unethical processes, as in compromising with host-country corruption and waste; or counterproductive outcomes—for example, crowding out local initiatives and indigenous entrepreneurship. But merits outweigh the deficiencies in view of the outstanding economic performances of Asian recipients of Japanese aid and investment.

The basic source of Japan's—or any country's—hegemony is economic growth. A major source of growth is the propensity to save. High savings, via trade surplus, translate into foreign investment. Foreign economic aid is also a transfer from the national savings. Should the Japanese propensity to save decline drastically, Japanese hegemony would be stillborn.

Successful Japanese-owned and Japanese-controlled firms outside of Japan can grow on their own without drawing upon Japan's domestic savings. On the one hand, this liberates the offshore Japanese firms from Japan's domestic constraints. Then the Japanese propensity to save can be allowed to decline so as to help reduce the chronic trade surplus. On the other hand, a fuller use of host-country capital and labor contributes to the expansion of the host-country economy.

The globalization of Japanese firms inevitably globalizes Japanese government policy. In effect, Japan acquires another Japan outside of Japan proper. In its economic policy-making, the Japanese government now has to pay attention to the effects of its domestic policy on the other Japan. Concurrently, the Japanese government cannot be indifferent to host-country policy, which is bound to affect the other Japan. At the minimum, these countries should be deterred from adopting policy that adversely affects the interests of the other Japan. As a quid pro quo, Japan's own policy should not be prejudicial to the interests of the host countries of the other Japan. Thus policy-making everywhere would be woven into a web of interdependence and complementarity.

In terms of a primitive notion of sovereignty, this kind of interdependence or interpenetration at the policy-making level would be an unacceptable interference in the internal affairs of sovereign states. It is precisely this notion of sovereignty, however, that comes to an end with the end of history.

The host countries for the other Japan are of two kinds, developed and less developed. With the developed host countries, the Japanese government should promote policy coordination over a wide range of international economic problems based on the international public goods of principles, norms, rules, and procedures consistent with global free markets. The extent to which Japan exercises the initiative over policy coordination between developed countries is a measure of Japan's hegemony vis-à-vis these countries. At present, such initiatives still appear to be the exclusive privilege of the United States.

Another group of hosts for the other Japan are the less developed countries. They are entitled to Japan's foreign economic aid. Here the Japanese government cannot avoid being involved in planning, designing, and analyzing host-country development. Leadership is expected, and the quality of leadership determines whether Japan is a good hegemon or a bad one. In Asia, Japan has been cautiously expanding its leadership role that affects Asian countries' economic policy. At the same time, Asian countries themselves are vigorously taking advantage of the global markets, including Japanese, and are playing Japan's own catch-up game.

None of the strategic maneuvers that has been mentioned here is sinister or unethical. In fact, they constitute the interactive process by which mutual benefits are identified and exploited. Japan is increasingly adept at such strategic maneuvers. But how countries may benefit from strategic interdependence with Japan and how they may guard themselves against the possible hazards of such interdependence require a closer look at certain specifics of the Japanese system.

BUSINESS AND GOVERNMENT IN HEGEMONIC EXPANSION

Japan's rise to a hegemonic position is by accretion of influence through trade, aid, and investment and through participation in the world order already in place thanks to the work of the previous—and still incumbent—hegemon, the United States. Unlike shifts in previous hegemonic cycles, which were mediated by war, hegemonic transition under way today is a gradual process closely tied to differential rates of economic growth among countries.

Quantitative aspects of Japan's potential hegemony are already well known. But hegemony is also qualitative; it covers such issues as how leadership is perceived by the led or whether influence is welcomed by the influenced. These qualitative aspects of hegemony generate heated debate. For example, foreign direct investment in the United States may begin innocuously as "buying into" America, but after a point, it may be seen by some irate Americans as "buying up" America itself.

In any country, foreign firms based in another country tend to be viewed collectively as an extension of their home country. [Jean-Jacques] Servan-Schreiber offered a classic example of this view: U.S.-based firms doing business in Europe were seen as an "American challenge." Today, Japan-based firms are likewise a Japanese challenge. Given such presumptions in the host country, foreign investors must carefully aim at the maximization of both their presence and host-country welcome.

Japanese business has a long tradition of cooperation with the government for mutual benefits. This behavior is repeated abroad in relation to the host-country governments. The record shows that Japanese business is remarkably well adapted to the rules and processes of host-country politics, especially in the realm of so-called influence buying, and has largely succeeded in promoting a political climate advantageous to it. The Japanese success in having the California unitary tax on foreign firms repealed is a well-known example. Further, many former high officials of the U.S. government, now in the private sector, are on Japanese payrolls as certified lobbyists on behalf of Japanese business interests.

The achievement of such advantages is what nationalists everywhere condemn as foreign interference in their national affairs. To see the same thing from the foreign companies' standpoint, however, some effort to influence host-country policy-making is an aspect of business insurance. Influence becomes an interference when sought after crudely or illegally.

Japanese influence is not all negative even from the standpoint of the host country's narrowest national interest. The managerial excellence of large Japanese firms is legendary. It also makes good sense at the rigorous level of the "theory of the firm."

Simplified, Japanese management techniques nurture group solidarity and encourage teamwork by combinations of egalitarian intragroup socialization—industrial democracy—and positive differential between a firm's material benefits and the next best opportunities available outside. This incentive structure encourages employee commitment to the employment relationship. In the language of economic analysis, this amounts to no more than the use of efficiency wages. With considerable enthusiasm, Japanese firms export this type of what might be called groupist management to their subsidiaries and affiliates—transplants—in host countries. Success stories already abound.

Nevertheless, a caveat is called for. The success of Japanese management techniques is potentially subversive of host-country values and ways of life because the thrust of this personnel policy is a microcorporatism, an autonomous community within the firm distinct from the surrounding society. Under groupist management, the employees become members—even called "children" in Japan—of the firm, sheltered against influences of a broader world outside. Japanese firms operating in foreign countries regularly send their host-country employees to Japan for training and indoctrination. In Japan, not only do they acquire work skills, but they pick up a taste for Japanese-style living and habits.

Add to this the inevitable policy involvement of Japanese business in the host country. The consequence may well be to redirect the loyalty of the host-country employees away from their nation toward Japanese business and eventually toward Japan. Japan acquires enormous centrality in their consciousness. As offshore operations of Japanese firms expand in this way and as their management styles generate a demonstration effect on indigenous firms, a japanization of the host-country economy takes place.

It is also well known that in Japan, business and government share a common national interest. Japan's unusually close business-government relationship has given rise to the notion of Japan, Inc., supported by the ideology of *kanmin ittai* ("government-people solidarity"). Japanese subsidiaries and affiliates are closely controlled by their headquarters in Tokyo, which in turn closely cooperate with the Japanese government. Thus the global spread of Japanese business may be synonymous with the global reach of Japan, Inc.

When summarized in a hurry, the characteristics of Japanese management may sound highly alarming. Fortunately, in the real world, economic processes and outcomes diffuse over time and space through micro-adjustments and complex configurations, instead of being concentrated in a clear-cut form in a given place at a given time. The diffusion of Japanese influences will be no exception. Host countries will have time to absorb and modify them so that indigenous sociocultural integrity may be maintained.

PROMOTION FROM WITHIN THE PAX AMERICANA

That the Pax Americana is on the wane does not automatically imply that a Pax Nipponica is on the rise. If Japanese hegemony should replace American, the test would be whether Japan can successfully play a leading role in the management of the international public goods that ensure the working of global market forces.

Much has already been learned about ways of managing the global economy from the well-structured hegemony of the United States. The global market forces are watched and assisted by international organizations—the General Agreement on Tariffs and Trade, the International Monetary Fund, the World Bank, the Organization for Economic Cooperation and Development, the United Nations, and so on. In designing, organizing, and maintaining these institutions, U.S. leadership has been indispensable. Because of its transparency and objectivity, U.S. hegemony has given rise to theories of hegemony that can be learned and applied by any hegemonic pretenders.

Today these international organizations collectively constitute a rudimentary form of international government. The hegemon that comes after the United States will be spared the pains of having to start from scratch. An important part of hegemony today is a leading role in international government through the existing international organizations. A new hegemon will be able to rise through the ranks in the established international order, rather than through a succession war as in the past.

In terms of economic contributions to the maintenance of the existing international organizations, Japan can clearly afford an extensive involvement. But the actual role Japan plays is considerably below the potential. Part of the reason for this discrepancy is historical, namely, the grandfathers who won the last war are still in control. If voting power in international organizations were aligned according to various countries' economic weight in the world and their ability and willingness to contribute, it would be strange for Britain, China, and the USSR to still be among the permanent members of the U.N. Security Council, arguably the most prestigious political organ of the world, while Germany, Italy, and Japan would not be.

Generally, Japan's money is welcome, but its voice is not. Often international organizations forgo benefits from Japan's larger contributions because money translates into voice through rules that tie voting power to the quota of capital subscription. Japan's money was for a long time not welcomed by the incumbents whose voting power was to decrease in the shuffle. Only as recently as 1990 was Japan promoted to the long-overdue second rank in voting power in the International Monetary Fund, equal to West Germany and next to the number-one United States. The political economy of hegemonic transition understandably involves both political and economic considerations even in well-established economic organizations. The participation of Japanese nationals in the bureaucracies of world organizations is extremely low, further disadvantaging Japan through office politics.

There is one international economic organization where Japan is clearly in the leading position, the Asian Development Bank. Whether Japan's position makes any difference may be discovered by a comparative analysis of the performance of the Asian Development Bank and other similar institutions. Unfortunately, such comparative studies are not available. In Asia, Japan's leadership is generally acknowledged. Japan itself is quite explicit, if cautious, about its hegemonic role in Asia, while it is reticent about global leadership.

TOWARD OVERCOMING ALL FORMS OF HEGEMONY

In the global arena, the United States still is the hegemon. Its political leadership and military power are unmatched. Its domestic economy, however, is debt-ridden and falling behind Japan in growth rates. The nature of a world order caught in the strange chemistry of Japan's economic power and the political and military power of the United States stimulates diverse speculations.

A nation cannot be a hegemon unless it demonstrates the ability and will to be one and unless its hegemony is accepted as legitimate by the world community. Of the three requisites—ability, will, and legitimacy—Japan meets only the economic requirements of the ability to lead. Japan's will to lead is' not firm. It is also doubtful that the world accepts Japan's hegemony as legitimate. On the other hand, the United States clearly desires to lead and the world accords legitimacy to U.S. leadership. Only the weaker macroeconomic performance of the United States casts a pall of doubt over the effectiveness of U.S. hegemony.

Given Japan's uncertain score card on hegemonic requirements, many Japanese find it both comfortable and advantageous to be number two, trailing the United States. It would be cost-effective for Japan to keep the Pax Americana as a world order and to help America from time to time by means of economic and technological cooperation. In other words, Japan should contribute to world peace and prosperity but should not attempt to lead the world by its own vision and designs. The choice of second fiddle for Japan is most clearly spelled out by Shinji Fukukawa, former vice-minister of the Ministry of International Trade and Industry. Fukukawa urges a "philosophy of contribution" (*Kōken no tetsugaku*) and an "economics of contribution" such that Japanese prosperity and world development may find optimal compatibility.

U.S. leadership, even vis-à-vis Japan itself, is amply demonstrated by the U.S. Structural Impediments Initiative (SII) [the effort to persuade Japan to remove economic barriers that result from Japan's domestic practices, such as interlocking companies that only buy from each other]. The Japanese know that the measures pointed out by the United States should have been implemented long ago at Japan's own initiative. But the Japanese political process has consistently failed to generate the desired remedies due essentially to the lack of innovative political leadership. The Japanese have long since given up on their own government, summing up their frustrations by a cynical adage: "third-rate politics in a first-rate economy."

External pressures like SII would have induced visceral reactions on the part of the Japanese as interferences with Japan's internal affairs or as disrespect for Japan's sovereignty. The popularity of "a Japan that can say 'no'" is a symptom of such reactions. But sober analyses prevail. A high Foreign Office official, Koji Watanabe,... observes that SII is technically an interference with Japan's internal affairs, but he immediately emphasizes that "we have to overcome thoughts like that by the principle of 'inter-dependence.'"

The SII dialogue is a two-way street; Japan, too, is invited to voice its complaints about the U.S. economy. This was apparently a novel experience for Japanese officials. Says Watanabe:

> Frankly, we were not used to complaining about America. At first we were at a loss and did not know what to say. Rather, I might say, we felt that America would not listen to us anyway. Now it is quite clear that America is serious about learning Japanese views on America....

Watanabe's revelations are astonishing in that national sovereignty is made subordinate to international interdependence and that Japan apparently has some psychological disadvantage in dealing with the United States. Under the circumstances, the United States must take a nurturing approach toward Japan, encouraging it to be more outspoken as a true moral equal of the United States. This means that Japan has much more to learn about the art of hegemony and needs time before it becomes an effective leader.

The impact of SII on Japanese thinking is far-reaching. The structural reforms that SII calls for are seen by some writers to be as significant as two major historical reforms that were also initiated by the United States: the modernization of Japan following Commodore Perry's visit in 1853 and democratization under General MacArthur's administration of occupied Japan. Now the same scale of reform is called for under America's SII. For Japan, this particular historical law of Japan's dependence on the United States for major reforms seems more important than grandiose hegemonic cycles. For the time being, then, Japan remains a junior partner, even a pupil for new lessons, of the United States under the Pax Americana.

A kinder view would be to say that Japan and the United States have complementary strengths and weaknesses, which require closer cooperation for the stability of the world order. American opinion leaders, appreciating Japan's economic strengths, suggest that a closer economic integration of the two countries—*nichibei* economy—would generate a more effective hegemony. Instead of lamenting the further fall of the U.S. share of world GNP, which was widespread in the 1970s, American policymakers now link the strategy of the United States to the sum of Japanese and U.S. economies. It is no longer a matter of either U.S. or Japanese hegemony; it is co-hegemony or what the Japanese call Pax Consortis. A preferred term for Americans would be "Pax Americana II."

For the world, then, the crucial factor over a medium term is the quality of U.S.–Japanese cooperation. America as number one claims a maximum freedom in the pursuit of its strategy based on its global vision, which is well known and even credited for bringing history to an end. But Japan's economic power is a critical factor that may make or break the success of America's world strategy. Thus, for its own good, the United States cannot ignore Japan. Neither the United States nor Japan can afford the luxury of a nationalist notion of sovereignty. When production depends on interdependence and teamwork, the parties involved must subordinate themselves to superordinate goals. The strategic interactions between the United States and Japan are much like a duopoly in economic analysis.

We reach a rather obvious conclusion. The weight of the Japanese economy is hegemonic in scale, but a hasty transition to Japanese hegemony would be counterproductive from the standpoint of world peace and stability. The world's need for a hegemonic state for the sake of a stable world order, however, may well be one of the history-bound concepts due to disappear with the end of history. When all political units, including the nation-states, are thoroughly democratized and disarmed, all political power devolves to the individual. Then all the individuals of the world might wish to reorganize a superordinate world community by a new social contract. The world community may still be divided into geographical units of administration—the former nation-states—but hegemonic competition between these units will be checked by global forces of democracy and market. The dialectic of contradictions will finally come to rest under permanent peace and will lose its history-making power.

POSTSCRIPT

Does Japan Represent a Worldwide Economic Threat?

In the past year or two, Japan has undergone significant shocks. The economy is not longer the untouchable juggernaut it once was. The Tokyo stock exchange suffered dramatic losses, in the 50 percent range, and has been slow to recover. A number of factors are hampering internal prosperity, and for the first time in decades, Japanese plants are laying off workers. One factor is increased competition from newly industrializing countries, especially those around the Pacific Rim such as South Korea, Taiwan, Singapore, and Malaysia. Improvements in quality in American cars has weakened the demand for Japanese imports; other "Japanese" cars (such as the Honda Accord) are now made (or at least assembled) in the United States. There has also been a dramatic shift in the exchange rates. As recently as 1985, the ratio between the Japanese yen and the U.S. dollar was approximately ¥250=$1. It has since declined and hit a post–World War II low of ¥101=$1 in August 1993. This means that goods produced in Japan have increased in price drastically when measured in U.S. dollars and are, therefore, much more expensive to buy for Americans.

Political changes have occurred as well. The dominant Liberal Democratic Party (LDP) lost power in August 1993 for the first time since a civilian government was formed after World War II. The new prime minister, Morihiro Hosokawa has indicated that his approach would be to encourage more consumption in Japan, thus increasing imports, rather than restraining exports.

While there are winds of change buffeting Japan, there can be little doubt that Japan is, and will remain, an economic power, as discussed in Edward J. Lincoln, "Japan in the 1990s: A New Kind of World Power," *Brookings Review* (Spring 1992). Moreover, with the end of the cold war, the political ties that bound Japan, the United States, and Western Europe together and made them willing to overlook, to some degree, economic rivalries have diminished. Japan has increasingly set its own foreign policy line, rather than following the American lead. The Japanese have been lobbying to change the membership of the UN Security Council to include Japan as a permanent member. Such changes and economic difficulties have led to charges and countercharges that Japan is aiming to eclipse U.S. leadership. These arguments can be reviewed in Robert B. Reich, "Is Japan Really Out to Get Us?" *New York Times*, Book Review Section (February 9, 1992).

ISSUE 10

Should the Developed North Increase Aid to the Less Developed South?

YES: Ivan L. Head, from "South-North Dangers," *Foreign Affairs* (Summer 1989)

NO: Peter Bauer, from "Creating the Third World: Foreign Aid and Its Off-spring," *Encounter* (April 1988)

ISSUE SUMMARY

YES: Ivan L. Head, president of the International Development Research Center of Canada and former foreign policy adviser to Canadian prime minister Elliott Trudeau, contends that the South's continued poverty constitutes an economic, environmental, and political threat to the developed countries. It is, therefore, in their interest to increase their efforts to help the South develop economically.

NO: Professor of economics Peter Bauer maintains that foreign aid goes to the wrong recipients and that it usually does not help, and may in fact be detrimental to, economic development.

One stark characteristic of the world system is that it is divided into two economic classes of countries. There is the North, which is industrialized and relatively prosperous. Then there is the South, which is mostly nonindustrial and relatively, and sometimes absolutely, impoverished. The countries that comprise the South are also called the Third World, or less developed countries, or developing countries. By whatever name they are known, however, Third World countries have conditions that are unacceptable. At a macroeconomic level, approximately three-quarters of the world's people live in the Third World, yet they possess only about one-seventh of the world's wealth (measured in gross national products, GNPs). On a more personal level, if you had been born in the South (compared to the North), your life would be almost 25 percent shorter; you would earn less than 8 percent of what you earn in the North; your children would be almost 8 times as likely to die before age 5; and it would be 11 times harder to find a physician.

Despite the rhetoric of the North about the Third World's plight, the countries of the North do relatively little to help. For example, U.S. economic foreign aid in 1990 was $11.4 billion, which amounted to only about half of what Americans spent in retail liquor stores. Canada's foreign aid in 1990

($2.5 billion) was equivalent to only about a third of what its citizens spent on tobacco. Foreign investment in the Third World is also extremely limited, and, especially since the onset of the international debt crisis, new loans to the Third World have declined, and repayment of existing loans is draining capital away from many less developed countries. Trade earnings are another possible source of development capital, but the raw materials produced and exported by most Third World countries earn them little compared to the cost of importing the more expensive finished products manufactured by the North.

There are a number of ways of approaching this issue of greater aid by the North for the South. One approach focuses on morality. Are we morally obligated to help less fortunate humans? A second approach explores more aid as a means of promoting the North's own self-interest. Some, including Ivan L. Head, contend that a fully developed world would mean greater prosperity for everyone and would be more stable politically. A third avenue pursues the causes for the Third World's poverty and lack of development in order to assess who or what is responsible.

It is possible to divide views on the origins and continuance of the North-South gap into three groups. One group believes that the uneven (but un-intended) spread of the Industrial Revolution resulted in unequal economic development. From this point of view, the answer to the question "Who is at fault?" is: "Nobody, it just happened." A second group finds the Third World itself responsible for much of its continuing poverty. Advocates of this view charge the Third World with failure to control its population, with lack of political stability, with poor economic planning, and with a variety of other ill-conceived practices that impede development. This group, which includes Peter Bauer, believes that foreign aid is wasteful and destructive of the policies needed to spur economic development.

A third group maintains that the North bears much of the responsibility for the South's condition and, therefore, is obligated to help the Third World. Those who hold this view contend that the colonization of the Third World, especially during the 1800s when the Industrial Revolution rapidly took hold in the North, destroyed the indigenous economic, social, and political organizations needed for development. The colonial powers then kept their dependencies underdeveloped in order to ensure a supply of cheap raw materials. Even though virtually all former colonies are now independent, this view continues, the developed countries continue to follow political and economic strategies designed to keep the Third World underdeveloped and dependent. This is called *dependencia* theory, which is also sometimes referred to as *neoimperialism*.

YES

Ivan L. Head

SOUTH-NORTH DANGERS

The North has discovered the South any number of times; we have given it—or parts of it—a variety of names (sometimes in error), and have defined its interests almost always from our own exclusive perspective. Curiosity, greed, fear, evangelic fervor and the zeal to civilize; the motivation for contact or disengagement has ranged from the loftiest to the basest. Northern observers have generally chosen the more generous interpretation; Southerners have less often shared that point of view.

North-South economic linkages have proved the most enduring and have taken several forms. Trade has been foremost. Trade generally consisted of commodities from the South—spices, fibers, precious metals and gems, beverages, slaves, sugar and tobacco; and manufactured goods from the North—trinkets, cloth, weaponry, implements and machinery. During the Industrial Revolution a global pattern of trade evolved; not vis-à-vis the Southern trading partners, which was assumed, but against Northern competitors. This was followed by the North's need to protect and secure its interests, initially against other Northern rivals and adversaries, local ruling classes and occasional brigands, and later against religious sects and sometimes entire local populations. From time to time the North settled segments of its surplus population in the South: sometimes forcibly, as to America and Australia, and other times peacefully, as to Canada and parts of Africa.

The direction and the result of these settlements were always the same: from North to South, infrastructure was installed, principles of governance were introduced and technologies were transferred. It was assumed that the North's techniques and technologies were superior, relevant and sustainable. Much more frequently than admitted, these assumptions have proved false.

In North-South terms, the year 1945 was a turning point both in activities and in expectations. Throughout the South, long-festering independence movements burgeoned into prominence. In the North, where interests are increasingly defined in terms of security and stability, a sterile bifurcation began to divide East and West. Not surprisingly, the definitions of security and the criteria for stability differed when viewed from the North or from the South. Of the human attributes, arrogance has not been absent in either hemisphere. Humility, however, has seldom been present in the North when it looks South. The absence of this trait, unless overcome, will continue to weaken the North both in image and in substance and will be critical to Northern welfare as the century turns.

The North-South relationship is a diverse and confusing web. To understand, to respond effectively and to ensure a constructive outcome is as demanding a task as any that faces humankind. It is demanding not only in terms of substance, but also because of attitudes well entrenched in both North and South. It is moreover the most important task, since it subsumes—or inevitably will subsume—all the others. We in the North may be most in peril (as those in much of the South have long been) because the momentum of events impacting upon us is in excess of our willingness to respond. If we are not willing to become aware, to change our unsustainable attitude of superiority, and to take action to reduce dramatically in the South the broad incidence there of absolute poverty, then our own economic welfare, our own social tranquility and our own political stability will not simply be at risk—increasingly they will be in jeopardy.

The phrase "North-South relations" was reportedly first used in the late 1950s by Sir Oliver Franks, then British ambassador to the United States. In the three decades since, the definition of the term has become as elastic as the relationship it describes has been turbulent.

This has happened, perhaps, because of the multitude of variables encompassed in the phrase: the formation of 100 or so newly independent states; the desire on the part of governments rich and poor that broad disparities in wealth be reduced; the hard evidence in a variety of places that violence is still all too often regarded as an acceptable option; the

stark reminders of the strengths of tribalism, feudalism and fundamentalism; and the ubiquitous obstacles to change—lack of awareness, absence of preparedness, inadequacy of commitment, retention of privilege.

Though imprecise, even inaccurate, the term "North-South" is resonant of human expectations and by far richer in its range of connotations than its contemporary, "East-West."

The notion of "development" has been consistently present in those connotations. The word itself is now permanently associated with the nonindustrialized, often recently independent countries. Gradually, the concepts of "economic advancement and social security" included in the 1941 Atlantic Charter by Churchill and Roosevelt, and reformulated in the U.N. Charter in 1945, have come to occupy a central position in international relations, but without a uniform interpretation. Politicians, popes, academics and journalists have all put forward definitions and proposals, some quite contradictory.

II

Policymakers in the immediate postwar period grappled with development issues framed by the experience of the colonial era and the anxieties of an increasingly polarized world. Initial development efforts emphasized, on the one hand, flows of technical assistance and improved market access for primary commodities and, on the other, efforts to bolster friends and strategically located countries against the perceived threat of communist aggression or subversion.

Environmental awareness was generally absent. In all too many instances there was a failure to respond effectively to the underlying social and economic problems facing the developing countries. In the absence of accurate diagnosis, the tendentious policies of the industrialized countries were not surprising. In particular the rapid and vigorous employment by Europe of generous U.S. assistance in the late 1940s led to assumptions that similar programs in developing regions would be equally successful. The Marshall Plan was not applicable, however, to the dissimilar circumstances of the developing countries.

The turmoil of governments in Western Europe in the seventeenth and eighteenth centuries, as they grappled with governance issues, appears minimal compared with the plight of the new postwar states. In the twentieth century, modern communications technologies have acquainted even the most remote communities with a knowledge of the much higher standards of living enjoyed elsewhere. Alternative social and economic images are projected and debated with the ferocity of the antagonists within Europe during the Reformation, but today's images are joined by an excess of weaponry and an intrusion of ideology that turns local dissidents into pawns on a global chessboard.

As they attained independence, developing countries found themselves wooed by East and West, not always in benign fashion. Many were alternately confused and exhilarated by the apparent choices open to them. To governments ill-equipped to shape their own societies, and impotent to respond to such indignities as the [U.S. Senator Bourke B.] Hickenlooper Amendment [1961], which required suspension of U.S. assistance to countries that nationalized U.S. property without speedy compensation, the planetary struggle for hearts and souls appeared in many instances as a bargaining card.

The development debate soon transformed itself from local social and economic imperatives into broad political divisions argued out in regional and interregional assemblies. Western politicians saw that more was involved here than the provision of rural health clinics or the importation of unprocessed primary commodities. The North-South relationship was no longer an engagement of cooperative activity; it had become a battlefield in which human ideals, vested interests and concepts of strategic security tussled and jousted. Throughout the 1950s the legal basis for U.S. development assistance was security—The Mutual Security Act. South Korea and Taiwan became major aid recipients, and Western financing for the Aswan High Dam was withdrawn when Egypt presumed to accept Soviet military assistance.

Then the United Nations declared the 1960s a "Development Decade," and the Organization for European Economic Cooperation became the Organization for Economic Cooperation and Development (OECD) [which now includes most developed countries]. The creation of the United Nations Conference on Trade and Development (UNCTAD) in 1964 eloquently signaled that the South regarded its plight as one anchored in the current international economic structure. "Trade, not aid" became a rallying cry, one which led to the formation of the Group of 77 and a determination by the nations of the South that they would form and maintain a unified bargaining position. If the North controlled the economic agenda, the South moved to assert the political agenda.

Throughout the 1970s, with mixed results, that agenda remained. The General Agreement on Tariffs and Trade (GATT) added Part IV to accommodate the particular problems of developing countries, and UNCTAD produced a resolution on a generalized system of preferences that was later adopted by OECD members. The strident call for a New International Economic Order issued from a nonaligned summit in Algiers in 1973 on the eve of the success of the Organization of Petroleum Exporting Countries in quadrupling oil prices within a year.

The intensity of the North-South debate escalated during the two special sessions of the General Assembly, and led to efforts to mute the language and restore some orderliness to the dialogue. The World Bank and the International Monetary Fund [IMF] introduced new facilities to meet the needs of those countries grievously wounded by the rise in oil prices. The Common Fund emerged in mid-decade as the dominant demand of the South, but diminished in importance as its complexity proved to be unmanageable and as the attention of the world turned increasingly to the fate of the low-income, oil-importing countries. The South, wearied by the reluctant responses of the North, turned to South-South cooperative initiatives but found its unity shattered with the second oil shock of 1979.

At the end of the 1970s the Brandt Commission signaled alarm that Northern interests were imperiled by the inability of the South to better meet its needs, but it was unable to attract the attention of the new U.S. administration. The 1980s ushered in the great debt crisis of the developing countries, with coincidental circumstances of extreme drought and famine in much of Africa, and unprecedented economic vitality and export performance in the newly industrialized countries of Asia. The [Norwegian Prime Minister Gro Harlem] Brundtland Commission warned that, in the absence of sustainable development practices, the planet would lose its life-support abilities.

... [I]t seems clear that the governments of the North have not yet been able to muster resolve and effective response to these bewildering circumstances.

There are a number of reasons. First, much as we in the North lose patience with our efforts to eradicate pockets of poverty in our midst and turn our attention elsewhere, the North seems unable to muster the stamina needed for the lengthy period of transformation in the South. The nations of the North evolved over many centuries as they tackled problems associated with the absence of infrastructure, inadequate education and social diversity. The struggles in the South are no less challenging and require a continuing commitment.

Second, arrogance and ignorance combine to prescribe inept remedies. Technologies that are inappropriate and ineffective continue to be transferred from North to South. When they fail, the South is blamed. Third, outrageous abuses of human rights, corruption and privilege in some developing countries are ready excuses for reluctance to respond adequately anywhere. And fourth, a latent fear of competition from low-wage producers deters full cooperation. In the end, evolving economies are often denied access to Northern markets, or are forced to absorb subsidized agricultural produce from the North at the expense of their own farm sector.

III

... [I]n the supercharged atmosphere of development, sheer quantity of activity can leave the false impression of accomplishment.[1] In most developing countries individual standards of living have dropped, political instability has increased, and the likelihood of sustained economic growth has now diminished. From the perspective of hundreds of millions of inhabitants of developing countries, life remains a wretched, uncertain prospect. One out of five persons lives in "absolute poverty"—the World Bank's definition of the state of those persons suffering from malnutrition "to the point of being unable to work." For all too many, the likelihood of a dignified, fulfilling livelihood is as distant as it was a generation earlier.

North-South relations are now in a state of disequilibrium, which makes the status quo unsustainable. The most obvious of the disequilibriums are environmental degradation, economic uncertainty, social unrest and political instability.

Population.

On July 11, 1987, the world's population passed the five-billion mark. In the first full year following, a net growth of another 83 million took place, an increase greater than the entire population of Mexico. The size of the planet did not increase, nor will it. In some respects, the planet has become smaller. The amount of arable land is actually decreasing. In those same 366 days, arable land diminished by 8,700 square miles—more than twice the size of the island of Jamaica....

The World Bank states that the best estimate for the year 2000—just 11 years from now—is an increase of 1.2 billion, for a total world population of 6.2 billion at the close of the century.

Those figures are difficult to digest. They work out to an annual increase of close to 100 million persons. One hundred million is about the population of Bangladesh. From now to the turn of the century, then, the world's population will grow by the equivalent of one new Bangladesh every year. Accepted projections distribute the population for the year 2000 as 4.9 billion for the developing countries and 1.3 billion for the industrialized countries. This is disequilibrium....

By the year 2000, 51.2 percent of the world's population will be urban. Forty-five of the 60 largest cities will be in the South, 18 of them larger than ten million. While populations are aging in the North, the reverse is the case in the South. The residents of Southern cities will be overwhelmingly young. In the developing countries, 35 percent of the total population will be under the age of 14. In ever-increasing numbers these youths find themselves on the streets: abandoned, uneducated, unemployed, alienated from any societal norms, without any loyalties except to their own gang or their own ideology or their own religious zealotry.

The rural populations find themselves forced to degrade the environment in an incessant quest for food, firewood and forage. Planetary forest cover was reduced from 25 percent of the earth's surface to 20 percent in two decades, according to the [former West German Chancellor Willie] Brandt Commission. Today, the Brundtland Commission estimates, for every tree planted in the tropical regions, ten are destroyed; in sub-Saharan Africa, the ratio is one to 29.

Economic Wealth.

The broad interstate disparities in wealth and income have long been recognized. A new factor has recently reemerged: financial transfers from South to North. Reemerged, for it was also a common occurrence in earlier colonial periods.

Capital flows to developing countries fall into two broad categories, private and official. The latter may be on concessional or commercial terms and found in both bilateral (national) and multilateral (international) institutions. Funding of these kinds is as targeted as is the case within industrialized countries, and takes several different instrumental forms: export credits, direct investment, grants and loans.

Until recently, the volume of capital flows to and from developing countries represented only a small proportion of the international total. The composition of those flows has varied considerably. Prior to World War I, the only countries then independent but regarded as developing were in Latin America. Virtually the only capital flows to the South were from private sources; overwhelmingly they were employed to finance the construction of railroads and utilities. In the interwar period, government borrowings became common, and sometimes loans were obtained to finance commodity stocks in the face of falling prices. With the Great Depression came defaults often spurred by protectionist trading policies that effectively prevented debtor countries from earning export-generated surpluses with which to service foreign debt.

The Bretton Woods Conference in 1944 sought to address the frailties of the international system through the creation of the World Bank and the IMF. A third, critically important institution, the proposed International Trade Organization, failed to emerge.

In the post-World War II period, financial flows to the poorest of the developing countries began to emerge from the new multilateral sources, initially from the International Development Association, then from the new regional development banks. With trade liberalization, both trade finance and private direct investment increased. The IMF began to finance restructuring efforts.

The oil-shock-induced current account deficits were in most instances financed from the unprecedented liquidity in the oil-producing countries, increasingly through the intercession of private banks. Since 1970 developing countries' external liabilities of all kinds, including obligations to the IMF, increased significantly. The current total is in excess of $1.3 trillion, the greater part of it denominated in U.S. dollars. Debt service payments have risen more than tenfold in the same period. Rising interest rates have resulted in interest payments accounting for more than 50 percent of debt servicing. What was once a condition of illiquidity in much of the South has now become a condition of insolvency.

The unprecedented exposure of the private banks has considerably reduced fresh credits. This—combined with the successful, though painful, servicing efforts of the majority of debtor countries—has led to a sharp reversal of the earlier transfers, with negative net transfers recorded successively since 1983. In 1988 the net negative flow (i.e., from South to North) from the 17 most highly indebted countries was $31 billion. The figure for all developing countries last year was in excess of $43 billion. . . .

A factor contributing to the growing magnitude of this imbalance is found in the terms of trade between developing and industrialized countries. It is more acute in some regions than others. The Economic Commission for Latin America and the Caribbean found that terms of trade for Latin American countries deteriorated 16.5 percent between 1980 and 1985.

Relative to gross domestic product, the external debt of the developing countries in the western hemisphere was 44.5 percent in 1988 (up from 34.5 percent in 1980); in Africa, 54.4 percent (up from 28.3 percent); and in Asia, 26.4 percent (up from 17.2 percent).

In the same period the ratio of external debt to exports was 322.4 percent for developing countries in the Western Hemisphere (up from 183.6 percent), 237.7 percent for Africa (up from 92.5 percent) and 81.8 percent for Asia (up from 72.1 percent). The economic downturn in the South in the past seven years has led to the loss of 130,000 Canadian jobs and some $24 billion (in Canadian dollars) in export revenues. In the United States, diminishing exports to Latin America alone has meant the loss of 340,000 jobs.

Scientific Activity.

In the late 1960s the inquiries launched by the Pearson Commission revealed that expenditures committed to research and development [R&D] in Latin America, Asia and Africa lagged far behind the outlays in the industrialized countries. An earlier U.N. study estimated, on the basis of admittedly uncertain data, that of all the funds committed to R&D worldwide, less than three percent were expended in the developing countries. Expenditure at these levels means that the indigenous scientific communities are inadequate in size even to identify problems, let alone deal with them effectively across the entire spectrum of natural and social sciences. In an age where technological advances are occurring with breathtaking speed, the gap in capacity between North and South is rapidly widening.

This lack of capacity is particularly distressing in light of the incontestable fact that technology, throughout history, has been the most effective of all agents for change. Contrary to popular opinion, the knowledge now available with respect to agricultural production, primary health care, pedagogy and economic analysis is not simply transferable; rather, it needs to be understood, then revised and absorbed by developing countries in order to be utilized in a geographically and culturally sensitive fashion. Developing countries must acquire the means to pursue the newer biological and physical science technologies and adapt them to their own needs. In their absence, the employment and benefit opportunities that these technologies promise will not be obtained.

UNCTAD figures show that the distribution of scientists and engineers worldwide is overwhelmingly concentrated in the North. The rate per 10,000 inhabitants is 95 in the developing countries compared with 285.2 in the industrialized market economy countries and 308.2 in the East European countries. That average figure of 95 for the South, not surprisingly, is not evenly distributed. The range is from 157.6 in Asia to 9.6 in Africa. The figure for technicians is even more dramatic, revealing a difference between North and South of an order of magnitude of ten.

The numbers of scientists, engineers and technicians engaged in R&D in the developing countries is less than 1.5 per 10,000 inhabitants, compared with 16.6 in the market economies of the North. It follows that R&D expenditures as a percentage of GNP heavily favor the North. In Africa and Latin America the figure is only 0.2 percent, and in Asia 0.5 percent. These figures have shown no significant increase in the past two decades.

No form of public-sector investment has paid greater dividends over time than investment in people through education and training. Yet no investment is slower in its returns (an entire generation is needed at minimum) and few are more controversial; witness the funding crisis now faced by school boards and universities throughout the United States and Canada. Even the most enlightened of developing countries' governments are unable to muster and retain the political courage required to invest in the future while denying immediate needs of a basic kind to populations that are not, historically, acquainted with the advantages of education. In the result, these countries are condemned for the foreseeable future to pursue outmoded, low-valued economic activity of a kind that is increasingly irrelevant to world market demand. In human terms it means that the grip of absolute poverty will not be eased and that the scourges of malnutrition and ill health will persist.

The impact of this disequilibrium takes many forms, many of them with negative effect upon the North: in the current Uruguay Round of GATT negotiations as developing countries resist the inclusion of services and proprietary knowledge in trade preferences; in the world's stock markets as they reflect the decreasing absorptive capacity of developing countries for imports of high-price, high-tech manufactures; in the health care systems of Europe and North America where tens of billions of dollars must be dedicated each year to life-support systems for incurably ill patients; in community concern over the spread of narcotics imported from regions unable to earn foreign exchange from any other economic activity; and in climate changes which are attributed in many instances to unsustainable agricultural practices and tropical rain forest destruction.

Military Power.

In contrast to the three previous sectors of activity, this one suffers not from neglect but from too active a stimulus. The issue is not so much that the North is enormously more richly endowed in military prowess than the South; it is that the countries of the South in many instances choose to mimic the industrialized states in placing high priority on defense-related expenditures at the expense of social needs. The result is a perverse imbalance. In the North are quantities of nuclear weapons, many mounted on long-range delivery systems of great accuracy, supported by highly trained personnel and sophisticated techniques for command, control and communications. These are weapons that are intended not to be used. In the South are increasingly available arsenals of conventional weapons ranging from rockets through aircraft and tanks to machine pistols, the specter of chemical weapons in some instances, much of this too often within the reach of inadequately trained or commanded troops. These are weapons that are intended to be used.

The sheer volume and transportability of modern weapons guarantees the porosity of once impervious membranes. No longer are deadly devices tightly held by national armed forces. The arsenals of heavy weaponry now in the hands of informal, sometimes unidentifiable, groupings is the equivalent of those in many legitimate armies. The firepower available to street gangs in some American cities exceeds that of World War II infantry platoons. And from both sides of the North-South divide, weapons and munitions make their way into the hands of terrorists.

The industrialized states are not entirely to blame for these circumstances, but neither are they entirely without responsibility. The conscious extension of East-West rivalries into the developing countries has certainly encouraged the latter to dedicate scarce resources to military activities. The perception that interregional rivalries are not only worthy of armed conflict but are also subject to military resolution (both assumptions highly questionable in most instances) is still another reason for high defense spending. The assumption that strong military forces are the best guarantee of a nation's ability to govern itself further supports these expenditures. Until relatively recently, the military academies of Europe and the United States were preferred training institutions for future leaders in the South, often with the active encouragement of Northern governments.

Not only have the military capacities of a number of Southern countries become considerable, including arsenals of increasingly potent weapons and delivery systems, but there has also been a tendency to rely on military force to the detriment of democratic processes. The combination of eager buyers in the South and willing sellers in the North has created a North-to-South weapons market of tens of billions of dollars annually, and

the proliferation of an unhealthy community of arms brokers and military advisers.

Still another anomaly has emerged. The high cost of arms imports and the images of successful defense industries, projected unconsciously by such countries as the United States and France, have encouraged increasing numbers of developing countries to become weapons manufacturers. The result is an increasing South-South arms trade, and an economic dedication in the South to defense industries, to the disadvantage of the civilian sector. Some countries are more successful than others in their search for markets. The Jaffee Centre for Strategic Studies at Tel Aviv University has calculated that arms exports represent nearly 20 percent of all Israeli manufactured exports and some ten percent of all exports.

Even as Northern policy analysts express alarm at the current chemical and the emerging nuclear capabilities of increasing numbers of developing countries, there is precious little evidence that Northern governments are willing to address seriously the underlying social and economic conditions that have spawned subversive movements and prompted armed retaliation.

This form of disequilibrium—military disequilibrium—is not one that should be balanced by major increases in expenditures and activity in the developing countries. The entry into a developing region of new types or levels of weaponry can be as destabilizing as would be the case in central Europe, and undoubtedly more destructive. Yet the tendency is in that direction.

As East-West tensions relax in the NATO region, the possibility of a power vacuum in the developing countries into which the East-West conflict could move is distressingly high, despite the welcome assurances of the Soviet Union to the contrary. To military planners in the North and South, security is often defined in military terms with consequences all too evident in any number of developing countries where defense expenditures rival or exceed expenditures on basic social requirements, to the detriment—not the enhancement—of political stability and, often, of military security as well: Lebanon, Afghanistan, El Salvador, Ethiopia—the tragic list goes on and on.

IV

The consequences of these and other disequilibriums are not always predictable, and sometimes not even discernible during real-time human observation. The political unit of time measurement in the industrialized democracies is four or, at most, five years. Events that mature on a longer cycle are seldom visible, and are certainly not influential, in the time frame occupied by decision-makers. Absent a political equivalent of time-lapse photography, governments of the North are unlikely to commit resources now to influence or control events in the distant future. If development is investment, as we encourage the developing countries to believe, we in the North offer little evidence of our own commitment to invest in the South's development.

Population, properly supported, is an immense natural resource and an incomparable source of accomplishment. Wretchedly poor people, however, without basic necessities or the hope of attaining them, turn upon themselves and upon their landscape with distressing results. Governments in North and South alike must acknowledge that population pressures are inconsistent with a wholesome environment and demeaning to human dignity, make a social contract impossible, and contribute to political and economic insecurity. Humane, effective programs of fertility control must attract sustained support, as must programs for the development and enhancement of individual human beings.

Sustainable economic growth is no longer severable as between North and South. Development assistance programs that are designed primarily for the benefit of the Northern donors—to reduce agricultural surpluses, to create employment in sluggish sectors of the economy, or to spur the export of military hardware—must be recognized for their inherent cynicism and their eventual ineffectiveness. In the interests of the North, the economic well-being of all countries must be accepted as a policy goal to be factored into all resource allocations.

Scientific activity must be encouraged within the developing countries to permit them to identify their own problems and gain the competence to resolve many of them. This approach demands programs designed to permit Third World scientists to engage in research of their own choosing in their own institutions on problems seen by them to be of priority. It demands as well a dedication to the sharing of knowledge and a utilization of the new computer and satellite technologies to permit a worldwide dissemination of information now in the public domain. The new biotechnologies promise to meet the food production requirements of many developing countries as well as utilize, for the benefit of North and South, the rich genetic biomass resources that can be cultivated only in the tropical regions and that have immense potential in so many sectors of application.

Military prowess in the North intended primarily for deterrence of worst-case fears has now surpassed the economic ability of either superpower. Technological spin-offs into the civilian sector have long since ceased to be cost-effective. Each new threshold in technology results in the release to Third World markets of massive quantities of powerful obsolescent weaponry. Governments North and South must accept that military prowess is not the normative indicator of accomplishment, that military prescriptions for the symptoms of socioeconomic distress reveal ignorance, not resolve.

What is needed is an attitudinal change of profound quality, of the kind that visits humankind only infrequently. To encourage a fresh perspective, we might borrow from Cornwallis' decision at Yorktown to order his bands to play "The World Turned Upside Down." We could begin by abandoning the misleading term "North-South" and substitute for it the now more accurate "South-North."

The South-North matrix is extensive and complex; it does not translate readily into simple patriotic imagery. It does not respond to simplistic "if only they were like us" solutions. It cannot even be defined in purely statistical terms. It is an embarrassment to Northern governments for it is at once a reminder of barren colonial legacies, compelling evidence of the failure of humankind to accomplish even a passing degree of social equity and proof that international arrogance is, in the end, hollow. And all the while, time is not on the side of the North any more than it favors the South.

Measured against the relentless momentum of current phenomena, indifference is not benign. Humility is needed, as is sustained dedication, if there is to be any reduction in magnitude of the disequilibriums now evident. The crafting of mutually beneficial dynamic relationships cannot wait for the emergence of a brilliant universal accord; it must emerge from a series of what Saburo Okita called "creative patchworks." In their absence, the present and growing imbalances threaten an uncontrollable Newtonian reaction of the kind prophesied a few years ago by François Mitterrand: "I am convinced that the balance between the two parts of the world, the industrialized nations and the others, will be one of the causes of the most serious tragedies at the end of the century, to be explicit, of world war."

NOTE

1. In a number of sectors, accomplishment has resulted. In the 24-year period 1960–84, the average annual per capita growth of GDP [gross domestic product] for all developing countries, excluding China and the oil-exporting countries, was 2.8 percent. If those countries were included, the average would be 3.4 percent. In that same period, remarkable gains were recorded in literacy, in reducing infant mortality and in increasing life expectancy. Cereal grain production increased; smallpox was eradicated.

NO

Peter Bauer

CREATING THE THIRD WORLD: FOREIGN AID AND ITS OFFSPRING

The Third World as a concept is the creation of foreign aid. Without aid there is no such collectivity as the Third World or the "South." Aid is the source of the North-South conflict, not its solution.

The Third World and its predecessor synonyms—the less-developed world, the underdeveloped world, the developing world, the non-aligned world—are no more than names for the countries whose governments, with occasional exceptions, demand and receive official transfers of aid from the West. (Practically all Third World governments are aid recipients, but not all aid recipients are in the Third World.)

The peoples of Asia, Africa, and Latin America live in the most diverse physical, cultural, social and political environments. They differ in many respects—in cultural, technical, and commercial sophistication, in political arrangements, and in income, wealth, and rate of economic progress. They were not aggregated into a single category of supposedly common characteristics and interests until the beginning of aid.

The peoples of the Third World constitute a rich variety of humanity. It is condescending for people in the West to regard them as being a largely undifferentiated and stagnant mass. It is even more unwarranted condescension to argue or act as if they were helpless victims who crave material progress but must depend on Western donations to achieve it.

Aid has produced the Third World or the underdeveloped world, but it cannot achieve its declared purpose of development and the relief of poverty. Yet the case for foreign aid is usually taken for granted, especially in Europe. Larger aid flows are described as improved aid performance. Giving more means doing better. The use of the term aid to describe these transfers has obscured realities, prejudged results, and disarmed critical discussion. Who could be against helping the less fortunate? The supporters of aid lay claim to a monopoly of compassion, and dismiss critics as ignorant, bigoted, uncaring.

From Peter Bauer, "Creating the Third World: Foreign Aid and Its Offspring," *Encounter* (April 1988). Copyright © 1988 by *Encounter*. Reprinted by permission. Some notes omitted.

If the aid policy were to be described by its appropriate name—*government to government subsidies*—it would lose much of its emotional appeal. Then, too, it would be more readily apparent that aid has been and remains a major factor in the politicisation of life in less-developed countries.

In current parlance, foreign aid means official government economic assistance in the form of grants, heavily subsidised loans, or unpaid technical assistance—as distinct from commercial investment, military aid, or the activities of voluntary organisations. Although the term aid is misleading, it would be pedantic to avoid this widely used expression, and in this article I use aid, subsidies, and transfers interchangeably.

Bilateral aid goes direct from donor government to recipient government; multilateral aid goes through the international organisations for subsequent reallocation by them. This terminology also misleads, because the words bilateral and multilateral imply a reciprocity which is absent—the donors give and the recipients receive without reciprocity. Having entered this *caveat,* I fall in with the accepted terminology.

Ever since the 1940s, it has been the consensus of mainstream development economists (including Nobel Laureates) that foreign aid is indispensable for reasonable progress in the less-developed countries. This has also been the opinion of leading academic economists in other fields when they occasionally wrote on development. The consensus was succinctly summarised a few years ago by Professor Hollis B. Chenery of Harvard, a former Vice-President of the World Bank in charge of economic development: "Foreign aid is the central component of world development."

Yet a vast amount of development has taken place—and still takes place—without foreign aid. Aid played no part in the development of Western Europe, or of large areas of Asia, Africa and Latin America, which progressed very rapidly long before the policy of aid was invented.

Although the case for aid is rarely questioned, its advocates occasionally buttress their pleas by specific arguments. Over the years the most influential has been that aid is necessary for relief of misery in the Third World. This is to be achieved through one or other of two routes: transfers to the poorest countries in the hope that this will help directly to improve the lot of the very poor; and transfers to these countries in the hope that this will promote development, thereby eliminating acute poverty.

These two objectives—development and relief of poverty—imply quite different criteria of allocation and quite different expected results, much in the same way as subsidised loans to promising youngsters for their education or to help them set up in business differ from giving alms to a beggar or financial support to an invalid. Aid to the helpless is not the same as support to the promising. Since around the mid-1970s, direct relief of human need has been especially prominent in aid advocacy; over a longer period, the promotion of economic development has been the more durable selling-point.

1. THE REAL RECIPIENTS

Aid transfers do not go to the pathetic creatures pictured in the publicity campaigns of the aid lobbies. The money goes to their governments: that is, their rulers.[1] And all too often these rulers are directly responsible for the gruesome conditions that we wish to alleviate. Aid helps, even enables, such governments to pursue policies which are extremely harmful to their people.

1. Maltreatment of the most productive groups, especially minorities, and sometimes their expulsion.

2. Enforced movements of population.

3. Coercive collectivisation and other forms of expropriation.

4. Suppression of private trade.

5. Underpayment of farmers.

6. Restriction of the inflow of capital, enterprise, and skills.

7. Voluntary or compulsory purchase of foreign enterprises, thus absorbing scarce capital and depriving the country of skills which are helpful to development.

8. Massive spending on prestige projects or on the support of uneconomic activities, especially manufacturing.

Such policies, even singly but much more so when pursued together, can undermine or cripple the economy. Viet Nam, Ethiopia, Tanzania, and Uganda are conspicuous examples of destructive policies, and in a large measure also of the neglect of the basic tasks of government: notably the protection of people's lives and property. This neglect of the basic functions of government amidst wholesale politicisation of life is widespread in aid-recipient countries.

Extreme cases apart, many aid recipients pursue policies which directly reduce incomes by such practices as the persecution of productive groups or the restriction of the employment of women. Such governments can qualify for more aid, since the allocation of much Western aid is determined by per-capita incomes. It is a notable paradox that official transfers reward policies of impoverishment.

The misery brought about by the aid-recipient rulers in Black Africa and the massive persecution practised by many of them have forced hundreds of thousands of their subjects to flee their countries. Substantial appeals by international organisations have collected many millions of dollars to alleviate their conditions. But the flight of these refugees was a result of the conduct of their rulers, whose political survival has often depended on aid.

Over most of the Third World there is no machinery for relief of poverty by the state. Even if a recipient government wanted to use official transfers to help the very poorest, this could be difficult, even impossible. More important, such help may not accord with the political or ideological priorities of a Third World ruler, or, indeed, with local mores.

This situation is particularly clear in multi-racial, multi-tribal, or multi-cultural countries. Will an Arab-dominated Sudanese government help the poorest blacks in the southern Sudan, hundreds of miles away, with whom it is in persistent armed conflict?... Would a Sinhalese-dominated government [of Sri Lanka] help the poorest among the Tamils? Such questions can be asked about practically every government in Asia and Africa.

The priorities of Third World rulers are reflected in their massive spending on prestige projects. Brand-new capitals, built from scratch at the cost of many billions of dollars, are often incomplete many years after construction first began—Abuja in Nigeria, for instance, or Dodoma in Tanzania. Even more grotesque is the lavish expenditure on the activities of the inappropriately-named "Organisation of African Unity", located in Addis Ababa.

From Viet Nam to Brazil, from Sri Lanka to West Africa, the Third World is littered with monuments and relics of unviable and grandiose schemes, undertaken for the political and personal purposes of the rulers and their local allies—and, at times, of Western commercial interests. Such projects are not abandoned even when it has become evident that they are wasteful and cannot achieve their declared objective. They are often a substantial drain on local economies.

These programmes and policies, evident for decades, continue to this day. For instance, the *Financial Times*... has described in detail the origins and cost of Air Lanka, the state-owned and state-run airline which is a major burden on a poor country oppressed by civil conflict. Because it is the pride of President Jayawardene, Air Lanka has not been put into liquidation.

On the same theme, *The Economist*... carried a lengthy review of two books describing the operation of aid to Tanzania and Mozambique. Their Swedish authors, once supporters of aid but now disillusioned, gave vivid examples of hopeless and expensive aid-financed projects. As one of them wrote of Tanzania: "The assistance was part of the making of the crisis...."

Black Africa has been perhaps most afflicted. Many of its programmes were never feasible from the outset, because of lack of skilled personnel, materials, and components. "White Elephants in Black Africa", an article in *The New Republic*, ... describes a number of such projects, and notes the forces (including pressure by Western commercial interests) that lay behind them.

Official transfers go to governments. They expand the resources, privileges, patronage, and power of the government in relation to the rest of society. This promotes politicisation of life; and politicisation, in turn, increases the stakes—both gains and losses—in the struggle for power.

Foreign aid has helped to unleash the forces that lie behind the recurrent or persistent civil wars of the Third World. The tensions resulting from extensive politicisation frequently erupt into armed conflict, even in countries where in the past the different communities have lived together peaceably for generations: witness Malaysia and Sri Lanka. Recurrent civil wars contribute to the Third World's heavy spending on arms: in 1981 the West German Ministry of Economic Cooperation estimated that Third World spending on arms was about one-fifth of the total world spending for this purpose. And these arms are intended for use against their own subjects, or against other Third World countries.

When life is extensively politicised, and civil conflict widespread, people's economic lot—even their economic survival—depends on what happens in the political and military arena. People come to be much more concerned with what will happen to them as a result of political, administrative, or military action than with devoting attention, energy and resources to productive economic activity.

Over large areas of Asia and Africa the population has been pushed back into subsistence production, or has been held in that precarious state of existence.

The coercive collectivisation of agriculture, the enforced mass migration in Tanzania ($3 [billion] in foreign aid from 1980–84), the large-scale and protracted civil war in the Sudan ($2.3 [billion]), the numerous expensive and unviable prestige projects in these countries, the underpayment of farmers, and the role of aid in sustaining the rulers have been described in detail in the Western press.

Such reports have appeared in quality newspapers notably sympathetic to the rulers responsible for these situations— including *The Times*, the *Financial Times* and the *New Statesman* in Britain, and *The New York Times*, the *Washington Post,* and the *Christian Science Monitor* in the USA.

Ethiopia's misery has been brought to the notice of tens of millions of people in the West. How many of them know that its Marxist-Leninist government [overthrown in 1991] regularly received... large-scale Western subsidies? These totalled about $1.3 [billion] over the five years from 1980–84. Throughout this period, the Ethiopian government pursued every single one of the policies I have instanced. Large-scale subsidies continue, even though the government persists in policies which, in the West, are recognised across the political spectrum as destructive for the people at large.

But what has happened to all the money? The inflow of aid has not prevented widespread famine, acute shortage of basic necessities, especially in the poorer areas, and scarcity of seeds and simple agricultural implements. It has, however, helped the government to fight its several civil wars, and to finance the Organisation of African Unity.

Could we avoid such perverse effects by giving money direct to the poorest? This is not possible on any significant scale, since Third World governments insist on retaining control over the allocation of aid, including major forms of voluntary charity. To the extent that direct allocation to the poor is possible, it creates another problem: sustained aid encourages chronic dependence, a persistent reliance on handouts. For various cultural and social reasons, this outcome is likely in much of Asia and Africa. For instance, in the 1980s dependence was readily observable in the Sahel, as has been acknowledged by both administrators and advocates of aid. It has also been noted in Micronesia, the US trust territory in the Pacific.

To adapt the language of the 19th-century English Poor Law, sustained official donations promote global pauperisation through world-wide outdoor relief. To use a Marxist term, handouts to governments which promote or perpetuate poverty reward immiseration.

2. THE DOUBLE ASYMMETRY

What of aid as an instrument of development? The misconception that money is necessary for development, and possibly also sufficient for it, has been a leitmotif in the advocacy of development aid since its inception in the early post-War years. The most familiar formulation of this idea, based on "the vicious circle of poverty", insists that without donations a society cannot emerge from backwardness. As we have seen, this proposition is inconsistent with evident reality: both the West and much of the Third World advanced greatly without external donations.

Large-volume and low-cost investible funds (i.e., money available for capital outlay) are not critical for economic advance. If they were, millions of very poor people—individuals, family groups, and whole societies—would not have risen from poverty to riches in a few years (or decades), as has happened the world over. Much research by leading scholars has confirmed that investible funds play a very limited causal role in development.[2]

Lack of money is not the *cause* of poverty: it *is* poverty. Conversely, to possess money is the *result* of economic achievement, not its *precondition*.[3] This confusion between cause and effect underlies the uncritical, axiomatic approach to official aid. Whatever happens in the recipient countries can be adduced as argument for further transfers. If the countries progress, this is seen as evidence of the efficacy of aid, and as ground for giving more. If the recipient countries stagnate or retrogress, then obviously the aid must have been insufficient—and more is needed.

Governments and enterprises in the Third World which are able to use capital productively can borrow abroad as well as at home. External funds are available to both private and official Third World borrowers who conduct their finances responsibly. For instance, Western and Levantine trading enterprises have regularly lent substantial amounts to trustworthy borrowers, even in very poor African countries. Recent experience has shown that Third World governments can borrow in the West very readily (perhaps too readily).

This applies also to borrowing for infrastructure. If harbours, bridges, roads are productive, they increase incomes and therefore taxable capacity, so that governments can readily service the borrowed funds.

The maximum contribution that foreign aid can make to development is, therefore, no more than the avoided cost of borrowing in the market-place: that is, the interest charges and amortisation (repayment of principal) which would have been paid on commercial loans. This conclusion is not affected by differences in local conditions, government policies, or the type of aid given.

However, any contribution which aid can make to development by reducing the cost of borrowing is likely to be offset by certain adverse repercussions. Most of these operate on personal, cultural, social, and political factors—which, unlike the amount and cost of investible funds, are indeed critical for economic performance.

1. The most important adverse repercussion is the promotion of politicisation, with its attendant baleful effects.

2. The belief that economic improvement depends on external factors is another adverse repercussion. Advocacy and inflow of official subsidies promote this misconception, which diverts attention from the basic determinants of development and from the possibilities of improving them. In the advanced countries, people developed unaided the attitudes, conduct and institutions which lie behind their economic progress. Preoccupation with external subsidies ignores these realities. The familiar shibboleth that aid helps people to help themselves is very nearly the complete opposite of the truth.

3. Some strands of aid advocacy encourage blackmail and beggary, attitudes not helpful to economic development. The argument that a reduction of aid will result in hostility to the West is a form of political blackmail. Acceptance of demands for debt write-offs as a form of aid favours in this context the imprudent and dishonest over those who are ready to meet their obligations.

4. Foreign aid tends to encourage the adoption of inappropriate external models in development and planning, often with considerable drain on the recipient country's resources.

5. A further significant result needs to be noted, even though its exposition is slightly technical. The inflow of official transfers drives up the real rate of

exchange, and this adversely affects a recipient country's competitiveness in foreign trade. This effect can be offset to the extent that the subsidised transfers increase productivity in the country. But such an increase is in practice unlikely—and even if it did occur, could take place only after a time-lag of years. In the meantime, the higher real exchange rate makes for continued dependence on external assistance. This particular effect of external subsidies follows from the well-established proposition of international trade theory: an inflow of capital supports the real exchange rate.

These adverse repercussions (the list could readily be extended) are compounded by anomalous criteria and policies in the allocation of aid, and by the practice of Western donors in favouring governments who try to establish closely controlled economies. Extensive state control is often thought to reflect the determination of Third World governments to accelerate economic progress. In reality it obstructs development in various ways, including restriction of external contacts.

The major adverse repercussions arise because aid does not simply descend like manna from heaven. It accrues to the government. It adds to government revenues, and to its external balances. Aid is generally significant compared to these magnitudes, and often exceeds them.

In its effects on development, the operation of official subsidies involves a double asymmetry.

First, any favourable effect is on a resource which is not critical for development, whereas the adverse effects operate on critical determinants.

Second, an amount of subsidy which is insufficient to benefit development appreciably (by reducing the cost of investible funds) is amply sufficient to set in train the adverse effects. This is so because a given volume of aid is smaller in relation to the Gross Domestic Product [GDP] than it is to the government budget or the foreign exchange earnings of the recipient country. It is the relationship to GDP that is relevant for the favourable effects, and the relationship to budgets and foreign earnings that is relevant for the unfavourable effects.

Aid is demonstrably not necessary for economic development. This is evident from the progress both of the West and of much of the Third World long before the advent of aid. Whether it is helpful or damaging to development cannot be established conclusively, but the reasons presented here strongly suggest that aid is much more likely to inhibit development than to promote it.

Here it may be useful to forestall two objections. First, the argument is in no way refuted by the progress of some aid recipients, or by the success of particular aid projects. The maximum contribution of aid to such success stories can never exceed the avoided cost of borrowing, and the adverse repercussions still operate.

Second, although aid can do little or nothing for development, or for the improvement of the lot of the poorest, it can at times ameliorate shortages, especially of imported goods. Relief of acute shortages, however, by augmenting supplies serves to conceal from the population—at least temporarily—the worse effects of destructive policies. Western aid, under such conditions, confers spurious respectability on the rulers, which gain assists them in maintaining their position.

Western aid was critical in maintaining [President Julius] Nyerere in power in Tanzania from the early 1960s to the mid-1980s—amidst forcible collectivisation and villagisation, and suppression of private commerce and industry. It... propped up Colonel Mengistu in Ethiopia and (at various times since the early 1960s) Milton Obote in Uganda.

3. BITING THE HAND...

Advocates of aid often use various *ad hoc* arguments. These arguments shift according to the audience addressed and the vagaries of politics and public discourse. Here are three currently much-canvassed examples.

1. *Without further subsidies, Third World debtors would be forced to default on their loans, and the resulting Western banking crisis would endanger the entire financial system of the West.*

If taxpayers' money is to be used to bail out the banks, this should be done directly, rather than by laundering the money through debtor governments—who might not, in the event, actually use it to service their debts. Indeed, why should they, when they are not pressed to do so by their creditors? Even open default by the debtors would not endanger the Western financial system, since default need not result either in a domino effect or in a substantial contraction in the money supply. If large-scale open default really carried serious risks for the financial system, shouldn't the monetary authorities encourage the lending banks to strengthen their capital base by reducing dividends and raising new money, rather than force them to lend further sums to defaulting debtors? Throwing good money after bad simply wastes more capital.

2. *Subsidies to foreign governments are necessary to maintain exports, output, and employment in the West.*

If government spending were required for this purpose, it could be achieved far more effectively by increased domestic spending.

3. *Aid serves Western political and strategic interests.*

But to serve this end, transfers would have to be geared both to the strategic importance of the recipients and to their conduct. In fact, many of the recipient countries are of no political or military significance. And many of the recipient governments are openly hostile to aid donors, whom they attempt to embarrass and oppose whenever they can. The West feeds the mouths that abuse it.

Receipt of official subsidies provides the only common characteristic and bond of the varied constituents of the Third World. What else is there in common between Malaysia and Mozambique, Nepal and Argentina, India and Chad, Tuvalu and Brazil, Burma and Nigeria? The common bond has enabled their governments to act as a collectivity in demanding subsidies from the West.

The Third World, since its emergence as a collectivity, has been consistently hostile to the West, although individual Third World countries have been neutral, or even friendly.

Such hostility is hardly surprising. The Third World, as a collectivity, exists to extract resources from the West. A hostile posture is apt for this purpose, since it can take advantage of national conflicts of interest among the Western nations, and the widespread feeling of guilt about Third World poverty. Hence the antagonism of many Third World delegates towards Western aid donors at the United Nations and on other platforms; hence the close ties to the Soviet bloc of many recipients of Western aid; hence the virulent attacks by [India's Indira]

Gandhi, Julius Nyerere, and [Ghana's] Kwame Nkrumah at times when their countries were heavily dependent on Western donations. The practical effects of this hostility are aggravated by the tendency of the West to overrate the political importance of the Third World in general, and often of specific countries in that collectivity.

In the field of international politics, the effects of politicisation of life extend beyond the countries directly involved....

Western aid [sometimes] goes to governments openly hostile to other aid-recipient governments, or even at war with them. This anomaly enables anti-Western groups to claim that the West, and especially the USA, supports the enemies of their countries. This reaction has been conspicuous in India, Pakistan, and Sri Lanka.

From very small beginnings, multilateral transfers have become a major component of Western aid; they now exceed one-third of aid from the OECD countries, and greatly enhance the resources and standing of the international organisations involved, some of which are instruments and platforms for hostility to the West. This is undisguised in the UN and in FAO, UNESCO, and UNCTAD.

Examples, often bizarre, abound of this hostility and of the impotence of Western donors. For instance, on the centenary of Lenin's birth in April 1970, UNESCO... passed by an overwhelming majority a resolution calling on all member governments to pay tribute to him as a great humanitarian.

This hostility is likely to endure, because of the built-in majority of the Third World... in these organisations, and because of the political sentiments and loyalties of many staff members.

Influential aid-advocates and administrators are apt to regard the international aid organisations, including the International Monetary Fund and the World Bank, as forming the fiscal core of an embryonic World Government, a major objective of which would be global egalitarianism, large-scale international income-redistribution. Perhaps they are not aware that this policy would involve the use by the organisations of quasi-totalitarian powers over an indefinite period.

There has also grown up around foreign aid, and with its help, a substantial literature critical of the West and of the market system. Insistence, in much of this literature, that the prosperity of the West has been extracted from the Third World stirs up or reinforces Western feelings of guilt. This both promotes the extraction of more aid and often serves unacknowledged political and ideological purposes.

Another consequence of foreign aid, different from those already discussed, has been to generate a new branch of economics. World-wide preoccupation with foreign aid and the underdeveloped world has produced modern development economics. Before World War II, development economics did not exist as a distinct subject, or even as a term. There is an umbilical link between foreign aid and the hundreds of university departments, institutes, and centres of development economics which have proliferated throughout the world. Many of these organisations, including some of the largest, are supported by aid funds. This link may have shaped the subject beyond policy proposals. It may have contributed to the emphasis on aid, planning, and related topics at the expense of economic history, of the many phenomena and sequences in Third World countries which can be helpfully studied by economists, and of exploration of the interaction between political and cultural factors and the conventional variables of economics.

4. PROPOSALS AND PROSPECTS

I have argued that foreign aid is more likely to inhibit than to promote development and relief of Third World poverty. It should be terminated....

In this context... what are the potentialities of voluntary charities?

The objections to official aid hardly apply to the work of voluntary charities, provided they are genuinely apolitical. (This qualification is necessary because some major Western charities seem to be concerned quite as much with political objectives as with relief of need.) The activities of voluntary organisations do not politicise life in recipient countries, and therefore are much less likely to contribute to tension and conflict. They also arouse less suspicion about the donors' motives.

Throughout most of the Third World, voluntary efforts are the only way to reach the poorest of the poor. Administered by people familiar with local conditions, these humane efforts can minimise the effect of permanent dependence on external help. Experienced personnel are necessary, since novices find it difficult to act effectively in unfamiliar cultural and social conditions. Small-scale operations are preferable to larger operations; they are likely to be more effective, and are less likely to be subjected to control by the recipient government.

What lies behind economic achievement and progress? The answer, often shirked or ignored, may appear obvious, even trivial. It lies in the conduct of people, including that of governments—on personal, cultural, and social factors, and on political arrangements. Access to external markets can be a significant factor; but in practice many benefits derived from this nearly always depend on these primary factors.

Economic achievement and advance do not depend on financial or natural resources. I have noted the relative unimportance of the volume of investible funds. I must add that abundant natural resources—including land—do not generate sustained prosperity, although mineral resources yield occasional windfalls. This point is underlined by the wide income differences, within one country, between the persons and communities who have access to the same natural resources.

The contemporary Third World is not short of natural resources. Most of Africa and Latin America and much of Asia are sparsely populated. Many millions of extremely poor people have abundant cultivable land—witness among others the tribes-folk of Black Africa and the Amazonian Indians, who live in areas where land is a free good. Conversely, many of the most prosperous areas of the Third World (Taiwan, Hong Kong, Singapore, and parts of Malaysia) are very densely populated, even where the land is not inherently fertile.

Such phenomena are not new. Amidst abundant, indeed unlimited, land and vast natural resources, the American Indians were wretchedly poor at the time when the first European colonies were established and when much of Europe with far less land was already rich.

Poverty and riches depend on man, his culture, his motivations, and his political arrangements. Herein lies the wealth and the poverty of nations.

NOTES

1. In some cases the transfers go *through* the governments rather than to them, but this distinction does not affect my argument, since these transfers still require the approval of the recipient government.

2. The need for more capital has always been the principal argument for official development aid. This underlines an anomaly: most aid recipients, perhaps all aid recipients, restrict the inflow of foreign private capital. Although the volume of investible funds is not critical for development, inflow of private capital is undoubtedly helpful, especially as it is usually accompanied by an inflow of skills, and of new ideas and methods of production.

3. Some individuals become rich through windfalls, privileged incomes, and the like. Such occurrences do not affect the argument, and do not promote sustained development.

POSTSCRIPT

Should the Developed North Increase Aid to the Less Developed South?

There can be no argument that most of the people in most of the countries of the South live in circumstances that citizens in the developed countries of the North would find unacceptable. There is also no question that most of the Third World was subjugated and held in colonial bondage by the developed countries. In most cases, that colonialism lasted into the second half of this century. Apart from these points, there is little agreement on the plight of the South in the selections by Head and Bauer.

Many Third World specialists blame colonialism for the Third World's lack of development, past and present. This view is held in much of the Third World and also is represented widely in Western scholarly opinion. Johan Galtung's "A Structural Theory of Imperialism," *Journal of Peace Research* (1971), is a classic statement from this perspective. This belief has led to the Third World's demand for a New International Economic Order (NIEO), in which there would be a greater sharing of wealth and economic power between North and South. (You will find that Galtung's ideas are also discussed in Issue 15, the debate on whether women in combat would weaken national security.) It is also possible to argue that continued poverty in the Third World, especially amid the general prosperity of the economically developed countries, will increase anger among the people of the economically less developed countries, decrease global stability, and have a variety of other negative consequences. For discussions of this aspect, see Nicole Ball, "Militarized States in the Third World," in *World Security: Trends and Challenges at Century's End*, edited by Michael T. Klare and Daniel C. Thomas (St. Martin's, 1992), and Donald M. Snow, *Distant Thunder: Third World Conflict and the New International Order* (St. Martin's, 1993)

Other analysts argue that colonialism actually benefited many dependencies by introducing modern economic techniques, and they say that those former colonies that have remained close to the industrialized countries have done the best. Still others have charged that some Third World countries have followed policies that have short-circuited their own development. This point of view sees calls for an NIEO as little more than an attempt by the South to reorder the international system to gain power. Steven D. Krasner's *Structural Conflict: The Third World Against Global Liberalism* (University of California Press, 1985) is written from this point of view.

There are also disagreements about how much the North should aid the South, irrespective of who has caused the problems. Humanitarian concerns, as well as a sense that all the world's people will eventually be more prosperous if the 80 percent who live in poverty in the South can develop, argue for greater aid, a view represented in David Aronson, "Why Africa Stays Poor and Why It Doesn't Have To," *The Humanist* (March/April 1993). But there are those who suggest that actually creating an NIEO will require a massive redistribution of resources away from the developed countries, a change that is neither in those countries' interests nor likely to be supported by their citizens. Like many issues, then, it is only partly a question of what is right; there is also the matter of how much we are willing to sacrifice to change things.

ISSUE 11

Should the Global Arms Trade Be Severely Restricted?

YES: William D. Hartung, from "Why Sell Arms? Lessons from the Carter Years," *World Policy Journal* (Spring 1993)

NO: John F. McDonnell, from "Pax Pacifica: Defense Exports," *Vital Speeches of the Day* (April 1, 1992)

ISSUE SUMMARY

YES: William D. Hartung, a senior research fellow at the World Policy Institute, contends that controlling the proliferation of weapons throughout the world by restricting arms sales should be a top foreign policy priority.

NO: John F. McDonnell, chairman and chief executive officer of McDonnell Douglas aircraft corporation, argues that selling weapons to allies enhances the security of both the seller and the buyer and promotes economic prosperity in the seller country.

The international transfer of weapons through direct arms sales and other, less direct, programs, such as foreign aid, has important economic and political ramifications. Foreign arms sales in 1992 alone were $32 billion; sales during the years 1982–1992 amounted to approximately $161 billion. Many billions of dollars of weaponry also moved through covert channels, ranging from the CIA and the KGB to rebel groups to shadowy arms dealers and drug dealers. Over this period, the United States and the Soviet Union were by far the largest arms suppliers, each accounting for about a third of all transfers. In 1989, of the top 100 corporations that sold weapons internationally, 47 were U.S.-based, 42 were Western European, 6 were Japanese, and 5 were located in Third World countries. State-owned enterprises in the Soviet Union, China, Czechoslovakia, and other communist countries also sold a huge amount of weaponry. About 60 percent of these weapons were imported by Third World countries. Within that group of countries, those in the Middle East were by far the largest importers, accounting for about one-third of all sales to Third World countries.

Several factors promote this flow of weaponry. Economic benefit is one. Selling weapons supplies profits for U.S. corporations and jobs for workers. It is often assumed that the flow of weapons is governed primarily by political considerations, with weapons going to countries that a government wishes to support. There are certainly many political strictures that promote or impede arms transfers, but they are not as important as the economic considerations. During the long war between Iran and Iraq during the 1980s, for example, there were 6 countries that supplied weapons to Iraq only; 7 countries that sold weapons to Iran only; and 28 countries that sold weapons to both countries. While there is no evidence to support the old "merchants of death" theory that arms manufactures seek to promote conflict to enhance their profits, there is little argument that foreign conflict can promote profitable sales.

The economic benefit of arms sales has always been important and, ironically, has become even more so in the post–cold war era of declining defense budgets. One way to avoid layoffs at defense plants that are no longer selling weapons to their home government is to sell weapons to other governments. That is certainly true in the United States and other Western industrialized countries; it is even more true in Russia. In the political and economic turmoil of post-Soviet, post-Communist Russia, arms are one of the few things that Russia produces well enough and in enough quantity to earn it foreign capital, which it desperately needs.

Arms sales are also important sources of export capital to a number of Third World countries seeking to expand their economies. China, for instance, is a major arms exporter, with sales equal to those of Great Britain.

Countries also give and sell weapons to promote their foreign policy goals. There are times when the transfer of arms helps accomplish the goals behind the policy. The supply of U.S. arms to Afghan rebels during the 1980s played a strong role in driving Soviet forces out of the country and toppling its communist government. At other times, the policy fails. Massive arms shipments could not stave off the end of the government of South Vietnam in 1975.

There are, however, objections and drawbacks to the sale of weapons. Some people make the moral objection, for example, that the transfer of weapons promotes violence and continues warfare unnecessarily. Another drawback is that you or your friends may one day be the target of weapons that you have supplied. When coalition forces confronted Iraq, they found themselves facing many of their own weapons. These had been either sold directly to Baghdad or had come to Iraq through third countries who had received the weapons and later sold them to Iraq or to international arms merchants. A third drawback is that, if a country is engaged in worldwide arms sales, it makes it hard for that country to persuade others not to sell weapons. It is worth noting for this debate that weapons have no conscience, they do not recognize their former owners, and they have no allegiance to their makers.

William Hartung and John McDonnell debate the wisdom of arms sales in the following two selections. Hartung favors tight restrictions on arms sales as part of an effort to control the proliferation of sophisticated weaponry throughout the world. McDonnell replies that it is neither good business nor good politics to overly restrict arms sales.

YES

William D. Hartung

WHY SELL ARMS? LESSONS FROM THE CARTER YEARS

From the moment that he won the election, Bill Clinton has gone out of his way to show that he's no Jimmy Carter. The popular mythology holds that the Carter administration was a "failed presidency," characterized by poor stewardship of the domestic economy and indecisive leadership in world affairs, so, clearly, President Clinton wants to head off any suggestion that his administration will be "Carter II." And because he has selected a number of Carter alumni for critical foreign policymaking positions, he is even more anxious to prove that he will be "a different kind of Democrat."

But President Clinton should avoid taking this "I'm not Carter" approach too far. The Carter experience offers important lessons for the new administration, none more relevant than the president's effort to exert U.S. leadership in controlling the proliferation of advanced armaments. Although Carter's arms-transfer control initiative ultimately fell victim to the rightward drift of his foreign policy and the collapse of superpower détente, it remains the most serious international effort to date to negotiate limits on the conventional arms trade. As such, it offers important insights into how the Clinton foreign policy team should approach this increasingly critical security issue.

The problem of conventional arms proliferation may be more complex now that it was in 1977, but it is also a much more urgent priority for U.S. military strategists. Many of them see ambitious regional powers like Iran or Iraq as the most likely threats to U.S. security in the post–Cold War era. Even hard-liners in the Pentagon can be persuaded by common sense: that a plan for limiting arms proliferation is a logical way of reducing the dangers U.S. military forces will face over the next decade. And at a time when peacekeeping efforts to deal with armed chaos in places like Yugoslavia and Somalia are an increasingly critical and contentious security issue, it makes sense to curb the flow of armaments to regions of conflict *before* the fighting breaks out.

For a multilateral effort to control arms sales to have any chance to succeed, the United States will have to play a leadership role. Why? Because the United States now sells more arms to regions of potential conflict than all other suppliers combined. In 1991, the United States accounted for 57 percent of all

From William D. Hartung, "Why Sell Arms? Lessons from the Carter Years," *World Policy Journal*, vol. 10, no. 1 (Spring 1993). Copyright © 1993 by *World Policy Journal*. Reprinted by permission. Notes omitted.

arms sales to the Third World. According to a prominent industry lobbyist, the U.S. share of the entire world arms market could top out at 70 percent or more by the mid-1990s, in the absence of "undue" government regulation. Gone are the days when the (often exaggerated) threat of Soviet arms supplies to its erstwhile Third World clients could be used as a justification for U.S. sales to its allies in volatile regions: Russia has eliminated billions of dollars worth of subsidized sales to the Third World, its total exports dropping to just 20 percent of the world market in 1991. As a result, the United States now has no serious rival for the dubious honor of serving as the world's number-one arms dealer. China, which is widely denounced as a "rogue proliferator" for its sales of missile and nuclear technology to regimes in the Middle East and South Asia, is no match for the United States in the overall Third World arms market. For 1991, total Chinese arms sales to the Third World were less than *one-fortieth* the level of U.S. exports. As for the western European suppliers, *total* exports to the Third World from all of western Europe were roughly one-third of the U.S. total for 1991.

While arms-industry lobbyists and their allies in the Pentagon have welcomed this overwhelming U.S. dominance of the international arms market as if it restored a natural order to the world, this trend is both a short-term political embarrassment and a long-term diplomatic obstacle to obtaining the cooperation of other suppliers in any meaningful system of multilateral arms-transfer controls.

If President Clinton doesn't take concrete action to restrain arms sales early in his term, he may lose the opportunity to do so later. Other arms-supplying nations will assume that he is continuing Bush's policy of using the rhetoric of arms-sales restraint as a political smokescreen for a policy aimed at helping U.S. firms corner the world arms market. To forge genuinely new economic and foreign policies, Bill Clinton will have to see beyond the special-interest pleading of the arms industry and the outmoded strategic thinking of the Pentagon. At this critical turning point in world affairs, the United States cannot afford to conduct business as usual in arms-sales policy. In charting a course past the political and economic minefield that will surely confront any serious attempt to control the arms trade, President Clinton could hope for no better guide to the hazards that lie ahead than Jimmy Carter's experiment in fostering arms-transfer restraint.

THE CARTER EXPERIMENT: MYTHS AND REALITIES

The first obstacle to understanding the relevance of the Carter arms-transfer policy to today's proliferation problems is the myth that it was an exercise in "naive idealism." ...

Contrary to the claims of its critics, the Carter arms-transfer restraint initiative was *not* merely a quixotic personal crusade, it was *not* an attempt to eliminate all arms sales, and it was *not* a unilateral initiative. It was a logical outgrowth of the arms-control politics of its era, at once a response to the uncontrolled acceleration of U.S. arms sales that occurred under the Nixon Doctrine and an extension of the principles enunciated in the landmark Arms Export Control Act of 1976 (AECA). Rep. Bill Richardson (D-NM), who worked to pass the AECA, notes that the creation of the 1976 law was motivated by "a feeling that the

Nixon/Kissinger policy was just out of control, and we had no handle on it."

So, when Jimmy Carter pledged during the 1976 presidential campaign to "increase the emphasis on peace and reduce the commerce in arms," he wasn't speaking in a political vacuum. Similarly, when President Carter promised to take steps to stem the "virtually unrestrained spread of conventional weaponry," he was echoing the equally strong language contained in the preamble of the Arms Export Control Act, which states that it should be the policy of the U.S. government to "exert leadership in the world community to bring about arrangements for reducing the international trade in implements of war."

When Carter put forward his arms-transfer restraint policy in Presidential Directive 13 (P.D. 13) in May 1977, he made it clear that it was his intention to work toward *multilateral* arrangements to limit the weapons trade, but he also noted that "because we dominate the market to such a degree, I believe that the United States can and should take the first step." Carter's proposed first step was in fact a remarkably comprehensive set of recommendations that targeted the critical components of what had clearly become a runaway arms trade under the auspices of the Nixon Doctrine:

- Limits on the sophistication of armaments that could be sold to regions of potential conflict in the developing world;
- Restrictions on sales of arms-production technology, a particularly dangerous and irreversible form of conventional-arms proliferation that had been encouraged by Nixon and Kissinger;

- A ceiling on total U.S. arms sales to the developing world, with a commitment to gradually reduce that volume each year;
- Changes in the role played by the U.S. government in the promotion of weapons sales abroad, most notably by placing restrictions on what U.S. embassy personnel could do to help U.S. defense firms market their systems.

Carter's approach encompassed both large issues of policy, such as what volume of arms the United States should sell in a given year, and smaller issues of day-to-day implementation, such as how U.S. personnel should interact with arms manufacturers seeking to sell weapons abroad. In so doing, Carter seemed to be setting the stage for an effective reversal of the pro-arms-sales attitude of the Nixon/Ford years. But his promising prescription for a new arms-sales policy ran aground on a series of strategic, conceptual, and bureaucratic obstacles.

WHY THE CARTER POLICY FAILED

The most important lesson to be gleaned from the Carter experiment in promoting arms-transfer restraint is a simple one: undertaking a fundamental shift in arms-sales policy requires forceful, persistent presidential leadership. After an early spurt of attention to his arms initiative during his first year in office, Carter delegated responsibility for the effort to a group of mid-level bureaucrats in the State Department and the Arms Control and Disarmament Agency (ACDA). A former Carter official who was involved in the arms-transfer negotiations with the Soviet Union has noted that "he [President Carter] started them in motion and then abandoned them."

This lack of consistent presidential interest and support was to prove fatal to the Conventional Arms Transfer talks, the most pathbreaking initiative within the overall Carter arms-transfer restraint policy....

[The] hopeful outlook for the CAT talks was abruptly reversed by Jimmy Carter's national security adviser, Zbigniew Brzezinski, who decided that the prospect of even *discussing* limits on U.S. sales to critical regions such as the Middle East and Asia would interfere with his larger anti-Soviet agenda. Brzezinski wanted a free hand to continue to offer unlimited U.S. arms supplies to the embattled Shah of Iran, *and* he wanted to use the promise of U.S. military technology as leverage in his secret negotiations aimed at normalizing relations with China. With these other priorities in mind, Brzezinski launched a successful bureaucratic attack on the CAT talks, and by December 1978 they were dead in the water....

In addition to the need for strong presidential leadership, the second key lesson of the Carter experience is that to have any hope of success, a policy of arms-transfer controls must be integrated with an administration's larger vision of what constitutes U.S. national security. Time and again, President Carter and his advisers cast aside their commitment to arms-sales restraint to promote mammoth arms deals that they justified on the basis of a traditional, geopolitical view of U.S. national security interests. Despite his commitment to controlling the arms trade on grounds of morality and arms control, Carter never fundamentally questioned the Cold War era proposition that arms sales are a legitimate and effective instrument of diplomacy and military strategy, rather than a potential danger to peace that fuels regional arms races and undermines the prospects for democracy and human rights.

There are numerous examples of how this failure of strategic vision subverted the Carter arms-transfer control policy:...

- *Arms for Access:* Particularly in the second half of his term, after the overthrow of the Shah and the Soviet invasion of Afghanistan, Carter used military aid and arms transfers as bargaining chips to win access to military bases in Somalia, Kenya, Oman, and other nations in and around the Persian Gulf for his proposed Rapid Deployment Force. Carter's seemingly innocuous decision to send substantial military aid to Somalia in exchange for access to military facilities is a textbook example of the long-term dangers of arms transfers. The Carter administration's Somalia aid program began a decade-long U.S. arms-transfer relationship with the Siad Barre regime, a strategy that helped create such armed chaos in Somalia that President Bush sent in the Marines in December 1992 to stop the fighting and protect humanitarian relief efforts.

The third major lesson from the Carter arms-transfer policy is the importance of defining a clear negotiating strategy in discussions with other suppliers over limiting weapons exports. As if the bureaucratic and geopolitical factors working against the Carter arms-transfer control initiative weren't sufficiently daunting, there was also a distinct division within the U.S. negotiating team at the CAT talks about the underlying purpose of the negotiations. One faction, spearheaded by officials in the

Bureau of Politico-Military Affairs in the State Department, saw the talks as a tool for raising larger political issues about superpower behavior in the Third World. They hoped the talks would lead ultimately to some sort of superpower code of conduct governing military intervention in developing nations.

While some officials at State were interested in what the CAT talks could do for the larger U.S.-Soviet relationship, a second group, centered in the Arms Control and Disarmament Agency, saw the talks as important in their own right. This group believed that, if pursued deliberately over a period of years, the CAT process could build a common vocabulary and bureaucratic infrastructure for achieving incremental controls over specific aspects of the arms trade.

This division over goals was rendered moot by the larger problems facing the initiative—most notably the rapid rightward shift in Carter policy and the adamant opposition of National Security Adviser Zbigniew Brzezinski—but it could have become a sticking point if the talks had proceeded. A related and equally important problem was that the CAT talks were just one of *eight* significant arms-control negotiations the United States was conducting with the Soviet Union at the time, with the result that relevant staff and high-level attention were stretched thin....

In the final analysis, Jimmy Carter's arms-transfer restraint policy failed for three principal reasons.

- He underestimated the difficulties involved in making such a major shift in policy;
- He didn't use the power of his office to make arms-transfer controls a priority

within the foreign policy and national security bureaucracies;
- He never made arms-transfer controls an overriding priority on national security grounds.

The question now is whether Bill Clinton, a skilled politician who is nothing if not persistent, is prepared to tackle the problem of conventional-arms proliferation; and if so, whether he can learn from the mistakes of the Carter approach.

THE CLINTON PROMISE

Unfortunately, the one way in which Bill Clinton clearly differs from Jimmy Carter on the arms-sales issue is that he is unencumbered by any significant campaign pledges to do something about the problem. Although he ran on a Democratic platform that promised to "press for strong international limits on the dangerous and wasteful flow of weapons to troubled regions," Clinton was strongly silent when Bush announced nearly $20 billion in new arms sales to the Third World during September and October 1992. In fact, in the case of the controversial sale of F-15 fighter planes to Saudi Arabia, Clinton came out in favor of the deal two weeks *before* President Bush announced his decision to go ahead with it.

There could be a silver lining in Clinton's "blank slate" on the arms-transfer issue: as analyst Lee Feinstein of the Arms Control Association has observed, "While Clinton doesn't have a mandate to pursue arms-transfer controls, he also doesn't have a straightjacket." The president is free to develop a pragmatic, forward-looking approach to the problem if he so chooses. And there is some hope that Clinton may in fact choose to do so. During the transition, he pledged to "review our arms-sales policy and take it up with the other major arms sellers of the world as part of a long-term effort to reduce the proliferation of weapons of destruction in the hands of some very dangerous people." If nothing else, controlling the arms trade should appeal to Clinton's pragmatic side: in a post–Cold War world in which ethnic, religious, and territorial conflicts waged with conventional armaments are the greatest immediate threat to peace, a case can be made that pursuing multilateral arms-transfer controls is even more important now than it was when Jimmy Carter was president.

The outlines of a new arms-transfer policy can be built around three broad elements: a recognition of arms-transfer controls as a central organizing principle of U.S. national security planning; a reversal of the economic incentives to export weapons that have been built into the administrative machinery of the U.S. government during the Reagan/Bush era; and a commitment to increased accountability in the arms-transfer decisionmaking process, so that Congress *and* the public have a voice about whom the Executive Branch is arming.

To assert arms-transfer controls as a priority national security issue, the president should move swiftly to revive and reinvigorate the Big Five arms-transfer controls between the United States, Russia, the United Kingdom, France, and China. As a meeting place for the nations that control the vast bulk of the world arms market, the talks are well worth pursuing—even if China continues to boycott them in protest over the U.S. decision to sell F-16s to Taiwan. To signal the seriousness of his intent in a new round of the talks, Clinton should con-sider imposing a moratorium on new U.S. arms sales to the Middle East for a period of six months to a year, to provide time for the discussions to bear fruit. And he should send his representatives to the table with concrete proposals, including the following: limits on the total volume of new sales to regions of potential conflict; strict limits on the transfer of combat aircraft, ballistic missiles, main battle tanks, and other offensive weaponry; and bans on the sale of antipersonnel weapons like land mines, napalm, and cluster bombs that are particularly devastating to civilian populations....

The elevation of arms-transfer controls on the national security agenda must be matched by a commitment to deal with the economic consequences of curbing U.S. weapons exports. Any semblance of a credible U.S. commitment to arms-transfer controls collapsed under the weight of the pork-barrel pressures of the 1992 election campaign. As a result, President Clinton's first priority must be to develop an economic strategy that will reduce the arms industry's incentives to aggressively pursue overseas arms sales as an alternative to converting to the production of nonmilitary goods and services.

He should begin by dismantling the "arms-export infrastructure" that has been woven into the fabric of government by the Bush and Reagan administrations for the specific purpose of promoting arms sales on economic grounds. Doing so will require a reduction in federal government subsidies for arms exports, as well as a prohibition on the use of U.S. government personnel or publications to promote weapons exports to regions of potential conflict.

To address the demand side of the arms-proliferation problem, the president should also exert U.S. influence in bilateral and multilateral aid programs to promote reductions in military spending on the part of aid recipients. Promoting arms sales by the government may save a few jobs in the short run, but in the long run it is an obstacle to restructuring and reducing the military-industrial complex. And those changes are urgently needed to free up the resources required to make the United States more competitive in the global economy.

At the same time, President Clinton should also promote much deeper cuts in military spending than he currently envisions: his campaign pledge to spend just 5 percent less on the military over the next five years than George Bush proposed would lock in Cold War levels of spending at a time when the country can't afford them. A serious commitment to limiting the spread of conventional armaments will reduce the military capability in regions of potential conflict, thereby further undercutting the rationale for sustaining the massive U.S. interventionary apparatus and paving the way for substantial cuts in military spending.

Finally, to restore public trust in the integrity of the government's national security decisionmaking processes (and avoiding another Iran/contra or Iraqgate scandal), the Clinton administration should move to increase the accountability of government arms-transfer decisions. On covert sales, that means, at a minimum, advance notification of Congress that exceeds the vague promises entailed in current law. Ultimately, covert sales should be eliminated as an instrument of national policy except in extreme cases where the president can demonstrate that the basic security of the nation is at stake. On sales of dual-use technologies of the kind that were used to help arm Iraq during the latter half of the 1980s, Commerce Department licensing decisions should be made public, and an independent nonproliferation agency should have veto power over questionable exports. And in the interest of fostering a vigorous national debate over all arms-sales decisions, Congress should be required to vote on major sales of fighter planes, tanks, and other major weapons systems.

WHAT TO LEARN

Probably the most important lesson that President Clinton can and should learn from the Carter arms-transfer experience is that controlling the arms trade will require both U.S. leadership and sustained presidential support. Arms-transfer controls can no longer be viewed as a noble goal to be cast aside when other pressing political or security concerns come to the forefront: controlling the proliferation of the weapons of war must become a first principle of U.S. national security planning. The costs of a business-as-usual strategy on arms sales are simply too high—for long-term U.S. security *and* economic interests—for President Clinton to pursue a status-quo policy. If he truly wants to revive the U.S. economy, convert the defense industry, and promote peacekeeping and conflict resolution, President Clinton has to pursue a serious, long-term strategy for reducing the transfer of arms and military technology to regions of potential conflict. In doing so, he should not feel defensive about drawing on the lessons of the last attempt to achieve multilateral arms-transfer restraint, Jimmy Carter's arms-transfer control policy.

NO

John F. McDonnell

PAX PACIFICA: DEFENSE EXPORTS

The U.S. has not had a coherent defense trade policy since the Carter administration, when the policy was one of actively discouraging defense exports. For too long now, U.S. policymakers have exhibited a great deal of ambivalence and schizophrenia about defense exports. Generally, they want to encourage exports to friendly nations, but they are concerned about the transfer of U.S. technology—and hamstrung by a set of restrictive regulations left over from the Carter administration.

... I intend to make the case that there is an urgent need for a new set of U.S. policies aimed at promoting U.S. defense exports through closer cooperative arrangements with other nations....

The development of a coherent U.S. arms transfer policy would serve a number of important objectives:

- putting U.S. weapons into the hands of U.S. allies dedicated to the preservation of world peace,
- keeping U.S. production lines warm that will otherwise go cold years before replacement weapon systems are delivered,
- allowing the U.S. to remain active in the years ahead as a supplier of front-line fighter planes, tanks, helicopters, and other weapons to friendly nations, while providing our own government with a much shorter procurement lead time in the event of future conflicts,
- reducing the cost to the U.S. government of improving and extending existing programs, through cost sharing with foreign partners,
- and, lastly, providing the U.S. defense industry with some much-needed sustenance at a time of declining U.S. spending on defense procurement.

The formation of a new set of policies must start with a recognition of how much the world has changed over the last couple of decades—and especially over the last couple of years.

When the first Pacific Command Security Assistance Conference was held here at Camp H. M. Smith in 1968, it was several months after the Tet Offensive in Vietnam. The much-maligned domino theory was about to be put to the test—with results that validated the theory at a great and tragic cost in human misery. After the fall of Vietnam came Cambodia and Laos and communist

From John F. McDonnell, "Pax Pacifica: Defense Exports," *Vital Speeches of the Day*, vol. 58, no. 12 (April 1, 1992). Copyright © 1992 by John F. McDonnell. Reprinted by permission.

insurgencies threatening the Philippines, Thailand, and Malaysia. All of these were poor countries, and U.S. military assistance took the form of a loan or a gift. The containment of communism was the principal objective.

Thanks to the ultimate success of our containment policy, our principal military customers today—particularly in the Pacific region—are no longer in such dire straits economically and strategically. They are willing to provide for their own security by paying cash for weapons and military know-how, and they are perfectly willing to take their business to suppliers in other parts of the world if we are unable or unwilling to give them what they need. Their willingness to provide for their own defense allows the U.S. to reduce its regional commitment, thereby saving U.S. defense dollars.

Speaking at a press conference in Singapore in July [1991], Admiral Larson [Commander in Chief, U.S. Pacific Command] did an excellent job of summing up the broad changes in the global defense structure that have occurred over the past few years with the end of the Cold War and the collapse of communism as a credible alternative to democracy and capitalism. I quote:

"Today, the threat of a short notice global war has receded, and the bipolar competition (with the Soviet Union) which divided the world into two armed camps appears to be ending.

"The multipolar world which is taking its place offers new opportunities for cooperation.... This is especially true in Asia, where Singapore (and other nations) have benefited from a wave of prosperity and economic expansion based on careful investment, innovative ideas, hard work, and foreign trade.

"But this new multipolar world of opportunity and promise has its own set of security issues and concerns. These include:

"—a resurgence of nationalism and religious conflict,

"—growing populations and economic frictions,

"—the proliferation of sophisticated offensive weapon systems, especially weapons of mass destruction,

"—the continuing presence of narcotics traffickers,

"—and the danger of international terrorism."

Because of reduced global tensions and the improved strategic situation, our government has announced the redeployment of 7,000 military personnel from South Korea, 5,000 from Japan, and 3,000 from the Philippines by the end of 1992. Three weeks ago, the U.S. Air Force pulled out of Clark Air Force Base in the Philippines, and the U.S. Navy is planning to pull out of Subic Bay Naval Station in 1993.

However, as Admiral Larson also observed, we cannot delude ourselves into thinking that violence and conflict have been banished from the world state. The disintegration of the Soviet empire and the collapse of a number of communist governments have created a witch's brew of political, religious, and cultural instabilities. Nevertheless, I believe that the U.S. now has an opportunity almost unparalleled in history to cooperate with other nations in ways that can benefit world peace and stability. It is even possible that we will see a Pax Pacifica—built on economic interdependence and military cooperation—to compare with the Pax Britannica that followed Napoleon's defeat at Waterloo. That is saying a lot, because there was not another major war in

Europe until the outbreak of World War I one hundred years later.

What will it take to create a Pax Pacifica? Let us take a brief backward look at Pax Britannica.

British hegemony rested on two main pillars—one economic, the other military. Britain was able to dominate world trade with its manufacturers—and it had total command over the world's sea lanes. The British navy ruled the waves for British commerce and imperialism.

Today's world is more complicated. The U.S. cannot dominate world trade as Britain did in the 19th century. Economically, we live in a multipolar world—and the real center of gravity for the world economy is shifting from the Atlantic region to the Pacific. Military power must ultimately shift in the same direction. But for now—and as far as the eye can see—the U.S. will remain the one great military power capable of defending the freedom and order upon which an open world trading system depends.

A Pax Pacifica, as I see it, will therefore rest on twin pillars. The first is the increasing linkage of the U.S. economy with that of the Asia/Pacific nations, with benefits to people on both sides of the ocean. The second is continued primacy of the U.S. in the military sphere. While encouraging other nations to take a more active role in their own defense and that of neighboring countries, the U.S. must take the lead in dealing with bullies like Saddam Hussein. In a crisis situation, the U.S. should be able to take control of the action, serving both as playmaker and leading scorer—the military equivalent, if you will, of a Michael Jordan on the world champion Chicago Bulls basketball team.

If the Gulf war proved anything, it proved the need for a U.S. force structure that is unrivalled in its ability to project power—and a U.S. command that is capable of leading other nations in the preservation of peace.

Though vanquished for now, Saddam Hussein is the perfect example of the dangers of a multipolar world—the dangers that were enumerated by Admiral Larson. For a brief moment, he convinced a great many people that a single madman—the leader of a country of just 17 million people—could reduce an entire region to fear and trembling and wreak immense havoc on the world economy. To put him in his place was an extraordinary feat requiring the best efforts of the superbly equipped and motivated forces under the command of... General Norman Schwarzkopf [in the Persian Gulf War].

How prepared are we to launch another Desert Storm against another madman later on in this decade—or in the early part of the next century? Will we be able to meet the challenge of another test similar to the one that we passed with flying colors earlier this year?

Those are troubling questions, because the answer is "probably not"—not unless we devise a strategy for plugging some gaping holes in our defense posture over the near term. Under current U.S. procurement plans, many of the same weapons that starred in Operation Desert Storm are scheduled to go out of production in the next few years. That includes the F-15, F-14, F-16, AV-8B, AH-64 Apache helicopter, M-1 tank, and the Patriot and Harpoon missiles. Of the combat aircraft that starred in Operation Desert Storm, the F/A-18 Hornet may be the only one still in production five years from now. And it will be almost a decade before next-generation fighters and other weapon systems can be delivered in quantity.

Operation Desert Storm was an "inventory war" in the sense that the U.S. and allied forces were not forced to step up present production to meet the requirement for fighter planes and other weapon systems. The next time, we may not be so fortunate—and if that happens we will be in danger of being unable to replace the weapons that are lost in battle.

There is another matter that should be of further concern to U.S. policymakers. Do we want to concede the field to the Europeans (and Russians and Chinese) when it comes to supplying weapons to other nations? Is world security better served by European weapons than it is by American weapons?

The point is: The Advanced Tactical Fighter and other next-generation U.S. weapon systems like the LH helicopter will not be available for export for several decades, if ever. If production of our current front-line fighters and helicopters is discontinued, the U.S. will indeed be conceding the field to other suppliers in equipping friendly nations with the means to defend themselves. In turn, that will cause a reduction in U.S. influence and a loss of control over the use of advanced weapons by other nations. If the U.S. is the supplier, it can cut off support, spares, and know-how.

I am not arguing that we should rob Peter to pay Paul by eliminating next-generation programs to keep older programs going a little longer. Indeed, I believe the Administration and the Pentagon are doing the right thing in defying the critics and continuing to support advanced technology weapon systems. It is imperative that the U.S. maintain technological leadership. It has been our trump card ever since World War II, when the U.S. won the race to develop an atomic bomb.

In remembering Pearl Harbor, we should remember the millions of American lives that were saved as a result of President Truman's decision to use the bomb to bring the war with Japan to an early conclusion. Many more Japanese lives as well would have been lost if the U.S. had been forced to invade the Japanese homeland.

In much the same way, U.S. technological superiority allowed allied forces to win the recent war in the Persian Gulf with minimal loss of life on our side—and with at least some containment of the casualties on the other side that would have come from a war of attrition. We will always need to have some "silver bullets" in our arsenal—weapon systems that are the most advanced and most capable in the world.

Given a declining U.S. defense budget, the U.S. government can and should do more to generate additional business for the U.S. defense industry by promoting exports and cooperative arrangements with other nations. Three things are lacking here.

First is a clear strategy. The AV-8B Harrier II—jointly developed by British Aerospace and McDonnell Douglas—is a good example of both the potential and the difficulties involved in developing an export-oriented program through international collaboration.

British Aerospace developed the original AV-8A Harrier I, the first vertical take-off and landing aircraft, and hoped to sell a variant of the aircraft to the U.S. Navy and Marines. However, the Marines were only interested in an aircraft with greater range and payload, and they didn't want to foot the bill for developing a new and much more efficient engine. McDonnell Douglas had the technology required to double the payload-range capability of the aircraft by redesigning the system for more efficient vertical power and control and by making maximum use of advanced lightweight materials. By forming an alliance, British Aerospace and McDonnell Douglas were able to meet the customer's requirement with a highly cost-efficient solution.

But how far is our government prepared to go in supporting collaborative ventures of this sort?

Right now, our company and British Aerospace are working on a radar-equipped upgrade of the AV-8B with broad export potential. The Spanish and Italians are committed both to sharing a substantial portion of the development cost and to purchasing a number of radar-equipped Harrier IIs. However, it is unclear at this time whether our own government will commit the relatively minor development and procurement funds needed to turn the improved Harrier into a sure winner in export markets....

A second set of obstacles preventing the export of U.S. arms for good and practical purposes involves a lack of political will—or outright political opposition. This problem is especially evident in sales to the Middle East.

Five years ago, Saudi Arabia sought to purchase 48 F-15 Eagles from the U.S. It was turned down, with the result that the Saudis then went to Great Britain for a $29 billion purchase of Tornados and the infrastructure to support them. Recently, the Saudis came back with another request for 72 F-15's. This one order could keep the F-15 line going three or four additional years. If the Saudis are turned down yet again, it will probably mean that the last F-15 will be delivered in 1994, with the elimination of tens of thousands of U.S. jobs. And again the Saudis will go to Europe for their weapon systems and ongoing support.

The third main factor restricting the export of U.S. weapons is concern regarding a loss of control over critical technologies. The problem here, as I see it, is that we are still protecting some technologies that are long in the tooth and readily available from other suppliers.

A couple of years ago, the U.S. Senate came within one vote of rejecting a major sale by General Dynamics to Japan for fear of a loss of control over key technologies. Under the sale, Japan is co-developing an improved version of the F-16—which has been in production for 17 years—and spending several billions of dollars in purchasing U.S.-made equipment.

In addition, U.S. Export Control Laws restrict the export of a number of technologies where the U.S. is not even a leader. For instance, an export license is required for fiber optic cable with a transmission speed of 140 megabytes or more, even though fiber optic cable of that speed is available from Japan, France, Canada, the U.K., Sweden and Germany—not to mention Russia. Similarly there are clamps on the export of composite manufacturing technology available from other sources in Europe and Japan.

Old habits are hard to break, and the U.S. is in the habit of regarding technology—even mature technology—as something that should be hoarded as long as possible. This is a self-defeating attitude. In general, once a technology enters full-scale production, it becomes a perishable commodity—something that is likely to lose its value if it is not traded or upgraded. If U.S. companies are restricted in their ability to capitalize on mature technologies, they will be limited in their ability to invest in new technologies. In the long run, that can only hurt U.S. competitiveness....

In short, we see cooperation as a means of better meeting the challenge of global competition....

Everywhere you look in the business world, companies are forming international strategic alliances. This includes not just weak companies but the biggest and best names in many industries. A strategic alliance in the business world is successful when it brings about a more efficient deployment of capital, technology, and people. It can be a means of avoiding costly duplication of development efforts—the endless reinventing of the wheel and all of its component parts. It can be a means of moving quickly in response to changing customer requirements.

U.S. policymakers should take note because many of the same benefits can be achieved from cooperation in defense procurement. I am not suggesting that U.S. defense contractors can and should cooperate with other nations in developing the most advanced technology weapon systems like the Advanced Tactical Fighter or the LH helicopter. It is imperative that we maintain technological leadership in advanced weaponry. However, there is wide scope for cooperation with other nations in the development and production of defense products utilizing technologies that are mature or non-critical.

In closing, I want to restate the point that I made at the outset. There are good and compelling reasons why the U.S. should encourage the export of U.S.-made weapons to friendly nations around the globe. This would serve U.S. strategic interests and it would help to shore up the U.S. defense industrial base at a time of declining defense spending. When it is allowed to compete, the U.S. defense industry is not only competitive but is almost always the first choice of the most knowledgeable customers around the world.

But in order to achieve the multiple objectives I have outlined, there has to be a greater recognition by U.S. policymakers of the importance of defense exports. Congress, the executive branch, and the defense industry need to work together in fashioning a coherent defense trade policy which not only permits but encourages closer cooperative arrangements with other nations. And one more thing: Cooperation should begin at home—with the development of a less adversarial relationship between the government and the defense industry.

It is within our power to create a better future—a future marked by peace, harmony and growing prosperity. With increased economic and military cooperation, we can create a true Pax Pacifica—to the benefit of the U.S., the Pacific region, and the entire globe.

POSTSCRIPT

Should the Global Arms Trade Be Severely Restricted?

Whether or not arms sales are for good or ill, they remain a major area of international commerce, and the debate continues. For a recent article dealing with the history of the trade, see Stephanie G. Neuman, "The Arms Market: Who's On Top," *Orbis* (October 1989). The debate about arms sales and international conflict is something of a chicken-and-egg argument. Proponents of arms sales maintain that, in a dangerous world, it only makes good sense to supply friendly governments and, sometimes, favored rebel groups with weapons. That not only creates stability, it also allows allies to defend themselves without your having to come to their aid. Opponents believe that this argument is essentially backwards. The view of the opponents is that the buildup of arms around the world drives anxiety, perceptions of mutual hostility, and arms races in an escalating spiral that too often leads to military conflict. By contrast, arms sales opponents say, restraint by one party leads to eased tension, fewer imports by others, less conflict, and so on, in a de-escalating series of actions and reactions. Many analysts who are opponents of large-scale arms trade are especially concerned about the impact of arms transfers on stability in the Third World. More on this view can be found in Michael T. Klare, "Deadly Convergence: The Arms Trade, Nuclear/Chemical/Missile Proliferation, and Regional Conflict in the 1990s," *World Security: Trends and Challenges at Century's End*, edited by Michael T. Klare and Daniel C. Thomas (St. Martin's, 1991).

What does research show about purported arms races? The answer is somewhat unclear as yet. As a general phenomenon, there is no good evidence that arms races occur. That is not to say that arms acquisitions by a neighbor might not spur a country to increase its own armaments. Rather, it means that such a causal factor is but one of many, which may also include bureaucratic pressures, domestic politics, and the overall international political climate. This is discussed in Robert E. Looney, "Defense Expenditures and Economic Performance in South Asia," *Conflict Management and Peace Science* (January 1991). See also Gary Zuk and Nancy R. Woodbury, "U.S. Defense Spending, Electors Cycles, and Soviet-American Relations," *Journal of Conflict Resolution* (January 1986).

ISSUE 12

Does the Global Environmental Movement Threaten Economic Prosperity?

YES: James M. Sheehan, from "The UN's Environmental Power Grab," *The World & I* (March 1993)

NO: Thea Browder, from "Good Environmentalism Is Good Business," *The World & I* (October 1992)

ISSUE SUMMARY

YES: James M. Sheehan, a research associate at the Competitive Enterprise Institute in Washington, D.C., charges that many ecological zealots want to use central planning to create strict environmental restrictions, which will negatively affect economic activity, causing national prosperity and individual standards of living to be diminished.

NO: Thea Browder, a Washington, D.C.–based analyst, contends that concerns about the economic costs of protecting the environment are overdrawn, that creative planning can drastically reduce the adverse economic effects of environmental protection, and that environmentalism can even be good business.

We live in an era of almost incomprehensible technological boom. In a very short time—less than a long lifetime in many cases—technology has brought about some amazing things. If you talked to a 100-year-old person, and there are many, he or she would remember a time before airplanes, before automobiles were common, before air conditioning, before electric refrigerators, and before medicines were available that could control polio and a host of other deadly diseases. A centenarian would also remember when the world's population was 25 percent of what it is today, when uranium was considered to be useless, and when mentioning something like ozone depletion, acid rain, or global warming would have been met with uncomprehending stares.

Technology and economic development have been a proverbial two-edged sword. Most people in economically developed countries (EDCs) and even many people in less developed countries (LDCs) have benefited mightily from modern technology. For these people, life is longer, easier, and materially richer. Yet we are also endangered by the by-products of progress.

The world's population now exceeds 5 billion people. Resources are being consumed at an exponential rate. There is the threat of global warming and its attendant problems—the polar icecaps could partly melt, the seas could consequently rise, and weather patterns could be dramatically altered. Cities have smog alerts and mountainous piles of trash in overused landfills, which leak their effluent into the groundwater. Acid rain is damaging forests; extinction rapidly claims an alarming array of species of flora and fauna. Can the globe stand a hundred more years of this?

Sustainability is a term that is important to this debate. Sustainable development means progress that occurs without further damaging the ecosystem. *Carrying capacity* is another key term. The question is whether or not there is some finite limit to the number of people that the Earth can accommodate. Carrying capacity is about more than just numbers. It also involves how carefully people manage the planet's resources—the life-styles they develop. In a hundred years, the Earth's population could be 10 billion, twice what it is today. Can the world carry 10 billion people while using resources as we do today? Further complicating this issue is the disparity in global economic development. There are relatively few people, mostly living in Europe, North America, and Japan, who account for a relatively large percentage of resource consumption and waste production. This creates two problems. One of these is that the majority of the world population still needs and deserves to develop economically. Can we ask them to forgo what we have attained in order to protect the environment? Secondly, because of the disparity of resource consumption and waste production, the cost of change will fall more heavily on people in the developed countries.

In June 1992 most of the world countries and numerous private organizations gathered in Rio de Janeiro, Brazil, to attend the United Nations Conference on Environment and Development (UNCED), popularly called the Rio Conference. The conference, under the direction of Canadian diplomat Maurice Strong, represented a major international effort to address sustainability. Among other things, UNCED reached two agreements: a convention to cut down emissions that create global warming and a convention to protect biodiversity. But the agreements were controversial. The EDCs, for example, rejected LDC demands that a strict timetable be set for the reduction of the emission of carbon dioxide and other gases that promote global warming. Many countries, such as those with extensive logging industries, sought to water down the biodiversity treaty and were successful.

That is where matters stood when James Sheehan and Thea Browder wrote the selections that follow. Sheehan views the work of UNCED as a power grab by the UN and environmental zealots ("econuts," as they are sometimes derisively called) who seek to restrict economic activity so stringently that it will eventually lead to "the green road to serfdom." Browder disagrees strongly. She claims that such arguments are wildly overstated and that good environmentalism is good business.

YES
James M. Sheehan

THE UN'S ENVIRONMENTAL POWER GRAB

With President Bush's signing of the UN–brokered Global Climate Treaty, the United Nations was granted unprecedented authority over the global environment. As the Senate made the United States the first industrialized nation to ratify the treaty on October 7, 1992, the United Nations was planning to follow through with an international conference on population and the environment, to be held in 1994. The United Nations has found a powerful issue, and it is on a roll.

The June 1992 UN Conference on Environment and Development (UNCED), otherwise known as the Earth Summit, represented the most ambitious attempt ever to globalize environmental policy. The summit has been called a cross between an environmental Woodstock and the historic Yalta Conference. Indeed, it contained elements of both; as the pulsing masses in the sandals-and-beads crowd celebrated the occasion with dancing, singing, and drum beating, the world's leaders went behind closed doors to determine the fate of the earth. The agenda endeavored to lower a green iron curtain around portions of the world in service to the mob's call for a unique and all-compassing ideology, a new world order to replace the destructiveness of Western capitalism.

This Earth Summit was considerably larger than the first, called the Stockholm Conference on the Human Environment and held in 1972, which prompted most nations to create environmental ministries and agencies such as the UN Environmental Programme. Environmental activists would like to see a similar impact from Rio, preferably a full-scale integration of environmental and economic ministries worldwide.

The concept of "sustainable development" supported by the summit's organizers is a vision of the world in which environmental and economic planning is combined as a single government function, driven by changes in economic and fiscal policies. [Canadian diplomat] Maurice Strong, UNCED secretary-general, describes sustainable development as "the integration of the environmental dimension into every aspect of our economic life from planning and policy-making to patterns of production and consumption."

From James M. Sheehan, "The UN's Environmental Power Grab," *The World & I* (March 1993). Copyright © 1993 by *The World & I*, a publication of The Washington Times Corporation. Reprinted by permission.

At the summit's opening ceremony, Strong called the human race "a species out of control." Rio was convened largely to provide more control over this destructive pest. To Strong, the Earth Summit represented "not an end in itself but a new beginning—a new beginning in bringing about transformations rooted in our deepest spiritual, moral and ethical values." As the United Nations expands its scope over the environment, the fortunes of various connected interests can be expected to rise.

THE LOBBYFEST

Attending the summit were thousands of bureaucrats, politicians, special interests, and environmental pressure groups. Thus, it was more of a lobbyfest than a summit, and the environment took a backseat to an assortment of ideological causes. The aptly named Global Forum, an alternative summit for environmentalists, represented thousands of nongovernmental organizations (NGOs) from around the world, with roughly 100 from the United States. Each wanted to leave its own imprint on the Rio proceedings.

"Our biggest goal is to make sure that the summit recognizes the importance of women. We're planning to lobby that one to death," said Bella Abzug, former New York congresswoman and head of a women's environmental organization. Sustainable development is seen by its proponents as a veritable panacea for all of the world's social maladies. An important objective of the summit, according to Strong, was "to incorporate gender concerns into all areas of its work and generate global awareness about the important role of women and children in promoting sustainable development."

Group after group set up booths at the Global Forum to hawk wares and antique ideologies. One could find every angle on the environment, from the essential role of vegetarianism, New Age music, and art in pursuing sustainable development to the need to give animals complete dominion over the earth.

The most visible gains for the environmental groups are to be found in the perpetuation of their lobbying and fundraising efforts. "We're less concerned with what happens at Rio as what will happen after it's over," admitted one activist from the Natural Resources Defense Council. The summit laid the basis for a whole new level of international collaboration by environmental lobbyists, unifying their goals and strengthening their positions. The politicization of the environment will allow the NGOs to reap the rewards of increased bureaucratic expenditures orchestrated by the United Nations, which has pledged since the summit to increasingly involve them in the decision-making process.

The emphasis on special interests at the summit was a major disappointment for the more forthright environmentalists. "The emphasis is on more 'management,' but whose environment is to be managed by whom, and in whose interests?" asked Nicholas Hildyard, editor of the British environmental journal the *Ecologist*. In his view, the elites in the developing world would benefit from new environmental foreign aid resulting from the Earth Summit. In times of high national debt, they depend on such capital inflows. But the underlying problems have not been addressed by aid transfers. "For the poor, the landless, those who have been marginalized by the development process, 'new and additional funds' hold no attractions," said Hildyard. "The solutions they seek are not financial, but political and cultural."

The Latin American Pact for Ecological Action questioned the summit's goals, saying that "we feel the social problem of poverty should receive the same weight as pure discussions of ecology." The NGO environmental peoples coordinator of Venezuela also dissented, vocally opposing taxes on the poor's energy and fuel-wood sources, as well as the forceful internationalization of Amazon resources. Many people whose lives are affected by greater government control of the environment recognize that it can be a recipe for disaster.

Malaysia, home to a large and valuable rain forest, took particular issue with the Rio agenda. Ting Wen Lian, Malaysia's ambassador to the UN Food and Agriculture Organization, accused the industrialized nations of being high-handed in asking countries like Malaysia to restrain the use of natural resources needed for economic development.

Gilberto Mestrinho, the controversial governor of the Brazilian state of Amazonas, created a stir at the summit with his contention that "when there is a choice between trees and man, I prefer man, and I will stand with him." Many Amazonas residents depend on the rain forest for their economic well-being. To them, a harmonious relationship between civilization and the forest only can be achieved with the use and management of the forests by local people. Mestrinho invites open trading of technology from the United States to enhance the efficiency of the harvesting of rain-forest resources, thereby maintaining the quality of life and the environment simultaneously.

America's $150 million forest initiative, pledged at the summit, offers loans to governments in return for leaving rain forests unharvested. All this will accomplish, according to Mestrinho, is the subsidization of cartels in the industrialized nations for forest products, gold, tin, and other minerals. Brazil will be cut out of lucrative markets in which it could compete effectively to reduce prices. The resulting economic hardship will foster wasteful forestry practices much worse than those existing today. Little of the U.S. aid is realistically expected to reach the people.

That lesson is lost on the United Nations, however. Instead of listening to the needs of the world's people, the summit only heard calls for more government, more bureaucracy, and more economic control. One such call came from Paulo Soleri, a famous Italian architect who spoke for Architects/Designers/Planners for Social Responsibility at the Global Forum. "The largest environmental threat is unlimited consumption, typified by the 'American Dream' of a single-family home with a two-car garage, basement, attic, and garden," said Soleri. "If we try to multiply this dream for the whole of humanity, we will need at least 10 more planets to deal with the environmental stress."

The guidance offered by UNCED Secretary-General Strong is similarly antiprosperity. Strong warned apocalyptically in his opening statement to the conference, "No one place on the planet can remain an island of affluence in a sea of misery. We're either going to save the whole world, or no one will be saved."

REDISTRIBUTION OF WEALTH

Underneath the environmental veneer of the summit was a grand egalitarian scheme for global redistribution of wealth. "The 1992 Earth Summit must produce a new political commitment to a global war on poverty as central priority of the world community in the remainder of the 1990s and into the 21st Century," wrote Strong. Because the money fails to reach its intended beneficiaries in most cases, the UN aims are falsely egalitarian. Yet the theme of equalizing the rich nations of the north with the impoverished nations of the south remains a potent justification for the United Nations' expanded environmental operations.

Several justifications have been put forth for the argument that industrialized nations, with the United States at the forefront, must pay for a global "cleanup." Because countries like the United States are accused of having created most of the ecological damage in the first place, it is logical to make the "polluter" pay. The industrial model of development is seen as severely flawed and "unsustainable." The industrialized nations have exploited all of their natural "capital," leaving none for the Third World. Now, they must pay for a global perestroika, providing the Third World with the wealth and technology to adopt environmentally "sustainable" modes of living.

Strong has estimated that developing nations require $70 billion per year in additional foreign assistance for the environment. Massive foreign aid from north to south is envisioned by the Earth Summiteers, overseen by a green bureaucracy staffed by the ecologically sensitive. Clearly, a belief that only a wise, elite class can structure the use of resources remains the dominant tenet of the green religion.

The conceptual framework of "sustainable development" serves as effective cover for restrictions on conventional economic growth, couched in terms of regulating only the unsustainable consumption patterns—"the code language for overconsumption by the rich," writes Stephen Collett in *Environment* magazine. Global redistribution of wealth is the ultimate, if somewhat hidden goal of the United Nations, which sees pollution as merely a subset of wider social injustice. Capitalism, by exploiting natural capital, is responsible for global poverty. "[Summit initiatives] will begin to eliminate the inequities between rich and poor nations, and perhaps someday, the rich and poor within countries," writes Michael McCoy in *Buzzworm: The Environmental Journal*.

The principal funding source for a global sustainable development initiative in the Third World will be the Global Environmental Facility (GEF), a joint project of the World Bank, the UN Environment Programme, and the UN Development Programme. The GEF currently is a three-year pilot project being tested for its effectiveness in financing sustainable development projects to reduce global warming, protect the ozone layer, protect biodiversity and preserve international waters. It has been supplied with a $1.3 billion fund primarily by several European countries and Japan. Early in 1992, the Bush administration committed to providing $50 million in U.S. funds to the GEF. Other proposals to raise money for international environmental programs include taxation on commerce in international waters, taxes on the use of the atmosphere by airplanes, and the issuance of postal Earth Stamps. Debt for nature swaps, already in use, involve the exchange of Third World debt for land ownership in rain forests and other natural resources.

FREE MARKETS?

The need to move toward global sustainable development is a reasonable-sounding platitude. The world does have many environmental problem—most stemming from the same factors that are making the world unnecessarily poor—the lack of the institutions of capitalism: private property, contracts, security of profits, and a stable rule of law. The free market is, of course, an obvious model for sustainability. No resource that has been brought within the system of private property and the market economy has become more scarce. Copper, oil, wood, and even privately managed wildlife are doing well.

Scarcity is not a product of demand, but rather a product of the failure to link demand into a responsive system. Thus, resources in many nations are being economically depleted because of a refusal to integrate these resources into a system of localized, decentralized control, that is to say, into a market economy. Yet the free market, the only form of sustainable development, was not really discussed in Rio.

To UNCED Secretary-General Strong, however, sustainable development is a security issue. "Life-styles of the rich—who make up a small part of the global population—are the source of the primary risks to our common future. They are simply not sustainable. We who enjoy these life-styles are all 'security risks,' warns Strong. He insists he is not against economic growth, prosperity, however. In fact, he sees sustainable development in neo-Keynesian terms, arguing that eradication of world poverty "would provide a major stimulus to the world economy."

The preference for greater government control of international environmental resources should be viewed in the context of its use in the United States. The EPA [Environmental Protection Agency] has expanded its role enormously in the last several years, and its regulations take $125 billion from the domestic economy. Environmental legislation now costs each American family more than $1,000 a year, according to the Center for the Study of American Business. Yet the growing use of bureaucratic and regulatory procedures to protect the environment has not proved very effective in curbing pollution.

A prosperous economy, on the other hand, is essential for environmental protection; that is the conclusion of a study for the National Bureau of Economic Research by Gene Grossman and Alan Krueger of Princeton University. Their analysis of air-quality data in a cross section of countries reveals that higher per capita incomes, starting at about $4,000–$5,000 per year, generally provide the economy with the capacity to invest in environmentally sound techniques of production. Because economic growth alleviates pollution problems, the economically stifling proposals from the United Nations surely represent the wrong approach.

The Earth Summit laid the groundwork for a huge boondoggle for political interests but did little to address the underlying causes of environmental problems. Free markets, property rights, and individual liberty were ignored and even ridiculed as oppressive anachronisms. They were pushed aside in the mad rush to form a global EPA-style superbureaucracy known as the Sustainable Development Commission, to be headquartered in New York.

Today, the ideology of centralized economic planning is in disrepute. But its basic tenets—a hatred of private action and private property—remain in place. Thus, the centralizers have shifted from the economic to the ecological sphere. There is little tolerance for the concept that the ecologies of the world are best protected by an extension of the classical liberal order—not by viewing the world in market failure terms, but rather by noting our persistent failure to extend markets to these newly valued areas. Markets work, it is grudgingly admitted, but they fail in the environmental arena. There, only the enlightened hand of the state, tempered by the majoritarian instincts of the mob, should govern. The goal is clear: Ecological central planning must control the fate of the world. The result of this plan is equally clear: It is the green road to serfdom.

NO

Thea Browder

GOOD ENVIRONMENTALISM IS GOOD BUSINESS

The corporate world is "greening." The environment, once perceived as being incompatible with economic growth, is gaining popularity among corporate executives who view waste reduction and efficiency as basic business sense and who realize that environmental liability can have a powerful impact on the bottom line.

Corporations are adopting a wide range of measures to confront environmental issues in their operations. In part, they are being forced to do so by increasingly stringent environmental regulations. But companies are also realizing that even in areas where regulations are not yet in place, voluntary efforts pay off financially as well as environmentally. Being ahead of the regulatory curve can help them save some of the costs incurred later by inability, retrofitting, and penalties.

"Protecting the environment is not only good for the planet, it's good for business," says AT&T's A. Lee Blitch. Companies that are perceived as being "greener" than others also win points with concerned consumers and investors. Moody's Investor Service has warned that environmental liabilities may affect credit ratings. And companies are finding that the environmental changes they make, whether by cutting waste in response to EPA regulations or by reducing packaging in response to consumer demand, are good for the bottom line.

CONCERN AT THE TOP

As a result of this awareness, leading U.S. companies are elevating environmental responsibilities right to the top. In a recent Investor Responsibility Research Center (IRRC) survey of nearly 200 companies, two-thirds of the respondents had a board of directors committee responsible for addressing environmental issues, and a majority said that environmental performance had become a consideration in executive or operating manager compensation. A full 83 percent said they had a written environmental policy in place.

Because environmental awareness is relatively new to the boardroom, most companies are still working to integrate environmental concerns throughout their operations and to coordinate the exchange of information among their many divisions. Environmental audits are widely used: More than 80 percent of the IRRC survey respondents had audit programs in place, and most companies said they audited facilities every one to three years. Usually the audit staff are internal to the company, but sometimes environmental consultants are brought in. Only 6 percent used environmental units from financial auditing firms.

INDUSTRY ENVIRONMENTAL CODES

Worldwide, environmental codes of business conduct are also proliferating, currently numbering more than 25. All these codes are voluntary, developed by industry or other business groups. The codes most frequently mentioned by survey respondents were the Chemical Manufacturers Association's (CMA) Guiding Principles for Responsible Care, the International Chamber of Commerce's (ICC) Business Charter for Sustainable Development, and the American Petroleum Institute's Guiding Principles. About one-third of the respondents subscribe to one or more such codes.

The public's low opinion of the chemical industry was a prime factor in the formation of the Responsible Care program. Surveys showed low confidence m the industry and widespread belief that laws should be more stringent and more strictly enforced. "We said, 'Look out, guys. We are going to end up in worse shape than the atomic industry if we don't do something,'" says CMA chairman John Johnstone, Jr., also chairman of Olin Corporation.

More than 185 companies in the chemical industry have signed onto the Responsible Care code, which the industry hopes will improve environmental performance across the industry and communicate the improvements to the public. Dow Chemical Chairman Paul Oreffice says that "in an atmosphere of intense public scrutiny, it is an approach that recognizes that the only way for the chemical industry to survive and prosper is to perform in a manner that is responsive, and is seen as being responsive, to public concerns."

The program's work includes identifying positive environmental management practices, communicating these practices throughout the CMA membership, establishing reporting milestones to measure industry improvement and identify areas where companies need help, working with policymakers to share information and obtain feedback, and reporting to the public on industry activities and success. Each signatory company adapts to its own program certain codes of management practices, which take the form not of prescribed standards but of goals and objectives. A public advisory panel of environmental, health, and safety experts assists companies to identify and develop programs.

The program has gotten results. For instance, Huntsman Chemical Corporation developed a solid-waste recycling program that it says has diverted more than 57 million pounds of waste from landfills, saving 2.67 million cubic feet of space, and saving Huntsman $5.5 million.

But like most self-monitored industry efforts, the Responsible Care program has been criticized by environmental groups, which call it too vague and question the lack of outside oversight. "The codes are nothing but a bunch of aimless words," Environmental Defense Fund (EDF) attorney Karen Florini told the *New York Times*. Florini continues, "Without them specifying their accounting procedures, data collection methods, and auditing, it is hard to take them seriously." Joan Bavaria, a leader in the socially responsible investment community, said that clear implementation of changes and public disclosure of information are needed for the public to believe in the industry initiative. The CMA says it is developing a third-party review system.

The ICC's 16-point, nonbinding Business Charter for Sustainable Development has been signed by more than 200 companies from 56 countries. The charter's first point is to "recognize environmental management as among the highest corporate priorities." Corporations view favorably the charter's focus on "sustainable development," a term that implies environmental protection without economic sacrifice.

The ICC charter, too, has its critics. Representatives of developing countries have noted that the charter's third principle, which seeks "to apply the same environmental criteria internationally," might not be compatible with the current practice of some companies from the industrialized countries of exporting chemicals that are banned in their country of origin. Jack Doyle, an analyst with the environmental group Friends of the Earth, expressed broader reservations about the effectiveness of signing a nonbinding charter. Doyle said a neutral third party is needed to verify that a company is following the principles, echoing public skepticism about industry's ability to monitor its own performance. Some corporations might agree: Robert Kennedy, chief executive officer at Union Carbide, said that having an independent environmental board with outside directors and independent audits had contributed greatly to the company's environmental management. And in fact, Waste Management, Inc., found the ICC charter not to be as strong as its own existing environmental policies and declined to sign it. Nonetheless, the charter is a sign that international industry is increasing its focus on environmental management issues.

European automakers, prompted by a legislative trend requiring them to take back cars at the end of their useful lives, have made rapid advances in recycling technology for cars. Mercedes-Benz, for instance, has invested some $80 million in a pilot plant for auto recycling. Parts that have value, such as the engine, glass, electrical wiring, large plastic parts, and tires, are removed and the shell is crushed and smelted to obtain high-grade industrial steel. Carbon dioxide is the only by-product. Based on tests conducted in Austria, Germany, and Switzerland, Mercedes expects to process more than 100,000 cars per year by the mid-'90s. Other companies exploring auto recycling are BMW, Peugeot, Renault, Volkswagen, and Volvo.

POLICY AND PRACTICAL RESULTS

What are the policy results of these management initiatives? Recycling is the most widespread environmental activity among corporations, according to the IRRC survey. Other common practices are pollution-control activities, environment management and policy actions, and waste minimization. While companies have been putting together conservation and waste-reduction programs for some time, they are now getting help from the experts.

An attitude shift by the EPA toward voluntary initiatives rather than command-and-control strategies has produced several programs that help companies make environmental advances. "I am tremendously excited by industry's willingness to make ambitious voluntary commitments to environmental protection," EPA Administrator [for President George Bush] William Reilly says of industry's response to the agency's 33/50 program.

Under the 33/50 program, more than 300 companies have voluntarily agreed to reduce their emissions of 17 high-priority toxic chemicals by 33 percent by 1992 and by 50 percent by 1995, using 1988 as a baseline year. The EPA estimates the program could prevent 700 million pounds per year of releases and transfers of those chemicals. A number of companies have committed to more ambitious goals than those the 33/50 program sets out. For instance, Baxter International expects to reduce the 17 listed chemicals by 80 percent by 1996 and by another 80 percent for air emissions of all 189 chemicals covered by the 1990 Clean Air Act amendments. Merck & Co., besides meeting the 33/50 goals, will also reduce by 90 percent by 1995 the toxic releases companies are required to report. Many companies have extended their commitments to facilities outside the United States. Martin Marietta commented to the EPA that "from our experience, we have concluded that substantial pollution prevention and/or reduction can be achieved cost-effectively."

Another EPA program, "Green Lights," is geared toward conservation and could help reduce annual emissions of carbon dioxide by 232 million tons, sulfur dioxide by 2.7 million tons, and nitro-

gen oxide by 900,000 tons, according to the agency. More than 180 companies, including Boeing, Kerr-McGee, and Shell Oil, have agreed to audit light use in all their facilities and to provide, within five years of joining the program, documentation that they have completely upgraded the lighting system with equipment that is as energy efficient as possible without being excessively costly and still providing adequate light.

The program benefits the company as well as the environment. By replacing a fluorescent lighting system at just one warehouse and distribution center with a high-pressure sodium system, Johnson & Johnson actually increased light levels by 25 percent while realizing annual energy savings of $14,000. The system paid for itself in three and one-half years.

INDUSTRY-ENVIRONMENTALIST COOPERATION

Not only is industry cooperating with government, but the longtime enemies are burying the hatchet in the name of environmentalism. In 1990, in a ground-breaking move, two historical adversaries, the EDF and McDonald's, signed an agreement to cooperate in an effort to reduce the solid waste generated by McDonald's restaurants. The EDF first approached McDonald's in 1989 to discuss the fast-food chain's solid-waste issues. The company then was under pressure from the public and from grass-roots environmental campaigns that opposed its use of Styrofoam packaging. Once the 1990 agreement was in place, a task force that included four representatives from McDonald's and three from the EDF spent six months visiting the company's restaurants, conducting surveys and audits, studying distribution and supply systems, and compiling statistics on waste generation. Shelby Yastrow, senior vice president, general counsel, and chief environmental officer at McDonald's, says that "the goal was to turn the company inside out. Every corner of McDonald's was subject to EDF's scrutiny." In April 1991, the task force released a 150-page report concluding that McDonald's could feasibly reduce its on-site waste generation by 80 percent without disrupting company operations. The report provided a 42-point plan whereby McDonald's could achieve this goal.

One of the central points of the waste-reduction plan was a switch from Styrofoam containers to paper-based wrapping, a move that reduced packaging volume by between 70 and 90 percent. According to an independent consulting firm, the wraps not only use less landfill, they also significantly reduce energy used and pollutants released during the wrap's life cycle. Other task force recommendations include recycled brown paper carryout bags and coffee filters bleached with oxygen to reduce the water pollution accompanying white paper production, and a switch to reusable shipping containers where possible and recycling of corrugated boxes.

Indeed, there have been other alliances between corporations and environmental groups, but the McDonald's-EDF agreement was the first to have such far-reaching effects on company policy. And while public pressure on McDonald's was an important incentive to change, credit for the success of the joint venture belongs to the attitudes of both parties. They say that mutual respect created what the EDF's Fred Krupp called a "relationship of trust." The EDF found McDonald's to be well-managed, open-

minded, flexible, and truly interested in getting results. Yastrow says McDonald's found in EDF the technical expertise it needed and the bonus of credibility with the public that the project might not have had with a consulting firm.

Some environmental groups criticized the EDF's participation with McDonald's, claiming it legitimized a fast-food life-style that is not compatible with environmental goals. Others, however, believe that although care must be taken that corporations actually achieve concrete results, environmental groups have no choice but to work with corporations if they are to make gains. And Neil Sampson, executive vice president of the American Forestry Association, wrote that "when it comes to the task of improving the world's environment, it is silly to ask who is righteous enough to join in the effort. The work's too important. It needs everyone."

As the environment continues to move to the forefront of policy making and public concern, corporations are sure to make further changes. With knowledgeable and concerned management, with the help of noncorporate experts, corporations can greatly reduce the adverse impact they make on the environment. And that is, at any rate, the first step toward a sustainable society.

POSTSCRIPT

Does the Global Environmental Movement Threaten Economic Prosperity?

"You can't have your cake and eat it too" is a trite phrase. Such bits of folk wisdom, though, often get to be trite because there is a kernel of truth to them that is worth repeating. The environment is akin to our common cake. People have been consuming it gluttonously during the past century, and that certainly cannot go on any longer. The question is whether or not we have to go on a bread and water diet. Also, can we ask the world's less developed countries to forgo cake when we have already consumed so much?

Questions such as these have brought environmental issues much closer to the forefront of world political concerns. See, for example, Stephen Viederman, "Sustainable Development: What It Is and How Do We Get There?" *Current History* (April 1993).

The point is that environmental protection is not cost free. This is because environmentally safe production, consumption, and waste disposal techniques are frequently much more expensive than current processes. It is also because poorer people will generally do what they must to survive, whether it is environmentally safe or not. Moreover, the less developed countries have precious few financial resources to devote to developing, constructing, and implementing environmentally safe processes. Therefore, if the changes that need to occur are going to be put in place before further massive environmental degradation occurs, there will have to be a massive flow of expensive technology and financial assistance from the developed countries to the less developed ones. The EDCs resisted LDC demands for vastly increased aid at the Rio Conference. You can learn more about UNCED and its aftermath by reading James Gustave Speth, "A Post-Rio Compact," *Foreign Policy* (Fall 1992), and the symposium issue "Environment & Development: Rio and After," *International Journal* (Autumn 1992).

A final note: President Clinton reversed the stand of his predecessor and signed the biodiversity convention when he became president. Which presidential stand do you support? Would you be willing, for example, to pay an environmental protection tax of, say, one percent of your earnings to the United Nations for global programs? Would you be willing to drive only 3 or 4 days a week? Are you willing to accept UN mandated restrictions on economic activity? If not, what is the answer? The bottom line, then, is what are the costs, and are you willing to bear them?

PART 3

International Security and World Politics

Whatever we may wish, war, terrorism, and other forms of physical coercion are still important elements of international politics. Countries both calculate how to use the instruments of force and how to implement national security. There can be little doubt, however, that there are significant changes underway in this realm as part of the changing world system. Strong pressures exist to reduce arms spending drastically, to expand the mission and strengthen the security capabilities of international organizations, and to end the almost exclusively male responsibilities and opportunities associated with service and combat units in the United States. This section examines how countries in the international system are addressing these issues, as well as the question of whether or not criminal suspects can be justifiably kidnapped from foreign countries in order to be prosecuted.

- Is It Possible to Drastically Reduce Defense Expenditures and Remain Secure?

- Should the United Nations Take on Greater Military Capabilities and Roles?

- Would Women in Combat Weaken National Security?

- Is the Kidnapping of Criminal Suspects from Foreign Countries Justifiable?

ISSUE 13

Is It Possible to Drastically Reduce Defense Expenditures and Remain Secure?

YES: Jerome B. Wiesner, Philip Morrison, and Kosta Tsipis, from "Ending Overkill," *The Bulletin of the Atomic Scientists* (March 1993)

NO: Colin L. Powell, from "U.S. Forces: Challenges Ahead," *Foreign Affairs* (Winter 1992/1993)

ISSUE SUMMARY

YES: Jerome B. Wiesner, Philip Morrison, and Kosta Tsipis, all faculty members at the Massachusetts Institute of Technology, maintain that U.S. defense expenditures can be reduced dramatically, while still ensuring the physical safety of the United States and protecting its vital interests.

NO: General Colin Powell, in an article written when he was serving as chairman of the U.S. Joint Chiefs of Staff, argues that drastic cuts will harm national security and are unacceptable.

The cold war is over; that much we know. Whether or not the world is safer is controversial. It is surely a relief that there has been an end to the occasionally eyeball-to-eyeball hostility between the Soviet Union and the United States. The once-feared Soviet army has fallen into disarray; its successor, the Russian army, does not at present possess the capability of fighting an extended, aggressive war. The United States and the Soviet Union, now Russia, have signed several major agreements to restrain or reduce their nuclear weapons inventories. Of these, the most important are the two Strategic Arms Limitation Talks treaties (SALT I, in 1972; SALT II, in 1979) and the two Strategic Arms Reduction Talks treaties (START I, in 1991; START II, in 1993). When the START II treaty becomes fully effective in the year 2003, the maximum U.S. nuclear inventory will be 3,500 nuclear devices, including 1,272 bombs, 1,723 warheads on submarine-based missiles, and 500 warheads on land-based missiles. The Russian inventory will be roughly equivalent.

Still, dangers persist. Both the Americans and Russians have, and will probably retain into the foreseeable future, a massive array of nuclear weapons. And the potential for mass destruction, including the possible proliferation of nuclear weapons and the persistence of chemical and biological weapons controlled by a number of countries, remains.

Hardly anyone, even in the military, disputes the idea that the United States and other countries can dramatically reduce their military spending (both as a proportion of their budgets and as a proportion of their gross national products, GNPs) by discarding current weapons systems, slowing the acquisition of new systems, and reducing uniformed personnel. Most analysts even agree that the country can reduce its real dollar (adjusted for inflation) defense expenditures. However, how to accomplish reductions in military inventory involves controversial choices. How far can reductions proceed before security is compromised? What are the domestic economic consequences of military reductions?

The structure of any military forces should be determined by the interplay between security needs and budgetary constraints. With a staggering budget deficit, combined with the new security context occasioned by the end of the cold war, the Administration has recommended a significant series of cuts in U.S. spending and forces.

The military cuts have also led to revisions in defense planning regarding the number and types of wars that the U.S. military should be ready to fight. In mid-1993, Secretary of Defense Les Aspin announced a plan informally labeled the "win-hold-win" strategy. Basically, it anticipates a U.S. force able to defeat one regional power while simultaneously being able to fend off a second regional power in another conflict until the first war is won and forces can be shifted to the second conflict. During the 1992 presidential race, Clinton told an audience that "our forces must be more mobile, more precise and more flexible, and they must have the technologically advanced weapons they need to prevail and to prevail quickly." Ironically, this means acquiring new, highly sophisticated military capabilities, which are very expensive.

Military cuts have also had an economic impact on many workers and localities. The U.S. Office of Technology Assessment has predicted that during the 1990s the reductions in military forces, in civilians working directly for one of the military services, and in civilians working in defense industries could eliminate 2.5 million jobs. Cuts have also raised concern that the country could lose its weapons-building capabilities. If, for example, submarine production is ended, then the many specialists that design and build submarines will eventually find other work, replacements will not be trained, and facilities will be converted to other uses or be dismantled.

The issue is not whether to reduce military spending, equipment, and personnel. Virtually everyone agrees that can and should be done. The question is how much can be done while ensuring national security. In the first article, Jerome Wiesner, Philip Morrison, and Kosta Tsipis argue that cuts well beyond those projected by President Clinton can be made safely. General Colin Powell disagrees, claiming that the already projected cuts will reduce U.S. forces as far as they can go while still retaining the ability to meet potential threats to U.S. national security.

YES

Jerome B. Wiesner, Philip Morrison, and Kosta Tsipis

ENDING OVERKILL

Twenty-four hours a day for 30 years without end, one or another of a carefully tended group of specially equipped jets was somewhere aloft, high over North America or the adjoining seas. Within that far-off plane on its determinedly random track, a dozen or two technicians attended the panels and screens of secure long-range communications. A general officer of the U.S. Strategic Air Command (SAC) and his staff endured long hours airborne until word came that the next such plane and crew in an unceasing rotation had safely taken off. Only upon confirmed replacement could the men aloft return to a SAC runway, only to take their place in the perpetual vigil a few days later.

That was "Looking Glass," an airborne surrogate command post. If the White House, the Pentagon, and the buried center of SAC at Omaha were destroyed or isolated by a sudden nuclear strike, the grave and anonymous officers of Looking Glass, prepared by long training and strict orders, were to send from on high the same coded commands their vanished president might have used to loose the awesome retaliation of the United States. This provision for catastrophic revenge would, it was held, deter a vaporizing attack from the blue: mutual destruction was assured.

Looking Glass took up its unending rounds in February 1961. SAC brought its anxious, ceaseless, airborne rotation to an end in July 1991. The thread of thermonuclear confrontation is no longer drawn taut.

There is hardly a more hopeful symbol. Even more, it is plain that the two superpowers are now well beyond merely symbolic change; they are moving awkwardly toward an enduring coexistence. This essay seeks to outline practical assurances against the fading apocalypse of large-scale nuclear war, and to draw from the universal and profound relief the implications that it bears for lesser instances of armed conflict.

REAL MONEY

... Nuclear weapons and their launchers, in spite of their dread potential, account for less than a fourth of total U.S. military expenditures. The bulk of

U.S. military costs have been—and are today—incurred in maintaining large, non-nuclear forces.

It is those forces, after all, that have fought the several bloody wars in the 50 years since World War II, while nuclear war has remained grimly potential. Now, the end of the bilateral Cold War between the nuclear superpowers presents an unmatched opportunity to begin a step-by-step process toward a world of nations that, if not free of conflict, is by and large determined to keep the peace. Peaceful international cooperation, promised in 1945 with the creation of the United Nations, was all but vitiated by five decades of the Cold War. In the coming years, the promise of the United Nations Charter can be realized, but not in a world armed with modern weapons at the present scale. To begin the tricky passage to a more cooperative, more reasonable international order, a start must be made to reduce the annual half-trillion dollars spent on arms procurement worldwide.

The best beginning would be a strong, sensible, and prompt reduction of American military forces, the largest and most comprehensive fighting force in the world—but one designed to meet an adversary now in national ruin. Such a reduction would send the best signal abroad. It would also free funds to help solve thorny problems at home—problems of unemployment, the cities, health, education, infrastructure, investment, and the deficit.

Peace is the first and most precious of all the outcomes from these reductions, but a secondary dividend is ... that shrinking military expenses will bring a budget saving of not a mere $50 to $100 billion dollars over the next decade, but $800 to $900 billion—real money.

Money is important, but the first question must be, is it safe to save? The answer is yes.

SCALING BACK

The Cold War-era hypertrophy of U.S. armed forces and the precarious instability of hair-trigger nuclear defenses carried three dangers. The greatest danger was living at the brink of nuclear catastrophe. No longer at that cliff edge, most people now recognize the economic damage—the dollars lost and the opportunities foregone. But the third danger was and is the Cold War frame of mind, and the inherently alarming signal it sends to anxious nations everywhere. What we need now is the slow construction of a cooperative defense of the peace.

For the foreseeable future, U.S. forces need to reflect the real world and its risks, not the shadowy images we once anxiously saw in the mirror. But how much force is enough? The balance must be reckoned afresh, starting with the huge U.S. inventory of weapons and trained forces.

Prudence implies that change cannot be too sudden, nor should it go beyond all possibility of reversal. But within those constraints, the American defense structure should be steadily and sharply reduced, both in nuclear weaponry—so terrible but so cheap—and in the grand panoply of expensive hardware known as conventional: planes, ships, tanks, and missiles. Of the 5 million men and women in uniform and out who now build, organize, and bear U.S. arms, most will need to be given new and constructive tasks by the end of the decade.

Of course, any reckoning of adequate nuclear and conventional military power 10 or more years from now depends on a realistic assessment of the missions and functions the U.S. military will be expected to perform. It is improbable, for instance, that the United States will become involved in a land war with a nuclear-armed China. Therefore, we need not match the size of its army, the world's largest. (Indeed, the United States has never done so, although it fought the fraction of the Chinese army sent to Korea.)

We must also overcome the Pearl Harbor syndrome. For 50 years that stunning attack on the U.S. fleet in Honolulu has been invoked to urge unfailing military preparedness. But one battle is not a war. Pearl Harbor was a tactical triumph for the Japanese navy and a strategic disaster for Japan. No other event could have so completely mobilized the United States for war. Pearl Harbor was not a Japanese success; it was a great American strategic victory, bitterly won by default.

That is not to advocate unreadiness or complacency. But a wider view of military aims and consequences must be considered. For example, Desert Storm's month of victories in the sky over Kuwait and Iraq carries its own seductively false lesson. Smart bombs are not the whole story. The engagement drew on a huge arsenal, an inventory of weapons—from earth orbit to the deep sea—designed to be mobilized against an enemy far more powerful than Iraq. The United States faced almost no aerial opposition, then conducted a lightning ground war across a trackless desert, against an adversary without a single effective ally or source of resupply. The Persian Gulf was a theater as suited for U.S. weapons as Vietnam was not. Victory over Baghdad could lead to conclusions as wrong as those drawn from the defeat at Pearl Harbor.

But American forces are now so large that for years to come they will have no rivals in power, once the geography of plausible combat is accounted for. In restructuring its forces, the United States should consider what sort of armed conflicts may occur and where—allowing latitude for misjudgment. A smaller force should still be able to deter war against this country and its allies, with sufficient strength to make the risks and costs of attack manifest to adversaries. At the same time, the United States must open new paths to the peaceful resolution of international conflict. While the country must avoid sudden change, the status quo—with bloated militaries around the world—is not a reasonable standard. U.S. policy and force structure ought to depend on an analysis of those against whom it might fight, including where and how.

MISSIONS FOR A NEW CENTURY

A military establishment defined by mission rather than service seems more amenable to reasoned restructuring. The division of the U.S. military forces into land, sea, and air components is the product of a long tradition as well as of differing tactics, technologies, and training that each environment requires. But tradition has been overtaken by the experience of joint operations. The Air-Land Battle doctrine developed in the 1970s and the Gulf War, in which land, air, naval, and space-borne weapons and communications systems were successfully combined, suggest that future U.S. military forces may be more advantageously structured along functional lines.

It is possible that six distinct military functions could one day be recognized as organized commands. They are:

- **Nuclear deterrence.** A triad of land-based intercontinental ballistic missiles, submarine-launched missiles, and intercontinental bombers, integrated to insure nuclear retaliatory capability.
- **Air-Land Battle.** Heavily armored troops, tanks, artillery, and armored helicopters working in concert with planes designed for ground attack, which are free to roam at will because of U.S. air superiority. The forces would be employed in the defense of overseas allies; U.S. shores are not vulnerable to ground attack.
- **Sea control.** Capital ships, both aircraft carriers with their surface escorts, and the new, nuclear-powered hunter-killer submarines, which can be used to clear sea lanes or impose blockades.
- **Land-sea interface.** Light, mobile, over-the-beach infantry, including marines, with small helicopter carriers and special transport, including landing craft and heavy helicopters, and nuclear-powered submarines prepared for assault and interdiction operations. This is the command most likely to be charged with carrying out increasingly frequent internationally sanctioned or mandated peacekeeping or punitive operations, or to provide humanitarian assistance.
- **Intelligence and space capabilities.** The National Reconnaissance Office, which procures military satellites; the Space Command, with its early warning functions and orbital worldwide monitoring; the Central Intelligence Agency; the Defense Intelligence Agency; the National Security Agency; and all other information-gathering agencies. Their task: to gather the data and provide the analyses to insure that the United States is seldom surprised.
- **Research, development, testing, and evaluation.** The Directorate of Defense Research and Engineering, the Defense Advanced Research Projects Agency, and the current military and Energy Department laboratories, test ranges, and other facilities would take responsibility for weapons research and development by the other five commands.

The six-part structure outlined on these pages would provide an opportunity for a truly "zero-based" restructuring of the military. Here, we suggest force structures appropriate for the year 2000.

NUCLEAR DETERRENCE

U.S. nuclear warheads would be divided among the familiar triad in the year 2000: on land-based missiles (ICBMs), on submarine-launched missiles (SLBMs), and on long-reach bomber aircraft. All three delivery systems would be integrated—as they are today—to insure appropriate retaliation to any nuclear attack. Strategic nuclear weapons are meant to destroy enemy homeland targets, military or civil, at any distance. But their possible use in war-fighting has steadily lost credibility. In June 1991, just before the great changes in Moscow, American forces deployed not just 100, or even 1,000, but about 9,750 warheads on strategic nuclear weapons, many with yields a hundred times greater than the first nuclear bombs of World War II. "Overkill" was really authentic.

Statesmen of nuclear-armed nations often describe the total elimination of weapons of mass destruction as their goal. But the possibility of an adversary retaining small, hidden stocks of nuclear weapons, and the need to deter reckless leaders mesmerized by the mythic attributes of such weapons, suggest that no quick end to all nuclear weapons is ahead.

The nuclear powers have been slow to move toward nuclear disarmament. Nor are they likely to pursue that goal. Moreover, in spite of the legalities, all sovereign states are not equal; the powerful have sought power, in part, to coerce the weak, and they will not relinquish that power lightly. Institutions dedicated to ending the nuclear threat must be joined by other institutions that temper the world's inequities in wealth and power. Those conditions must be nurtured; they will not arise from academic or legal pronouncements alone, however equitable or appealing.

The Strategic Arms Reduction Treaty (START), signed in Moscow in July 1991 and lately ratified by the U.S. Senate, calls for the first meaningful reduction in the number of nuclear weapons in history. START I will reduce U.S. and Russian strategic arms to about 6,000 "accountable" warheads for each nation, with monitored, on-the-spot dismantling and destruction by 1999. It has been plainly in the spirit of the times to do more, as indeed Presidents George Bush and Boris Yeltsin did in 1991 and 1992, with informal agreements on tactical missiles, and most recently, by signing START II in Moscow in early January. If ratified, START II will further reduce each country's strategic arsenal to fewer than 3,500 warheads. That is still overkill. A more rational U.S. nuclear arsenal for the year 2000 should include no more than 780 strategic nuclear warheads.

The nuclear arsenal would include:

Land-based intercontinental ballistic missiles (ICBMs). One warhead in each land-based ICBM would end the main incentive for preemptive attack on easily located and immobile silos. A first strike would offer no clear gain in damage capability, because at least one warhead would be expended for each warhead destroyed, and some of them would miss. The Defense Department intends to maintain the current number of Minuteman III ICBMs, downloaded to a single warhead, but 300 would be adequate.

Submarine-launched ballistic missiles (SLBMs). Only the 10 newest missile submarines, some still to be built, all able to patrol far offshore, should be retained. But warheads would be limited to one on each of the 24 missiles aboard each of these Ohio-class submarines. Submarines and crews could be rotated to insure that six of the 10 submarines are always safe on sea patrol—about the same readiness level the United States now maintains.

Strategic nuclear bombers. The bomber brings commander and crew close to the target and into harm's way, where danger and admiration alike have dwelt since modern war began. These "slow," air-breathing aircraft need hours to reach their target, not the half hour that an intercontinental missile takes. Therefore, the decision to strike can be reconsidered and recalled for some time after takeoff, and airborne crews have time to exercise some judgment.

But in recent years, a compromise has been struck with the old image of heroic pilots penetrating deep into enemy territory: today's bombers may carry gravity bombs all the way in, or small ballistic ("stand-off") missiles to be launched from a few hundred miles away, or long-range cruise missiles that may not even require crossing an enemy border. The mix of bomber payloads can be chosen mission by mission. The new B-2 aircraft are acclaimed by their friends for their speed and low visibility to the waiting radars. But they have more than a few technical flaws that are not easily remedied, and they have a dauntingly high cost. Their "stealth" is not invisibility; radar will pick them up all the same, although at shorter range—perhaps half the usual early-warning distance.

START counting rules were written to favor the aircraft mode of delivery, since bombers were seen as unlikely first-strike weapons. But why augment a nuclear bomber force, vulnerable on the runways, expensive to keep aloft, and ungainly as a deterrent? Instead of building a fleet of expensive B-2s, the least costly and least provocative bombers—older B-52s armed with existing stand-off weapons—should be kept. No nuclear-armed "stealthy" B-2s and no advanced cruise missiles are needed in a rational force for the year 2000. A number of airborne nuclear warheads comparable to that of the other two legs of the triad would seem enough.

Tactical nuclear weapons, with smaller yields, were meant for battlefield use against combat forces or their forward support—airfields, bases, and transportation nodes as far away as a few hundred miles behind the lines. Whoever coined the cynical definition that a tactical nuclear weapon was one "intended to explode within Germany" was not far off the mark. The United States deployed these weapons in Europe as a symbol of its commitment to European defense. Interest in tactical nuclear weapons has declined sharply now that Germany has been reunited.

In September 1991, President Bush wisely ordered the elimination of nearly all U.S. sea or land-based tactical nuclear weapons. Only the carrier-borne attack bombers of longer range (mainly A-6 Intruders) were exempted; about 50 or fewer of these weapons remain on each active carrier, or about 600–700 in total. This floating ability to initiate nuclear war against even non-nuclear states far overseas is hardly tolerable, and it poses its own dangers. All these weapons should be set ashore and dismantled by the year 2000.

There is little military purpose for the nearly 1,000 nuclear gravity bombs the United States deploys in Europe. But there are diplomatic issues: France and Britain have comparable arms in similar numbers. Negotiations to end deployment of all tactical nuclear weapons in Europe should start at once, with our nuclear allies inviting Germany and states to the east to attend as acutely interested parties.

Pending allied agreement, U.S. nuclear deployments in Europe should be reduced—not to zero at once, but to about 250 gravity bombs on tactical aircraft, a number comparable to those our two nuclear-armed allies now hold. However, all the states involved are likely to agree on a nuclear-free Europe well before the end of the decade. Such an initiative would make a splendid contribution to the 1995 Review Conference on the Nuclear Non-Proliferation Treaty (NPT), damping the enthusiasm of nuclear-weapon aspirants who have long argued that they have been victimized by a double standard.

Although the nuclear forces proposed here for the year 2000 are far more modest than those envisioned by START II, they are still too large and ominous for long-term world safety. This is a cautious and conservative plan, one that recognizes that profound changes can come only slowly. Nevertheless, even though the ink has not yet cured on START II, the leaders of the nuclear club must proceed with further reductions.

Strategic defenses. A modest U.S. defense against intrusive bomber aircraft and stand-off cruise-missile carriers (but not against their missiles) is now assigned to 160 modern fighter-interceptors of the Air National Guard, joined by about 50 Canadian fighters. Jointly, they watch over the Arctic approaches where an automated radar net, North Warning System, is newly in service. A limited ballistic missile defense system is still planned, although such a system would be useless against terrorist attack. As unlikely as a terrorist attack may seem, it is surely more likely than an attack by intercontinental ballistic missiles.

The study of anti-missile systems should certainly continue, but without the large expenditures necessary for either development or procurement. The resources consumed by the Strategic Defense Initiative Office have been excessive; they should be cut to a pre-SDI level (about $1 billion for R&D) before the end of the century, unless conditions clearly change.

The elaborate and indispensable satellite systems in orbit that connect our forces, guide them, and warn of nuclear attack, are so thoroughly useful for conventional war that they should be discussed within that wider context.

Building bombs. The largest military expenditure of the United States missing from the Defense Department budget is the cost of building nuclear weapons,

or reworking old ones into new. Nuclear weapons research and testing are included among the military tasks assigned to the Energy Department. Details of the Energy Department's weapons budget are secret, but a rough estimate would put the department's long-term annual nuclear weapons costs at some $2 billion. (The bill for cleaning up the nuclear plants, however, will be high, and the work will have to continue for many years.) With more than 1,000 U.S. tests on record, continuing to test is more of an addiction than an essential activity.

Further, although the United States has declared that it will end all tests in 1996—that action is contingent on whether or not another power is testing. That's senseless. The United States already has such a staggering technological lead in nuclear weapons that no other nation would be remotely able to "catch up." But the signal that a resumption of U.S. tests would send to aspiring nuclear powers *would* be a real source of danger.

In 1993, the production of weapons and essential nuclear explosives, including tests and the reprocessing of nuclear fuel, will cost about $8 billion, spent in some 16 specialized plants (many of which are contaminated) in a dozen states. Three large Energy Department laboratories carry out design, development, engineering, and testing. Plainly, these activities will drop sharply, while disassembly of weapons for storage or disposal, conducted at the Pantex plant near Amarillo, Texas, will increase. Even now Pantex is working solely on disassembly; no new warheads are in production. Meticulous technical efforts are needed throughout this dangerous cycle.

By the end of the decade, the United States should neither develop nor produce nuclear weapons. Spent naval reactor fuel can be stored, just as the country stores much larger amounts of spent civilian fuel. The three bomb laboratories should be cut to two—Los Alamos and Sandia, both in New Mexico. The Lawrence Livermore National Laboratory in California might switch entirely to civilian work. The costs of various control, surveillance, and safety activities would remain.

AIR-LAND BATTLE

Ground forces. U.S. Army ground forces now stand at approximately 1.8 million men and women. The Defense Department plans to reduce the army from 16 divisions to 12 by 1995. (In wartime, U.S. army divisions measure 17,000 men and women, with a choice of ample supplementary units.) These numbers do not include Marine Corps divisions.

There is no real need to maintain such a large standing force. A sufficient force for the year 2000 would consist of a single full armored division, an airborne division, and six independent brigades with roughly 6,000 soldiers each, two with two main battle tank battalions each, and the others with a mix of lighter units. This force should include two armored cavalry regiments (faster, lighter armored units intended for easier mobility and reconnaissance). The present plan now deploys three such units. The slimmed-down force would deploy about 500 main battle tanks for Europe and a similar number for other theaters. An additional 1,000 would be kept in storage.

The United States needs a flexible, mobile, ground force equivalent to about four and a half divisions, with a heavy core at a little under two full armored

divisions. Under this plan, the active army would number about 180,000.

Air: Tactical forces. Tactical air strength should be cut in concert with the deep cuts in ground forces. But remaining U.S. airpower should not be proportionally reduced—the size, technical prowess, and superb training of American aviation continues to make a special contribution to the overall security of our allies.

The air force plans to deploy about 56 combat squadrons of fighter and ground-attack fixed-wing aircraft in 1993—or about 1,160 planes, if only "primary aircraft authorized" for these units are included. The present active strength of tactical combat aircraft supports an army of about 16 divisions. With ground forces cut by a factor of 3.5, the tactical air force should be reduced to about one-third the size of the current force. This force would consist of 18 squadrons armed with the newest aircraft types—stealthy F-117s, top-of-the-line F-15 and F-16 fighters, and the tough, battlefield-tested A-10.

SEA CONTROL

Of all U.S. military services, the navy now receives the largest share of the budget if only by a little. So much money is spent maintaining 14 active aircraft-carrier battle groups that a stringent reduction in that force alone would sharply reduce naval costs. The Defense Department projects that in 1995 the navy will still include 12 carrier battle groups—an amazing number. The surface support for carriers now includes six warships, mostly cruisers and frigates, for each carrier at sea. Instead, twelve anti-air and anti-ship missile cruisers (most nuclear-propelled, some the newer but smaller gas-turbine Ticonderoga class); and 18 of the newer anti-submarine destroyers (Spruance or newer) and frigates would furnish ample surface escort for five carriers. The surface ships in each battle group would be supplemented by two nuclear-power attack submarines.

The U.S. Navy needs to remain recognizably second to none, but it should not be larger than any two other forces combined. A U.S. fleet of 30 or more destroyers and frigates, in addition to the 18 assigned to carrier battle groups, would be ample. The surface fleet would include 12 cruisers, 50 destroyers and frigates, and five big carriers. The Defense Secretary's 1992 report projected a surface combat fleet of 145 ships in 1995, but 65 combat ships of the newest types would represent a cut comparable to that proposed for the army.

The auxiliaries needed to support blue water aircraft carriers are called Underway Replenishment Groups. Three such groups are needed with five specialized ships in each. Adding another 15 would still equal only half of the 60 combat support ships in the current Defense Department plan. Many other support ships fulfill a range of purposes farther from combat—tenders, floating dry docks, and hospital ships. The Defense Department plan sets the 1995 level for these support ships at 50, but a reduction to 30 may well be possible. New naval shipbuilding should all but end; by 2000 the navy should operate not the 420 active ships and submarines now planned, but about 160. (These figures exclude nuclear-armed strategic submarines.)

Naval air strength consists principally of carrier-borne combat wings. With five rather than 14 aircraft carriers, naval air strength should be reduced, although not in direct proportion to the carrier number. These powerful units can be based on land as well as at sea. But the 1993 tally of 620 active naval fighter and attack aircraft (56 carrier-borne combat squadrons) should be reduced to 18 squadrons, or about 210 planes.

The large, land-based force of long-range maritime patrol aircraft, aimed mostly against submarines, but used generally for surface surveillance on the high seas, should be retained near full strength in this world of surprises. About 250 active turboprop patrol planes (Orion P-3s) are available to survey the ocean, supplemented by counterpart patrols of maritime allies.

LAND-SEA INTERFACE

By tradition and origin the marines are an elite ship-borne force prepared to land on distant shores. But the Marine Corps has grown so large, with its own air force and relatively heavy weapons, that it is now one-fourth the size of the U.S. Army. Operations requiring quick, forcible entry on the multi-division scale seem unlikely; in "Desert Storm," a landing by two brigades was ostensibly prepared, but proved to be an offshore feint.

The marines' specialty is over-the-beach amphibious operations. One Marine Expeditionary Unit (MEU) numbers about 2,500 men and women, with 10 tanks and artillery batteries, half a dozen vertical-takeoff attack aircraft, and 30 helicopters. The marines now have a dozen or more helicopter and assault carriers, each able to carry and launch its aircraft, and to dispatch up to 2,000 troops and their armor at any beach. This force offers the flexible, speedy, small-scale response needed for the missions the future appears to hold for the marines—whether they are sent to intervene militarily or for humanitarian purposes, such as in "Operation Restore Hope" in Somalia.

This ability seems worth preserving. Even if entry by force becomes rare (as it should), marine forces should include up to a dozen distinct expeditionary units, which could be grouped if needed with some help from naval aircraft carriers and prepositioned ships. The Marine Corps would be reduced from a force of almost 200,000 to one augmented division and its air support, a force of about 50,000. This force would retain about 25 of 65 amphibious warfare ships, mainly new ones.

Two Marine Expeditionary Brigades— each with a half-dozen MEUs—would receive appropriate air support from 150 fixed-wing combat aircraft (including 40 of the service's unique vertical-takeoff Harrier jets), and a similar number of gunship and transport helicopters. These can be borne by helicopter carriers as well as by big carriers.

INTELLIGENCE AND SPACE CAPABILITIES

The costs of the key military function related to information-gathering of all kinds, including valuable hardware in orbit, are more or less secret. They are spread and split up so that no official budget figures are available. There are, of course, informal estimates, based on information as it is made publicly available. That is the basis for this proposal.

The largest single item is tactical intelligence—the reconnaissance aircraft, radio monitoring, and a dozen more organized activities that bring short-term battlefield information directly to combat forces. These activities could be reduced

more or less in concert with the reduction in the size of the forces themselves.

A similar sum is divided between the diverse military satellites and the signal-decrypting organization, the National Security Agency. Without an opportunity to examine the books, it seems prudent to limit budget cuts in this area in order to retain a strong global flow of hard information. Smaller intelligence agencies serve the uniformed services, the Defense Department itself, and other departments of government. These should be somewhat reduced. The celebrated CIA—estimated to cost about one-tenth of the present total—should be cut by half, in an effort to curtail doubtful covert operations everywhere.

The overall result is to decrease the total costs of intelligence, including space, from the estimated 1992 sum of $29 billion to $16 billion (in 1990 dollars) by the year 2000. All these items deserve study by an independent commission with access to the secret record. Serious consideration should be given to sharing intelligence and its costs with our allies and with the United Nations.

WEAPONS RESEARCH AND DEVELOPMENT

The research and development of new weapons, nuclear and conventional, have given the U.S. military an unsurpassed technological edge on the battlefield as well as an undoubted deterrence to nuclear aggression. In 1991, weapons research totaled $42 billion, consuming 60 percent of all federal R&D funds. Of this total, $37 billion, or 90 percent, went for development, testing, and evaluation of new weapons.

continued on p. 233

Table 1

Proposed U.S. Forces in the Year 2000

	Numerical strength	$ billions (1990 dollars)
Nuclear Deterrence	>1,000	15.7
Air-Land Battle		
Active divisions	5	14.0
(with 2,000 main battle tanks; 300 ground support aircraft; 700 combat helicopters)		
Reserve divisions	10	4.8
Fighter aircraft		
Active	400	8.0
Reserve	400	2.5
Sealift	(chartered)	
Land-Sea Interface		
Marines		
Active divisions	1	1.3
Reserve divisions	1	0.5
Aircraft	150	2.0
Amphibious ships	50	3.3
Airlift	500	5.0
Sea Control		
Carrier groups	5	15.0
(each with 1 aircraft carrier, 40 primary aircraft, 1 cruiser, 3 destroyers, 2 frigates, 2 attack submarines, 6 fast supply ships)		
Mine warfare ships	15	0.3
Anti-submarine warfare		
Attack submarines	40	4.9
P-3C patrol aircraft	260	2.6
Surface combatants	47	3.0
(7 cruisers, 40 frigates and destroyers)		
Auxiliary ships	50	1.2
Total combat forces		84.1
Intelligence & Space		16.0
Research, Development, Testing & Evaluation		15.0
TOTAL		115.0*

*Does not include $21 billion for military pensions.

Forty years of such investments have paid off. U.S. arms are now technologically superior overall to what an opponent could deploy a decade from now. The race to stay ahead can slow down. At $15 billion a year, a military R&D program would still equal the sum of all current civilian R&D programs, with the exception of the space program. This amount is still nearly 10 times the combined investment in military R&D of Germany and Japan. R&D money should be spent on the communications, electronic countermeasures, and surveillance-and-attack systems that will keep American arms immune to obsolescence; it should not be spent on unneeded weapons such as the V-22 Osprey tilt-rotor aircraft and the Seawolf submarine, the C-17 transport, or on new antisubmarine and early-warning systems or even on upgrades to existing advanced aircraft.

A SUFFICIENT FORCE

Now we come to the forces we propose for the year 2000, summarizing both their nature and annual outlays in billions of 1990 dollars (see table 1). These forces are adequate to undertake six or eight Somalia-like operations at the same time, or to mount a force somewhat larger than the American part of "Desert Storm." Broadly they would be more capable and more versatile than any other in the world, at a cost reduced from that of 1992 by about 60 percent, down to $115 billion.

* * *

We believe that Americans, along with the citizens of all other nations who live with some degree of comfort and safety, will have, step-by-step, to replace mutual fear with mutual aid, or enter into a fiercely unstable world. The task is surely long, but it is worthwhile. In a stable world most people, even the myriad poor—many in a wealthy United States—need to see some path that promises them safety, justice, and even well-being. Those few who will not accept the promise must encounter high barriers against violent international change, barriers that will be well guarded by the many.

We have perhaps five decades to nourish that outcome from our present world of bitter division and its implied conflicts. Certainly violent conflict will not disappear, nor will military forces, but both need to dwindle greatly in scale; the terrible weapons of mass destruction can sleep.

Great hope comes from one great fact: the economic, technical, and human resources now sequestered annually in the unproductive world of arms amount to the major part of a trillion dollars a year worldwide. In nature and size these resources are capable of bringing profound change to the lives of most of the world's people. Among those billions a working solution to our acute environmental and human problems rests not less (and with good judgment, not more) than one long lifetime ahead.

NO

Colin L. Powell

U.S. FORCES: CHALLENGES AHEAD

America is a remarkable nation. We are, as Abraham Lincoln told Congress in December 1862, a nation that "cannot escape history" because we are "the last best hope of earth." The president said that his administration and Congress held the "power and... responsibility" to ensure that the hope America promised would be fulfilled. Today, 130 years later, Lincoln's America is the sole superpower left on earth.

Often I wonder what Lincoln would think were he here to see us and to marvel at our strength. There are aspects that would make him shudder—the turmoil of our inner cities, our still unresolved racial inequalities, the rising crime and continued drug use—but on balance I believe he would be pleased. Democracy is the most powerful political force at work in the world today. Our values, our persistence, our determination helped bring about this situation. America is not perfect by any means, but the nation does offer its citizens the individual and collective opportunity to strive to be better.

America is still the last best hope of earth, and we still hold the power and bear the responsibility for its remaining so. This is an enormous power and a sobering responsibility, especially since America is no longer alone but is accompanied by a free world growing ever larger and more interconnected.

As chairman of the Joint Chiefs of Staff of the U.S. armed forces, I share the responsibility for America's security. I share it with the president and commander in chief, with the secretary of defense and with the magnificent men and women—volunteers all—of America's armed forces. In truth, we share it also with every citizen of the nation, for that is one of the unique aspects of America; while many other nations constantly lay claim to "peoples' armies," our nation actually has one.

America's armed forces are as much a part of the fabric of U.S. values—freedom, democracy, human dignity and the rule of law—as any other institutional, cultural or religious thread....

From Colin L. Powell, "U.S. Forces: Challenges Ahead," *Foreign Affairs,* vol. 72, no. 5 (Winter 1992/1993). Copyright © 1992 by The Council on Foreign Relations, Inc. Reprinted by permission of *Foreign Affairs.*

These wonderful young men and women of America's armed forces are crucial to the future of the nation and, ultimately, to the future of the world. The reasons are worth pondering.

OBLIGATED TO LEAD

No other nation on earth has the power we possess. More important, no other nation on earth has the trusted power that we possess. We are obligated to lead. If the free world is to harvest the hope and fulfill the promise that our great victory in the Cold War has offered us, America must shoulder the responsibility of its power. The last best hope of earth has no other choice. We must lead.

We cannot lead without our armed forces. Economic power is essential; political and diplomatic skills are needed; the power of our beliefs and our values is fundamental to any success we might achieve; but the presence of our arms to buttress these other elements of our power is as critical to us as the freedom we so adore. Our arms must be second to none.

Today our armed forces are second to none. Ninety-seven percent of our men and women are high school graduates as opposed to 77 percent in the nation at large. Minorities enjoy better opportunities in the military than anywhere else in America. Our young volunteers are the best and the brightest of the wide diversity that makes up America. And anyone who doubts our ability to wage war decisively needs only to look at our recent triumph in the Gulf War.

In 1989, because of dramatic changes looming over the horizon, we began looking at how to restructure these high-quality armed forces without doing harm to their excellence; in fact, we wanted to improve them even further. Only a fortune-teller could have predicted the specific changes that occurred—the fall of the Berlin Wall, the demise of the Warsaw Pact, the failed coup in the Soviet Union and the eventual disappearance of that empire. But in the Pentagon we did recognize the unmistakable signs of change—the kind that leaves in history's dust those who cling to the past....

President Bush saw this historic change. Working together with his advisers, the president and the secretary of defense outlined a new national security strategy. In the Pentagon we took the new national security strategy and built a military strategy to support it. Then, in August 1990, as President Bush made the first public announcement of America's new approach to national security, Saddam Hussein attacked Kuwait. His brutal aggression caused us to implement our new strategy even as we began publicizing it. Every American was able to see our strategy validated in war.

Today there are other Saddam Husseins in the world. There is one in North Korea, and there is the original still in the Middle East—and no reason to believe his successor would be any different. Moreover, the instability and uncertainty that always accompany the fall of empires are growing rather than diminishing. In the Pentagon we believe our military strategy fits the world we see developing like a tight leather glove.

In the fall of 1992 we are fine-tuning that strategy, restructuring our armed forces so that they are ideally suited to executing it, and proposing a much-reduced multiyear defense budget to pay for it all.

REGIONAL RATHER THAN GLOBAL CONFLICT

The new national military strategy is an unclassified document. Anyone can read it. It is short, to the point and unambiguous. The central idea in the strategy is the change from a focus on global warfighting to a focus on regional contingencies. No communist hordes threaten western Europe today and, by extension, the rest of the free world. So our new strategy emphasizes being able to deal with individual crises without their escalating to global or thermonuclear war.

Two and a half years ago, as we developed the new strategy, we saw the possibility of a major regional conflict in the Persian Gulf—and it turned out we were right—and a major regional conflict in the Pacific, perhaps on the Korean peninsula, where the Cold War lingers on. We knew then, and we know now, that prudent planning requires that we be able to deal simultaneously with two major crises of this type, however unlikely that might be. In our judgment, the best way to make sure their coincidence remained unlikely was to be ready to react to both, so that if we were involved in one, no one would tempt us into the other.

Moreover we can see more clearly today that danger has not disappeared from the world. All along the southeastern and southern borders of the old Soviet empire, from Moldova to Tajikistan, smoldering disputes and ethnic hatreds disrupt our post–Cold War reverie. In the Balkans such hatreds and centuries-old antagonisms have burst forth into a heart-wrenching civil war. The scenes from Sarajevo defy our idea of justice and human rights and give new meaning to the word "senseless." In Somalia, relief operations are underway amid the chaos and anarchy of another civil war that wracks our idea of justice, human rights and the rule of law. Ruthless warlords make money from donated food and medical supplies. Relief workers are threatened if they do not comply with a local dictator's whims.

We cannot tell where or when the next crisis will appear that will demand the use of our troops. . . . To deal with such a wide range of possibilities, our armed forces must be capable of accomplishing a wide range of missions.

FUTURE MISSIONS AND CLEAR OBJECTIVES

What sorts of missions can we envision? I believe peacekeeping and humanitarian operations are a given. Likewise our forward presence is a given—to signal our commitment to our allies and to give second thoughts to any disturber of peace. It is in the category of the use of "violent" force that views begin to differ.

Occasionally these differences in view have been categorized quite starkly as the "limited war" school and the "all-out war" school. For the man or woman in combat, however, such academic niceties are moot. . . . But while such distinctions as limited and all-out war mean little to a soldier who is clutching the ground while bullets whiz by his ears, they do serve to illuminate our debate.

All wars are limited. As [the nineteenth-century German military thinker] Carl von Clausewitz was careful to point out, there has never been a state of absolute war. Such a state would mean total annihilation. The Athenians at Melos, Attila the Hun, Tamerlane, the Romans salting the fields of the Carthaginians may have come close, but even their incredible ruthlessness gave way to pragmatism before a state of absolute war was achieved.

Wars are limited by three means: by the territory on which they are fought (as in Korean or Vietnam); by the means used to fight them (no nuclear weapons in Korea; no massive mobilization for Vietnam); or by the objectives for which they are fought—the most significant limitation in political terms and therefore the limitation that is most often discussed and debated.

Objectives for which we use "violent" force can range from hurting an enemy enough so that he or she ceases to do the thing that is endangering our interests (air strikes against Libya in 1986 to prevent further Libyan-sponsored terrorism), to unseating the enemy's government and altering fundamentally his or her way of life (World War II).

The Gulf War was a limited-objective war. If it had not been, we would be ruling Baghdad today—at unpardonable expense in terms of money, lives lost and ruined regional relationships. The Gulf War was also a limited-means war—we did not use every means at our disposal to eject the Iraqi Army from Kuwait. But we did use overwhelming force quickly and decisively. This, I believe, is why some have characterized that war as an "all-out" war. It was strictly speaking no such thing.

To help with the complex issue of the use of "violent" force, some have turned to a set of principles or a when-to-go-to-war doctrine. "Follow these directions and you can't go wrong." There is, however, no fixed set of rules for the use of military force. To set one up is dangerous....

When a "fire" starts that might require committing armed forces, we need to evaluate the circumstances. Relevant questions include: Is the political objective we seek to achieve important, clearly defined and understood? Have all other nonviolent policy means failed? Will military force achieve the objective? At what cost? Have the gains and risks been analyzed? How might the situation that we seek to alter, once it is altered by force, develop further and what might be the consequences?...

Over the past three years the U.S. armed forces have been used repeatedly to defend our interests and to achieve our political objectives. In Panama a dictator was removed from power. In the Philippines the use of limited force helped save a democracy. In Somalia a daring night raid rescued our embassy. In Liberia we rescued stranded international citizens and protected our embassy. In the Persian Gulf a nation was liberated. Moreover we have used our forces for humanitarian relief operations in Iraq, Somalia, Bangladesh, Russia and Bosnia....

Today American troops around the world are protecting the peace in Europe, the Persian Gulf, Korea, Cambodia, the Sinai and western Sahara. They have brought relief to Americans at home here in Florida, Hawaii and Guam. Ironically enough, the American people are getting a solid return on their defense investment even as from all corners of the nation come shouts for imprudent reductions that would gut their armed forces....

FUTURE MILITARY STRUCTURE

Because of the need to accomplish a wide range of missions, our new armed forces will be *capabilities* oriented as well as *threat* oriented. When we were confronted by an all-defining, single, overwhelming threat—the Soviet

Union—we could focus on that threat as the yardstick of our strategy, tactics, weapons and budget. The Soviet Union is gone. Replacing it is a world of promise and hope—exemplified by the former Soviets themselves as they struggle mightily to make a transformation that the world has never witnessed before. But the U.S.–Soviet standoff imposed a sort of bipolar lock on the world and, in many ways, held the world together. That lock has been removed. Now tectonic plates shift beneath us, causing instability in a dozen different places.

In a few cases, such as Korea and southwest Asia, we can point to particular threats with some degree of certainty; otherwise, we cannot be exact. Most of us anticipated very few of the more than a dozen crises our armed forces have confronted in the past three years. That will not change. We must be ready to meet whatever threats to our interests may arise. We must concentrate on the capabilities of our armed forces to meet a host of threats and not on a single threat. This is a very different orientation. It is so different that some of us have trouble adapting to it; we are so accustomed to the past. Indeed most of our lives were dedicated to the old way of thinking. But in the Department of Defense I believe we have made great progress in changing to this new emphasis on capabilities as well as threats.

Conceptually we refer to our new capabilities-oriented armed forces as "the Base Force." This concept provides for military forces focused on the Atlantic region, the Pacific region, contingencies in other regions and on continued nuclear deterrence.

Across the Atlantic—in Europe, the Mediterranean and the Middle East— America continues to have vital interests.

We belong to the most effective alliance in history, NATO [North Atlantic Treaty Organization]. In light of the changes that have taken place in Europe, NATO has revamped its strategic outlook and restructured its forces as dramatically as we have our own.

One of the key features of NATO's changed posture is its new focus on the east. For over forty years NATO underwrote the security and prosperity of western Europe. Now it is time for NATO to underwrite the security and prosperity of the east. This may be the most important post–Cold War task we undertake.

America cannot accomplish this task without active participation in NATO. U.S. ground troops in Europe are still vital. Although far fewer troops will be necessary, now that the Warsaw Pact has dissolved, America needs enough troops to meet its commitments. This "enough" will be debated hotly in the months to come. Proposals range from 75,000 to 150,000. But I believe our political leaders understand that the debate is about the numbers and not the presence.

In 1990 we deployed massive U.S. forces to the Persian Gulf. Using those forces in 1991 we fought an overwhelmingly decisive war. We did this to liberate Kuwait and to strip a regional tyrant of his capacity to wage offensive war and thus destabilize the region. With two-thirds of the world's oil reserves in the region, this action was certainly in our vital interest.

Nothing has changed about the importance of the Middle East. What has changed is that Kuwait is free, oil is flowing and Saddam Hussein threatens no one outside his own borders. A U.S. military presence is crucial to ensuring that this stability continues.

American forces in the Atlantic region—on land and at sea—are part of our conceptual package of Atlantic forces. Also part of that package are forces based in the United States whose orientation is toward the Atlantic; should a crisis in the region demand more forces than we have forward-deployed, these forces would reinforce them as rapidly as possible.

In our Base Force we have provided for the same sort of conceptual force package focused on the Pacific region. There too America continues to have vital interests, our security relationships with Japan and the Republic of Korea being at the top of the list.

We have also provided for what we call a "contingency force package." Troops and units in this conceptual package will be located in the United States and be ready to go at a moment's notice. The time from their alert to their movement will be measured in hours and minutes, not in days.

Finally, we provided for a conceptual package of strategic nuclear forces. Notwithstanding the historic reductions proposed for the world's strategic nuclear stockpile, when and if these reductions are complete, we will still have nuclear weapons in the world. We must continue to deter the use of these weapons against America or its friends and allies. This can only be done with a modern, capable and ready nuclear force. We will rely heavily on the most secure leg of our nuclear triad, the ballistic missile submarines. But we will maintain a resilient and capable triad with forces in the other two legs as well, manned bombers and land-based ballistic missiles.

Our Base Force is dynamic. There is nothing sacrosanct about its number of tanks, ships or missiles, its structure or its manpower. We can decrease or increase weapons numbers; we can add or delete structure, and we can mobilize manpower—all depending on how our interests evolve and what threats to those interests develop over time. But as we develop our Base Force, we must avoid making two serious mistakes. First, our military must not become "hollow" as it was in the early 1970s. A hollow force has lots of structure—divisions, squadrons, ships—but no trained manpower to fight in them. In other words we pay for weapons, equipment, ships and aircraft with the money we would have used for our people. If we do this, maintaining the high-quality force we now have will be impossible. Second, we must not go too far, too fast. This is the easiest mistake to make and, therefore, the one that troubles me most.

In the last three fiscal years America has already released 431,000 people from active duty and civilian rolls. This has caused a direct loss of 400,000 jobs in related defense industries across the nation. Stunningly it has also cost the loss of almost 800,000 jobs in the nondefense sector. In sum, we have released into an already severely challenged job market over 1.6 million people. Couple this economic cost with the absolute certainty that accelerated reduction rates will destroy the high morale of our armed forces, and it becomes easy to understand my deep concern. Neither [Bush administration] Secretary of Defense Dick Cheney nor I want a future president to turn tc the armed forces and discover that they are unready for action. I firmly believe the American people are of the same mind.

If we proceed prudently along the path mapped out by the Department of Defense, we will make neither of these mistakes, we will not become a hollow force and we will not break the force while making worse an already weakened economy. In the exciting but still dangerous days that lie ahead, presidents, Congresses and the American people will be able to count on their armed forces for whatever task they want them to accomplish.

A FOURTH RENDEZVOUS WITH DESTINY

Today, unlike that December day in 1862 when President Lincoln spoke to Congress, the prospects for America are anything but bleak. It is true we have substantial economic challenges facing us, as well as a burning need to reaffirm some of our basic values and beliefs. But if Lincoln were alive today, I do not believe he would trade December 1992 for December 1862.

I believe Mr. Lincoln would be especially excited by the prospects that now lie before his nation. Only three times in our history have we had a "rendezvous with destiny," as President Franklin D. Roosevelt called our challenge in World War II. The American Revolution was one such historical moment because it gave birth to America. The Civil War was another because it made our revolution complete; it made America what it is today. World War II, as Roosevelt so clearly recognized, and the Cold War that followed—which he could not see—combined to provide us the third such occasion. These two wars cleansed the world of tyrannies bent on hegemony and began the spread of democracy and free markets and, as the Soviet Union finally disappeared, accelerated their spread at a dizzying rate.

The summons to leadership that we face at present is our fourth rendezvous with destiny. Answering this summons does not mean peace, prosperity, justice for all and no more wars in the world—any more than the American Revolution meant all people were free, the Civil War meant an end to racial inequality, or World War II and our great victory in the Cold War meant the triumph of democracy and free markets. What our leadership in the world does mean is that these things have a chance. We can have peace. We can continue moving toward greater prosperity for all. We can strive for justice in the world. We can seek to limit the destruction and the casualties of war. We can help enslaved people find their freedom. This is our fourth rendezvous with destiny: to lead the world at a time of immense opportunity—an opportunity never seen in the world before. As Lincoln said in 1862, America could not escape history. In 1992, we must not let history escape us.

POSTSCRIPT

Is It Possible to Drastically Reduce Defense Expenditures and Remain Secure?

Defense planning is one of the toughest of all policy-making areas. If you make a mistake in domestic policy, it can hurt you; if you make an error in defense policy, it can kill you. One factor that makes defense planning difficult is the fact that there are disputes about how military spending fits in with national priorities. Some people argue that the first duty of government is to protect citizens' lives. From this perspective it follows that defense needs should be handled first (along with internal security, such as the police), and funds should be allocated to meet those needs before money is spent on other programs. Other people argue that national security is just one of many needs and that military funding has to give way to appropriations for domestic programs. A related argument, which is one especially associated with feminist thought, is that male political leaders all too often define security in terms of security from physical attack, whereas security from hunger, disease, and other deprivations are also part of maintaining life.

Domestic economic circumstances present another conundrum. Few dispute the reality that defense spending cuts create unemployment and other forms of short-term economic dislocation. There are many, however, who argue that shifting spending from military to civilian production will, in the long run, be beneficial. Defense proponents reply that such figures are, at best, highly debatable. For a recent study of the evidence, see Steve Chan and Alex Mintz, eds., *Defense, Welfare and Growth: Perspectives and Evidence* (Routledge, 1992).

Another complication in defense planning is that the future is unclear. Yes, the cold war is over. And, yes, Russia represents little threat for now. Yet it is also the case that a new, peaceful world order has not arrived and that perils persist and may proliferate in the future.

For an illustrative argument that countries could safely get rid of all their ballistic (long-range) missiles, see Alton Frye, "Zero Ballistic Missiles," *Foreign Policy* (Fall 1992). The idea of drastic reductions are considered in Gene Sharp, *Civilian-Based Defense: A Post-Military Weapons System* (Princeton University Press, 1991). Such advocacy for dramatic reductions is disputed by Colin S. Gray in *House of Cards: Why Arms Control Must Fail* (Cornell University Press, 1992).

ISSUE 14

Should the United Nations Take on Greater Military Capabilities and Roles?

YES: Boutros Boutros-Ghali, from *An Agenda for Peace: Preventive Diplomacy, Peacemaking and Peacekeeping* (United Nations, 1992)

NO: Jeffrey R. Gerlach, from "A U.N. Army for the New World Order?" *Orbis: A Journal of World Affairs* (Spring 1993)

ISSUE SUMMARY

YES: United Nations Secretary General Boutros Boutros-Ghali contends that both the scope of the United Nation's security mission and the extent of the UN's military capabilities should be expanded significantly in the interest of world peace.

NO: Jeffrey R. Gerlach, a foreign policy analyst at the Cato Institute in Washington, D.C., criticizes the recommendations of Boutros-Ghali on several grounds. Gerlach is concerned that such expansion would lead to the United Nations imposing its "international collectivist" will on others, especially small, Third World countries.

More than any single purpose, the United Nations was established with the hope that it could help save "succeeding generations from the scourge of war which ... has brought untold sorrow to mankind." These opening words of the UN Charter reflect a realization born of World War I, World War II, and the advent of the atomic age, that, whatever the horrendous past toll of warfare, the future cost could be far, far worse.

The UN seeks to maintain and restore peace through a variety of methods. These include creating norms against violence, providing a forum to debate questions as an alternative to war, efforts to prevent the proliferation of weapons, diplomatic intervention (such as mediation), and the establishment of diplomatic and economic sanctions. Additionally, and at the heart of the issue here, the UN can dispatch troops under its banner or authorize member countries to use their forces to carry out UN mandates.

United Nations forces involving a substantial number of military or police personnel have been used more than two dozen times in the organization's nearly half-century history, and have involved troops and police from more than 75 countries. UN forces have helped maintain or restore the peace in many locations; almost 900 blue-helmeted UN soldiers have died in the quest of international peace, and UN forces received the Nobel Peace Prize in 1988. Nevertheless, recent events and changes in attitudes have renewed the debate over the military role of the UN.

Of all UN operations, about half are currently active. Several of these, including the UN presence in Bosnia-Herzegovina, Cambodia, and Somalia, involve large numbers of troops and collectively cost approximately $2 billion annually. Often UN forces have played an important part in the peace process; other times they have been unsuccessful. The limited mandate and strength of UN forces have frequently left them as helpless as any bystanders, unable to stop the slaughter in Bosnia-Herzegovina, for example. The change in the international system has also added to the controversy over the UN's role. The cold war has ended; some people hope for and are trying to promote a new world order (see Issue 1). What this means is that collective action under UN auspices is becoming more acceptable, unilateral action by a country more the exception.

There are several provisions in the UN Charter that are especially important to understanding how the troops are used and some of the points that are debated in the following selections. All UN members that have signed the Charter agree to act in accordance with Article 2: "to fulfill . . . the obligations assumed by them in accordance with the present Charter." Article 24 gives the Security Council "primary responsibility for the maintenance of international peace and security." Then Article 42 says that the Council may take "action by air, sea, or land forces as necessary to maintain or restore international peace and security . . . [using the] forces of Members of the United Nations [to do so]." This raises the question of whether or not the dispatch of a country's forces to a UN operation is mandatory.

The immediate debate in this issue was touched of by a summit meeting of the leaders of the 15 countries with seats on the Security Council in January 1992. The leaders called on the UN secretary-general to report on ways to enhance UN ability "for preventative diplomacy, for peacemaking, and for peacekeeping." The response of Secretary-General Boutros Boutros-Ghali is the first of the two articles that follow. In it, Boutros-Ghali makes far-reaching recommendations to strengthen and expand the UN's role in promoting, maintaining, and restoring peace. Jeffrey Gerlach, in the second article, argues that the secretary-general's recommendations are mostly ill-conceived and should not be supported.

YES

Boutros Boutros-Ghali

AN AGENDA FOR PEACE: PREVENTIVE DIPLOMACY, PEACEMAKING AND PEACEKEEPING

INTRODUCTION

In its statement of 31 January 1992, adopted at the conclusion of the first meeting held by the Security Council at the level of Heads of State and Government, I was invited to prepare, for circulation to the Members of the United Nations by 1 July 1992, an "analysis and recommendations on ways of strengthening and making more efficient, within the framework and provisions of the Charter, the capacity of the United Nations for preventive diplomacy, for peacemaking and for peacekeeping."

The United Nations is a gathering of sovereign States and what it can do depends on the common ground that they create between them. The adversarial decades of the Cold War made the original promise of the Organization impossible to fulfill. The January 1992 Summit therefore represented an unprecedented recommitment, at the highest political level, to the Purposes and Principles of the Charter.

In these past months a conviction has grown, among nations large and small, that an opportunity has been regained to achieve [one of] the great objectives of the Charter—a United Nations capable of maintaining international peace and security.... This opportunity must not be squandered. The Organization must never again be crippled as it was in the era that has now passed.

I welcome the invitation of the Security Council, ... to prepare this report. It draws upon ideas and proposals transmitted to me by Governments, regional agencies, nongovernmental organizations, and institutions and individuals from many countries.... [But] the responsibility for this report is my own.

The sources of conflict and war are pervasive and deep. To reach them will require our utmost effort to enhance respect for human rights and fundamental freedoms, to promote sustainable economic and social development for wider prosperity, to alleviate distress and to curtail the existence and use of massively destructive weapons.... I bear them all in mind as, in the present report, I turn to the problems that the Council has specifically requested I consider: preventive diplomacy, peacemaking and peacekeeping—to which I have added a closely related concept, post-conflict peace-building.

The manifest desire of the membership to work together is a new source of strength in our common endeavor. Success is far from certain, however. While my report deals with ways to improve the Organization's capacity to pursue and preserve peace, it is crucial for all Member States to bear in mind that the search for improved mechanisms and techniques will be of little significance unless this new spirit of commonality is propelled by the will to take the hard decisions demanded by this time of opportunity....

THE CHANGING CONTEXT

In the course of the past few years the immense ideological barrier that for decades gave rise to distrust and hostility—and the terrible tools of destruction that were their inseparable companions—has collapsed. Even as the issues between States north and south grow more acute, and call for attention at the highest levels of government, the improvement in relations between States east and west affords new possibilities, some already realized, to meet successfully threats to common security.

Authoritarian regimes have given way to more democratic forces and responsive Governments. The form, scope and intensity of these processes differ from Latin America to Africa to Europe to Asia, but they are sufficiently similar to indicate a global phenomenon. Parallel to these political changes, many States are seeking more open forms of economic policy, creating a worldwide sense of dynamism and movement.

To the hundreds of millions who gained their independence in the surge of decolonization following the creation of the United Nations, have been added millions more who have recently gained freedom. Once again new States are taking their seats in the General Assembly. Their arrival reconfirms the importance and indispensability of the sovereign State as the fundamental entity of the international community.

We have entered a time of global transition marked by uniquely contradictory trends. Regional and continental associations of States are evolving ways to deepen cooperation and ease some of the contentious characteristics of sovereign and nationalistic rivalries. National boundaries are blurred by advanced communications and global commerce.... At the same time, however, fierce new assertions of nationalism and sovereignty spring up, and the cohesion of States is threatened by brutal ethnic, religious, social, cultural or linguistic strife....

The concept of peace is easy to grasp; that of international security is more complex, for a pattern of contradictions has arisen here as well. As major nuclear Powers have begun to negotiate arms reduction agreements, the proliferation of weapons of mass destruction threatens to increase and conventional arms continue to be amassed in many parts of the world. As racism becomes recognized for the destructive force it is and as apartheid is being dismantled, new racial tensions are rising and finding expression in violence.

Technological advances are altering the nature and the expectation of life all over the globe. The revolution in communications has united the world in awareness, in aspiration and in greater solidarity against injustice. But progress also brings new risks for stability: ecological damage, disruption of family and community life, greater intrusion into the lives and rights of individuals....

So at this moment of renewed opportunity, the efforts of the Organization to build peace, stability and security must encompass matters beyond military threats in order to break the fetters of strife and warfare that have characterized the past. But armed conflicts today, as they have throughout history, continue to bring fear and horror to humanity, requiring our urgent involvement to try to prevent, contain and bring them to an end.

Since the creation of the United Nations in 1945, over 100 major conflicts around the world have left some 20 million dead. The United Nations was rendered powerless to deal with many of these crises because of the vetoes—279 of them—cast in the Security Council, which were a vivid expression of the divisions of that period.

With the end of the Cold War there have been no such vetoes since 31 May 1990,* and demands on the United Nations have surged. Its security arm, once disabled by circumstances it was not created or equipped to control, has emerged as a central instrument for the prevention and resolution of conflicts and for the preservation of peace. Our aims must be:

- To seek to identify at the earliest possible stage situations that could produce conflict, and to try through diplomacy to remove the sources of danger before violence results;
- Where conflict erupts, to engage in peacemaking aimed at resolving the issues that have led to conflict;
- Through peacekeeping, to work to preserve peace, however fragile, where fighting has been halted and to assist in implementing agreements achieved by the peacemakers;
- To stand ready to assist in peacebuilding in its differing contexts: rebuilding the institutions and infrastructures of nations torn by civil war and strife; and building bonds of peaceful mutual benefit among nations formerly at war;
- And in the largest sense, to address the deepest causes of conflict: economic despair, social injustice and political oppression....

The Security Council has been assigned by all Member States the primary responsibility for the maintenance of international peace and security under the Charter. In its broadest sense this responsibility must be shared by the General Assembly and by all the functional elements of the world Organization....

The foundation-stone of this work is and must remain the State. Respect for its fundamental sovereignty and integrity are crucial to any common international progress. The time of absolute and exclusive sovereignty, however, has passed; its theory was never matched by reality.... The United Nations has not closed its door. Yet if every ethnic, religious or linguistic group claimed statehood, there would be no limit to fragmentation, and peace, security and economic well-being for all would become ever more difficult to achieve.

---

* [This has now changed.—Ed.]

One requirement for solutions to these problems lies in commitment to human rights with a special sensitivity to those of minorities, whether ethnic, religious, social or linguistic.... The General Assembly soon will have before it a declaration on the rights of minorities. That instrument, together with the increasingly effective machinery of the United Nations dealing with human rights, should enhance the situation of minorities as well as the stability of States.

... The sovereignty, territorial integrity and independence of States within the established international system, and the principle of self-determination for peoples, both of great value and importance, must not be permitted to work against each other in the period ahead.... Our constant duty should be to maintain the integrity of each while finding a balanced design for all.

DEFINITIONS

The terms preventive diplomacy, peacemaking and peacekeeping are integrally related and as used in this report are defined as follows:

Preventive diplomacy is action to prevent disputes from arising between parties, to prevent existing disputes from escalating into conflicts and to limit the spread of the latter when they occur.

Peacemaking is action to bring hostile parties to agreement, essentially through such peaceful means as those foreseen in Chapter VI of the Charter of the United Nations.

Peacekeeping is the deployment of a United Nations presence in the field, hitherto with the consent of all the parties concerned, normally involving United Nations military and/or policy personnel and frequently civilians as well.

Peacekeeping is a technique that expands the possibilities for both the prevention of conflict and the making of peace.

The present report in addition will address the critically related concept of post-conflict peace-building—action to identify and support structures which will tend to strengthen and solidify peace in order to avoid a relapse into conflict....

These four areas for action, taken together, and carried out with the backing of all Members, offer a coherent contribution towards securing peace in the spirit of the Charter. The United Nations has extensive experience not only in these fields, but in the wider realm of work for peace in which these four fields are set.... The world has often been rent by conflict and plagued by massive human suffering and deprivation. Yet it would have been far more so without the continuing efforts of the United Nations. This wide experience must be taken into account in assessing the potential of the United Nations in maintaining international security not only in its traditional sense, but in the new dimensions presented by the era ahead.

PREVENTIVE DIPLOMACY

The most desirable and efficient employment of diplomacy is to ease tensions before they result in conflict—or, if conflict breaks out, to act swiftly to contain it and resolve its underlying causes. Preventive diplomacy may be performed by the Secretary-General personally or through senior staff or specialized agencies and programs, by the Security Council or the General Assembly, and by regional organizations in cooperation with the United Nations. Preventive diplomacy requires measures to create confidence; it needs early warning based on information gathering and informal or formal fact-finding; it may also involve preventive deployment and, in some situations, demilitarized zones....

Preventive Deployment

United Nations operations in areas of crisis have generally been established after conflict has occurred. The time has come to plan for circumstances warranting preventive deployment [of UN forces], which could take place in a variety of instances and ways. For example, in conditions of national crisis there could be preventive deployment at the request of the Government or all parties concerned, or with their consent; in inter-State disputes such deployment could take place when two countries feel that a United Nations presence on both sides of their border can discourage hostilities; furthermore, preventive deployment could take place when a country feels threatened and requests the deployment of an appropriate United Nations presence along its side of the border alone. In each situation, the mandate and composition of the United Nations presence would need to be carefully devised and be clear to all.

In conditions of crisis within a country, when the Government requests all parties consent, preventive deployment could help in a number of ways to alleviate suffering and to limit or control violence. Humanitarian assistance, impartially provided, could be critical importance; assistance in maintaining security, whether through military, police or civilian personnel, could save lives and develop conditions of safety in which negotiations can be held....

In these situations of internal crisis the United Nations will need to respect the sovereignty of the State; to do otherwise would not be in accordance with the understanding of Member States in accepting the principles of the Charter.... In this context, humanitarian assistance should be provided with the consent of the affected country and, in principle, on the basis of an appeal by that country....

In inter-State disputes, when both parties agree, I recommend that if the Security Council concludes that the likelihood of hostilities between neighboring countries could be removed by the preventive deployment of a United Nations presence on the territory of each State, such action should be taken....

In cases where one nation fears a cross-border attack, if the Security Council concludes that a United Nations presence on one side of the border, with the consent only of the requesting economy, would serve to deter conflict, I recommend that preventive deployment take place....

Demilitarized Zones

In the past, demilitarized zones have been established by agreement of the parties at the conclusion of a conflict. In addition to the deployment of United Nations personnel is such zones as part of peacekeeping operations, consideration should now be given to the usefulness of such zones as a form of preventive deployment, on both sides of a border, with the agreement of the two parties, as a means of separating potential belligerents, or on one side of the line, at the request of one party, for the purpose of removing any pretext for attack. Demilitarized zones would serve as symbols of the international community's concern that conflict be prevented.

PEACEMAKING

Between the tasks of seeking to prevent conflict and keeping the peace lies the responsibility to try to bring hostile parties to agreement by peaceful means. Chapter VI of the Charter sets forth a comprehensive list of such means for the resolution of conflict. These have been amplified in various declarations.... The United Nations has had wide experience in the application of these peaceful means. If conflicts have gone unresolved, it is not because techniques [for a] peaceful settlement were unknown or inadequate. The fault lies first in the lack of political will of parties to seek a solution to their differences through such means as are suggested in the Charter, and second, in the lack of leverage at the disposal of a third party if this is the procedure chosen. The indifference of the internal community to a problem, or the marginalization of it, can also thwart the possibilities of solution. We must look primarily to these areas if we hope to enhance the capacity of the Organization in achieving peaceful settlements....

Use of Military Force

It is the essence of the concept of collective security as contained in the Charter that if peaceful means fail, the measures provided in Chapter VII should be used, on the decision of the Security Council, to maintain or restore international peace and security in the face of a "threat to the peace, breach of the peace, or act of aggression." The Security Council has not so far made use of the most coercive of these measures—the action by military forces foreseen in Article 42. In the situation between Iraq and Kuwait, the Council chose to authorize Member States to take measures on its behalf. The Charter, however, provides a detailed approach which now merits the attention of all Member States.

Under Article 42 of the Charter, the Security Council has the authority to take military action to maintain or restore international peace and security. While such action should only be taken when all peaceful means have failed, the option of taking it is essential to the credibility of the United Nations as a guarantor of international security. This will require bringing into being, through negotiations, the special agreements foreseen in Article 43 of the Charter, whereby Member States undertake to make armed forces, assistance and facilities available to the Security Council for the purposes stated in Article 42, not only on an ad hoc basis but on a permanent basis. Under the political circumstances that now exist for the first time since the Charter was adopted, the long-standing obstacles to the conclusion of such special agreements should no longer prevail. The ready availability of armed forces on call could serve, in itself, as a means of deterring breaches of the peace since a potential aggressor would know that the Council had at its disposal a means of response. Forces under Article 43 may perhaps never be sufficiently large or well enough equipped to deal with a threat from a major army equipped with sophisticated weapons. They would be useful, however, in meeting any threat posed by a military force of a lesser order. I recommend that the Security Council initiate negotiations in accordance with Article 43, supported by the Military Staff Committee, which may be augmented if necessary by others in accordance with Article 47, paragraph 2, of the Charter. It is my view that the role of the Military Staff Committee should be seen in the context of Chapter VII, and not that of the planning or conduct of peacekeeping operations.

Peace-Enforcement Units

The mission of forces under Article 43 would be to respond to outright aggression, imminent or actual. Such forces are not likely to be available for some time to come. Cease-fires have often been agreed to but not complied with, and the United Nations has sometimes been called upon to send forces to restore and maintain the cease-fire. This task can on occasion exceed the mission of peacekeeping forces and the expectations of peacekeeping force contributors. I recommend that the Council consider the utilization of peace-enforcement units in clearly defined circumstances and with their terms of reference specified in advance. Such units from Member States would be available on call and would consist of troops that have volunteered for such service. They would have to be more heavily armed than peacekeeping forces and would need to undergo extensive preparatory training within their national forces. Deployment and operation of such forces would be under the authorization of the Security Council and would, as in the case of peacekeeping forces, be under the command of the Secretary-General. I consider such peace-enforcement units to be warranted as a provisional measure under Article 40 of the Charter. Such peace-enforcement units should not be confused with the forces that may eventually be constituted under Article 43 to deal with acts of aggression or with the military personnel which Governments may agree to keep on standby for possible contribution to peacekeeping operations.

Just as diplomacy will continue across the span of all the activities dealt with in the present report, so there may not be a dividing line between peacemaking and peacekeeping. Peacemaking is often a prelude to peacekeeping—just as the deployment of a United Nations presence in the field may expand possibilities for the prevention of conflict, facilitate the work of peacemaking and in many cases serve as a prerequisite for peace-building.

PEACEKEEPING

Peacekeeping can rightly be called the invention of the United Nations. It has brought a degree of stability to numerous areas of tension around the world.

Increasing Demands

Thirteen peacekeeping operations were established between the years 1945 and 1987; 13 others since then. An estimated 528,000 military, police and civilian personnel had served under the flag of the United Nations until January 1992. Over 800 of them from 43 countries have died in the service of the Organization. The costs of these operations have aggregated some $8.3 billion till 1992. The unpaid arrears towards them stand at over $800 million, which represent a debt owed by the Organization to the troop-contributing countries. Peacekeeping operations approved at present are estimated to cost close to $3 billion in the current 12-month period, while patterns of payment are unacceptably slow. Against this, global defense expenditures at the end of the last decade had approached $1 trillion a year, or $2 million per minute.

The contrast between the costs of United Nations peacekeeping and the costs of the alternative, war—between the demands of the Organization and the means provided to meet them—would be farcical were the consequences not so damaging to global stability and to the credibility of the Organization. At a time when nations and peoples increasingly are looking to the United Nations for assistance in keeping the peace—and holding it responsible when this cannot be so—fundamental decisions must be taken to enhance the capacity of the Organization in this innovative and productive exercise of its function. I am conscious that the present volume and unpredictability of peacekeeping assessments poses real problems for some Member States. For this reason, I strongly support proposals in some Member States for their peacekeeping contributions to be financed from [countries' national] defense, rather than foreign affairs, budgets and I recommend such action to others....

New Departures in Peacekeeping

The nature of peacekeeping operations has evolved rapidly in recent years. The established principles and practices of peacekeeping have responded flexibly to new demands of recent years, and the basic conditions for success remain unchanged: a clear and practicable mandate; the cooperation of the parties in implementing that mandate; the continuing support of the Security Council; the readiness of Member States to contribute the military, police and civilian personnel, including specialists, required; effective United Nations command at Headquarters and in the field; and adequate financial and logistic support. As the international climate has changed and peacekeeping operations are increasingly fielded to help implement settlements that have been negotiated by

peacemakers, a new array of demands and problems has emerged regarding logistics, equipment, personnel and finance, all of which could be corrected if Member States so wished and were ready to make the necessary resources available.

Personnel

Member States are keen to participate in peacekeeping operations. Military observers and infantry are invariably available in the required numbers, but logistic units present a greater problem, as few armies can afford to spare such units for an extended period. Member States were requested in 1990 to state what military personnel they were in principle prepared to make available; few replied. I reiterate that request to all Member States to reply frankly and promptly. Standby arrangements should be confirmed, ... concerning the kind and number of skilled personnel they will be prepared to offer the United Nations as the needs of new operations arise.

Increasingly, peacekeeping requires that civilian political officers, human rights monitors, electoral officials, refugee and humanitarian aid specialists and police play as central a role as the military. Police personnel have proved increasingly difficult to obtain in the numbers required. I recommend that arrangements be reviewed and improved for training peacekeeping personnel—civilian, police, or military—using the varied capabilities of Member State Governments, or nongovernmental organizations and the facilities of the Secretariat....

Logistics

Not all Governments can provide their battalions with the equipment they need for service abroad. While some equipment is provided by troop-contributing countries, a great deal has to come from the United Nations, including equipment to fill gaps in underequipped national units. The United Nations has no standing stock of such equipment. Orders must be placed with manufacturers, which creates a number of difficulties. A pre-positioned stock of basic peacekeeping equipment should be established, so that at least some vehicles, communications equipment, generators, etc. would be immediately available at the start of an operation. Alternatively, Governments should commit themselves to keeping certain equipment, specified by the Secretary-General, on standby for immediate sale, loan or donation to the United Nations when required.

Member States in a position to do so should make air- and sea-lift capacity available to the United Nations free of cost or at lower than commercial rates, as was the practice until recently.

POST-CONFLICT PEACE-BUILDING

Peacemaking and peacekeeping operations, to be truly successful, must come to include comprehensive efforts to identify and support structures which will tend to consolidate peace and advance a sense of confidence and well-being among people. Through agreements ending civil strife, these may include disarming the previously warring parties and the restoration of order, the custody and possible destruction of weapons, repatriating refugees, advisory and training support for security personnel, monitoring elections, advancing efforts to protect human rights, reforming or strengthening governmental institutions

and promoting formal and informal processes of political participation....

COOPERATION WITH REGIONAL ARRANGEMENTS AND ORGANIZATIONS

The Covenant of the League of Nations, in its Article 21, noted the validity of regional understandings for securing the maintenance of peace. The Charter devotes Chapter VIII to regional arrangements or agencies for dealing with such matters relating to the maintenance of international peace and security as are appropriate for regional action and consistent with the Purposes and Principles of the United Nations. The cold war impaired the proper use of Chapter VIII and indeed, in that era, regional arrangements worked on occasion against resolving disputes in the manner foreseen in the Charter....

SAFETY OF PERSONNEL

When United Nations personnel are deployed in conditions of strife, whether for preventive diplomacy, peacemaking, peacekeeping, peace-building or humanitarian purposes, the need arises to ensure their safety. There has been an unconscionable increase in the number of fatalities. Following the conclusion of a cease-fire and in order to prevent further outbreaks of violence, United Nations guards were called upon to assist in volatile conditions in Iraq. Their presence afforded a measure of security to United Nations personnel and supplies and, in addition, introduced an element of reassurance and stability that helped to prevent renewed conflict. Depending upon the nature of the situation, different configurations and compositions of security deployments will need to be considered. As the variety and scale of threat widens, innovative measures will be required to deal with the dangers facing United Nations personnel.

Experience has demonstrated that the presence of a United Nations operation has not always been sufficient to deter hostile action. Duty in areas of danger can never be risk-free; United Nations personnel must expect to go in harm's way at times. The courage, commitment and idealism shown by United Nations personnel should be respected by the entire international community. These men and women deserve to be properly recognized and rewarded for the perilous tasks they undertake. Their interests and those of their families must be given due regard and protected.

Given the pressing need to afford adequate protection to United Nations personnel engaged in life-endangering circumstances, I recommend that the Security Council, unless it elects immediately to withdraw the United Nations presence in order to preserve the credibility of the Organization, gravely consider what action should be taken towards those who put United Nations personnel in danger. Before deployment takes place, the Council should keep open the option of considering in advance collective measures, possibly including those under Chapter VII when a threat to international peace and security is also involved, to come into effect should the purpose of the United Nations operation systematically be frustrated and hostilities occur.

FINANCING

A chasm has developed between the tasks entrusted to this Organization and the financial means provided to it. The truth of the matter is that our vision cannot really extend to the prospect opening before us as long as our financing remains myopic....

To remedy the financial situation of the United Nations in all its aspects, my distinguished predecessor repeatedly drew the attention of Member States to the increasingly impossible situation that has arisen and, during the forty-sixth session of the General Assembly, made a number of proposals.... with which I am in broad agreement.... [One] suggested the adoption of a set of measures to deal with the cash flow problems caused by the exceptionally high level of unpaid contributions as well as with the problem of inadequate working capital reserves:

(a) Charging interest on the amounts of assessed contributions that are not paid on time;

(b) Suspending certain financial regulations of the United Nations to permit the retention of budgetary surpluses;

(c) Increasing the Working Capital Fund to a level of $250 million and endorsing the principle that the level of the Fund should be approximately 25 percent of the annual assessment under the regular budget;

(d) Establishment of a temporary Peacekeeping Reserve Fund, at a level of $50 million, to meet initial expenses of peacekeeping operations pending receipt of assessed contributions.

(e) Authorization to the Secretary-General to borrow commercially, should other sources of cash be inadequate....

In addition..., others have been added in recent months in the course of public discussion. These ideas include: a levy on arms sales that could be related to maintaining an Arms Register by the United Nations; a levy on international air travel, which is dependent on the maintenance of peace; authorization for the United Nations to borrow from the World Bank and the International Monetary Fund, for peace and development are interdependent; general tax exemption for contributions made to the United Nations by foundations, businesses and individuals; and changes in the formula for calculating the scale of assessments for peacekeeping operations.

As such ideas are debated, a stark fact remains: the financial foundations of the Organization daily grow weaker, debilitating its political will and practical capacity to undertake new and essential activities. This state of affairs must not continue. Whether decisions are taken on financing the Organization, there is one inescapable necessity: Member States must pay their assessed contributions in full and on time. Failure to do so puts them in breach of their obligations under the Charter....

AN AGENDA FOR PEACE

The nations and peoples of the United Nations are fortunate in a way that those of the League of Nations were not. We have been given a second chance to create the world of our Charter that they were denied. With the cold war ended we have drawn back from the brink of a confrontation that threatened the world and, too often, paralyzed our Organization.

Even as we celebrate our restored possibilities, there is a need to ensure that the lessons of the past four decades are learned and that the errors, or variations of them, are not repeated. For there may not be a third opportunity for our planet which, now for different reasons, remains endangered....

Never again must the Security Council lose the collegiality that is essential to its proper functioning, an attribute that it has gained after such trial. A genuine sense of consensus deriving from shared interests must govern its work, not the threat of the veto or the power of any group of nations....

Power brings special responsibilities, and temptations. The powerful must resist the dual but opposite calls of unilateralism and isolationism if the United Nations is to succeed. For just as unilateralism at the global or regional level can shake the confidence of others, so can isolationism, whether it results from political choice or constitutional circumstance, enfeeble the global undertaking....

Reform is a continuing process, and improvement can have no limit. Yet there is an expectation, which I wish to see fulfilled, that the present phase in the renewal of this Organization should be complete by 1995, its fiftieth anniversary. The pace set must therefore be increased if the United Nations is to keep ahead of the acceleration of history that characterizes this age. We must be guided not by precedents alone, however wise these may be, but by the needs of the future and by the shape and content that we wish to give it.

... The United Nations was created with a great and courageous vision. Now is the time, for its nations and peoples, and the men and women who serve it, to seize the moment for the sake of the future.

NO

Jeffrey R. Gerlach

A U.N. ARMY FOR THE NEW WORLD ORDER?

The U.S. decision to intervene in Somalia created nearly universal approbation among policy makers, analysts, and members of the media. American troops, acting under the authority of the U.N. Security Council, led the effort to ensure relief supplies were delivered to Somalis threatened by starvation and disease.... [P]roponents [also] hoped the mission would provide a model for handling future international crises.... If the organization is to succeed in this ambitious mission, many proponents of a Pax United Nations argue, it must be endowed with a military force capable of preventing or reversing such horrors as those that have occurred in Somalia....

Though controversial, support for a U.N. military has grown rapidly since the release last June of the U.N. Secretary-General's report to the Security Council, *An Agenda for Peace*. Responding to the Council's request for a proposal to strengthen the U.N.'s ability to resolve world conflicts, Boutros Boutros-Ghali argued that his organization needs a military force if it is to maintain international peace and stability. He proposed a plan aimed at establishing a de facto U.N. army, with each member state making available up to 1,000 troops for peace-enforcement and deterrent operations. Missions using U.N. armed forces would be conducted under the authority of the Security Council and at the command of the Secretary-General.

If accepted by the U.S government, this proposal would inevitably represent a major step away from a security policy based on American national interests. Nevertheless, Boutros-Ghali's proposal has garnered widespread support in the United States.

THE SUPPORTERS

In a *New York Times* article, Senator David Boren (Democrat of Oklahoma) suggested that 40 to 50 U.N. member nations contribute to a rapid deployment force of 100,000 volunteers. He argued that such a force would "help discourage regional conflicts, violations of basic justice, the proliferation of weapons and international terrorism." His Senate colleague, Joseph Biden

From Jeffrey R. Gerlach, "A U.N. Army for the New World Order?" *Orbis: A Journal of World Affairs* (Spring 1993). Copyright © 1993 by The Foreign Policy Research Institute. Reprinted by permission. Notes omitted.

(Democrat of Delaware) introduced Senate Joint Resolution 325, the "Collective Security Participation Resolution," that urged "the president to take all appropriate steps to negotiate, under Article 43 of the United Nations Charter, 'a special agreement or agreements' with equitable terms under which designated forces from various countries, including the United States, would be 'available to the Security Council... for the purpose of maintaining international peace and security.'"...

President Bill Clinton, in a major foreign policy address of his campaign, pledged his support for the creation of a U.N. military force. A Clinton administration, he promised, would "stand up for our interests, but we will share burdens, where possible, through multilateral efforts to secure the peace, such as NATO and a new, voluntary U.N. Rapid Deployment Force. In Bosnia, Somalia, Cambodia, and other war-torn areas of the world, multilateral action holds promise as never before, and the U.N. deserves full and appropriate contributions from all the major powers." Former president Bush, whose use of the United Nations during the Gulf War helped to reinvigorate the organization, was less enthusiastic about Boutros-Ghali's proposed army. However, he did pledge stronger U.S. support for peacekeeping operations and offered to make U.S. military facilities and expertise available to the United Nations. In addition, he suggested that the Security Council meet to discuss the proposals outlined by Boutros-Ghali.

Influential members of the media have also supported various versions of the U.N. army. An editorial in *The New York Times* proclaimed: "With a force capable of responding quickly, the United Nations could save lives, check massive tides of refugees and discourage warlords. In the world, as on a city street, the mere presence of a cop on the beat matters." A *USA Today* editorial argued that the alternative to supporting Boutros-Ghali might be disastrous: "If the world community doesn't learn to resolve ethnic rivalries loosed by the Cold War's end, hundreds of Yugoslavias could crater the future."...

Support for a U.N. army has been even stronger within the academic and policy community. Bruce Russett, a political scientist at Yale, and James S. Sutterlin, a fellow at Yale's International Security Program, argue that "the Security Council should be able to mobilize a force to serve under U.N. command for enforcement purposes." Harvard University's Joseph S. Nye, Jr., has suggested a rapid deployment force of 60,000 troops built around a professional core of 5,000 U.N. soldiers. A blue-ribbon panel convened by the Carnegie Endowment for International Peace concluded that "the United Nations must take steps to prepare better for military enforcement actions.... If collective security is to be taken seriously, the UN must be prepared, in the end, to use force." Brian Urquhart, scholar in residence at the Ford Foundation, suggests that "A third category of international military operation is needed, somewhere between peacekeeping and large-scale enforcement." Such views are not held by a tiny minority but represent the thinking of many analysts.

Members of the international community have likewise voiced support for similar schemes. German foreign minister Klaus Kinkel has argued that the system of collective security of the United Nations and other regional organizations, must be made "powerful instruments of a new world domestic policy." The French government has offered, with certain conditions, to make one thousand troops available to the Security Council on forty-eight hours' notice and another thousand within a week. Russian president Boris Yeltsin has stated his country's support for the French plan.

THE REASONS WHY NOT

Evidently, in the post–cold war debate about U.S. foreign policy, advocates of a U.N.-based collective security system will have one of the strongest voices. Casting their own views as moderate and centrist, these advocates denounce one set of their opponents as isolationists seeking a Fortress America and another set as global hegemonists bent on imposing a Pax Americana. With an armed United Nations, they say, Americans can promote democracy, protect human rights, and maintain stability, without paying the full costs or looking like bullies.

The vision has its attractions, no doubt. But it is fraught with dangerous complications and contradictions. Pursuit of global collective security is likely to enmesh the United States in a myriad of complex and costly operations that have little to do with its national interest, and that will ultimately fail.

Strategic objections. The most general objection to a U.N. army is that it may run counter to U.S. national interests, which are not always compatible with the interests of other major powers, idealists to the contrary notwithstanding. NATO, often cited as an exemplary alliance, was bound together by one constant, common, overwhelming threat: the Soviet Union. Now that it lacks such

an overwhelming common interest, even NATO may prove incapable of maintaining its close security relationships over the long run. And when one turns from NATO to contemplate an alliance whose main pillars include the United States, Russia, and China, it is difficult to find any sufficient common ground to maintain a collective security system. If the Security Council were expanded to include diverse world powers such as Germany, Japan, or India, as many analysts have proposed, the difficulty would be even greater. Inevitably, countries will view events differently and formulate their policies accordingly. For this reason, the formation of ad hoc coalitions in response to particular international problems seems to be a much more promising security policy than a permanent worldwide security structure.

Political objections. Under Boutros-Ghali's proposal, the Security Council would have broad guidelines to intervene throughout the world, and would control a U.N. military as the means to do so. The Council would, in turn, be accountable only to leaders of the governments represented on the Council. According to the U.N. Participation Act, which authorizes a U.S. role in that organization, the president has the authority to engage in negotiations to make available American troops for U.N. activities. If an agreement were ratified by majorities in both houses of Congress, the Security Council would need only the approval of the president to send Americans into combat. As long as U.S. troops were used only for limited peacekeeping missions, that would present little problem. However, if they become engaged in U.N. wars, with only the consent of the president, is the power of Congress to declare war effectively abolished? Admittedly, Congress's constitutional role has been much attenuated in the last fifty years, but substantial vestiges remain in the pressure Congress can exert on the president. Without even those vestiges, the potential for an executive abuse of power is enormous.

If one were to circumvent the problems posed by Security Council control of U.N. operations by putting the army under the authority of the General Assembly, the result would probably be worse. The composition of the General Assembly (with a majority of authoritarian states) and its historical record (voting for numerous resolutions Americans consider abhorrent, notably the resolution declaring that Zionism is racism) do not inspire confidence in that body.

Military objections. Another important question concerning a proposed U.N. army regards its composition. Peacekeeping missions, in which the parties to a conflict have agreed to a U.N. presence, generally entail few casualties. Peace-imposing missions, involving uninvited intervention that seeks to halt aggression and domestic repression, raises the specter of serious conflict and adds a dangerous new dimension to U.N. missions. In those situations, the United Nations forces are likely to face a determined opposition.

And so the question arises: Who is going to fight, and possibly die, for this new world order? There is a long tradition, right or wrong, under which countries have sent their young people to fight for the national interest, as determined by the country's leaders. But that tradition does not apply here, given the tenuous links that may exist between a U.N. operation and a country's national interest. Thus, it is surely a minimum ethical requirement for a U.N. army that it be all-volunteer. But that raises other problems. For example, can one speak of true volunteers being drawn from a member-state's conscripted military? If not, the pool of potential soldiers is going to be small indeed.

Whatever U.S. soldiers did end up in the U.N. army would probably be placed under the command of foreign officers. The U.N. Charter authorizes a Military Staff Committee (MSC), charged with directing any armed forces placed at the disposal of the Security Council. The MSC is composed of the Chiefs of Staff of the permanent members of the Security Council. That body was largely dormant throughout the cold war, but pressure has been building recently to revive the MSC. The notion of U.S. troops serving under foreign command is one that the Pentagon views with great concern. A truly international force would have to overcome technical military problems such as differences in training, command, and equipment among the participating nations. In addition, there are questions regarding the competency of any international military command. John F. Hillen III, a veteran of Operation Desert Storm now at the department of war studies at King's College in London, argues that "You need narrowly defined objectives, unity of command, a small narrow-based interest, to make the tough decisions and the tough calls. The U.N. has just too much plurality of opinion to accomplish any of that."

Financial objections. Proponents of a vastly strengthened U.N. coercive arm tend to avoid discussions of its cost, or even to claim the issue as a plus for the United States, because it represents burden-sharing. Consider, however, that the United Nations is currently maintaining thirteen peacekeeping operations at an annual cost of over $3 billion. In order for the United States to pay its share (it is required to pay 30 percent of all peacekeeping costs), the Bush administration requested an additional $810 million for peacekeeping operations in 1992 and 1993, much of it to pay for the ambitious U.N. program for Cambodia. Congress was extremely reluctant to authorize even that relatively modest expenditure. And rightly so, one might well argue, given the U.S. budget deficit and the poor prospects for peace in Cambodia. Would the United States be required to pay a similar share of the far more expensive U.N. military operations? Would Congress be morally or even legally bound to authorize such expenditure— even if the operation were undertaken without its consent? And, if so, what then becomes of the congressional power of the purse?

One proposal seeks to smooth the way for U.S. funding of the United Nations by moving it from the State Department to the Department of Defense. The hope is that, given the massive budget of the latter, U.S. officials would find it easier to spend the billions of dollars required for a collective security regime. Perhaps so. Yet the American people would bear the costs of such efforts regardless of which department provided the funds.

Another proposal seeks to avoid the whole problem of balky legislatures that are accountable to their citizens and to acquire the funds for a U.N. military through a special "dedicated" tax. Two forms of commerce have been offered up as the most promising subjects of this tax: international arms sales and international travel. In either case, of course, the cost of the U.N. military operations would be shifted from the countries that support such actions to individuals and businesses who might be utterly uninvolved with them.

COLLECTIVE INTERNATIONALISM

Although the proposal for a U.N. army has its own flaws, its greatest failing is the underlying principle it nourishes, which may be called collective internationalism. Collective internationalism envisions a world in which regional and global organizations are charged with solving a vast array of international and even domestic problems. Richard N. Gardner, Professor of Law and International Organization at Columbia University, describes it as "the construction of a peaceful world order through multilateral cooperation and effective international organization." Though regional organizations would be important players in such a world order, the United Nations is today the centerpiece of most of these proposals.

Much of the collective internationalist vision is quite benign. Few people, for example, would argue with efforts to increase international cooperation. However, advocates of collective internationalism generally go well beyond support for incremental efforts aimed at developing peaceful relations among states. The goals of a full-fledged international collective security system are quite ambitious: addressing the roots of insecurity, such as economic, ethnic, and racial injustice; preventing human rights violations and political repression; reducing military threats; organizing preventive diplomacy and crisis prevention efforts; and developing an enforcement mechanism for maintaining peace. The last point is the most critical as it constitutes the means to ensure the collective international vision.

Transnational authorities would have a number of different tools in their fight against injustice. The most powerful of those are economic sanctions and military intervention. Economic sanctions are widely recognized as legitimate means for promoting security interests, and have been used by the United Nations on several occasions. But the results of economic sanctions have been notoriously poor. Until now, therefore, the United Nations has generally been seen as a non-option when frustrated policy makers decided to get serious. This is why a U.N. military force has become such a critical step in developing a genuine theory of international collective security.

Virtually all parties to the debate recognize that the post–cold war world is likely to produce numerous regional disputes, domestic and cross-border, sometimes leading to conflict. The main point of contention among American analysts is the proper reaction to such conflicts. With the possibility of a U.N. army in view, advocates of collective internationalism can now present their position as a serious "middle path between bearing too much and too little of the international burden." They seek to limit turmoil through intervention, they say, but without embracing the high costs and risks involved in unilateral U.S. intervention. Flora Lewis calls the strategy "a way to resolve the dilemma between dangerous global unilateralism and sulky, equally dangerous, isolationism. It is neither utopian nor meanly narrow realpolitik."

THE SLIPPERY SLOPE

Isolationist, collective internationalism certainly is not. Whether it leads to utopianism is another matter, for it sets the policy maker on a very slippery slope. Rather than assess a dispute's impact on American society, collective internationalists are tempted to target all grievances and all injustice.

The avowed move from peacekeeping to peace-imposing operations is the first step down this slope. With two notable exceptions (the Korean "police action" and the Gulf War), preventing or reversing aggression by force would be a dramatic reversal of U.N. tradition. Yet that is the direction in which collective internationalists are taking us.

The second major step down the slippery slope is the blurring of the traditional distinction between international and primarily domestic affairs. In fact, several recent U.N. actions have served to erode the concept of sovereignty. U.N. Resolution 688, for example, passed on April 5, 1991, authorized member states to protect and assist the Kurdish population within Iraq's borders. Columnist Charles Krauthammer argues, "The world needs to declare a new international principle: Where sovereignty has broken down and barbarism broken out—sorry, there are no Euclidian rules for this: The Security Council will determine when that happens—the world will step in and provide protection. It is a grand violation of the principle of sovereignty, and long overdue." ...

[This] would require Washington to intervene in scores of places throughout the world. Americans may hope that governments around the world respect the rights of their citizens, but that hope disregards not only current international conditions, in which barbarism is widespread, but virtually the entire history of human existence.

A third step down the slope is taken by commentators who suggest collective security ranges beyond the issues of political and economic oppression. Alan K. Henrikson suggests that environmental damage would be an appropriate reason for international intervention. "The most conceptually novel, though not historically unprecedented, kind of international intervention in internal affairs that might be justified... would be helpful intercession, and perhaps even forcible intervention, for the purpose of stopping serious damage to the environment, within as well as beyond national boundaries." Indar Jit Rikhye, senior advisor for U.N. Affairs at the U.S. Institute of Peace, adds drug interdiction and patrolling the world's oceans to the list of issues that should involve the United Nations.

Enthusiastically, a recent assistant secretary of state for international organization affairs, John R. Bolton, sums up the vision this way: "We have an opportunity to do great things: help stabilize fledgling democracies in countries that have known only tyranny for decades; promote human rights on a global scale; use the U.N. and the relevant regional organizations to help create greater international peace and stability than the world has ever known."

A less sanguine interpretation is that a U.N. army is a recipe for fighting endless enemies in intractable situations. Virtually every region of the planet populated by human beings contains areas in which turmoil is already occurring or threatens to break out.... To seek to right every injustice would be quixotic; even to address a relatively small percentage would require an enormous expenditure of blood and treasure. Conflicts now occurring in the Balkans [and elsewhere] are but the tip of the iceberg compared to potential sources of conflict. Even areas that are generally considered stable, such as Western Europe, have their Irish Republican Army and Basque movements.

Though many proponents of collective internationalism view the Gulf War as a prototype of the conflicts a U.N. army would fight, more likely the United Nations would be faced with quite different kinds of problems. The Gulf War was fought with conventional tactics on desert terrain against an overmatched enemy. Such conflicts, in which the aggressor is clearly identifiable, are likely to be the exception. The messy U.N. intervention in the Belgian Congo (now Zaire) is probably a more realistic example of the conflicts that the future will bring. That mission, which lasted from 1960 to 1964, involved a total of over 93,000 troops, cost $411 million, and ultimately proved disastrous.

The United Nations found itself in the midst of a very complex situation. The Belgian Congo was an area the size of Western Europe, created by Belgian colonizers, and inhabited by numerous ethnic groups. After de-colonization, the country was faced with many difficult problems, including economic hardships, continued Belgian interference, a lack of indigenous leadership, and the prospect of civil war among feuding ethnic groups.

The United Nations, with assistance from a number of countries, including the United States, did achieve one of its goals in that conflict: maintaining the territorial integrity of the country. But Michael G. Schatzberg of the School of Advanced International Studies at Johns Hopkins University argues, "From [Zaireans'] perspective, the results have been damaging and disheartening, not least because popular political will was never given a chance to register." In fact, the United Nations managed to inhibit the growth of freedom in Zaire and to ensure that a corrupt dictator would reign for nearly three decades. Barry M. Schutz writes, "The Congo Operation taught the UN that interventions in countries where social/ethnic elements are at war with each other and with their government are virtually impossible to contain, let alone resolve." But that assumption about U.N. wisdom is probably inaccurate, as the United Nations now contemplates using force in a virtually limitless number of similar situations.

THE U.N. SUPERPOWER

For theoretical and practical reasons, then, it appears that a U.N. army would have to be far larger than Boutros-Ghali envisions. A more realistic view of the requirements is provided by Alan K. Henrikson, Director of the Fletcher Roundtable on a New World Order at The Fletcher School of Law and Diplomacy, [who suggests a U.N. force]

> ... large and powerful enough—with, say, 500,000 troops equipped with modern weapons—to deal with all but major international aggression, possibly involving nuclear weapons and conducted at the superpower level.

Henrikson's proposal represents the level of force needed to begin to undertake the ambitious missions described by collective internationalists. Other analysts, however, propose even larger international military forces....

Robert C. Johansen, senior fellow at the University of Notre Dame's Institute for International Peace Studies, argues that "there is some military logic to the idea that the United Nations eventually should have more power than any single country if it intends to prevent an aggressive nation from disrupting the peace....

The Security Council will need more enforcement power than any member can wield against it...."

A United Nations endowed with more military power than any single country would have very few restraints placed on its actions. No country, acting alone, would be able to defend itself against a U.N. mission, even an unfair or unwise one. That could even place the sovereignty of the United States at risk. Since the purpose of U.S. foreign policy should be to protect the sovereignty and territorial integrity of the United States, thus ensuring that the liberties of the American people are not imperiled by external threats, the "logic" of proposals to make U.N. military power superior to that of the United States should be firmly rejected.

Even short of such extreme proposals, however, it is clear that a U.N. security system would require every state to cede in some degree its right to make independent security decisions based on its own national interest. To those concerned with the U.S. national interest, it is thus among the most disconcerting outcomes of collective internationalism to wonder how often the U.S. view would and would not prevail in the international system. If General Assembly precedents are any indication, the United States would rarely get its way in that body's decisions. For example, during the 46th General Assembly, which held its plenary session from September 17, 1991, to December 20, 1991, the average overall voting coincidence by U.N. members with the United States was 27.8 percent. And even that dismal number is a significant improvement compared to earlier years. If the General Assembly were to play a strong role in future U.N. operations, the United States should be prepared to see many of its national security wishes overridden.

THE SYSTEM IN OPERATION

Lastly, apart from questions of policy, one must ask how the collective internationalist scheme would be likely to operate in practice.

Consider the promotion of democracy and respect for human rights—goals that in the abstract seem unassailable. In fact, they present a number of complications. For one thing, the terms themselves are quite contentious. A number of U.N. documents purport to explain the two concepts, but their definitions remain vague and even contradictory. In the Universal Declaration of Human Rights, the United Nations has adopted a very broad notion of "rights," declaring: "1. Everyone has the right to work, to free choice of employment, to just and favourable conditions of work and to protection against unemployment.... 3. Everyone who works has the right to just and favourable remuneration ensuring for himself and his family an existence worthy of human dignity, and supplemented, if necessary, by other means of social protection." Such "rights" are not only different from the traditional U.S. interpretation of individual liberty, they are incompatible with it.

Then, too, how would the United Nations decide which situations are worthy of intervention? Since it could not get involved in every fray, criteria for determining when to intervene must be developed. Is the repression of ethnic groups in Sudan more worthy of rectification than the overthrow of a democratically elected government in Haiti or Peru? Does the plight of the Kurds supersede that of the Tibetans? Is

repression in Cuba more significant than abuses in Algeria, Iran, or Guatemala? How would one even go about deciding, lacking any standards of national interest?

In practice, the Security Council would decide, and, although the Security Council is composed of fifteen members, the permanent five would hold the vast majority of the power. Once the five had agreed on a policy, they would probably be able to impose their views on the non-permanent members. Edward C. Luck and Toby Trister Gati of the United Nations Association of the United States, both strong proponents of collective security, admit, "In practical terms, then, most of the responsibility for deciding when, where, and how these sweeping principles will be applied rests with the members of the Security Council. Theirs necessarily must be a subjective rather than an objective judgment."

Though advocates of a U.N. collective security system admit there is a problem in the subjective nature of such decisions, they believe it can be overcome. David J. Scheffer argues that "international lawyers need to remain vigilant in their examination of the legitimacy of interventions authorized by collective decision-making bodies, particularly the Security Council." Other commentators suggest that case law, and the precedents established by previous interventions, will provide appropriate guidelines for decisions. However, lawyers can be wrong and previous interventions, despite their legitimacy in international law, provide little guidance for future actions. More to the point, neither proposal places any significant restraints on the power of the Security Council.

In practice, small, weak countries are most likely to be the target of

U.N. intervention. The Security Council would probably not authorize a peace-enforcement mission against a powerful state, simply because of the high risk involved. A large and populous country, especially if equipped with nuclear weapons (as India and Pakistan are), would be relatively free to commit actions that would cause a less powerful state to become the target of a U.N. army.

Inevitably, the five permanent members of the Council, and perhaps their clients, would be treated differently than other states. Since each permanent member could veto any particular action, states on good terms with at least one member would be likely to avoid sanctions. At the same time, regions of interest to the members of the Security Council would receive far more attention.

Proponents of collective internationalism must explain how these problems can be avoided; they must articulate the conditions under which the United Nations, or any other transnational authority, should involve itself in other countries' affairs. Otherwise, the opportunities for cynical double standards are nearly unlimited.

Furthermore, even if reasonable criteria could be developed regarding the use of armed forces, U.N. institutions would be required to execute them. Critics have long argued that corruption and inefficiency have marred the operation of the organization. And though the operations of the United Nations have expanded in recent years, it has not been able to solve the problems its critics have identified. William Branigan of *The Washington Post* recently characterized the organization as:

an enormous, largely uncontrolled bureaucracy, subject to abuses and deficiencies that impair its effectiveness....
In ways that reform advocates find both absurd and infuriating, the UN system appears to have careened out of control. Many of its programs and activities have become redundant or irrelevant. Their main beneficiaries often are the bureaucrats they employ.

Such descriptions do not inspire confidence in an organization that many hope will tackle the world's most pressing problems.

CONCLUSION

As a long-term goal, U.S. foreign policy should be directed toward encouraging the kind of peaceful, harmonious world envisioned by collective internationalists. They are right to believe that a world of that kind would pose little threat to the United States, and would offer far more benefits than the current one. But the long-range means to achieving such a goal should be the peaceful, negotiated removal of barriers that inhibit the free movement of people, ideas, and goods. The United States does not need a United Nations with the broad mission of imposing its vision of peace and prosperity on the world.

Arguably, a more benign world must come gradually, from the grass-roots level, as nations around the world accept democracy and a respect for individual rights. As Prime Minister of the Czech Republic Vaclav Klaus has stated, "Democracy, freedom and the market cannot be 'introduced.' They cannot be implanted into an unprepared or uncooperative soil from outside, by decree, by lecturing, by giving good advice."

If the members of the United Nations wish to join the United States in expanding peace and freedom, therefore, a sizable majority should start at home. Freedom House reports that 96 of the countries in the world and 13 territories (representing 75 percent of the world's population) are not free or only partly free, while 75 states and 48 territories (25 percent of the world's population) are considered free. The People's Republic of China, a permanent member of the Security Council, is a particularly poor choice to participate in a crusade for democracy, having killed and repressed millions of its own people.

As for the short-term: If U.S. vital interests are threatened, then it is the United States that must act, decisively, either by itself or in ad hoc concert with others who share the same interests. When those direct interests are not involved, policy makers should refrain from risking American lives. If Americans are called upon to bear the heavy burden of war, they should know they are fighting for the freedom of their country, not the quixotic schemes of U.S. politicians and pundits.

POSTSCRIPT

Should the United Nations Take on Greater Military Capabilities and Roles?

The idea of creating what could be the beginnings of a permanent international police force, or even an army, is being debated seriously in many forums. For more on the topic, two good sources are Edward C. Luck, "Making Peace," *Foreign Policy* (Winter 1992/93) and Lincoln P. Bloomfield, "Policing World Disorder," *World Monitor* (February 1993). For the cautious view that military solutions are only possible amid common political efforts, see Dan G. Loomis, "Prospects for UN Peacekeeping," *Global Affairs* (Winter 1993). Loomis is a Canadian general. For a skeptical view, see Eugene V. Rostow, "Should UN Charter Article 43 Be Raised from the Dead?" *Global Affairs* (Winter 1993). For an outright negative opinion, see Doug Bandow, "Avoiding War," *Foreign Policy* (Winter 1992/93).

One reason for the current debate on UN military operations is the increased use of the UN to intervene in all sorts of international and domestic clashes. During 1993 the UN will spend approximately $3.8 billion on peace-keeping, nearly quintuple its 1991 budget. In mid-1993, more than 60,000 troops were deployed under the UN flag. There were 14 proposals for peace-keeping operations pending before the Security Council. A second reason for the current debate is that some critics charge that it is difficult to field one, unified successful military force cobbled together from many armies. Many observers do not believe that the multinational armies now deployed by the UN can ever be effective. Like a pick-up athletic team that finds it hard to be effective when playing against a team that regularly practices together under a single coach, so, too, the UN forces face special difficulties. Multinational armies suffer from a lack of common training and differences in communications, weapons, and logistics. Fractured command structures and even basic language difficulties are additional complications. But the emerging support for a new world order and a weariness of bearing the physical and financial costs of unilateral action have brought more countries around to the idea of collective action through the UN and regional organizations.

Speaking at the UN in September 1992, President George Bush expressed a willingness to train U.S. troops for UN operations. Peacekeeping operations are now part of the curriculum at some U.S. military academies, and Bush offered to turn over Fort Dix in New Jersey for training international UN forces. More recently, President Bill Clinton's ambassador to the UN, Madeleine Albright, has commented that "ad hoc approaches dominate what should be

a far more efficient and regularized system of peacekeeping operations....
I do think a standby [UN] force is the way to go." There are other seeming
small shifts that are important. One of these occurred in Somalia. At first, the
commander of UN forces there was an American. Then command shifted to
a Pakistani general. For the first time, U.S. forces were operating under the
overall command of a foreign general.

A related matter involves the constitutional processes by which the United
States and other countries go to war. If the UN can authorize a war and can
require countries to supply forces, then those countries might be forced to
fight a war in which they would otherwise not participate. Could they be
forced to do so without going through the legal processes required by their
legal systems? Secretary of Defense Les Aspin summed up the constitutional
issue during his confirmation hearings. "The president is commander in
chief.... Congress has war powers... [but] if you second [transfer] these
forces to the UN, how do you maintain the Constitution?"

As a last point to ponder, the debate over UN military forces is also part of
a debate about how to regulate, perhaps govern, the world. There are many
views on the whether the sovereignty of states should decrease, whether
the role of the UN should increase, or even whether an effort should be
made to shift from national to world government. To further inform yourself
on these questions, read James Rosenau, *The United Nations In a Turbulent
World* (Lynne Rienner, 1992) and Harlan Cleveland, "Rethinking International
Governance," *The Futurist* (May/June 1991).

ISSUE 15

Would Women in Combat Weaken National Security?

YES: David Horowitz, from "The Feminist Assault on the Military," *National Review* (October 5, 1992)

NO: Sue Tunnicliffe, from "War, Peace and Feminist Theory," *Paper presented to the International Studies Association 33rd Annual Convention* (March/April 1992)

ISSUE SUMMARY

YES: Analyst David Horowitz maintains that there are many purposes behind the feminists' efforts to restructure the military, but national security is not one of them.

NO: Sue Tunnicliffe, a political scientist at Staffordshire Polytechnic College in England, contends that opposition to women in combat positions is *not* based on concerns about national security; rather, it is primarily an attempt to perpetuate male political domination.

Women make up 11 percent of the U.S. military, but they have been traditionally barred from serving on warships, flying in warplanes, or being assigned to infantry, artillery, or armor units. Over the last few years, administrative or legislative actions have opened the way for women to serve as combat pilots and in some other combat positions. Other roles, such as those in ground combat, remain off limits to women. The range of military occupational specialties (MOS) open to women in other countries varies greatly, but there is no country that routinely assigns women to ground combat units. Furthermore, apart from some short periods when a country was in crisis, there has never been a time or place where women served regularly in such roles. This is not to say that that is correct. Indeed, there are many people who argue that it is both discriminatory and deprives the military of personnel who could make valuable contributions.

The debate between David Horowitz and Sue Tunnicliffe needs to be put into perspective. This debate operates on several levels. At one level, some see this debate as limited to the specific issue of what would happen to a country's military operations and military defense capabilities if women served in combat. This is the most common frame of reference for the debate. Opponents of combat roles for women argue that such a role would undermine military capability. Former Marine Corps commandant General Robert Barrow, in testimony before Congress, said, "If you want to make a combat unit ineffective, assign women to it. It would destroy the Marine Corps—as simple as that—something no enemy has been able to do in over 200 years." Proponents of women in combat would reply, as did analyst Linda Grand de Pauw, that Barrow's position is akin to "the image they [white military leaders] used to have of blacks before they served with them." Other members of the presidential panel on women in combat disagreed. Marine Brigadier General Thomas Draude, whose daughter is a navy pilot, commented, "I'm asked, would you let your daughter fly in combat with the possibility of her becoming a POW? And my answer is yes, because I believe we should send in the best."

Horowitz and Tunnicliffe address these matters in part, but the two authors also argue this debate on another level. This level relates to the question of the role of women in the political system. Why are women excluded, legally or by custom, from certain roles? Is it truly a matter of ability, or physical strength, or are men simply trying to "keep women in their place" and maintain control? Those who see this debate as an issue of the social control of women would agree with the female U.S. Army captain who told a committee of the U.S. Congress that although male military officers who oppose women in combat "talk about sex and toilets," their real concern "is . . . privilege and power."

If the issue of women in combat is part of the larger struggle by men to keep political power and women to gain more of it, then, if the women succeed, what will be the effect on the way that political affairs—international as well as domestic—are conducted? There are some analysts who contend that women are less caught up in a culture of violence. Therefore a world in which women played an equal role in politics would be less violent. According to feminists, concepts such as peace and security are prime examples of how men and women conceive of issues differently. Scholar Betty Reardon, for example, contends that men stress "negative peace. . . . From the masculine perspective, peace for the most part has meant the absence of war and the prevention of armed conflict." By contrast, says Reardon, women emphasize "positive peace," that is, the "conditions of social justice, economic equity and ecological balance." Thus, in Reardon's view, women are more prone to see international security in broader terms than are men. According to Canadian scholar Christine Ball, "They see the broader needs [that must be met] if we are to attain a secure planet."

Thus, as the following selections by Horowitz and Tunnicliffe demonstrate, the debate over women in service in combat roles is not only about national security, it is also about the role of women in domestic and world politics. Horowitz believes that there is a feminist assault on the military that will ill serve the United States. Tunnicliffe suggest that men oppose women in combat in the interest of preserving male, not national, security.

YES

David Horowitz

THE FEMINIST ASSAULT
ON THE MILITARY

For nearly two decades after the Sixties, the military remained the one institution to withstand the baleful influences of the radical Left. Now that the cold war is over, this immunity appears to have ended. A series of relatively trivial incidents (a joke about women's sexual excuses, a skit mocking a female member of Congress) and a drunken party at which crotches were grabbed in a gantlet ritual have fueled a national hysteria about "sexual harassment" and a political witchhunt that is threatening to deconstruct the military in the way other institutions have been deconstructed before.

Fanning the fires are feminist legislators on the Armed Services Committee, led by Democrat Pat Schroeder, who want women assigned to combat roles. In a July 9 letter to Defense Secretary Dick Cheney, Representative Schroeder... called for investigations and prosecutions to purge the Navy of sexual miscreants and bad attitudes.

Mrs. Schroeder herself was the center of the second Navy "scandal," over the Tom Cat Follies at the Miramar Naval Station....

When the Navy brass was alerted to the contents of the show by a female officer who had been present, the reaction was swift. Five career officers present at the Follies had their commands terminated. (Subsequently, two were reinstated.) The Navy has also apologized to Mrs. Schroeder. Such appeasement, however, has only whetted the appetite of the feminist vanguard, which has stepped up its campaign to pass the Schroeder Amendment, allowing women to fly combat missions. It is seen by advocates as a "wedge" measure that would lead to expanded combat roles and true "institutional equality" for women....

MILITANTLY ANTI-MILITARY

It should come as no surprise that many advocates of the change have previously shown little interest in maintaining an effective defense. Representative Schroeder, for example, was an antiwar activist before entering the House. She has been a determined adversary of military preparedness on the Armed Services Committee, where she now serves as a ranking member....

Examples of this kind of double agenda abound in the current feminist campaign and can be found in testimony before the Presidential Commission on the Assignment of Women in the Armed Forces. Maria Lepowsky, a professor of Women's Studies, provided the commissioners with data to support a combat role for women. Then Professor Lepowsky asked herself: "What would be some possible consequences... —if women were put in combat—on American cultural values and American society...?" She answered her own question: "I think there might be increased concern about committing troops to combat, also perhaps a good thing...."

In other words, Professor Lepowsky was advocating that women be put in combat roles because to do so would make it *more difficult* to commit troops to combat. Now this is a kind of candor that is unusual for the Left.

REFORM, SOVIET STYLE

Moderate feminists generally want modest reforms in American society. Technological advances, like birth control, have dramatically changed women's social roles, requiring adjustments in the culture. The most constructive way for these changes to take place is deliberately, and with due respect for consequences that may be unforeseen. As the inhabitants of the former Soviet empire discovered, at great human cost, revolutionary cures can often be worse than the disease.

This is a lesson lost on feminism's radical wing. When advocates of current military reform speak of "gender integration" of the military, they are often involving the ideas of these radicals without recognizing them for what they are. Gender feminism is a bastard child of Marxism. It holds that women are not women by nature, but that society has "constructed" or created them female so that men could oppress them. Gender feminists are social engineers in the same way as Communists. They deny that human biology fundamentally influences who we are. For them, the solution to all social problems, conflicts, and disappointments in life is to manipulate laws and institutions so as to create liberated human beings, who will not hate, have prejudices, exhibit bad sexual manners, or go to war.

Gender feminists have little interest in questions of America's national security because they believe America is a patriarchal, sexist, racist oppressor whose institutions must be transformed beyond recognition. Of course, the gender feminists are not so naïve as to admit their radical agendas outside the sanctuaries of women's studies departments. In testifying before Presidential Commissions they will say that placing women in combat positions is merely an extension of women working outside the home, and of equal opportunity.

But placing women in harm's way and training them to kill one-on-one is not a mere extension of working outside the home. Furthermore, there are definite limits to equal rights and equal opportunity when biology is involved. Do American males have the right to bear children? Do they have an equal opportunity with women to do so? Do they have an equal aptitude for combat? Ninety per cent of those arrested for violent crimes are male. Obviously males have a distinct advantage over females in mobilizing an existing instinct for aggression for the purposes of organized combat.

The difficulty in confronting these issues on their merits is the emotional element that is introduced by the moral posturing of the Left. One of the leading advocates of equal military roles is Commander Rosemary Mariner, a 19-year career naval officer. Commander Mariner's testimony before the Commission is illustrative: "As with racial integration the biggest problem confronting gender integration is not men or women, but bigotry.... [S]exual harassment will continue to be a major problem in the armed forces because the combat exclusion law and policies make women institutionally inferior."...

Consider the proposition: ... According to the gender feminists, the U.S. military, by including women in combat positions, can solve this age-old problem. As soon as this law is changed, women's self-esteem will rise, men's respect for women will increase, and presto! sexual harassment will cease.

It is difficult to believe that a rational human being could propose such nonsense, but this is the fundamental idea that feminists advance *ad nauseam,* and that our military brass and political leadership are capitulating to at a disturbing pace....

Studies conducted at West Point have identified 120 physical differences between men and women that bear on military requirements. Yet the U.S. Naval Academy has been criticized for not moving fast enough to increase its female enrollment. Senator Barbara Mikulski has demanded "an attitude change" at the academy, and an official Committee on Women's Issues headed by Rear Admiral Virgil Hill has called for the "immediate dismissal of senior officers who question the role of women in the military." To question—to *question*—the

role of women in the military is now regarded as bigotry by the military itself.

The word "bigot" has resonance. It is meant to invoke the specter of racism and to appropriate the moral mantle of the civil-rights movement for feminist causes. This feminist attempt to hijack the civil-rights movement is both spurious and offensive, but it is highly effective in preventing opponents from laughing feminist arguments out of court.

As for the facts about women's suitability for combat, it is not always easy to discover them. In its Washington session in June, the Presidential Commission heard testimony from William S. Lind, former defense advisor to Gary Hart. Lind referred to the suppression of information vital to the decisions the Commission is being asked to make. According to Lind, the Army Personnel Office had detailed information on problems encountered with women troops in Desert Storm, which had not been released to the public. The information included the fact that, when the troops were called for battle, the non-deployability rate for women was three to four times higher than that for men. This had a negative effect on unit cohesion, a primary component of combat effectiveness. Pregnancy during Desert Shield was the primary reason for non-deployability.

Also covered up are the consequences of the way women are treated in the service academies. The official position at West Point, for example, is that there have been no negative effects. The facts are different, as a recent Heritage study by Robert Knight reveals. According to the sworn testimony of a West Point official taken in a Roanoke court, when men and women are required to perform the same exercises, women's scores are "weighted" to compensate for their deficiencies; women cadets take "comparable" training when they cannot meet the physical standards for male cadets, and peer ratings have been eliminated because women were scoring too low. "Gender norming"—the institutionalization of a double standard, so that women are measured against other women, rather than against men—is now the rule at all the service academies.

Even the *men's* training program has been downgraded: cadets no longer train in combat boots because women were experiencing higher rates of injury; running with heavy weapons has been eliminated because it is "unrealistic and therefore inappropriate" to expect women to do it; the famed "recondo" endurance week, during which cadets used to march with full backpacks and undergo other strenuous activities, has been eliminated, as have upper-body strength events in the obstacle course.

It is one thing to have second-rate professors because of affirmative-action quotas that lower standards. But a second-rate officer corps?

Not surprisingly, resentment on the part of male cadets is high. One indication is that more than 50 per cent of the women cadets at West Point reported that they had been sexually harassed last year.

It is a perfectly sinister combination. Rub men's noses in arbitrariness and unfairness, and then charge them with sexual harassment when they react. It is also a perfect prescription for accumulating power and controlling resources. Which is what this witchhunt is ultimately about. For every male who falls from grace there is a politically correct career officer or politician ready to achieve grace by prosecuting the cause. Rose-

mary Mariner is a candidate for admiral; Beverly Byron has been mentioned for Secretary of the Navy; Pat Schroeder has her sights set on being Secretary of Defense.

Another problem raised by William Lind is what happens when women troops are actually deployed. In combat situations, men will act instinctively to protect women, abandoning their tactical objectives in the process. The males' protective instincts will be increased by the knowledge of what other males will do to females taken prisoner. This is not theory, but the experience of the Israelis and other military forces that tried and then abandoned the practice of deploying women in combat.

No amount of sensitivity training, no amount of brainwashing can alter human nature. The Communists proved this at unbelievable cost. They could not make a new socialist man (or woman) who would respond as effectively and efficiently to administrative commands as to market incentives, who would be communist and not individualist. The Communists killed tens of millions of people and impoverished whole nations trying to change human nature, all the time calling it "liberation," just as radical feminists do. It didn't work.

And yet, the military leadership presses on. The Air Force has established a SERE program (Survival, Evasion, Resistance, and Escape), including its own "prisoner of war" camp in Washington state to desensitize its male recruits so that they won't react like men when female prisoners are tortured. In their infinite wisdom, Mrs. Schroeder and her feminist colleagues have enlisted the military in a program to brainwash men so they won't care what happens to women. That's consciousness raising, feminist style.

It is hardly necessary to have the detailed information that the military has decided to suppress, to see that America's ability to wage war has already been seriously weakened by the deployment of relatively large numbers of women to an overseas battlefield, even absent a combat role. Who does not remember the poignant stories the networks did, in lavish detail, about the children left behind by their mothers dispatched to war duty in the Persian Gulf? (In fact there were 16,337 single military parents who left anxious children behind.)

The net result is that an American President now is under pressure to win a war in four days or lose the war at home. What will be the temptation for dictators to test the will of America's liberated military and compassionate citizenry? These changes have implications for diplomacy and for long-term national-security interests that are literally incalculable.

The fabric of America's institutional and cultural life has already been shredded by the forces of the Left, with disastrous social consequences. Now the purpose and mission of the American military are held to be of less concern than the need to eradicate any possible injustice that might be associated with the exclusion of women from combat. The worst crimes of our century have been committed by crusades to eradicate injustice, stamp out politically incorrect attitudes, and reconstruct human nature. Let's not add the weakening of America's military to the depressing list of disasters of these utopias that failed.

NO

Sue Tunnicliffe

WAR, PEACE AND FEMINIST THEORY

In recent years a new approach has developed to the perennial question of why nations go to war. Those involved in this approach have shifted their focus away from the search for material causes of war to consider how cultural values and social practices sustain war as an institution.[1] This paper falls within this approach in seeking to draw attention to the links between cultural conceptions and constructions of gender and the ideology of militarism.

As the term militarism does not have a universally agreed meaning, I should state here that throughout the paper it is used in the sense of a general propensity to, and preparedness for, military action, real or threatened, to settle conflicts of interests. This paper is concerned with one of the processes that strengthen and maintain militarism—the recruitment and training of armed forces—and the gender ideology that underpins it. A considerable amount of feminist analysis of this process has been produced already but it tends to be ignored, overlooked or merely mentioned in passing by the majority of 'mainstream' authors. This paper seeks to demonstrate that any attempt to understand the cultural roots of war is seriously weakened by this omission. In particular, it will consider a recent article by Johan Galtung in which he explicitly claims that the cultural roots of militarism include "heavily nationalist, racist and sexist ideologies".[2] But while the influences of nationalism and racism are made relatively clear in his analysis this is not the case with regard to sexism. My claim is that his case would be strengthened considerably by the inclusion of a discussion of the feminist work outlined below.

'MANPOWER'

The sexist nature of the military is widely acknowledged and well-documented. As one commentator puts it, "to say that the combat branches of the armed forces are sexist is like remarking that gravity generally pulls downward."[3] The overall attitude of the military towards women is summed up in the words of General Robert H. Barrow, ex-commander of the U.S. marines:

From Sue Tunnicliffe, "War, Peace and Feminist Theory: An Expansion of Galtung's Theory of Cultural Violence," a paper presented to the International Studies Association 33rd Annual Convention, Atlanta, Georgia, USA (March/April 1992). Copyright © 1992 by Sue Tunnicliffe, Staffordshire University, Stoke-on-Trent, England. Reprinted by permission.

"War is a man's work. Biological convergence on the battlefield [i.e. women serving in combat] would not only be dissatisfying in terms of what women could do, but it would be an enormous psychological distraction for the male, who wants to think that he's fighting for that woman somewhere behind, not up there in the same foxhole with him. It tramples the male ego. When you get right down to it, you have to protect the manhood of war."[4]

General Barrow's comments demonstrate how the military version of masculinity, in which combat is the ultimate expression of manhood, is dependent on a complementary notion of femininity, according to which women should behave as passive creatures in need of protection. Feminists argue that this gender ideology is vital to the recruitment and training of armed forces. To quote Cynthia Enloe:

"Military forces past and present have not been able to get, keep and reproduce the sorts of soldiers they imagine they need without drawing on ideological beliefs concerning the different and stratified roles of women and men. Without assurance that women will play their 'proper' roles, the military cannot provide men with the incentives to enlist, obey orders, give orders, fight, kill, re-enlist, and convince their sons to enlist."[5]

Women as Other I

So "militaries need women"—but "they need women to behave as the gender 'women'... acting in ways women are supposed to act."[6] Most importantly, it is necessary for women to be seen as in need of protection. This notion of the 'protected' who are located on the 'home-front' serves to encourage in servicemen a preparedness to fight on the 'battlefront'. Women, as the 'protected', are necessary as symbols of 'the hearth and home' which the armed forces claim to be defending.

In order for women to play their 'proper' role of the protected to men as protectors, the battlefront/homefront distinction is essential. However, the presence of women in the armed forces makes this distinction hard to sustain. Militaries have always needed women to fill the nurturing and supportive roles—the 'feminine' occupations—necessary to their continuing operation. In order to preserve the myth of the battlefront/homefront distinction and the role of women as the protected it is the general case that women, as women, are banned from combat and largely confined to clerical, administrative and medical tasks, supporting the men who perform the proper task of the military—to protect. Wendy Chapkis notes the effect of this sexual division of labour:

"the ghettoization of women in traditionally feminine occupations in the military reinforces—even in the midst of the machine itself—the image of women as Other: nurturing, supportive and affectationally essential but practically dependent and therefore defenceless. Women then remain in need of male protectors which the military has been designed to create."[7]

Women serving in the military are marked as Other by different uniforms, different insignia and an emphasis on retaining their femininity by such means as the provision of lessons in make-up techniques.

It is a matter of fact, however, that even if they are not engaged in direct combat women do serve on the 'front'—the most obvious example is that of medical staff on the battlefield. During the recent Allied action in the Gulf, although they were not allowed to fly bombers, women were involved in the first air raids against Baghdad by flying mid-air refuelling planes. Clearly, being defined as non-combatants and restricted to support duties does not 'protect' any of these women from enemy fire. Nor does being based on the 'homefront' when it is targetted by long range bombers or missiles. During the Second World War, women in the British Auxiliary Territorial Service, the ATS, served in mixed ack-ack battalions where they "directed the searchlights and radio-located the enemy planes, yet were not allowed to fire the guns."[8]

It is also a matter of fact that women do, on occasion, engage in full combat roles, usually when the available manpower is insufficient.[9] Ruth Roach Pierson points to comparative studies which indicate that "women's exclusion from combat has been relaxed when societies have been undergoing social revolutionary struggle against repressive regimes, colonial or indigenous—as in wars of national liberation or 'people's wars', or when countries have mounted guerrilla resistance against invasion and conquest by a foreign enemy".[10] This challenge to the ideological link between combat and masculinity is rarely allowed to continue once stability is attained. For instance, Israeli women served as combatants in the war of independence of 1948–9 but since the regularization of the Israeli Defense Forces they have been excluded from "all jobs involving combat, jobs that have to be filled under bad conditions, and jobs where physical demands are regarded as too great for females".[11]

Women as Other II

The general exclusion of women from combat serves not only to maintain the distinction between the protected and the protector. It also serves to prevent the 'dilution' of the masculine nature of the military; to repeat General Barrow, "When you get right down to it, you have to protect the manhood of war." The military version of masculinity, then, involves the role of combat as the ultimate test of 'manhood', that is, to assert control, to dominate, to conquer, to kill if necessary is to be thoroughly masculine. The ideology is fuelled by positive images of the hero, the comrade-at-arms, the 'real' man. However, the realities of military life rarely live up to these romantic fantasies. Reliance on such images is not sufficient to ensure compliance to regulations and unquestioning obedience to orders by servicemen often living in harsh conditions and more often than not engaged in mundane activities. These positive images of masculinity are reinforced by negative images which rely on a conception of femininity which again sets up women as Other but in a more brutal sense. The use of female images in the training of recruits is by now familiar. Some link women with the enemy, others encourage brutal sexual behaviour as a sign of masculinity.[12] For a serviceman, the ultimate insult is to be considered feminine. Sharon Macdonald quotes an American marine recalling basic training:

"... one is continually addressed as faggot or a girl. These labels are usually screamed into the face from a distance of two or three inches by the drill instructor, a most awesome, intimidating figure. During such verbal assaults one is required, under threat of physical violence, to remain utterly passive."[13]

The drill instructor, in his aggressive use of power, embodies the masculinity required of a good soldier while the recruit is forced to take on the feminine role of passivity and ineffectiveness in the face of threatening behaviour. According to Macdonald, this tension serves to generate insecurity in the recruit about his sexual identity, forcing him to prove his masculinity "along the lines laid down by the military ideology".[14] So to prove one's manhood is to prove one is not a woman or, in other words, achievement of the military version of masculinity requires not only the fulfilling of masculine roles but the denigration of femininity; it requires women as the despised Other.

The gendered ideology on which militarism is based means, then, that women are needed to fulfill the feminine roles which support the military machine, but they must be banned, in general, from active combat lest they 'dilute' its masculine nature. Masculinity, as we have seen, is defined in terms of non-femininity, that is, it is based on the association of men with Self and women with Other. This involves at one level the determining of what are appropriate roles for women and at another level the denigration of what are seen as womanly qualities. Not surprisingly feminists have noted that "the more militarist a society tends to be the more sexist are its institutions and values", as in the examples of Nazi Germany and, more recently, Chile.[15]

CULTURAL VIOLENCE

I now want to turn to Galtung's account which offers a cultural approach to the legitimation of violation, including the direct violence of war. This he does by introducing the concept of 'cultural violence', defined as "those aspects of a culture, the symbolic sphere of our existence, that can be used to legitimate violence in its direct or structural form."[16] Galtung argues that cultural violence "makes direct or structural violence look and even feel right—or at least not wrong."[17] One way it can do this is by "changing the moral colour of an act from red/wrong to green/right or at least to yellow/acceptable."[18] For example, murder on behalf of oneself is wrong while murder on behalf of the country is right, and, in the United Kingdom, rape outside marriage is unacceptable while, until very recently, rape within marriage has been acceptable. Cultural violence can also work by making reality "opaque" so that, in fact, we do not see the violence as such. This is particularly true of structural violence which, in Galtung's words, "may be seen as about as natural as the air around us".[19] As Galtung puts it, "the culture preaches, teaches, admonishes, eggs on and dulls us into seeing exploitation and/or repression as normal and natural, or into not seeing them at all".[20] Eventually those who are subjected to this culturally legitimized structural violence may resort to direct violence in order to break out of the "structural iron cage" thereby triggering counter-violence to "keep the cage intact" which is also legitimized by cultural violence, that is, by the assumptions prevalent in the culture about such people.

But where do these assumptions come from? ...

CONCLUSION

By linking the work of feminists with Galtung's theory it becomes apparent that the allocation of specific roles and characteristics according to sex is a major form of cultural violence. This follows not only because it oppresses women—which is structural violence—but because the dualistic thinking which equates men with aggressiveness, dominance and activity and women with peacefulness, submission and passivity underpins the processes which support and legitimize direct violence in the form of war. Not only does this division sustain militarism by aiding the recruitment and training of armed forces but it encourages us to perceive men as less vulnerable and more hardened to war. This view allows them to be more readily sacrificed to military objectives, making the choice of military solutions to conflicts that little bit easier.

It has been claimed that "more thorough research on the social and ideological supports for war preparation would enable us to outline much more clearly the social changes which might assist the more narrowly focused processes of disarmament and international political change."[21] I would argue on the strength of thorough, feminist research already in existence that those social changes must include the dismantling of all oppressive masculine/feminine dichotomies. In practice, this would involve the promotion of women in society and the re-valuing of so-called womanly qualities. In other words, the achievement of the goals of feminism would take us some of the way down the road to peace.

NOTES

1. See, for example, Elise Boulding, Clovis Brigagao & Kevin Clements (eds.), Peace Culture and Society (Boulder: Westview, 1991). Martin Shaw & Colin Creighton, The Sociology of War and Peace (London: Macmillan, 1987).

2. Johan Galtung, 'Cultural Violence', in Journal of Peace Research, vol.27, no.3, (1990A), pp.291–305.

3. Gwynne Dyer, War (London: Bodley Head, 1986), p.123.

4. Nancy Hartsock, 'Masculinity, Heroism and the Making of War', in Adrienne Harris & Ynestra King (eds.), Rocking the Ship of State: Toward a Feminist Peace Politics, (Boulder: Westview, 1989), p.134.

5. Cynthia Enloe, Does Khaki Become You? The Militarization of Women's Lives (London: Pluto, 1983), p.212.

6. Ibid.

7. Wendy Chapkis, 'Sexuality and Militarism', in Eva Isaksson (ed.), Women and the Military System, (London: Harvester, 1988), p.111.

8. Di Parkin, 'Women in the Armed Services, 1940–5', in R. Samuel (ed.), Patriotism: The Making and Unmaking of British National Identity, (London: Routledge, 1989). p.169. Parkin includes a reproduction of an ATS recruiting poster which proclaims "THE MEN WILL DO THE FIGHTING—YOU MUST DO THE REST".

9. Recently, the governments of Canada and the Netherlands have relaxed the combat ban due to a combination of manpower shortage and pressure from demands for equal rights for women in the military. In Great Britain, it was announced in December 1991 that Flt Lt Sally Cox would be the first woman allowed by the RAF to train as a fighter pilot. In February 1992 it was reported that she had failed to complete her training course at RAF Chivenor where the failure rate is between 10–20%.

10. Ruth Roach Pierson, 'Did Your Mother Wear Army Boots? Feminist Theory and Women's Relation to War, Peace and Revolution', in Sharon Macdonald, Pat Holden & Shirley Ardener, (eds.), Images of Women in Peace and War, (London: Macmillan, 1987), p.222. See also Gwynne Dyer, op cit, p.125. It is estimated that women represented 25–30% of the Sandinista Liberation Front's combat troops in Nicaragua.

11. Ibid.

12. See, for example, Gwynne Dyer, op cit, p.123. Dyer quotes a Senior Drill Instructor in the US Marine Corps who employs the image of "Suzie Rottencrotch".

13. Quoted in Sharon Macdonald, 'Drawing the Lines—Gender, Peace and War: an Introduction', in Macdonald et al. op cit, p.16.

14. Ibid.

15. Betty Reardon, Sexism and the War System, (New York: Teachers College, 1985), p.14. See, for example, Maria Elena Valenzuela, 'Women Under Dictatorship and Military Regime: The Case of Chile', in E. Boulding, C. Brigagao & K. Clements, op cit, pp.229–238.

16. Johan Galtung, (1990A), op cit, p.291.

17. Ibid.

18. Ibid, p.292.

19. Johan Galtung, 'Violence and Peace', in Paul Smoker, Ruth Davies and Barbara Munske, A Reader in Peace Studies, (Oxford: Pergamon, 1990B), p.12.

20. Johan Galtung, (1990A), op cit, p.295.

21. Martin Shaw & Colin Creighton, op cit, p.11.

POSTSCRIPT

Would Women in Combat Weaken National Security?

The debate over the availability of combat roles to women is currently being conducted in the United States and other countries. To gain a sense of how the issue is being debated in Canada, see Ellen Symons, "Under Fire: Canadian Women in Combat," *Canadian Journal of Women and the Law* (Spring 1991). The controversy received new impetus from the Persian Gulf War, where women of the United States and other countries came under fire, were wounded, killed, and captured, along with men. By all accounts, the women served well. In the United States and other countries, military specialties are the last great exclusively male preserve from which women are legally barred. Is that discrimination or reasonable policy? If women become more fully integrated into the political power structures of countries, how will domestic and international policy be affected? Two readings that should be mentioned immediately are Betty Reardon, "Feminists Concepts of Peace and Security," in *A Reader in Peace Studies*, edited by Paul Smoker, Ruth Davies, and Barbara Munske (Pergamon Press, 1990) and Christine Ball, "Towards a Feminine Perspective on Peace," *Peace Research* (Spring 1991). Inasmuch as Johan Galtung's work is mentioned so prominently in Tunnicliffe's article, you might also wish to read some of his analysis. See "Cultural Violence," *Journal of Peace Research* (Fall, 1990).

One way that exclusion from combat service works against women is that it keeps them from advancing in rank equally with men. Most officers who achieve the rank of admiral or general come from their service's combat elements. Infantry officers may become the Army chief of staff; no supply officer has ever made it. Another point of discrimination, arguably against men, is that since women are barred from most combat roles, they do not in the United States have to register for the draft. Almost certainly, opening all or most combat roles to women would mean that the U.S. Supreme Court would strike down the gender discrimination in draft laws and require women to register and, if necessary, to be drafted on an equal basis with men. By extension, this means that serving in combat roles would not be voluntary for women. "If men can't get away with it [avoiding combat], neither can women," commented Professor Charles Moskos, an expert in military sociology.

To return to the more general question of women in politics, there is also the fascinating and important question of whether or not women in equal power to men would alter the basic tenets of domestic and international political

280

policy. If it is true, as some analysts claim, that women have a different, less violent political orientation, then their increased role in national and international political structures, including the military, will enhance security, in part by decreasing the overall level of violence in politics. The object of security, after all, is safety, whether that is brought about by having an invincible army or by having no army or no need for an army. This, needless to say, is very controversial, and even feminist scholars are split on the issue whether differing male-female approaches to politics are completely learned behaviors or not. For readings on this issue and the perspectives of women, consult J. Ann Tickner, *Gender in International Relations: Feminist Perspectives on Achieving Global Security* (Columbia University Press, 1992) and Nancy E. McGlen and Meredith Reid Sarkees, eds., *Women in Foreign Policy* (Routledge, 1993).

ISSUE 16

Is the Kidnapping of Criminal Suspects from Foreign Countries Justifiable?

YES: Robert Bork, from "The Reach of American Law," *The National Interest* (Fall 1992)

NO: Jack R. Binns, from "Reflections on Mr. Bumble: Extraterritorial Kidnapping," *Foreign Service Journal* (October 1992)

ISSUE SUMMARY

YES: Robert Bork, a scholar at the American Enterprise Institute and former judge of the U.S. Court of Appeals, contends that trying criminal suspects kidnapped from other countries does not violate the law and that the U.S. courts are wise to avoid inserting themselves into the controversy by barring such trials.

NO: Jack R. Binns, a retired professional diplomat and former U.S. ambassador to Honduras, argues that bringing suspects to the United States for trial by kidnapping them, rather than through the legal process of extradition, is bad law and worse foreign policy.

Sovereignty is one of the key concepts defining the international system. What this means is that each country is legally in control of what occurs within its territorial boundaries and free from outside interference or judgment. Sovereignty, not recognizing a higher authority, is more a legal than political reality, and even in the legal realm, it is not absolute. Yet the idea that each country should respect every other countries' sovereignty is central to international law.

This brings up the question, key to the debate here, what can and should a country do about an individual who is charged with having committed a crime but who lives in or has fled to another country? In most cases, this involves a matter where a person was present in one country, allegedly committed a crime, and then is found to be in another country. Sometimes it involves a crime that a country defines as illegal even though it did not occur in that country. The specific case debated here is one such example. Enrique Camarena-Salazar, an agent with the U.S. Drug Enforcement Agency (DEA), was working in Mexico with authorities there to break a drug ring operating from Guadalajara. He was tortured and murdered in 1990. Officials of the DEA charged that a Mexican physician, Huberto Alvarez-Machain, was one of those involved in Camarena's death. Alvarez was brought to the United States and charged with several crimes, including killing a U.S. federal agent. The United States defines that as a crime subject to U.S. criminal procedures, no matter where the act takes place. Similarly, after U.S. forces invaded Panama in 1989 to overthrow the government of strongman General Manuel Noriega, he was brought to the United States, tried, and convicted on a number of criminal charges that he committed in Panama.

Extradition is the normal procedure under international law whereby an individual is transferred from the jurisdiction of the state were he or she is to the state that has filed the charges. A country asks another to surrender an individual; there is usually a hearing in the second country to determine if there is reasonable cause; and if there is, then the individual is transferred. There is no right for one state to demand that another surrender an accused person. Indeed, most states, including the United States and Canada, have a long history of refusing to extradite individuals who are being sought for what is arguably political persecution.

In the first reading, Robert Bork, an eminent legal scholar who was once nominated for the U.S. Supreme Court, makes a fairly technical legal argument that the kidnapping of Dr. Alvarez-Machain was justified. Advocates of this point of view argue that a criminal suspect might be able to escape during extradition procedures, especially in a country that has little interest in bringing him to justice. Some countries shield those accused of crimes by other countries. Libya, for example, has refused to extradite two of its agents accused by the United States and Great Britain of masterminding the terrorist bombing that destroyed Pan American flight 103 over Lockerbie, Scotland, in 1988, which killed 270 passengers and crew.

Those who oppose kidnapping accused felons to bring them to trial argue that the practice is neither legally justifiable nor politically wise. The legal argument, which Jack Binns makes in the second article, is that abducting alleged criminals violates the standards of international law as well as precedents set in U.S. courts. Opponents of kidnapping also point out that such acts can create great resentment in countries whose territories have been violated. Mexicans, for example, were outraged when Alvarez-Machain was abducted and delivered into the hands of U.S. authorities, who had posted a reward for his delivery. Officials in other countries also took a dim view of the extralegal apprehension of Dr. Alvarez-Machain. A spokesperson for the Canadian government declared, "Any attempt by a foreign official to abduct someone from Canadian territory is a criminal act."

The issues involved in this debate, then, are many and complex. Sometimes what is just and what is legal are not the same. Kidnapping, even for some higher cause, is illegal for individuals. Are governments governed by differing standards? Political ramifications also have to be factored in, because countries react negatively to having someone, accused felon or not, forcibly taken out of their territories. On balance, Robert Bork approves of such abductions; Jack Binns does not.

YES

Robert Bork

THE REACH OF AMERICAN LAW

The Supreme Court made a great many headlines last term.... [F]ew attracted more press attention and scandalized commentary, both at home and abroad, than the holding that our courts can try a Mexican citizen whom the United States kidnapped from his own country.

The *New York Times* editorial page called the decision "astonishing" and agreed with the three dissenting justices that it was "monstrous." Senator Daniel Patrick Moynihan, who frequently sees violations of international law in American actions abroad, said, "The decision is manifestly wrong." In the *Los Angeles Times,* under the headline "The Supreme Court's Insult to Law-Abiding Countries," a law professor denounced the "moral shabbiness of both our nation's conduct and the court's approval" of it, the "intellectual poverty" of Chief Justice [William] Rehnquist's majority opinion, and an "intense and extreme... right-wing activism" that is "against individual rights." Canada, Switzerland, and nations all over Latin America protested.

The excitement is misplaced, for the decision is undoubtedly correct. It does, however, raise in a dramatic context the vexed issue of the respective duties of courts and the executive branch with respect to the reach of U.S. law abroad.

Pursuant to a joint effort to stop or lessen international drug trafficking, Mexico allows agents of the U.S. Drug Enforcement Agency [DEA] to operate on its territory. Enrique ("Kiki") Camarena-Salazar, one such American agent, was kidnapped by Mexican drug traffickers and tortured with a red hot pipe to make him reveal what information law enforcement officials had. He was then killed. The DEA had reason to believe that one Humberto Alvarez-Machain, a physician and citizen of Mexico, assisted in this grisly proceeding by prolonging Camarena's life, so that his torture and interrogation could be extended.

Lower-level DEA officials, determined to bring Alvarez to justice, offered a reward for his delivery to this country. Alvarez was seized in his office in Guadalajara, taken by private plane to El Paso, Texas, and arrested there by DEA officers.

Alvarez was indicted for several crimes, including conspiracy to kidnap and kidnapping a federal agent, and the felony murder of a federal agent. These are crimes under U.S. law wherever they occur. The district court,

From Robert Bork, "The Reach of American Law," *The National Interest* (Fall 1992). Copyright © 1992 by *The National Interest*, Washington, DC. Reprinted by permission.

however, held that it lacked jurisdiction because Alvarez's abduction at the insistence of the U.S. government violated the extradition treaty with Mexico. The court of appeals affirmed, but the Supreme Court reversed and remanded the case for trial.

THE OPINIONS

Of the three types of issues the Alvarez abduction raises—legal, diplomatic, and moral—the Supreme Court was properly concerned only with the first. Much of the criticism of the Court's decision, however, is made on grounds of morality. Quite aside from the fact that the decision can also be defended on moral grounds, such criticism rests on the increasingly popular supposition that it is the function of the Court to decide on the general "rightness" of matters brought before it—i.e., to decide as the critic would decide if he had combined judicial, legislative, and executive power. Our perception of the Court's role is less and less that of a group of lawyers striving to arrive at the better view of the meaning of law in ambiguous contexts than that of a body of philosophers seeking universal principles of natural justice. It must be admitted that the Court has often accepted just such an inflated view of its function, but in *Alvarez* it did not.

Both the majority opinion by Chief Justice Rehnquist and the dissent by Justice Stevens, joined by Justices Blackmun and O'Connor, engaged in close readings of the extradition treaty to determine whether it forbade the abduction. The dissent found additional support for its conclusion in customary international law, which the majority sloughed off rather quickly. A treaty is, of course, a form of international law, but a form far more definite than many branches of that subject. Customary international law, said to be derived from observation of the actual practices of nations, is frequently vague and internally inconsistent. But a treaty is a legal document rather than commentators' summaries of international practice or a statement of moral principle. The Court majority, therefore, set itself the mundane legal task of interpreting a contract between the United States and Mexico to determine whether the parties had ruled out such a kidnapping.

The terms of the treaty with Mexico, as the chief justice's opinion observed, do not purport to specify the only means by which either country may gain custody of a national of the other in order to prosecute him. The jurisdiction of the trial court had, therefore, to be determined by examination of other legal materials which might give meaning to the silence of the treaty.

There had never been a case quite like this one; it was, in legal parlance, a case of first impression. There were, however, precedents that shed some light.... [One such Court case decided in 1886 was] *Ker v. Illinois.... Ker* held that a fugitive abducted from Peru by a private person, a Pinkerton agent, could be tried in this country. In [this] case, the Court rejected the argument that the abductee had a right under the existing extradition treaty to be brought here for prosecution only according to the treaty's terms....

The difference between the kidnapping from Peru and *Alvarez*, of course, was that there was no American government involvement in the former case and the Peruvian government had not protested as Mexico did. Still, the principle is much the same. In the absence of a specific law whose protection the defendant is entitled to claim, it does not matter to an American court how the defendant was brought within its jurisdiction. This is perfectly sensible. The kidnapping of Alvarez undoubtedly violated Mexican law, and Mexico asked for the extradition of those it thought responsible for trial in its courts. But U.S. courts do not apply Mexico's criminal code. The request for extradition, moreover, was necessarily addressed to the executive branch; the judiciary would become involved only if the executive complied and the person to be returned appealed to the courts on the ground that his was not an extraditable offense.

The chief justice noted that the *Ker* decision, as well as the position of the United States that the case applied to forcible abductions made outside the United States–Mexico treaty, had been brought to the attention of the Mexican government as early as 1906. Nevertheless, in negotiating the current version of the treaty, Mexico did not attempt to limit the effect of *Ker*. This omission is relevant because the treaty did adopt [other limits on extradition]....

Justice Stevens' dissent [in the *Alvarez* case] argued from the comprehensiveness of the treaty that it must be read to govern all methods of obtaining the presence of a foreign national for prosecution here. But his reasoning from the treaty's provisions seems less than airtight:

> Article 9 expressly provides that neither Contracting Party is bound to deliver up its own nationals, although it may do so in its discretion, but if it does not do so, it "shall submit the case to its competent authorities for purposes of prosecution."

This certainly seems, as the dissent says, to cover the subject of extradition comprehensively, but it does not address the question of one nation's allowable actions if the other neither grants extradition nor initiates a prosecution. Though it is clear that Mexico, if asked, would not extradite Alvarez, it would be unfair to conclude that Mexico would not prosecute him. That nation had already prosecuted, convicted, and given the maximum sentence of forty years to others involved in Camerena's torture-murder. The Court did not address the question of Mexico's intention, which, for reasons to be developed, was a proper omission.

* * *

The dissent's citation of other treaty provisions—requiring "sufficient" evidence to grant extradition, withholding extradition for political, military offenses or when the person has already been tried, and the like—do not clarify what happens when these requirements have been satisfied but the country whose national is sought will neither extradite nor prosecute. Thus, it is not entirely true, as the dissent charges, that the majority "concludes that the Treaty merely creates an optional method of obtaining jurisdiction over alleged offenders, and that the parties silently reserved the right to resort to self-help whenever they deem force more expeditious than legal process." It would fit the facts of *Alvarez* more accurately to say that the Court concluded, albeit tacitly, that the option of self-help is available when the executive branch thinks the requested state has not complied with Article 9. Again, we have no way of knowing what the executive branch thought, and the Court did well not to inquire.

Alvarez claimed as well that he had been denied due process of law. The *Ker* Court rejected the defendant's argument that his kidnapping violated due process of law, a ruling reaffirmed in 1952 when the Court, in the case of a man kidnapped in Illinois by Michigan officers, held that

> due process of law is satisfied when one present in court is convicted of a crime after having been fairly apprized of the charges against him and after a fair trial in accordance with constitutional procedural safeguards. There is nothing in the Constitution that requires a court to permit a guilty person rightfully convicted to escape justice because he has been brought to trial against his will.

Finally, Alvarez invoked customary international law in an effort to defeat the jurisdiction of the U.S. courts, arguing not that international law applied directly but rather that international kidnappings are so clearly condemned by such law that its principles should guide the interpretation of the treaty. The Court found no principles, other than the most general and unspecific, that justified adding a term to the extradition treaty the parties had not adopted.

CONFLICTING PRINCIPLES

Actually, there is a fairly specific international law principle relevant to Alvarez's case. A nation's territorial integrity is considered a basic attribute of sovereignty, and that integrity, commentators generally agree, is violated when agents of a foreign nation enter the country to seize persons for trial in the foreign nation. Though it is commonly said that the principles of international law are embodied in the law of the United States, in fact violations are commonly handled not by courts but by the executive branch. Persons abducted abroad and brought here for trial have, upon the protest of the foreign government whose territory was invaded, often been returned.

Moreover, as is common in law, perhaps most particularly in international law, one seemingly firm principle is immediately countered by another. Here, the principle of Mexico's territorial integrity is countered by the U.S.' right of self-defense. Even forcible abductions have been justified on that ground. Alvarez's abduction may be justified on a similar principle of self-defense, a principle which would not seem to be affected by whether there was a protest by the nation in which the abduction took place. Abraham Sofaer, then the legal adviser to the State Department, testified to Congress in 1989 that among the factors to be considered are "the seriousness of the offense for which the apprehended person is arrested; the citizenship of the offender; whether the foreign government itself had tried to bring the offenders to justice or would have consented to the apprehension had it been asked; and the general tenor of bilateral relations with the United States." These are obviously not factors for consideration by courts but by the political branches of our government.

Drug traffickers, with whom Alvarez was allegedly working, constitute a major threat to this country, which in itself may justify unconsented action against such persons by the American government. Alvarez's specific offense, using his medical skills to keep an American agent alive for additional torture, is among the most heinous that can be imagined.

Whatever the validity of the self-defense argument, which seems tenuous to some, it seems clear that courts should not employ customary international law to limit the president's powers. In 1980, the Department's Office of Legal Counsel

(OLC) took up the question of the Federal Bureau of Investigation's authority under U.S. law to arrest a fugitive in a foreign country without that country's consent. The 1980 opinion concluded that the principles of customary international law deprived the FBI of any such power under domestic law. The 1980 opinion reasoned that the authority of the United States is limited by the sovereignty of other nations so that the president and Congress could not legally authorize action in a foreign country that ran counter to customary international law, and, it was thought, extraterritorial arrests by the FBI would violate such customary law.

In any event, whether or not the United States was free to depart from customary international law, the FBI itself was subject to its general enabling statutes, and these, while they do not themselves restrict the agency's authority in this regard, must be interpreted to prevent the FBI from departing from the principles of customary international law. The first argument was that the United States itself could never lawfully violate those principles; the second was that even if the United States could, our own statutes must be read not to allow extraterritorial arrests, though the statutes could be changed.

* * *

Since these conclusions would place our government under an absolute prohibition against bringing criminals such as terrorists to book under all circumstances, the subject was reexamined by Reagan's OLC, then headed by William Barr,... President Bush's attorney general. The conclusions were rather different. Barr's opinion did not quibble about the content of customary international law, but went directly to the issue of the power of the United States to violate or, as he put it, "depart from" those norms. Under our constitutional structure, Barr said, the legislative and executive branches are free to take or direct actions that are not in accord with principles of customary international law. That conclusion found support in an 1814 opinion by Chief Justice John Marshall which described the rule of customary international law as

> a guide which the sovereign follows or abandons at his will. The rule, like other precepts of morality, of humanity, and even of wisdom, is addressed to the judgment of the sovereign; and although it cannot be disregarded by him without obloquy, yet it may be disregarded.

The rule may also be one which cannot be disregarded without incurring not only obloquy but sanctions, challenges in the International Court of Justice, suits against the United States in the foreign nation whose law was violated, deterioration of relations with the country in which the abduction took place, and reduced law enforcement cooperation by other nations. But these consequences, however much they should count in making a decision to conduct an abduction abroad, are legally irrelevant to the authority of the United States under its own law to seize foreigners abroad for trial here. All these considerations properly fall within the discretion of the executive branch and Congress and are not properly the subject of judicial determination.

The Barr opinion also rejected the conclusion of the 1980 opinion with respect to the limitations customary international law places upon the FBI's enabling statutes. The Bureau is given authority to make arrests without any specification of a territorial limitation. Because the president has constitutional authority to act contrary to customary international law, the restrictions of that law should not be attached to general statutes in a way that prevents the president from exercising his authority. Barr's 1989 opinion seems correct. International law, including customary international law, should not affect our constitutional arrangements, however desirable it may be that the executive branch make every effort to act in conformity with internationally recognized principles.

The chief justice's opinion did not discuss the firmness of Mexico's determination to try Alvarez, the various principles and counter-principles of international law that might be brought into play, or the opposed views of OLC in 1980 and 1989. At first sight, this may seem cavalier, but it was probably deliberate and undoubtedly wise. Had the Court entered upon these subjects, it would have had to discuss such matters as Mexico's law enforcement. Assuming, as seems entirely likely, that judicial inquiry would have found that Mexico would prosecute and punish Alvarez, the Court would have committed itself to engage in such inquiries with regard to other countries in future cases. The mere fact of such an inquiry would be resented and an adverse determination would certainly heighten the strain of our relations with the country in question. [Chief Justice] Rehnquist's opinion closed, perhaps for that reason, with the observation that there are benefits in allowing these matters to be resolved by diplomacy.

THE EXECUTIVE'S CALL

Alvarez is best seen, therefore, as a sound separation of powers decision. That is the meaning of the Court's observation that "[Alvarez]... may be correct that [his] abduction was 'shocking'... and that it may be in violation of general international law principles. Mexico has protested the abduction of [Alvarez] through diplomatic notes... and the decision of whether [he] should be returned to Mexico, as a matter outside of the Treaty, is a matter for the Executive Branch."

One of the difficulties with the case is that the decision to kidnap Alvarez was not made by executive branch officials with no responsibility for our foreign affairs. That difficulty was cured in this instance because the abduction was ratified when the United States refused either to return the abducted Mexican or to amend the extradition treaty between the two countries to prohibit such kidnappings. It is now U.S. policy that such abductions may be made only with the agreement of the president and the Departments of State and Justice. The refusal to amend the treaty to ban kidnapping may reflect the judgment that this would require amending all extradition treaties to which the United States is a party. Our government could not very well pick and choose on the ground that some governments are trustworthy and some are not. The decision not to eschew kidnapping in all cases undoubtedly reflects a further judgment that this tactic must be held in reserve in an era with a rising incidence of terrorism and international drug trafficking that threatens Americans abroad and at home. There are, of course, very good reasons why the United States may resort to the forcible removal of a suspect in violation of foreign law and in opposition to the wishes of the foreign government involved. Some governments actively sponsor terrorism directed at Americans or have officials who are themselves heavily involved in drug trafficking; some display high degrees of corruption in law enforcement; some would find it politically unpopular to turn over their nationals to the United States for trial; some, having found on their own soil terrorists or drug traffickers of other nations, are afraid of violence against their own citizens in retaliation. Unless the United States is willing to render its citizens even more vulnerable, there will be occasions when it must seize foreigners on foreign soil or on ships or airplanes registered in or owned by other countries.

* * *

There are more U.S. laws that apply to actions taken abroad by foreign nationals than most people realize. Reacting to specific acts of terrorism, Congress has gradually expanded the list of crimes abroad that are punishable here. Initially, airline hijacking was covered; then, after the assassinations of President John F. Kennedy and Senator Robert Kennedy, Congress enacted a criminal prohibition on the murder of a president or vice president anywhere in the world. After the murder of a diplomat, Congress gave criminal jurisdiction to U.S. courts to try those who killed or assaulted designated diplomatic employees, and moved on a few years later to outlaw assaults, murders, and kidnappings of members of the Cabinet, the Supreme Court, and Congress. When terrorists began attacking or seizing Americans who held no government positions, Congress first provided criminal penalties for those who took American hostages, and finally went the whole route by providing criminal jurisdiction here over those who kill or assault Americans anywhere in the world in acts of terrorism. There is no real doubt concerning the legality of these exercises of jurisdiction. There is also no real doubt that if an American president were assassinated in Algeria by a citizen of that country, Americans would support the assassin's abduction—even those who now denounce the seizure of the accomplice to Camerena's assassination....

There are doctrines intended to mitigate the extent to which U.S. courts can interfere with our foreign relations by assuming jurisdiction over actors in or policies of other countries. One is the principle of comity, which means that the U.S. court whose jurisdiction is invoked by a private party will make a judgment about which state has the paramount interest in the matter and defer to its law. Another is the act of state doctrine, which holds that our courts will not question acts required to be done on its own soil by a foreign nation. Neither of these doctrines has provided a satisfactory resolution of the conflicts between our courts' assertions of extraterritorial jurisdiction and the desire of other nations not to have their policies hampered or their citizens harassed by our courts....

[There is good reason, however, why the act of state doctrine has not been accepted by U.S. courts. For example, if] the word of the United Kingdom about its policies had to be accepted, then, in the next case, the court might find itself urged to accept the word of a Muammar Qadaffi or a Leonid Brezhnev. There are duplicitous as well as reliable foreign governments. To accept the act of state argument in [one] case would place the court in the future position of leaving American plaintiffs at the mercy of corrupt foreign governments, or of having to decide which governments were trustworthy and which were not. The first alternative is difficult, perhaps impossible, to accept, while the second involves an even greater interference with the relations between the United States and other nations than the exercise of extraterritorial jurisdiction.

It may seem that the solution to such dilemmas is to have the executive branch, through the State Department, inform the court whether the exercise of jurisdiction is appropriate in such cases; but that, too, has serious problems. It is one thing for the executive branch to limit its own invocation of a court's jurisdiction for reasons of state; it is quite another for the executive branch to urge the courts to deny relief to an American citizen who has an otherwise valid claim. Fairness aside, there are apt to be domestic political repercussions. In the uranium cartel cases, repeated, but always unsuccessful, efforts were made to get the State Department to make representations to the courts about the impropriety of doubting the word and ignoring the policies of the foreign governments.

The State Department lawyers recognized the problems with the act of state doctrine, but even if there had been no doctrinal difficulties, for the Department to file on the side of the cartelists would have meant spending scarce political capital. Members of the Senate had expressed their outrage that the Department of Justice, recognizing the foreign relations problems, had let the companies off with a slap on the wrist.

Scholarly debate has swirled and will continue to swirl around exercises of extraterritorial jurisdiction by the United States. Given the nature of the problem, no entirely satisfactory resolution seems possible, at least where such jurisdiction is invoked by states or private parties. The indictment in August of fugitive Colombian drug trafficker Pablo Escobar by a New York federal court, and the announcement by the U.S. government of a $2 million reward for information leading to his capture, show how timely this issue remains. It is encouraging, however, that the Rehnquist Court, in the context of extraterritorial executive action, has resisted the impulse to insert the courts into what is best seen as a foreign policy question entrusted to the political branches.

NO

Jack R. Binns

REFLECTIONS ON MR. BUMBLE: EXTRATERRITORIAL KIDNAPPING

"If the law supposes that... the law is a ass, a idiot," said Dickens's Mr. Bumble in *Oliver Twist,* Bumble might have been describing our Supreme Court's recent 6 to 3 decision in *U.S. v. Humberto Alvarez Machain.* The court held that it was quite all right, thank you, for paid agents of the United States government (employees acting for the Drug Enforcement Administration [DEA]) to abduct a Mexican national from Mexico for a crime committed in that country, *sans* permission of the government of Mexico, and deliver him to U.S. authorities for trial. The existing bilateral extradition treaty, official protests of the Mexican government, and international law, the court said, are matters of no account. Evidently kidnapping by a sovereign power is not a crime, at least as long as it is carried out beyond U.S. frontiers.

The Supreme Court's majority (with a stinging dissent) held that there was nothing in the U.S.–Mexican extradition treaty about the parties' "refraining from forcibly abducting people from others' territory" and that "the principles of international law provide no basis for interpreting the treaty to include an implied term prohibiting international abductions." Thus the decisions of the District and Appeals Courts that Alvarez was to be returned to Mexico without trial should be reversed. In a stroke the court:...

- Ruled that key principles of international law, including the doctrine of sovereignty are not important considerations in matters of U.S. domestic law, at least as far as the Supreme Court is concerned;
- Implicitly sanctioned future "unfriendly acts" of this nature against friendly governments (much to their alarm), at least until President Bush promised Mexico that we would not exercise this newly approved power. But then why did the Department of Justice go to court and argue for the decision? Could it be that no one thought the Mexicans would be angry? Or was it that no one cared?;
- Turned reason on its head as regards the purpose and validity of extradition treaties to which the U.S. government has subscribed (more than 100

such are currently in force). If states may legally kidnap nationals of another state from that state, why are treaties needed?; and

- Brought our country into international disrepute (this, of course, is nothing new).

DO UNTO OTHERS

How the court's decision will affect our relations with Mexico, Latin America, generally, and other nations over the longer term remains to be seen. The administration appears to be trying to undo the damage, but in reality, the government's own hubris (or ignorance) gave rise to it. Everyone seems to have forgotten how the State Department's former legal adviser, Judge Abraham Sofaer, responded to a congressional committee in 1985 when questioned on the issue: "How would we feel if some foreign nation... came over here and seized some terrorist suspect in New York City, Boston, or Philadelphia because we refused through normal channels of international legal communication to extradite that individual?" Simple and to the point.

Chief Justice William Rehnquist surely gave substance to Mr. Bumble when he wrote that the decision might be "shocking" and "in violation of general international law [sic]" but held that the United States had the right to try Alvarez. Allow me to line up instead with the minority, Justices John Paul Stevens, Harry Blackmun, and Sandra O'Connor, and agree with Stevens's view that it was a "monstrous" decision that will "damage international respect for the rule of law."

Clearly the law in the Alvarez case, as interpreted by the majority (Justices Byron White, Antonin Scalia, Anthony Kennedy, Thomas Souter, Clarence Thomas, and Rehnquist), is an ass. But while the ultimate blame lies with the court, the administration is not blameless.

The Alvarez "snatch" itself was a rogue operation (i.e. not sanctioned at the political level), but it was ultimately supported by the highest levels. Perhaps most significantly, it was this administration, in the person of Attorney General William P. Barr, that pushed and argued hard for extending the extraterritorial reach of U.S. law.

ORIGINS OF THE ASS

Until a strange and controversial 1985 Justice Department opinion by then Assistant Attorney General Barr, who was heading the Legal Counsel's Office, both State and Justice had agreed that the kidnapping of suspects from foreign countries was unlawful. With this 1985 antecedent, asserting that such action was legal, it came as no surprise that Justice argued in support of DEA in the Alvarez case. Nor should it raise an eyebrow that now Attorney General Barr hailed the decision as "an important victory in our ongoing efforts against terrorists [sic] and narco-traffickers who operate against the U.S. from overseas." If that was true, why did President Bush assure the Mexicans we wouldn't do it again?

Being neither a lawyer nor a legal scholar, I am not qualified to comment on the finer legal points involved. But I can read the decision and comments of those who are qualified to judge the substance of the case. They may not have been unanimous, but an overwhelming majority has been severely critical.

Like my Foreign Service colleagues, I spent my career upholding and defending the Constitution, seeking to advance U.S. interests as defined by various administrations, and trying to strengthen comity among nations. That's why I joined the Foreign Service. To me, the *Alvarez* decision was a slap in the face, an ignorant, narrow decision. It repudiated many of the principles of our foreign policy to which I and thousands of others devoted much of our professional lives.

What, we may ask, is going on? What ever became of the "new world order" the Bush Administration claimed to be designing and constructing not long ago? Where does *Alvarez* fit in? What kind of order—world or otherwise—can proceed from vigilantism endorsed by our highest court? An observation by Justice William Brandeis comes to mind: "If government becomes a lawbreaker ... it invites every man to become a law unto himself." Substitute "nation" for "man."

SOVEREIGNTY FOR WHOM?

Beyond its narrow focus, the Supreme Court's decision is remarkable for its absence of historical context or perspective. It's as though the law were being invented at that point; the issue did not exist until 1990 in Mexico. Justice Scalia holds that legislation should be interpreted based on its pure text, without regard to the intent of legislators. It follows that he, and those who accept that line of reason, would have no problem with giving equally short shrift to history and the evolution of general international law.

A word also needs to be said in favor of the exercise of sovereignty and protection of citizens. Both are important attributes of nationhood and government. Goodness knows this administration has not been slow to stake out broad claims in either sphere. Moreover, these have not been minor factors in our history as a nation generally nor our diplomatic history specifically. We have conducted military operations from the 18th century (Barbary pirates) to the late 20th (attacks on Libya following the Berlin bombings) in the name of both. Within this same period it is possible to count at least one war (1812) and several crises (e.g., the Trent affair) that arose from attempts by one power to exercise extraterritorial rights over another. We were usually resisting such assertion.

In the *Alvarez* decision, we blithely ignored that history of resistance to incursions on our sovereignty. The decision lacked any recognition that other states might seek to exercise these same powers, any notion that international law has a role to play in the conduct of our international relations and usually serves U.S. interests, and any apparent awareness of its implications.

Whether the result was the product of hubris or ignorance, I leave to others to decide. Whatever the reason, the decision was bad law and bad foreign policy.

BUREAUCRACY ENDURES

The Supreme Court ruling was the latest example of our tendency to diverge from what we preach and ignore international law when we think it convenient. The decision is bound to affect our relations not only with Mexico but with other countries as well. But how might we reduce the decision's effects? The president's belated efforts to reassure the Mexicans (perhaps to save the North American Free Trade Agreement) were helpful, but may not persuade many others.

continued on p. 296

JUST DESSERTS AND NASTY SURPRISES

Living near the border in Arizona, I quickly perceived our Mexican neighbors' outrage at the Alvarez decision and got a taste of the possible consequences. Most were aware of the Mexican government's immediate protest, its "suspension" of cooperation with the DEA in Mexico (since rescinded), and its later rejection of all U.S. assistance in the "drug war." Relatively few, however, were aware that, within a week of the decision, armed Mexican authorities entered U.S. territory and seized several Mexicans at gunpoint before they could be processed for entry by U.S. officials. That the U.S. officials watched and did not respond showed restraint. That's to be praised.

President Bush's subsequent assurances to Mexican President Salinas helped to defuse, at least for now, what might have been a powder keg. But as one distinguished former ambassador under whom I once served noted correctly in an analogous situation, "Our hosts won't forget this matter and will turn it to their advantage when they judge the time is right." We now appear to have a bill due with the Mexicans.

On an unofficial basis, governments occasionally engage in extralegal practices by mutual consent. There is, for example, the "unofficial extradition" of alleged criminals. One common variation is the perfectly correct action of one country in returning an illegal or undesirable alien to the authorities of his or her country of origin. This is called deportation.

But another extralegal practice common with our Latin American neighbors involves U.S. law-enforcement officials' persuading their counterparts to detain and deliver to U.S. jurisdiction alleged criminals (usually American citizens and almost never host-country nationals) who are legally resident in the host country. Sweeteners—free transportation for the escorting officers, extra days in the United States at U.S. government expense, promises of increased cooperation and support—are usually part of the deal. Our embassies are usually witting participants in these arrangements. I certainly was, both as charge and ambassador. As regards clearance and coordination with our embassies, our law-enforcement agencies tend to be scrupulous.

It is usually argued in these cases that returning the fugitive to U.S. justice is in the national interest—hardly a proposition that, on its face, can be challenged. Besides, it saves time, expense, and the irritation of an extradition proceeding. These arguments are more dubious. The fact that I was once co-defendant (along with Cyrus Vance, Bill Bowdler, Marvin Weisman, Attorney General Griffin B. Bell, and dozens of other State and Justice officials) in a multi-million dollar lawsuit arising from one such "unofficial" action may make me somewhat more sensitive than some to the pitfalls and abuses of

Box continued on next page.

such procedures. This particular case was dismissed by federal court, but the fallout in the cooperating country was significant.

The fugitive in question was tried, convicted, and given a suspended sentence by the U.S. court. Within three months he was back and initiated legal action against host-country authorities. That's when the doo-doo hit the fan.

Once the dust (or whatever it was) settled, two local police officials were in jail and stayed there for several years; the supervising official in the Interior Ministry had been sacked; the minister had resigned; the United States had received a lot of very bad publicity (for "subverting" the host-country government, *inter alia*); and an arrest warrant had been issued for our legal attache. Not exactly a soaring diplomatic success. Fortunately, the natives were basically friendly and resilient. They also appeared to have short memories; and it helped that they weren't enthusiastic about American felons settling in their country.

There was, at least for me, a lesson in all this. I decided to be very skeptical of U.S. law-enforcement agencies when they wanted to "work deals" with our hosts. The old arguments of avoiding the time, expense, and energy of formal extradition no longer cut much ice. My response became, "If this is really a bad guy, let's extradite; if he's not that bad, let's just hope he makes a mistake that will drop him into our hands." Having made that decision, there were no more unpleasant surprises.

Thus, the issue of overseas fugitives is more complex than just extradition treaties and international law, though goodness knows they provide the legal bedrock. The round-up of offshore miscreants is not always as neat, legal, and consequence-free as we would like. It's not always easy to catch the guys in the black hats, but sometimes when you ignore the niceties (legalities) you create more problems and get soot on your white hat to boot.

—JACK R. BINNS

A broader, formal declaration that the United States will forego unilateral extraterritorial action in the future would be very helpful. But that seems highly improbable. Having been involved in similar efforts, I find it easy to predict the arguments that will come forth from those agencies wishing greater latitude for such action: "it will foreclose future options;" "it will diminish our credibility;" "it will reduce our leverage with Libya" (to cite a timely example); and "it's the law of the land." Anyone who has fought the bureaucratic wars knows the tired arguments that would be trotted out and also knows they are largely specious. Administrations come and go, but the rationales of the bureaucracy endure. And unless Congress sees *Alvarez* as a problem, the tired arguments will almost surely prevail.

Would a congressional resolution or, better yet, specific legislation stating the U.S. intention to eschew unilateral extraterritorial action and abide by international norms serve a constructive purpose? Would President Bush dare veto such legislation? The answer to the first question is clearly yes; that to the second is less clear.

Perhaps retired colleagues will join with me... to urge such a course of action on Congress. That would go some way toward reestablishing our credibility as a law-abiding member of the international community; it would also serve notice on those members of executive agencies who might be tempted to engage in similar future operations (the rogues), that it will not be tolerated. That won't remove the burden placed on us by the Supreme Court, but it's still something. Even Mr. Bumble might approve.

POSTSCRIPT

Is the Kidnapping of Criminal Suspects from Foreign Countries Justifiable?

Why the new level of awareness and debate about kidnapping criminal suspects from other countries? Because what were once widely accepted norms of behavior are undergoing changes. Because the flow of money and goods between countries, and the availability of modern transportation, allows criminals to operate internationally, and adds to the likelihood of greater efforts to bring accused criminals back for trial from other countries. Because the legal and political difficulties of extradition sometimes leads to kidnappings, or countries offer rewards for the abduction and delivery of criminal suspects. Such was the case with Mexican physician Huberto Alvarez-Machain.

Bringing alleged international criminals to justice involves many complexities, however. Evidence is often difficult to obtain or is ambiguous. In late 1992, the UN Security Council voted to investigate war crimes in the former Yugoslavia. The effort came to naught. After many frustrating months, Canadian Navy Commander Bill Fenrick, a lawyer working with the UN investigative commission, commented, "I think realistically it's going to be very difficult to get a senior political figure or a very senior military figure before a court unless there's a change in regime [in Serbia or among the Bosnian Serbs].... So I don't think that what we are going to end up with is a Nuremberg II." On the issue of international war crimes trials, see Allan Gerson, "Prosecuting War Crimes," *Foreign Service Journal* (May 1993).

In another place, the conviction of John Demjanjuk was overturned unanimoulsy by the Supreme Court of Israel based on the substantial doubt created by records released by the KGB (the secret police of the Soviet Union) showing that the real Ivan the Terrible was another Ukrainian, Ivan Marchenko. At this point, the rule governing extradition required Demjanjuk be returned to the United States. Yet further difficulties arose when (a) Israeli prosecutors appealed to the Israeli courts to keep Demjanjuk in custody on the grounds that he had been a guard at the Sobibor death camp, and (b) the U.S. Justice Department tried to revoke Demjanjuk's citizenship and block his return on the grounds that he had lied on his original application to enter the Untied States 41 years earlier. It was a very messy situation.

It may also occur that innocent people are abducted and taken across national boundaries. Alvarez-Machain was tried in U.S. federal court. He was acquitted. Sometimes, international prosecutions speak to revenge of the strong rather than justice. General Noriega claimed he was a prisoner of war.

Perhaps that claim had more validity than recognized by the courts of the victorious United States.

Finally, it is important to worry about precedent. If, for example, Americans can abduct others for trial in the United States, then is it acceptable for others to abduct Americans for trial in those countries? In July 1988, the USS *Vincennes*, commanded by Captain Will Rogers, shot down an Iranian plane, killing 290 people. The United States termed it a regrettable accident brought on by the failure of the Iranian airbus to identify itself properly. Rogers was later awarded a medal for meritorious command. The Iranians accused Captain Rogers of war crimes. How would Americans react if Iranian kidnappers seized Rogers and took him to Tehran for trial?

PART 4

Values and International Relations

We live in an era of increasing global interdependence, and, consequently, the state of relations among countries will become an ever more vital concern to all the world's people. In this section, we examine issues of global concern and issues related to the values that affect relations and policy-making among nations.

■ Should Morality and Human Rights Strongly Influence Foreign Policy-Making?

■ Are Global Standards of Human Rights Desirable?

■ Is There a World Population Crisis?

■ Can Modern War Be Just?

ISSUE 17

Should Morality and Human Rights Strongly Influence Foreign Policy-Making?

YES: Cyrus R. Vance, from "The Human Rights Imperative," *Foreign Policy* (Summer 1986)

NO: George Shultz, from "Morality and Realism in American Foreign Policy," *Department of State Bulletin* (December 1985)

ISSUE SUMMARY

YES: Former U.S. secretary of state Cyrus R. Vance contends that a commitment to human rights must be a central principle of foreign policy.

NO: Former U.S. secretary of state George Shultz asserts that foreign policy must avoid idealism if it conflicts with the national interest.

One of the classic debates among academics and policymakers is the debate over the degree to which morality should be a factor in formulating foreign policy. As the following articles by two U.S. secretaries of state show, few argue for either absolute *idealism*, adhering to morality and ignoring other aspects of the national interest, or absolute disregard of morality in pursuit of *realism*, or "realpolitik" national interest. The debate, then, is one of priority, or of emphasis.

Academically, the founder of the realist school was Hans Morgenthau, and Shultz's speech was occasioned by his acceptance of the Hans J. Morgenthau Memorial Prize awarded by the National Committee on American Foreign Policy. Most foreign policy practitioners have also followed the realist approach; Richard Nixon and Henry Kissinger are especially good examples, and George Bush is also strongly in the realist camp. As Shultz notes, realists do not reject morality. Instead, they argue that a country faced with enemies in an armed and dangerous world cannot always afford to be idealist if doing so threatens the national interest.

This approach is rejected by those who believe that foreign policy must be founded on moral principles. This approach is often labeled idealism. President Jimmy Carter and his secretary of state, Cyrus Vance, are the most recent notable idealists to have guided U.S. foreign policy. Idealists reject the idea that morality and national interest are incompatible. Instead, they argue that the United States and others are best served by setting high standards of international conduct. Such a policy, idealists maintain, is most likely to show the contrast between the United States and oppressive countries, such as China, and make U.S. leadership attractive to the people of the world.

Throughout most of history, realism has governed foreign policy. When Hitler's Nazi Germany invaded Stalin's communist Soviet Union, democratic Great Britain's Winston Churchill offered Stalin aid. When Churchill's decision was challenged in Parliament, he replied: "If Hitler had invaded Hell, ... [I would] make favorable reference to the devil." Churchill's American contemporary, President Franklin D. Roosevelt, was also a realist. When, for example, critics objected to U.S. support of Dominican Republic dictator Rafael Trujillo, FDR answered that "[Trujillo] may be an SOB, but he is our SOB."

The end of World War II and the founding of the United Nations marked the beginning of increased idealist influence on international conduct. The world was appalled by the war, the Holocaust, and other wartime tragedies, and countries pledged in the UN Charter to promote human rights and abandon violence except to defeat aggression. Other affirmations of human rights such as the Universal Declaration of Human Rights (1948), the International Covenant on Civil and Political Rights (1966), and the European-focused Helsinki Agreements (1975) followed. Thus, most of the world's countries have pledged to live in peace and to respect the civil rights and liberties of both their own citizens and those in other countries. It has become more difficult for countries to ignore their public pledges.

Modern communications, especially television, have also promoted concern with morality. Now, acts of oppression, such as those inflicted by the South African government on its black citizens or by China on its dissenters, are rapidly and graphically transmitted to the living rooms and consciences of the world. This has prompted debate on relations with those governments. Similarly, the use or support of violence is often vividly portrayed, spurring moral objection by idealists and counterarguments by realists. Whether or not to support rebels against governments the United States opposes is a related moral issue, and it is discussed by both Cyrus R. Vance and George Shultz in the following pieces.

YES

Cyrus R. Vance

THE HUMAN RIGHTS IMPERATIVE

The last 5 years have not been easy for those who believe that a commitment to human rights must be a central tenet of American foreign policy. The concept and definition of human rights have been twisted almost beyond recognition. Long-standing principles of international law and practice have been chipped away. Doublespeak has too often been the order of the day. Yet the time may be coming when Americans will be able to sweep aside the illusions and myths that have been used, often deliberately, to fog the human rights debate. The time may be coming when the opportunities presented by a strong human rights policy can again be seized.

These signs do not presage merely a belated recognition that former President Jimmy Carter was correct in committing U.S. foreign policy to human dignity and freedom. One can sense a rising desire among Americans to see a return to the fundamental beliefs on which their country's human rights policy must rest and from which it draws its strength. If so, and if their leaders will respond to this desire, Americans will be able again to pursue their ideals without sacrificing their traditional pragmatism.

[Former] President Ronald Reagan is fond of calling America a "city upon a hill." But the Puritan leader John Winthrop, who first uttered those words in the 17th century, intended them as a warning about the importance of adhering to the values that eventually shaped America's founding and development—particularly those later reflected in the U.S. Constitution in the Bill of Rights—not as a boast about military or economic power. As a country, America cannot be, as Reagan suggests, the "last, best hope of man on earth" unless it is prepared to restore to its rightful place in American national life respect for and protection of human rights at home and abroad.

Let me define what I mean by human rights. The most important human rights are those that protect the security of the person. Violations of such rights include genocide; slavery; torture; cruel, inhuman, and degrading treatment or punishment; arbitrary arrest or imprisonment; denial of fair trial; and invasion of the home....

Second is that bundle of rights affecting the fulfillment of such vital needs as food, clothing, shelter, health care, and education—in the scheme of President

Franklin Roosevelt's four freedoms, the freedom from want. Americans recognize that fulfilling these rights depends largely on the stage of a country's economic development. [T]he United States can and should help others attain these basic rights....

Third, there is the right to enjoy civil and political liberties. These include not only freedom of speech, freedom of the press, freedom of religion, and freedom to assemble and to petition the government to redress grievances,... but also the right that most Americans take for granted— the freedom to move freely within and to and from one's own country.

Civil and political rights also must include the liberty to take part in government;... the only just powers of a government are those derived from the consent of the governed. By exercising this freedom, citizens may insist that their government protect and promote their individual rights.

Finally, there is a basic human right to freedom from discrimination because of race, religion, color, or gender.

Almost all of these rights are recognized in the United Nations Universal Declaration of Human Rights, a document... that draws heavily on the American Bill of Rights, the British Magna Carta, and the French Declaration of the Rights of Man and of the Citizen. Each of these documents has played a vital role in the historical evolution of respect for human rights. But after World War II, the world witnessed an unprecedented human rights revolution, including measures to institutionalize the international enforcement of human rights.

Until then, the idea that a regime could be held accountable to international standards and to the world for the treatment of its people was regarded largely as an idiosyncrasy of the democratic West, invoked only when it served a Western power's interests. A sovereign government, tradition held, could rule its people or its territory as it saw fit....

[A]ttitudes changed radically after World War II, principally because of the horror felt around the world when the Holocaust was exposed and when the full extent of Joseph Stalin's purges became clear. Individuals and countries suddenly realized that without standards, there were also no limits. The war also revealed that the far-flung colonial systems were bankrupt. Great powers could no longer hold sway over peoples they had for so long considered, in the English writer Rudyard Kipling's words, "lesser breeds without the Law."

Against this historical background, substantial progress has been made over the last 40 years. Since 1945, the world has codified a wide range of human rights. That process is in itself an enormous achievement. The power of these codes is demonstrated when movements like Poland's outlawed independent trade union Solidarity cite international norms to justify population demands for greater liberty. Even countries that show little respect for human rights feel a need to pay lip service to them. But codes alone are not enough. It also has been necessary to develop international institutions to implement them.

First, in 1945, the United Nations Charter was adopted, enshrining human rights both as a basic objective of the newly created body and as a universal obligation....

In 1946, the Commission on Human Rights was established in the United Nations.... In 1948 came the Universal Declaration of Human Rights, a basic though nonbinding declaration of principles of human rights and freedoms. The 1940s and 1950s also saw the drafting of the Convention on the Prevention and Punishment of the Crime of Genocide and the preparation of two separate human rights covenants—one on political and civil rights and the other covering economic, social, and cultural rights.

During much of the 1950s, Washington stood aloof from treaties furthering those rights and limited itself to supporting U.N. studies and advisory services. But during the 1960s, America resumed its leadership, and in 1965–1966, the two covenants were finally adopted by the United Nations and presented for ratification by member states.

Largely in response to American pressure, the world moved to implement these codes more effectively. To this end, Western Europe, the Americas, and later, Africa, established their own human rights institutions. On another front, the U.N. system for several years confined its public human rights activities to only three cases: Chile, Israel, and South Africa. But beginning in the Carter years, further U.S. prodding led the international community to broaden its concern to include the examination of human rights violations in many countries, including communist countries. Progress, though sometimes halting, has been made in a process that has no precedent.

DANGEROUS ILLUSIONS

Many opportunities and obstacles lie ahead. But first the illusions that cloud, and fallacies that subvert, American human rights policy must be dispelled. Only then can a coherent and determined course be charted.

The first and most dangerous illusion holds that pursuing values such as human rights in U.S. foreign policy is incompatible with pursuing U.S. national interests. This is nonsense. As Reagan stated in March 1986: "A foreign policy that ignored the fate of millions in the world who seek freedom would be a betrayal of our national heritage. Our own freedom, and that of our allies, could never be secure in a world where freedom was threatened everywhere else."

Moreover, no foreign policy can gain the American people's support unless it reflects their deeper values. Carter understood this when, as president, he championed human rights. In addition to enabling millions of people to live better lives, this commitment helped redeem U.S. foreign policy from the bitterness and divisions of the Vietnam War. It reassured the American people that the U.S. role abroad can have a purpose that they could all support.

Human rights policy also requires practical judgments. Americans must continually weigh how best to encourage progress while maintaining their ability to conduct necessary business with countries in which they have important security interests. But the United States must always bear in mind that the demand for individual freedom and human dignity cannot be quelled without sowing the seeds of discontent and violent convulsion. Thus supporting constructive change that enhances individual freedom is both morally right and in America's national interest.

Freedom is a universal right of all human beings.... In a profound sense, America's ideals and interests coincide, for the United States has a stake in the stability that comes when people can express their hopes and build their futures freely. In the long run, no system is as solid as that built on the rock of freedom. But it is not enough simply to proclaim such general principles. The more difficult question remains: What means of support should be provided to those whose rights are denied or endangered? And to answer this question, two underlying groups of questions must be addressed.

First, what are the facts? What violations or deprivations are taking place? How extensive are they? Do they demonstrate a consistent pattern of gross violations of human rights? What is the degree of control and responsibility of the government involved? Will that government permit independent outside investigation?

Second, what can be done? Will U.S. actions help promote the overall cause of human rights? Can U.S. actions improve the specific conditions at hand, or could they make matters worse? Will other countries work with the United States? Does America's sense of values and decency demand that the country speak out or take action even where there is only a remote chance of making its influence felt?

If the United States is determined to act, many tools are available. They range from quiet diplomacy, to public pronouncements, to withholding economic or military assistance from the incumbent regime. In some cases, Washington may need to provide economic assistance to oppressed peoples and, in rare instances like Afghanistan, limited military aid. Where appropriate, the United States should take positive steps to encourage compliance with basic human rights norms. And America should strive to

act in concert with other countries when possible.

A second illusion that must be exposed is one pushed by many critics of Carter's human rights focus. Wrapping themselves in a rhetorical cloak of democracy and freedom, these critics pursue a curious logic that leads them to support governments and groups that deny democracy and abuse freedom. They insist on drawing a distinction for foreign-policy purposes between "authoritarian" countries that are seen as friendly toward the United States and "totalitarian" states seen as hostile. Authoritarian governments, the argument continues, are less repressive than revolutionary autocracies, more susceptible to liberalization, and more compatible with U.S. interests. Generally speaking, it is said, anticommunist autocracies tolerate social inequities, brutality, and poverty while revolutionary autocracies create them.

Sadly, this specious distinction, rooted in America's former U.N. representative Jeane Kirkpatrick's November 1979 *Commentary* article "Dictatorships and Double Standards," became a central element of the new human rights policy set forth at the start of the Reagan administration. Kirkpatrick's thesis damaged America's image as a beacon of freedom and a wise and humane champion of human rights. If it were simply an academic exercise, this version of the authoritarian-totalitarian distinction might cause little mischief. But it has a deeper political purpose. The implication that such a distinction provides a basis for condoning terror and brutality if committed by authoritarian governments friendly to the United States is mind-boggling.

The suggestion that America should turn a blind eye to human rights violations by autocrats of any stripe is unacceptable. Such thinking is morally bankrupt and badly serves U.S. national interests. To the individual on the rack it makes no difference whether the torturer is right- or left-handed—it remains the rack. In short, a sound and balanced human rights policy requires condemnation of such conduct, no matter who the perpetrator is....

A third human rights illusion, deriving from the second, is the fallacy inherent in the so-called Reagan Doctrine enunciated in the president's 1985 State of the Union address. Speaking about U.S. policy toward armed insurgencies against communist regimes, he declared: "We must not break faith with those who are risking their lives—on every continent, from Afghanistan to Nicaragua—to defy Soviet-supported aggression and secure rights which have been ours from birth.... Support for freedom fighters is self-defense."

No doubt there will be situations in which the United States should aid insurgencies—as in Afghanistan, where such aid promotes human rights and clearly serves American interests. There, the Soviet Union invaded a small neighboring country with overpowering military force, deposed the existing government, and imposed its own hand-picked government that, with the support of massive Soviet firepower, slaughtered tens of thousands of Afghans and turned millions more into refugees. It is critical to note that in supporting the Afghan rebels, Americans are not merely supporting an anticommunist rebellion. The United States is vindicating universal principles of international law and helping the Afghan people to determine their own future.

Yet the Reagan Doctrine, taking shelter under the banner of human rights, commits America to supporting anticommunist revolution wherever it arises. By implication, the doctrine offers no such assistance to opponents of other tyrannies. As the case of Nicaragua shows, the support the doctrine promises can include American arms....

This policy is both wrong and potentially dangerous to America's interests and its standing in the world. As with virtually all doctrines, it is automatic and inflexible by nature. That inflexibility blinds policymakers in a double sense. It blinds them to the realities and available alternatives in individual situations, and it blinds them to the principles of respect for national territorial sovereignty and nonintervention—cornerstones of international order.

The Reagan Doctrine's evident bias toward military options could easily prompt Washington to overlook better ways to achieve worthy goals. Even where economic incentives or restrictions may be sufficient, and even where U.S. policy may lack regional support and might work against broader U.S. interests, the Reagan Doctrine suggests that, at a minimum, America should fund military forces.

Beyond this strategic misconception, the Reagan Doctrine obscures the hard but essential questions of means and consequences. To avoid self-delusion, Americans must recognize that anticommunism cannot always be equated with democracy. Nor is anticommunism a shield against the consequences of unrealistic and imprudent action. At the very least, the United States must ask whom it intends to support. Do they believe in democratic values? Can they attract sufficient support in their country and region to govern if they take power? How would such a change affect the citizens of their country? Does America risk raising hopes or expectations that it cannot or will not fulfill? Can America deliver enough aid to decisively affect the outcome? Finally, will such a policy have the domestic support needed to sustain Washington's chosen course of action?

Ironically, many champions of the Reagan Doctrine call themselves realists. Yet any policy that tempts the country to ignore these basic questions cannot be called hardheaded or realistic. The doctrine's dogmatism and seductive ideological beckoning to leap before looking, are, in fact, strikingly unrealistic. So systematically ignoring the principles of sovereignty and nonintervention is not in America's national interest.

NEW HOPE FOR PROGRESS

A key strength of this country has always been its respect for law and moral values. To follow the Reagan Doctrine would undermine America's moral authority. What the United States and the Soviet Union have to offer the world must be distinguished by more than the simple declaration that, by definition, whatever Washington does is right and whatever Moscow does is wrong.

President John Kennedy once said that the United States is engaged in a "long, twilight struggle" in world affairs. But if that is so, America's principles and interests both are more likely to thrive if the country keeps faith with the ideals for which it struggles.

Principle must be the foundation of America's course for the future, but policy will be sustained only if it is also pragmatic. That must not mean

that pragmatism should dominate. U.S. foreign policy must never become realpolitik unconnected with principle. Yet promoting ideals that have no chance of being put into practice risks becoming mere posturing. Nor should Americans focus simply on the great issues and ignore the fact that, at heart, human rights concern individual human beings. Indeed, it matters greatly what America can do in concrete cases, in individual countries, for any one person to live a better life.

The charge to U.S. human rights policy has rarely been put more clearly than by Felice Gaer, executive director of the International League for Human Rights. Testifying before a subcommittee of the House Committee on Foreign Affairs in February 1986, she said: "The United States needs to do more than make declarations and to provide free transport for fleeing dictators.... The U.S. Government has leverage to use—if it chooses to use it. It has the power to persuade governments."

The United States has many opportunities, and faces many problems, in trying to advance human rights abroad. In a few countries, there is reason to give thanks for recent progress. In others, recent shifts in stated U.S. policy provide hope for future progress....

Encouraging news recently has come from the Philippines and Haiti as well. In Haiti, the heir to one of the world's worst traditions of government finally was driven from power. This island country remains desperately poor and faces a difficult future. But at least its destiny is being determined largely by men and women who seek a better life for all Haitians. America can and must help, beginning with immediate emergency food aid, while it urgently assesses Haiti's longer-term needs. In the Philippines, the problems are even more complex, but the victory achieved is even more inspiring. All Americans have marveled at the magnificent commitment of the Filipino people to freedom, at the physical and moral courage of President Corazon Aquino, at the support of the Roman Catholic church under the leadership of Jaime Cardinal Sin, and at the unforgettable sight of peaceful, unarmed men and women facing down tanks and guns with their "prayers and presence." The United States should offer whatever support it can as that country seeks to rebuild both politically and economically.

One of the most striking developments of the 1980s has been the answer to Stalin's question concerning how many divisions the pope has. From Poland to the Philippines, the world has heard the answer. Quite a few. Much remains to be done in the Philippines, and the doing will not be easy. But what has been shown in Buenos Aires, in Port-au-Prince, and in Manila is that peaceful, democratic change is possible in today's world, that such change carries with it great promise, and that there is much that American human rights policies can do to promote it.

In many other countries the pace of change has been maddeningly slow, and in some, nonexistent. Both opportunities and pitfalls abound. This is particularly true in Central America, and nowhere more so than in Nicaragua. Furnishing military aid to the *contras* is a disastrous mistake. The United States should listen to the virtually unanimous advice of its Latin American neighbors who urge it not to give such aid and to give its full support instead to the Contadora process. Despite temporary setbacks, this regional peace effort provides a framework for ending Central America's agony while safeguarding the hemisphere's security interests. But whatever their viewpoint, Americans all should be able to agree that human rights are denied and abused in Nicaragua, and have been for decades—by the late dictator Anastasio Somoza Debayle and his supporters and by the Sandinistas. Americans must continue to demand an end to all such abuses....

[Then] there is South Africa. The United States has maintained diplomatic relations with South Africa for many years.... South Africa is a source of important raw materials, occupying a strategic position along the sea routes running from the Indian Ocean and the Middle East into the Atlantic Ocean. Yet productive relations with South Africa are impossible because of sharp differences over apartheid, over the right of South Africa's blacks to live decent lives, and over their right to participate as full citizens in governing their country.

South Africa has institutionalized discrimination of the most vicious sort and resists fundamental change of this abhorrent system. What the United States seeks in the near term is clear: the dismantling of apartheid, root and branch, and the sharing of political power among whites, blacks, mixed-blood "Coloreds," and Asians alike.

The United States should make unmistakably clear to President P. W. Botha [South Africa's former president, succeeded by F. W. DeKlerk, who became president on August 15, 1989] and all South Africans that Americans are committed to the total abolition of apartheid and to genuine power sharing. The U.S. government must underscore that South Africa cannot adopt one policy for worldwide public consumption and a second, less stringent policy for private discussion in Pretoria. America must make unmistakably clear that time is running out and that major steps must be taken now.

The South African government also must be told that, without prompt action, the United States will impose more stringent economic restrictions.... And America should work with like-minded countries to pressure South Africa to make those decisions that are necessary now to stop further repression and a bloody civil war later.

The world has a long agenda in the pursuit of human rights. There will be, I fear, no final victory over tyranny, no end to the challenge of helping people to live decent lives, free from oppression and indignity. But this generation has set the highest standards for human rights in human history. It has achieved much; it has proved repeatedly that no idea is so compelling as the idea of human freedom. America was "conceived in Liberty, and dedicated to the proposition that all men are created equal." It is America's task, a century and a quarter after Abraham Lincoln spoke, to do its utmost to help redeem that promise for men and women everywhere.

NO

George Shultz

MORALITY AND REALISM IN AMERICAN FOREIGN POLICY

HANS MORGENTHAU'S LEGACY

Hans Morgenthau was a pioneer in the study of international relations. He, perhaps more than anyone else, gave it intellectual respectability as an academic discipline. His work transformed our thinking about international relations and about America's role in the postwar world. In fundamental ways, he set the terms of the modern debate, and it is hard to imagine what our policies would be like today had we not had the benefit of his wisdom and the clarity of his thinking.

As a professor of the University of Chicago,... in 1948 he published the first edition of his epoch-making text, *Politics Among Nations*. Its impact was immediate—and alarming to many. It focused on the reality of so-called power politics and the balance of power—the evils of the Old World conflicts that immigrants had come to this country to escape and which Wilsonian idealism had sought to eradicate.

Morgenthau's critics, however, tended to miss what he was really saying about international morality and ethics. The choice, he insisted, is not between moral principles and the national interest, devoid of moral dignity, but between moral principles divorced from political reality and moral principles derived from political reality. And he called on Americans to relearn the principles of statecraft and political morality that had guided the Founding Fathers.

Hans Morgenthau was right in this. Our Declaration of Independence set forth principles, after all, that we believed to be universal. And throughout our history, Americans as individuals—and, sometimes, as a nation—have frequently expressed our hopes for a world based on those principles. The very nature of our society makes us a people with a moral vision, not only for ourselves but for the world.

At the same time, however, we Americans have had to accept that our passionate commitment to moral principles could be no substitute for a sound

From George Shultz, "Morality and Realism in American Foreign Policy," *Department of State Bulletin* (December 1985).

foreign policy in a world of hard realities and complex choices. Our Founding Fathers, in fact, understood this very well.

Hans Morgenthau wrote that "the intoxication with moral abstractions... is one of the great sources of weakness and failure in American foreign policy." He was assailing the tendency among Americans at many periods in our later history to hold ourselves above power politics and to believe that moral principles alone could guide us in our relations with the rest of the world. He correctly worried that our moral impulse, noble as it might be, could lead either to futile and perhaps dangerous global crusades, on the one hand, or to escapism and isolationism, equally dangerous, on the other.

The challenge we have always faced has been to forge policies that could combine morality and realism that would be in keeping with our ideals without doing damage to our national interests. Hans Morgenthau's work shaped our national debate about this challenge with an unprecedented intensity and clarity.

IDEALS AND INTERESTS TODAY

That debate still continues today. But today there is a new reality.

The reality today is that our moral principles and our national interests may be converging, by necessity, more than ever before. The revolutions in communications and transportation have made the world a smaller place. Events in one part of the world have a more far-reaching impact than ever before on the international environment and on our national security. Even individual acts of violence by terrorists can affect us in ways never possible before the advent of international electronic media....

In our world, our ideals and our interests thus are intimately connected. In the long run, the survival of America and American democracy is essential if freedom itself is to survive. No one who cherishes freedom and democracy could argue that these ideals can be gained through policies that weaken this nation.

We are the strongest free nation on earth. Our closest allies are democracies and depend on us for their security. And our security and well-being are enhanced in a world where democracy flourishes and where the global economic system is open and free. We could not hope to survive long if our fellow democracies succumbed to totalitarianism. Thus, we have a vital stake in the direction the world takes—whether it be toward greater freedom or toward dictatorship.

All of this requires that we engage ourselves in the politics of the real world, for both moral and strategic reasons. And the more we engage ourselves in the world, the more we must grapple with the difficult moral choices that the real world presents to us.

We have friends and allies who do not always live up to our standards of freedom and democratic government, yet we cannot abandon them. Our adversaries are the worst offenders of the principles we cherish, yet in the nuclear age, we have no choice but to seek solutions by political means. We are vulnerable to terrorism because we are a free and law-abiding society, yet we must find a way to respond that is consistent with our ideals as a free and law-abiding society.

The challenge of pursuing policies that reflect our ideals and yet protect our national interests is, for all the difficulties, one that we must meet. The political reality of our time is that America's strategic interests require that we support our ideals abroad.

Consider the example of Nicaragua. We oppose the efforts of the communist leaders in Nicaragua to consolidate a totalitarian regime on the mainland of Central America—on both moral and strategic grounds. Few in the United States would deny today that the Managua regime is a moral disaster. The communists have brutally repressed the Nicaraguan people's yearning for freedom and self-government, the same yearning that had earlier made possible the overthrow of the Somoza tyranny. But there are some in this country who would deny that America has a strategic stake in the outcome of the ideological struggle underway in Nicaragua today. Can we not, they ask, accept the existence of this regime in our hemisphere even if we find its ideology abhorrent? Must we oppose it simply because it is communist?

The answer is we must oppose the Nicaraguan dictators not simply because they are communists but because they are communists who serve the interests of the Soviet Union and its Cuban client and who threaten peace in this hemisphere. The facts are indisputable. Had the communists adopted even a neutral international posture after their revolution; had they not threatened their neighbors, our friends and allies in the region, with subversion and aggression; had they not lent logistical and material support to the Marxist-Leninist guerrillas in El Salvador—in short, had they not become instruments of Soviet global strategy, the United States would have had a less clear strategic interest in opposing them.

Our relations with China and Yugoslavia show that we are prepared for constructive relations with communist countries regardless of ideological differences. Yet, as a general principle in the postwar world, the United States has and does oppose communist expansionism, most particularly as practiced by the Soviet Union and its surrogates. We do so not because we are crusaders in the grip of ideological or messianic fervor, but because our strategic interests, by any cool and rational analysis, require us to do so.

Our interests, however, also require something more. It is not enough to know only what we are against. We must also know what we are for. And in the modern world, our national interests require us to be on the side of freedom and democratic change everywhere—and no less in such areas of strategic importance to us as Central America, South Africa, the Philippines, and South Korea.

We understood this important lesson in Western Europe almost 40 years ago, with the Truman Doctrine, the Marshall Plan, and NATO; and we learned the lesson again in just the last 4 years in El Salvador: the best defense against the threat of communist takeover is the strengthening of freedom and democracy. The most stable friends and allies of the United States are invariably the democratic nations. They are stable because they exist to serve the needs of the people and because they give every segment of society a chance to influence, peacefully and legally, the course their nation takes. They are stable because no one can question their fundamental legitimacy. No would-be revolutionary can claim to represent the people against some ruling oligarchy because the people can speak for themselves. And the people never "choose" communism.

One of the most difficult challenges we face today is in South Africa. Americans naturally find apartheid totally reprehensible. It must go. But how shall it go? Our influence is limited. Shall we try to undermine the South African economy in an effort to topple the white regime, even if that would hurt the very people we are trying to help as well as neighboring black countries whose economies are heavily dependent on South Africa? Do we want to see the country become so unstable that there is a violent revolution? History teaches that the black majority might likely wind up exchanging one set of oppressors for another and, yes, could be worse off.

The premise of the President's policy is that we cannot wash our hands of the problem or strike moralistic poses. The only course consistent with American principles is to stay engaged as a force for peaceful change. Our interests and our values are parallel because the present system is doomed, and the only alternative to a radical, violent outcome is a political accommodation now, before it is too late.

The moral—and the practical—policy is to use our influence to encourage a peaceful transition to a just society. It is not our job to cheer on, from the sidelines, a race war in southern Africa or to accelerate trends that will inexorably produce the same result.

Therefore, the centerpiece of our policy is a call for political dialogue and negotiation between the government and representative black leaders. Such an effort requires that we keep in contact with all parties, black and white; it means encouraging the South African Government to go further and faster on a course on which it has already haltingly embarked. The President's Executive order a month ago, therefore, was directed against the machinery of apartheid, but in a way that did not magnify the hardship of the victims of apartheid. This approach may suffer the obloquy of the moral absolutists—of those opposed to change and of those demanding violent change. But we will stick to this course because it is right.

THE IMPORTANCE OF REALISM

A foreign policy based on realism, therefore, cannot ignore the importance of either ideology or morality. But realism *does* require that we avoid foreign policies based exclusively on moral absolutes divorced from political reality. Hans Morgenthau was right to warn against the dangers of such moral crusades or escapism.

We know that the spread of communism is inimical to our interests, but we also know that we are not omnipotent and that we must set priorities. We cannot send American troops to every region of the world threatened by Soviet-backed communist insurgents, though there may be times when that is the right choice and the only choice.... The wide range of challenges we face requires that we choose from an equally wide range of responses: from economic and security assistance to aid for freedom fighters to direct military action when necessary. We must discriminate; we must be prudent; we must use all the tools at our disposal and respond in ways appropriate to the challenge. Realism, as Hans Morgenthau understood it, is also a counsel of restraint and healthy common sense.

We also know that supporting democratic progress is a difficult task. Our influence in fostering democracy is often limited in those nations where it has never before taken root, where rulers are reluctant to give up their privileged status, where civil strife is rampant, where extreme poverty and inequality pose obstacles to social and political progress.

Moral posturing is no substitute for effective policies. Nor can we afford to distance ourselves from all the difficult and ambiguous moral choices of the real world. We may often have to accept the reality that advances toward democracy and greater freedom in some important pro-Western nations may be slow and will require patience.

If we use our power to push our non-democratic allies too far and too fast, we may, in fact, destroy the hope for greater freedom; and we may also find that the regimes we inadvertently bring into power are the worst of both worlds: they may be both hostile to our interests *and* more repressive and dictatorial than those we sought to change. We need only remember what happened in Iran and Nicaragua. The fall of a strategically located, friendly country can strengthen Soviet power and, thus, set back the cause of freedom regionally and globally.

But we must also remember what happened in El Salvador and throughout Latin America in the past 5 years—and, for that matter, what is happening today in Nicaragua, Cambodia, Afghanistan, and Angola, where people are fighting and dying for independence and freedom. What we do in each case must vary according to the circumstances, but there should not be any doubt of whose side we are on.

...[The Carter] administration took the position that our fear of communism was inordinate and emphasized that there were severe limits to America's ability or right to influence world events. I believe this was a council of despair, a sign that we had lost faith in ourselves and in our values.

...Our ideals must be a source of strength—not paralysis—in our struggle against aggression, international lawless-ness, and terrorism. We have learned that our moral convictions must be tempered and tested in daily grappling with the realities of the modern world. But we have also learned that our ideals have value and relevance, that the idea of freedom is a powerful force. Our ideals have a concrete, practical meaning today. They not only point the way to a better world, they reflect some of the most powerful currents at work in the contemporary world. The striving for justice, freedom, progress, and peace is an ever-present reality that is today, more than ever, impressing itself on international politics.

As Hans Morgenthau understood, the conduct of a realistic and principled foreign policy is an honorable endeavor and an inescapable responsibility. We draw strength from our ideals and principles, and we and our friends among the free nations will not shrink from using our strength to defend and further the values and principles that have made us great.

POSTSCRIPT

Should Morality and Human Rights Strongly Influence Foreign Policy-Making?

There are times when morality and realpolitik national interest support the same policy choice. Defeating dangerously militaristic and unconscionably evil Nazi Germany is a clear example. Usually, though, the choice is not that easy and presents a troubling dilemma. If you ignore morality and support oppression, even in the most indirect fashion by befriending those who practice it, you leave yourself open to the charge of guilt by inaction or association. Yet most people also have qualms about self-sacrificing morality.

To study the divergent realist and idealist approaches, review Hans Morgenthau's *Politics Among Nations* (Knopf, 1985) along with (leading idealist) Stanley Hoffmann's review of the book's latest edition in the *Atlantic Monthly* (November 1985). From the practitioner point of view, the realists are well represented by Henry Kissinger's memoirs *The White House Years* (Little, Brown, 1979) and *Years of Upheaval* (Little, Brown, 1982). Cyrus Vance's memoirs *Hard Choices* (Simon & Schuster, 1982) is an idealist counterpart.

Even if we try to apply realpolitik or morality, the choices are not always certain. If we take the realist approach, what is the "real" national interest? In the short term, supporting the white South African government may be in the amoral national interest because they are "our SOBs." But, in the long run, the blacks will probably prevail, and perhaps, morality aside, the smarter choice is to get on the winning side now. Similarly, what is moral is often uncertain. Should we, for one, intervene in the internal affairs of another sovereign country, be it South Africa or China? Also, is there really a universal morality on which we all can agree, or, by applying our own standards, are we practicing "cultural imperialism"? Finally, if we withdraw support from a friendly dictator or topple an unfriendly one, what is our responsibility for what happens next? The Shah of Iran was certainly a despot, but were the people of Iran better off under the Ayatollah Khomeini?

Further readings on this topic include: Robert W. McElroy, *Morality and American Foreign Policy.* (Princeton University Press, 1992); Felix Oppenheim, *The Place of Morality in Foreign Policy* (Lexington Books, 1991); Michael Walzer, *Just and Unjust Wars,* 2d edition (Basic Books, 1992); and Terry Nardin and David R. Mapel, *Traditions of International Ethics* (Cambridge University Press, 1992).

ISSUE 18

Are Global Standards of Human Rights Desirable?

YES: Rhoda E. Howard, from "Human Rights and the Necessity for Cultural Change," *Focus on Law Studies* (Fall 1992)

NO: Vinay Lal, from "The Imperialism of Human Rights," *Focus on Law Studies* (Fall 1992)

ISSUE SUMMARY

YES: Professor of sociology Rhoda E. Howard contends that some human rights are so fundamental to justice that they are universal. Generally, cultural differences should not be used as an excuse to deny these basic rights.

NO: Professor of humanities Vinay Lal argues that, to a significant degree, human rights are based on the cultural traditions of the West; therefore, pressuring countries to abide by global standards of human rights is mostly a tactic used by Western nations to maintain their power over weaker nations and regions.

Take a survey of your friends. Ask them if they are in favor of justice, in favor of morality, in favor of human rights. It would be surprising if any of the people you asked came out against human rights. Nevertheless, despite the regard most people say they have for justice, morality, and human rights, the fact is, these standards are not universally followed.

But why is there a gap between what people say regarding justice, morality, and human rights and what happens in practice? Some organizations or individuals really do not mean what they say, or practice what they preach, as the old saying goes. The second reason is a lot more complex and is the focus of this issue. It may be that violations of human rights are, to a degree, a matter of perception and culture. It may be that practices that we in the West sometimes condemn are not universally seen as abuses. Rather, they may be things we disapprove of because of our cultural biases.

Where do rights, concepts of morality, and standards of justice come from in the first place? Religion is often used as a higher source of human rights. There are people who believe that one or more deities bestowed rights on human beings. Other people would argue there are such things as "natural rights." These are based on the essence of being human and are theoretically possessed by people when they live in a true "state of nature," that is, before they join together into governments. This contention is central to Canadian scholar Rhoda Howard's argument in the first selection. She maintains that democracy and justice based on human rights are necessary to societies if they are to progress socially, economically, and politically.

Yet other people contend that rights are not inherent, at least for the most part. Instead, those who hold this view argue that rights, or at least many of them, are culturally based. Proponents of this view would point out that differing standards prove the cultural origins of rights. Western, especially American, culture, for example, places a high value on individual rights. The rights of the individual come before the good of the society or a class of citizens. Many other cultures place a much higher value on the rights of the community. This means that when the rights of the individual and the good of the society clash, the presumption is that societal good is the more important standard. When students protesting for democracy in China were attacked and killed by government troops in 1989 in Tiananmen Square, the West condemned China for violating the right to democracy, the right to free speech, and other human rights. From the point of view of the Chinese government, however, the students' rights did not extend to trying to undermine the socialist movement, which had done much to benefit Chinese society. Westerners largely dismissed this counterargument as mere propaganda.

The contention by Vinay Lal and others that rights are culture-based, and therefore not universal, leads to the charge by some analysts that trying to insist that others abide by your standards of justice, morality, and human rights leads to cultural imperialism. In many Muslim cultures, for example, the idea that women have rights, a Western idea, is very foreign. Is this an abuse of women or essential to the culture of Muslim countries? Should the United States, Canada, and other countries with different views of women's rights take action?

The issues are thus complex. Rhoda Howard argues that universally applicable human rights are basic to justice and ought to be encouraged and insisted upon. Vinay Lal rejects this view and contends that human rights have been used as little more than a cover for injustice.

YES
Rhoda E. Howard

HUMAN RIGHTS AND THE NECESSITY FOR CULTURAL CHANGE

Many critics of the concept of human rights argue that it undermines indigenous cultures, especially in the underdeveloped world (Cobbah, 1987; Pollis and Schwab, 1980; Renteln, 1990). I agree that the concept of human rights often undermines cultures. Cultural rupture is often a necessary aspect of the entrenchment of respect for human rights. Culture is not of absolute ethical value; if certain aspects of particular cultures change because citizens prefer to focus on human rights, then that is a perfectly acceptable price to pay.

Human rights are rights held by the individual merely because she or he is human, without regard to status or position. In principle, all human beings hold human rights equally. These rights are claims against the state that do not depend on duties to the state, although they do depend on duties to other citizens, e.g., not to commit crimes. They are also claims that the individual can make against society as a whole. Society, however, may have cultural preconceptions that certain types of individuals ought not to be entitled to such rights. Thus, culture and human rights come into conflict. The concept of cultural relativism recognizes this, but does not consider the possibility that, in such instances, perhaps the better path to choose is to change the culture in order to promote human rights.

Cultural relativism is a method of social analysis that stresses the importance of regarding social and cultural phenomena from the "perspective of participants in or adherents of a given culture" (Bidney, 1968). Relativism assumes that there is no one culture whose customs and beliefs dominate all others in a moral sense. Relativism is a necessary corrective to ethical ethnocentrism. But it is now sometimes taken to such an extreme that any outsider's discussions of local violations of human rights are criticized as forms of ideological imperialism.

In effect, this extreme position advocates not cultural relativism but cultural absolutism. Cultural absolutists posit particular cultures as of absolute moral value, more valuable than any universal principle of justice. In the left-right/North-South debate that permeates today's ideological exchanges, cultural absolutists specifically argue that culture is of more importance than

From Rhoda E. Howard, "Human Rights and the Necessity for Cultural Change," *Focus on Law Studies*, vol. 8, no. 1 (Fall 1992). Copyright © 1992 by The American Bar Association. Reprinted by permission. References omitted.

the internationally accepted principles of human rights.

Cultural absolutists argue that human rights violate indigenous cultures because they are Western in origin. But the origins of any idea, including human rights, do not limit its applicability. The concept of human rights arose in the West largely in reaction to the overwhelming power of the absolutist state; in the Third World today, states also possess enormous power against which citizens need to be protected. As societies change, so ideals of social justice change.

Cultures are not immutable aspects of social life, ordained forever to be static. Cultures change as a result of structural change: secularism, urbanization and industrialism are among the chief causes of cultural change both in the West since the eighteenth century and in the underdeveloped world today (Howard, 1986, chapter 2). Cultures can also be manipulated by political or social spokespersons in their own interest. Culturalism is frequently an argument that is used to "cover" political repression, as when Kenyan President Daniel arap Moi told a female environmental activist not to criticize his policies because it is "against African tradition" for women to speak up in public. This does not mean that all aspects of culture must necessarily be ruptured in order that human rights can be entrenched. Many aspects of culture, such as kinship patterns, art or ritual, have nothing to do with human rights and can safely be preserved, even enhanced, when other rights-abusive practices are corrected. Many aspects of public morality are similarly not matters of human rights. The existence or abolition of polygamous marriage, for example, is not an international human rights issue, despite objections to it in the West. Nor is the proper degree of respect one should show to one's elders, or the proper norms of generosity and hospitality. The apparent Western overemphasis on work at the expense of family is a cultural practice that Third World societies can avoid without violating human rights. Many other such matters, such as whether criminal punishment should be by restitution or imprisonment, can be resolved without violating international human rights norms.

Jack Donnelly argues that "weak" cultural relativism is sometimes an appropriate response to human rights violations. Weak cultural relativism would "allow occasional and strictly limited local variations and exceptions to human rights," while recognizing "a comprehensive set of prima facie universal human rights" (Donnelly, 1989, p. 110). This is an appropriate position if the violation of a human right is truly a cultural practice that no political authority and no socially dominant group initiates or defends. Consider the case of female genital operations in Africa and elsewhere. Governments do not promote these violations; indeed, through education about their detrimental health consequences, they try to stop them. Nevertheless there is strong popular sentiment in favour of the operations, among women as well as (if not more so than) men (Slack, 1988). Similarly, child betrothal, officially a violation of international human rights norms, is popularly accepted in some cultures (Howard, 1986, chapter 8). And certain forms of freedom of speech, such as blasphemy and pornography, are deeply offensive to popular sentiment in many cultures, whether or not the government permits or prohibits them.

Although a weak cultural relativist stance is appropriate in some instances as a protection of custom against international human rights norms, to implement human rights does mean that certain cultural practices must be ruptured. One obvious example is the universal subordination of women as a group to men as a group, backed up by men's collective economic, political and physical power over women. If women have achieved greater access to human rights in North America since the second wave of feminism began about 1970, it is largely because they have challenged cultural stereotypes of how they ought to behave. Feminist activists no longer believe that women ought to be deferential to men or wives subordinate to their husbands. Nor do they any longer hold to the almost universal cultural belief that women's divinely ordained purpose in life is to bear children. Feminists in other parts of the world such as India or Africa are making similar challenges to their cultures in the process of asserting their rights (on women's rights as human rights, see Bunch, 1990, and Eisler, 1987.)

Many critics of human rights find them overly individualistic; they point to the selfish materialism they see in Western (North American) society. But the individualism of Western society reflects not protection but neglect of human rights, especially economic rights (Howard, "Ideologies of Social Exclusion," unpublished). In the United States, certain economic rights are regarded as culturally inappropriate. A deeply ingrained belief exists that everyone ought to be able to care for himself and his family. Since the U.S. is or was the land of opportunity (at least for white people), anyone who lives in poverty is personally responsible for his being in that state. Thus the U.S. has the worst record of provision of economic rights of any major Western democratic state. The right to health is not acknowledged, nor is the right to housing or food. Before such rights are acknowledged and provided in the U.S., the cultural belief in the virtues of hard work and pulling oneself up by one's bootstraps will have to be replaced by a more collectivist vision of social responsibility. The culturally ingrained belief that blacks are inferior people not deserving of the respect and concern of whites will also need to be ruptured.

Critics of human rights sometimes argue that cultures are so different that there is no possibility of shared meanings about social justice evolving across cultural barriers. The multivocality of talk about rights precludes any kind of consensus. The very possibility of debate is rejected. Indeed, debate, the idea that people holding initially opposing views can persuade each other through logic and reason of their position, is rejected as a form of thought typical of rationalist and competitive Western society. Western thought, it is argued, silences the oppressed.

Yet it is precisely the central human rights premises of freedom of speech, press and assembly that all over the world permit the silenced to gain a social voice. Human rights undermine constricting status-based categorizations of human beings: they permit people from degraded social groups to demand social change. Rational discourse about human rights permits degraded· workers, peasants, untouchables, women and members of minority groups to articulate and consider alternate social arrangements than those that currently oppress them (see also Teson, 1985).

Human rights are "inauthentic" in many cultures because they challenge the ingrained privileges of the ruling classes, the wealthy, the Brahmin, the patriarch, or the member of a privileged ethnic or religious group. The purpose of human rights is precisely to change many culturally ingrained habits and customs that violate the dignity of the individual. Rather than apologizing that human rights challenge cultural norms in many societies, including our own, we should celebrate that fact.

NO
Vinay Lal

THE IMPERIALISM OF
HUMAN RIGHTS

The notion of human rights is deeply embedded in modern legal and political thought and could well be considered one of the most significant achievements of contemporary culture and civilization. Certain classes of people in all societies have, from the beginning of time, been endowed with "rights" which others could not claim. The immunity that emissaries (now diplomats) from one state to another have always received constitutes one of the norms of conduct that has guided relations between states. Likewise, most cultures have had, in principle at least, intricate rules to govern the conduct of warfare. Civilians were not to be taken hostage as a military strategy; a soldier was not to be shot as he was surrendering; and so on.

Some of these customary modes of conduct are now enshrined in the law, transmitted on the one hand into "rights" that the citizen can claim against the state, and on the other hand into restraints on the state's agenda to produce conformity and contain dissent. The individual has been given a great many more rights, and—what is unique to modern times—never before have such rights been placed under the protection of the law. States are bound in their relations to their subjects by a myriad of international agreements and laws, including the Geneva Conventions, the International Covenant on Civil and Political Rights, the United Nations Charter, the Universal Declaration of Human Rights, and the U.N. Body of Principles for the Protection of All Persons Under Any Form of Detention or Punishment.

Moreover, it is only in our times that the "international community" seems prepared to enforce sanctions against a state for alleged violations of such rights. With the demise of communism, the principal foes of human rights appear to have been crushed, and the very notion of "human rights" seems sovereign. Should we then unreservedly endorse the culture of "human rights" as it has developed in the liberal-democratic framework of the modern West, indeed even as a signifier of the "end of history" and of the emergence of the New World Order? On the contrary, I would like to suggest several compelling reasons why, far from acquiescing in the suggestion that the notion of

From Vinay Lal, "The Imperialism of Human Rights," *Focus on Law Studies*, vol. 8, no. 1 (Fall 1992). Copyright © 1992 by The American Bar Association. Reprinted by permission.

human rights is the most promising avenue to a new era in human relations, we should consider the discourse of human rights as the most evolved form of Western imperialism. Indeed, human rights can be viewed as the latest masquerade of the West—particularly America, the torchbearer since the end of World War II of "Western" values—to appear to the world as the epitome of civilization and as the only legitimate arbiter of human values.

To understand the roots of the modern discourse of "human rights," we need to isolate the two central notions from which it is derived, namely the "individual" and the "rule of law." It has been a staple of Western thought since at least the Renaissance that—while the West recognizes the individual as the true unit of being and the building block of society, non-Western cultures have been built around collectivities, conceived as religious, linguistic, ethnic, tribal or racial groups. As the *Economist*—and one could multiply such examples a thousand-fold—was to boldly declare in its issue of 27 February 1909, "whatever may be the political atom in India, it is certainly not the individual of Western democratic theory, but the community of some sort." In the West the individual stands in singular and splendid isolation, the promise of the inherent perfectibility of man; in the non-West, the individual is nothing, always a part of a collectivity in relation to which his or her existence is defined, never a being unto himself or herself. Where the "individual" does not exist, one cannot speak of his or her rights; and where there are no rights, it is perfectly absurd to speak of their denial or abrogation.

On the Western view, moreover, if the atomistic conception of the "individual"

is a prerequisite for a concern with human rights, so is the "rule of law" under which alone can such rights be respected. In a society which lives by the "rule of law," such laws as the government might formulate are done so in accordance with certain normative criteria—for example, they shall be non-discriminatory, blind to considerations of race, gender, class, and linguistic background; these laws are then made public, so that no person might plead ignorance of the law; and the judicial process under which the person charged for the infringement of such laws is tried must hold out the promise of being fair and equitable. As in the case of "individual," the "rule of law" is held to be a uniquely Western contribution to civilization, on the two-fold assumption that democracy is an idea and institution of purely Western origins, and that the only form of government known to non-Western societies was absolutism. In conditions of "Oriental Despotism," the only law was the law of the despot, and the life and limb of each of his subjects was hostage to the tyranny of his pleasures and whims. In the despotic state, there was perhaps only one "individual," the absolute ruler; under him were the masses, particles of dust on the distant horizon. What rights were there to speak of then?

Having briefly outlined how the notions of the "individual" and the "rule of law" came to intersect in the formulation of the discourse of human rights, we can proceed to unravel some of the more disturbing and unacceptable aspects of this discourse. Where once the language of liberation was religion, today the language of emancipation is law. Indeed, the very notion of "human rights," as it is commonly understood in the international forum today, is legalistic.

Proponents of the "rule of law," convinced of the uniqueness of the West, are not prepared to concede that customs and traditional usages in most "Third World" countries have functioned for centuries in place of "law," and that even without the "rule of law" there were conventions and traditions which bound one person to respect the rights of another. We expect rights to be protected under the law and the conformity of states to the "rule of law." Many obvious and commonplace objections to such a state of affairs come to mind. By what right, with what authority, and with what consequences do certain states brand other states as "outlaw" or "renegade" states, living outside the pale of the "rule of law," allegedly oblivious to the rights of their subjects, and therefore subject to sanctions from the "international community"?

There is, as has been argued, one "rule of law" for the powerful, and an altogether different one for those states that do not speak the "rational," "diplomatic," and "sane" language that the West has decreed to be the universal form of linguistic exchange. It is not only the case that when Americans retaliate against their foes, they are engaged in "just war" or purely "defensive" measures in the interest of national security, but also that when Libyans or Syrians do so, they are transformed into "terrorists" or ruthless and self-aggrandizing despots in the pursuit of international dominance. The problem is more acute: who is to police the police? The United States claims adherence to international law, but summarily rejected the authority of the World Court when it condemned the United States for waging undeclared war against Nicaragua. More recently, the U.S. Supreme Court, in an astounding judgment barely noticed in the American

press, upheld the constitutionality of a decision of a circuit court in Texas which, by allowing American law enforcement officers to kidnap nationals of a foreign state for alleged offenses under American law to be brought to the United States for trial, effectively proclaims the global jurisdiction of American law. As a noted Indian commentator has written, "We are thus back in the 15th, 16th, and 17th century world of piracy and pillage" (Ashok Mitra, "No Holds Barred for the U.S.," *Deccan Herald*, 3 July 1992). Were not the Libyans and Sandinistas supposed to be the pirates?

There are, however, less obvious and more significant problems with the legalistic conception of a world order where "human rights" will be safeguarded. The present conception of "human rights" largely rests on a distinction between state and civil society, a distinction here fraught with hazardous consequences. The rights which are claimed are rights held against the state or, to put it another way, with the blessing of the state: the right to freedom of speech and expression, the right to gather in public, the right to express one's grievances within the limits of the constitution, and so forth. The state becomes the guarantor of these rights, when in fact it is everywhere the state which is the most flagrant violator of human rights.

Not only does the discourse of "human rights" privilege the state, but the very conception of "rights" must of necessity remain circumscribed. The right to a fair hearing upon arrest, or to take part in the government of one's country, is acknowledged as an unqualified political and civil right, but the right to housing, food, clean air, an ecologically-sound environment, free primary and secondary education, public transportation, a high standard of health, the preservation of one's ethnic identity and culture, and security in the event of unemployment or impairment due to disease and old age is not accorded parity. When, as in the United States, certain communities are in a systematic and calculated fashion deprived of the basic amenities required to sustain a reasonable standard of living, when an entire economy is designed on a war footing, does not that constitute a gross and inexcusable infringement of the "human rights" of those who are most disempowered in our society? Is it not ironic that in the very week this year when rebellious demonstrators in Thailand were being hailed in the Western media as champions of human rights, martyrs to freedom, and foes of tyranny, the insurrectionists in Los Angeles were contemptuously dismissed by the same media as "rioters," "hooligans," "arsonists," and "murderers"? No doubt some were just exactly that, but that admission cannot allow us to obfuscate the recognition that the action of the insurrectionists was fueled by a deep-seated resentment at the violation of their social, economic, and cultural rights.

Certainly there are organizations, such as the Minority Rights Group (London) and Cultural Survival (Boston), which have adopted a broader conception of "human rights," and whose discourse is as concerned with the numerous rights of "collectivities," whether conceived in terms of race, gender, class, ethnic or linguistic background, as it is with the rights of "individuals." But this is not the discourse of "human rights" in the main, and it is emphatically not the discourse of Western powers, which have seldom adhered to the standards that they expect others to abide by, and would use even food and medicine, as the contin-

uing embargo against Iraq so vividly demonstrates, to retain their political and cultural hegemony even as they continue to deploy the rhetoric of "human rights." Never mind that state formation in the West was forged over the last few centuries by brutally coercive techniques—colonialism, genocide, eugenics, the machinery of "law and order"—to create homogeneous groups. One could point randomly to the complete elimination of the Tasmanian Aboriginals, the extermination of many Native American tribes, the Highland Clearances in Scotland, even the very processes by which a largely Breton-speaking France became, in less than a hundred years, French-speaking. We should be emphatically clear that what are called "Third World" countries should not be allowed the luxury, the right if you will, of pointing to the excesses of state formation in the West to argue, in a parody of the ludicrous evolutionary model where the non-Western world is destined to become progressively free and democratic, that they too must ruthlessly forge ahead with "development" and "progress" before their subjects can be allowed "human rights."

The idea of "human rights" is noble and its denial an effrontery to humankind. But it is only as an imagined idea that we can embrace it, and our fascination with this idea must not deflect us from the understanding that, as an ideological and political tool of the West, and particularly of the only remaining superpower, "human rights" is contaminated. Perhaps, before "human rights" is flaunted by the United States as what most of the rest of the world must learn to respect, the movement for "human rights" should first come home to roost. As Noam Chomsky has written, people in the Third World "have never understood the deep totalitarian strain in Western culture, nor have they ever understood the savagery and cynicism of Western culture." Could there be greater testimony to this hypocrisy than the fact that inscribed on the marble wall of the main lobby at CIA headquarters in Virginia is this quotation from John (VIII: 32): "And Ye Shall Know the Truth/And the Truth Shall Make You Free?"

POSTSCRIPT

Are Global Standards of Human Rights Desirable?

The points discussed in the selections by Rhoda Howard and Vinay Lal are not just matters of abstract concern; they are significantly related to the conduct of international relations. During the cold war, the United States and other Western countries were frequently willing to overlook abuses in allied countries because they were seen as lesser evils in the fight against the greatest evil, the Soviet communist menace. That is changing, and the view that morality should influence foreign policy decisions is getting renewed attention. For more insight on this, see Terry Nardin and David R. Mapel, eds., *Traditions of International Ethics* (Cambridge University Press, 1992) and Felix Oppenheim, *The Place of Morality in Foreign Policy* (Lexington Books, 1991).

More evidence of the controversy about human rights arose during the UN World Conference on Human Rights, convened in Vienna, Austria, in June 1993. It was attended by more than 5,000 delegates representing more than 170 countries and nearly 1,000 nongovernmental organizations, such as Amnesty International and the International Red Cross. The UN conference did draft language for the UN to consider in support of greater protection for women and children. See Rebecca J. Cook, "Women's International Rights Law: The Way Forward," *Human Rights Quarterly* (Spring 1993). However, the conference made less progress on the idea of appointing a UN commissioner to oversee human rights and on proposals to increase UN enforcement of human rights by imposing economic and diplomatic sanctions, and taking other actions, against abusive countries. Part of the resistance came from some Third World representatives who worried that the creation of universal human rights standards would mean that the dominant Western powers of Europe and North America would force their values on other cultures. Wong Kan Seng, the foreign minister of Singapore, said that the "universal recognition of the ideal of human rights can be harmful if universalism is used to deny or mask the reality of diversity" among world cultures and their values. Many Western delegates condemned this so-called cultural relativism approach. "The cultural argument is the threat at this conference," said Kenneth Roth, executive director of the New York–based group Human Rights Watch. "A watering-down of human rights is not something we can accept," added Gerhart Daum, a member of the German delegation.

ISSUE 19

Is There a World Population Crisis?

YES: Nafis Sadik, from "World Population Continues to Rise," *The Futurist* (March/April 1991)

NO: Julian L. Simon, from "Population Growth Is Not Bad for Humanity," *National Forum: The Phi Kappa Phi Journal* (Winter 1990)

ISSUE SUMMARY

YES: Nafis Sadik, executive director of the United Nations Population Fund, argues that more than 5 billion people are already straining the world's resources, but population continues to grow too fast in the regions of the world least able to support population increases.

NO: Julian L. Simon, a professor of economics and business administration, contends that claims of retarded economic growth and many other alleged harms from population growth have proved to be incorrect and that population growth should be viewed as beneficial to the development of humankind.

There is no debate over some of the basic statistics about the world population and its growth. First, on July 11, 1987, the estimated world population reached 5 billion people; by mid-1991 it was over 5.38 billion. Second, the rate of world population growth has expanded rapidly in this century. It took all of human history, about 14 million years, before the world population reached 1 billion in 1800. Another 130 years passed before the population rose to 2 billion in 1930. Just 30 years passed before 1960 and 3 billion people. That time span was halved to 15 years when the population reached 4 billion in 1975, and dropped to 12 years for the 5 billion milestone in 1987. If sustained, the annual 1987–1991 increase of 96 million works out to a world population of 6 billion people in October 1997. A May 1990 report issued by the UN Population Fund estimated that, by the beginning of the twenty-first century, the world population could triple to approximately 15 billion. In somewhat different terms, as Sadik points out, the world population is now actually expanding at over 94 million people a year, or 260,000 people a day, or 10,800 people an hour. If it has taken you two minutes to read this far, there are 360 more people in the world than when you began reading.

A third statistical fact is that the population growth is not evenly distributed across the globe. The regions that mostly include less developed countries (LDCs) are expanding the most rapidly. Africa has the highest regional annual growth rate at 3.00% (1985–1990). South Asia (including India) is expanding at 2.34% annually, and Latin America's annual growth rate is 2.09%. That contrasts sharply with annual growth rates of 0.23% in Europe, 0.90% in the United States, and 0.70% in Canada.

The causes of the still rapidly increasing population are more controversial, but there are hard statistics. The birthrate (annual live births per 1,000 population) is still high in some parts of the world, standing at 44.7 (1985–1990) in Africa, as compared to 13.0 in Europe. But the rate has declined from 33.9 (1965–1970) to a current 27.1 worldwide and from 47.7 to a current 44.7 in Africa. But earlier increases are bringing more people into childbearing years, so there are more births occurring despite the lower birthrate. Also, an ironic problem is that increases in Third World health standards are contributing to population growth. In Africa, for example, life expectancy at birth has improved from 44.1 years (1965–1970) to 51.9 years (1985–1990), while the death rate (per 1,000 population) has declined from 21.1 to 14.9. The population is therefore growing in part because improved health standards mean that fewer people are dying. Julian Simon sees this indication of a better quality of life as a source of celebration, but it also produces many more people.

It is also clear that population growth is related to economic circumstance. Especially in the absence of strong government programs, poorer countries have higher birthrates than wealthier countries. That does not mean that having babies makes you poor, as Simon notes. Studies have demonstrated that the opposite is true. Because of birth control ignorance, cultural reasons, the underemployment of women in paying jobs, and other factors, poverty causes babies.

Most controversial is the degree to which the world population and its projected growth are critical problems. In the following selections, Nafis Sadik views the population issue as a crisis that affects the entire globe. Julian L. Simon is much more optimistic, contending that many of the concerns are illusory, that population growth has many advantages, and that if countries work to develop their economies, the population can be sustained.

YES

Nafis Sadik

WORLD POPULATION
CONTINUES TO RISE

The 1990s will be a critical decade. The choices of the next 10 years will decide the speed of population growth for much of the next century; they will decide whether world population triples or merely doubles before it finally stops growing; they will decide whether the pace of damage to the environment speeds up or slows down.

The world's population, now 5.3 billion, is increasing by three people every second—about a quarter of a million every day. Between 90 and 100 million people—roughly equivalent to the population of Eastern Europe or Central America—will be added every year during the 1990s; a billion people—a whole extra China—over the decade.

No less than 95% of the global population growth over the next 35 years will be in the developing countries of Africa, Asia, and Latin America.

It has been more than 20 years since the population growth rate of developing countries reached its peak in 1965–70. But it will be during only the last five years of this century that the additions to total numbers in developing countries will reach their maximum. This 35-year lag is a powerful demonstration of the steamroller momentum of population growth.

Racing to provide services to fast-growing populations is like running up the down escalator: You have to run very fast indeed to maintain upward motion. So far, all the effort put into social programs has not been quite enough to move upward in numerical terms. The absolute total of human deprivation has actually increased, and unless there is a massive increase in family planning and other social spending, the future will be no better.

POPULATION TRENDS

Southern Asia, with almost a quarter of the current total world population, will account for 31% of the total increase between now and the end of the century; Africa, with 12% of the world's population today, will account for 23% of the increase. By contrast, eastern Asia, which has another 25% of the current world population, will account for only 17% of the total increase. Similarly, the developed countries—Europe (including the [former] Soviet

Union), North America, and Japan, which represent 23% of the current world population—will account for only 6% of the increase. The remaining 15% of the world's population, living in developing countries, will produce 23% of the increase.

By and large, the increases will be in the poorest countries—those by definition least equipped to meet the needs of the new arrivals and invest in the future.

Because of the world's skewed growth patterns, the balance of numbers will shift radically. In 1950, Europe and North America constituted 22% of the world's population. In 2025, they will make up less than 9%. Africa, only 9% of the world population in 1950, will account for just under a fifth of the 2025 total. India will overtake China as the world's most populous country by the year 2030.

Toward the end of the twenty-first century, a number of countries seem set to face severe problems if populations grow as projected. Nigeria could have some 500 million citizens—as many as the whole African continent had around 1982. This would represent more than 10 people for every hectare [about 2.47 acres] of arable land. Modern France, with better soils and less erosion, has only three people per hectare. Bangladesh's 116 million inhabitants would grow to 324 million, with density on its arable land more than twice as high as in the Netherlands today. This does not take into account any land that may be lost to sea-level rises caused by global warming.

It should be emphasized that these are not the most-pessimistic projections. On the contrary, they assume steadily declining fertility during most of the next 100 years.

FOOD

Between 1979–81 and 1986–87, cereal production per person actually declined in 51 developing countries and rose in only 43. The total number of malnourished people increased from 460 million to 512 million and is projected to exceed 532 million by the end of the century.

Developing countries as a whole have suffered a serious decline in food self-sufficiency. Their cereal imports in 1969–71 were only 20 million tons. By 1983–85, they had risen to 69 million tons and are projected to total 112 million tons by the end of the century. These deficits have so far been met by corresponding surpluses in the industrialized countries—of which the overwhelming bulk comes from North America.

World food security now depends shakily on the performance of North American farmers. Following the drought-hit U.S. harvest of 1988, world cereal stocks dropped from 451 million tons in 1986–87 to only 290 million tons in 1989, down from a safe 24% of annual consumption to the danger level of 17%.

POVERTY

The world produces enough food to feed everyone today—yet malnutrition affects as many as 500 million people. The problem is poverty and the ability to earn a livelihood. The total numbers of the poor have grown over the past two decades to around one billion now.

Absolute poverty has shown a dogged tendency to rise in numerical terms. The poorest fifth of the population still dispose of only 4% of the world's wealth, while the richest dispose of 58%. Economic recession, rising debt burdens, and mistaken priorities have reduced social spending in many countries.

But population growth at over 2% annually has also slowed social progress. So much additional investment has been required to increase the quantity of health, education, and other services to meet the needs of increased populations that the quality of service has suffered.

In many sectors, the proportion of deprived people has declined. But this is a reduced proportion of a higher total population swelled by rapid growth. As a result, the total numbers of deprived people have grown.

The growth of incomes may be affected by population growth. On a regional basis, there is an inverse relationship between population growth and growth of per capita income. There is a lag of 15–20 years between the peak of population growth and the peak growth in the labor force. Already there are severe problems in absorbing new entrants to the labor force in regions such as Africa or South Asia. Yet, in numerical terms, the highest rates of labor-force growth in developing countries lie ahead, in the years 2010–2020.

The labor force in developing countries will grow from around 1.76 billion today to more than 3.1 billion in 2025. Every year, 38 million new jobs will be needed, without counting jobs required to wipe out existing underemployment, estimated at 40% in many developing countries. Complicating the issue will be the spread of new, labor-saving technologies.

The land still provides the livelihood of almost 60% of the population of developing countries. But most of the best and most-accessible land is already in use, and what is left is either less fertile or harder to clear and work. The area available per person actually declined at the rate of 1.9% a year during the 1980s.

URBAN AND EDUCATION ISSUES

In recent decades, urban growth in developing countries has been even more rapid than overall population growth. Town populations are expanding at 3.6% a year—four and a half times faster than in industrialized countries and 60% faster than rural areas. Rural migrants swell the total, but an increasing share of this growth now comes from natural growth within the cities themselves.

The speed of growth has outpaced the ability of local and national government to provide adequate services. The number of urban households without safe water increased from 138 million in 1970 to 215 million in 1988. Over the same period, households without adequate sanitation ballooned from 98 million to 340 million.

The total number of children out of school grew from 284 million in 1970 to 293 million in 1985 and is projected to rise further to 315 million by the end of the century. Also between 1970 and 1985: The total number of illiterates rose from 742 million to 889 million, and total number of people without safe sanitation increased from about a billion to 1.75 billion.

EATING AWAY AT THE EARTH

These increasing numbers are eating away at the earth itself. The combination of fast population growth and poverty in developing countries has begun to make permanent changes to the environment. During the 1990s, these changes will reach critical levels. They include continued urban growth, degradation of land and water resources, massive deforestation, and buildup of greenhouse gases.

Many of these changes are now inevitable because they were not foreseen early enough, or because action was not taken to forestall them. Our options in the present generations are narrower because of the decisions of our predecessors. Our range of choice, as individuals or as nations, is narrower, and the choices are harder.

The 1990s will decide whether the choices for our children narrow yet further—or open up. We know more about population—and interactions among population, resources, and the environment—than any previous generation. We have the basis for action. Failure to use it decisively will ensure only that the problems become much more severe and much more intractable, the choices harder and their price higher.

At the start of the 1990s, the choice must be to act decisively to slow population growth, attack poverty, and protect the environment. The alternative is to hand on to our children a poisoned inheritance.

DANGER SIGNALS

Just a few years ago, in 1984, it seemed as if the rate of population growth was slowing everywhere except Africa and the parts of South Asia. The world's population seemed set to stabilize at around 10.2 billion toward the end of the next century.

Today, the situation looks less promising. Progress in reducing birth rates has been slower than expected. According to the latest U.N. projections, the world has overshot the marker points of the 1984 "most likely" medium projection and is now on course for an eventual total that will be closer to 11 billion than to 10 billion.

In 15 countries—13 of them in Africa—birthrates actually rose between 1960–65 and 1980–85. In another 23 nations, the birthrate fell by less than 2%.

If fertility reductions continue to be slower than projected, the mark could be missed yet again. In that case, the world could be headed toward an eventual total of up to 14 billion people.

Why should we be worried about this? At present, the human race numbers "only" 5.3 billion, of which about a billion live in poverty. Can the earth meet even modest aspirations for the "bottom billion," let alone those of the better-off and their descendants, without irreparable damage to its life-support systems?

Already, our impact has been sufficient to degrade the soils of millions of hectares, to threaten the rain forests and the thousands of species they harbor, to thin the ozone layer, and to initiate a global warming whose full consequences cannot yet be calculated. The impact has greatly increased since 1950.

By far the largest share of resources used, and waste created, is currently the responsibility of the "top billion" people, those in industrialized countries. These are the countries overwhelmingly responsible for damage to the ozone layer and acidification, as well as for roughly two-thirds of global warming.

However, in developing countries, the combination of poverty and population growth among the "bottom billion" is damaging the environment in several of the most sensitive areas, notably through deforestation and land degradation. Deforestation is a prime cause of increased levels of carbon dioxide, one of the principal greenhouse gases responsible for global warming. Rice paddies and domestic cattle—food suppliers for 2 billion people in developing countries—are also major producers of methane, another of the greenhouse gases.

Developing countries are also doing their best to increase their share of industrial production and consumption. Their share of industrial pollution is rising and will continue to rise.

At any level of development, larger numbers of people consume more resources and produce more waste. The quality of human life is inseparable from the quality of the environment. It is increasingly clear that both are inseparable from the question of human numbers and concentrations.

A CASE FOR CHANGE

Redressing the balance demands action in three major areas:

1. A shift to cleaner technologies, energy efficiency, and resource conservation by all countries is necessary, especially for the richer quarter of the world's population.

Carbon-dioxide emissions will be hardest to bring under control. If the atmospheric concentration of carbon dioxide is to be stabilized, cuts of 50% to 80% in emissions may be required by the middle of the next century. These will be difficult to achieve even with the most-concentrated efforts.

Four major lines of action will produce the greatest impact, especially if they are pursued in parallel. The first is improved efficiency in energy use. The second is a shift from fossil fuels, which currently account for 78% of the world's energy use, to renewable sources such as wind, geothermal, and solar thermal. The third

is halting deforestation. The fourth is slowing population growth.

There are no technological solutions in sight for methane emissions from irrigated fields and livestock. They have both expanded in response to growing rural populations and to meet expanding world demands for cereals and meat. The irrigated area has grown by about 1.9% a year since 1970, slightly faster than world population. Livestock and irrigation will both continue to expand in line with populations in developing countries. Reducing population growth is the only viable strategy to reduce the growth in methane emissions from these sources.

2. A direct and all-out attack on poverty itself will be required.

3. Reductions are needed in overall rates of population growth. Reducing population growth, especially in the countries with the highest rates of growth, will be a crucial part of any strategy of sustainable development.

Reducing the rate of population growth will help extend the options for future generations: It will be easier to provide higher quality and universal education, health care, shelter, and an adequate diet; to invest in employment and economic development; and to limit the overall level of environmental damage.

WHAT NEEDS TO BE DONE?

Immediate action to widen options and improve the quality of life, especially for women, will do much to secure population goals. It will also widen the options and improve the quality of life of future generations.

Education is often the means to a new vision of options.... For women, it offers a view of sources of status beyond childbearing. Because of this, education—especially for girls—has a strong impact on the health of the family and on its chosen size....

Education's impact on fertility and use of family planning is equally strong. Women with seven or more years of education tend to marry an average of almost four years later than those who have had none.

Yet, there remains a great deal to be done in women's education, even to bring it level with men's. Women make up almost two-thirds of the illiterate adults in developing countries....

SUPPORT FOR FAMILY-PLANNING EFFORTS

Political support from the highest levels in the state is essential in making family planning both widely available and widely used. Political backing helps to legitimize family planning, to desensitize it, and to place it in the forum of public debate. It helps win over traditional leaders or counter their hostility. It also helps to ensure that funding and staffing for family planning are stable and protected against damaging budget cuts or the competing demands of rival departments.

Support must extend far beyond the national leadership before programs take off. It may be necessary to involve a wide range of religious and traditional leaders in discussions before introducing population policies and programs on a wide scale....

Four main barriers block the way to easy access to family planning. The most obvious is geographical: How long do people have to travel to get supplies, and how long do they have to wait for service when they get there?

The second barrier is financial: While many surveys show that people are willing to pay moderate amounts for family-planning supplies, most poor people have a fairly low price threshold. Costs of more than 1% of income are likely to prove a deterrent.

Culture and communication are a third barrier: opposition from the peer group, husband, or mother-in-law; shyness about discussing contraception or undergoing gynecological examination; language difficulties; or unsympathetic clinic staff.

A fourth barrier is the methods available: There is no such thing as the perfect contraceptive. Most people who need one can find a method suited to their needs—if one is available. However, if high contraception use is to be achieved, suitable services must be not only available, but accessible to all who need them.

Suitable services mean high-quality services. In the long run, the quantity of continuing users will depend on the quality of the service....

DEVELOPING HUMAN RESOURCES

Investment in human resources provides a firm base for rapid economic development and could have a significant impact on the environmental crisis. It is essential for global security. But in the past, it has often commanded a lower priority than industry, agriculture, or military expenditure.

It is time for a new scale of priorities: There is no other sphere of development where investment can make such a large contribution both to the options and to the quality of life, both in the present and in the future. Whatever the future returns, investment is needed now.

NO   Julian L. Simon

POPULATION GROWTH IS NOT BAD FOR HUMANITY

The prospectus for this issue of *National Forum* that came to us authors included this: "Is the situation as desperate as Lester Brown [who edits the annual *State of the World* volume] says, 'by the end of the next decade... The community of nations either will have rallied and turned back threatening trends, or environmental deterioration and social disintegration will be feeding on each other'?"

This question is wholly miscast. The trends are *not* threatening. Rather, all the trends important to humanity point to benign directions, and have for centuries and perhaps millennia.

The prospectus also included a list of "ecological issues" to be discussed in this issue such as "soil erosion," "deforestation," "depletion of the U.S. wheat harvest," "poisoning the food supply," "the price of pesticides," and many more such descriptions which imply that conditions are getting worse.

Each of these issues is misstated. There are no data showing that the soil in the world is becoming more eroded than less eroded. The U.S. wheat harvest is one of the great success stories of all time and continues to be so. And so it is with other issues.

All of the other issues are supposedly related to the subject about which I am to write, "the consequences of overpopulation," insofar as the purported bad trends are supposedly the result of human beings, and therefore fewer human beings are supposed to alleviate the negative trends. But if the trends really are not negative—and the scientific evidence shows them not to be—then it does not make sense to ask whether population is growing too fast or too slow in the context of these issues.

Yet once again there is hysteria about there being too many people and too many babies being born. Television presents notables ranging from the late Andrei Sakharov to Dan Rather repeating that more people on earth mean poorer lives now and worse prospects for the future. The newspapers chime in. A typical editorial in the ... *Washington Post* says that "in the developing world... fertility rates impede advances in economic growth, health, and educational opportunities." Nobel-winner Leon Lederman says in his statement

From Julian L. Simon, "Population Growth Is Not Bad for Humanity," *National Forum: The Phi Kappa Phi Journal*, vol. 70, no. 1 (Winter 1990). Copyright © 1990 by The Honor Society of Phi Kappa Phi. Reprinted by permission of *National Forum: The Phi Kappa Phi Journal*. References omitted.

as candidate for the president of the American Association for the Advancement of Science that "overpopulation" is one of our "present crises."... The president of NOW [National Organization for Women] warns that continued population growth would be a "catastrophe."... The head of the Worcester Foundation for Experimental Biology calls for more funding for contraceptive research because of "Overpopulation together with continuing deterioration of the environment."... And this is just a tiny sample of one summer.

Erroneous belief about population growth has cost dearly. It has directed attention away from the factor that we now know is central in a country's economic development, its economic and political system. Economic reforms away from totalitarianism and central economic planning in poor countries probably would have been faster and more widespread if slow growth was not explained by recourse to population growth. And in rich countries, misdirected attention to population growth and the supposed consequence of natural resource shortage has caused waste through such programs as synthetic fuel promotion and the development of airplanes that would be appropriate for an age of greater scarcity. Our antinatalist foreign policy is dangerous politically because it risks our being labeled racist, as happened when [India's prime minister] Indira Ghandi was overthrown because of her sterilization program. Furthermore, misplaced belief that population growth slows economic development provides support for inhumane programs of coercion and the denial of personal liberty in one of the most sacred and valued choices a family can make—the number of children that it

wishes to bear and raise—in such countries as China, Indonesia, and Vietnam.

These ideas affect other public events, too. In 1973, [U.S.] Supreme Court Justice Potter Stewart's vote in *Roe v. Wade* was influenced by this idea, according to Bob Woodward and Scott Armstrong: "As Stewart saw it, abortion was becoming one reasonable solution to population control."... And in 1989, when hearing the *Webster* case, Justice Sandra Day O'Connor again brought the idea of overpopulation into a hypothetical question she asked of Charles Fried, former solicitor-general: "Do you think that the state has the right to, if in a future century we had a serious overpopulation problem, has a right to require women to have abortions after so many children?" No matter how one feels about abortion—I personally feel that it should not be illegal, though I regret its occurrence—it seems better that unsound arguments should not be adduced in the discussion; such idea pollution tends to cost dearly in the long run.

Unlike the earlier period of rampaging worry following Earth Day 1970, however, it is now well-established scientifically that population growth is not the bogey that conventional opinion and the press believe it to be. In the 1980s a revolution occurred in scientific views toward the role of population growth in economic development. By now the economic profession has turned almost completely away from the previous view that population growth is a crucial negative factor in economic development. There is still controversy about whether population growth is even a minor negative factor in some cases, or whether it is beneficial in the long run. But there is no longer any scientific support for the earlier view which was the basis for the U.S.

policy and then the policy of other countries.

For a quarter century our "helping" institutions misanalyzed such world development problems as starving children, illiteracy, pollution, supplies of natural resources, and slow growth. The World Bank, the State Department's Aid to International Development (AID), The United Nations Fund for Populations Activities (UNFPA), and the environmental organizations have asserted that the cause is population growth—the population "explosion" or "bomb," the "population plague." But for almost as long as this idea has been the core of U.S. theory about foreign aid, there has been a solid body of statistical evidence that contradicts this conventional wisdom about the effects of population growth—evidence which falsifies the ideas which support U.S. population policy toward less-developed countries.

The "official" turning point came in 1986 with the publication of a report by the National Research Council and the National Academy of Sciences (NRC-NAS), entitled *Population Growth and Economic Development*, which almost completely reversed a 1971 report on the same subject from the same institution. On the specific issue of raw materials that has been the subject of so much alarm, NRC-NAS concluded: "The scarcity of exhaustible resources is at most a minor constraint on economic growth.... the concern about the impact of rapid population growth on resource exhaustion has often been exaggerated." And the general conclusion goes only as far as "On balance, we reach the qualitative conclusion that slower population growth would be beneficial to economic development for most developing countries...." That is, NRC-NAS found forces operating in both positive and negative directions, its conclusion does not apply to all countries, and the size of the effect is not known even where it is believed to be present. This is a major break from the past monolithic characterization of additional people as a major drag upon development across the board. This revolution in thought has not been reported in the press, however, and therefore had had no effect on public thought on the subject.

There now exist perhaps two dozen competent statistical studies covering the few countries for which data are available over the past century, and also of the many countries for which data are available since World War II. The basic method is to gather data on each country's rate of population growth and its rate of economic growth, and then to examine whether—looking at all the data in the sample together—the countries with high population growth rates have economic growth rates lower than average, and countries with low population growth rates have economic growth rates higher than average.

The clear-cut consensus of this body of work is that faster population growth is *not* associated with slower economic growth. On average, countries whose populations grew faster did not grow slower economically. That is, there is no basis in the statistics for the belief that faster population growth causes slower economic growth.

Additional powerful evidence comes from pairs of countries that have the same culture and history, and had much the same standard of living when they split apart after World War II—East and West Germany, North and South Korea, and China and Taiwan. In each case the centrally planned communist country began with less population "pressure," as measured by density per square kilometer, than did the market-directed noncommunist country. And the communist and noncommunist countries in each pair also started with much the same birth rates and population growth rates.

The market-directed economies have performed much better economically than the centrally planned countries. Income per person is higher. Wages have grown faster. Key indicators of infrastructure such as telephones per person show a much higher level of development. And indicators of individual wealth and personal consumption, such as autos and newsprint, show enormous advantages for the market-directed enterprise economies compared to the centrally planned, centrally controlled economies. Furthermore, birth rates fell at least as early and as fast in the market-directed countries as in the centrally planned countries.

These data provide solid evidence that an enterprise system works better than does a planned economy. This powerful explanation of economic development cuts the ground from under population growth as a likely explanation. And under conditions of freedom, population growth poses less of a problem in the short run, and brings many more benefits in the long run, than under conditions of government planning of the economy.

One inevitably wonders: How can the persuasive common sense embodied in the Malthusian theory be wrong? To be sure, in the short run an additional person—baby or immigrant—inevitably means a lower standard of living for everyone; every parent knows that. More consumers mean less of the fixed available stock of goods to be divided among more people. And more workers laboring with the same fixed current stock of capital means that there will be less output per worker. The latter effect, known as "the law of diminishing return," is the essence of Malthus's theory as he first set it out.

But if the resources with which people work are not fixed over the period being analyzed, then the Malthusian logic of diminishing returns does not apply. And the plain fact is that, given some time to adjust to shortages, the resource base does not remain fixed. People create more resources of all kinds. When horse-powered transportation became a major problem, the railroad and the motor car were developed. When schoolhouses become crowded, we build new schools—more modern and better than the old ones.

As with man-made production capital, so it is with natural resources. When a shortage of elephant tusks for ivory billiard balls threatened in the last century, and a prize was offered for a substitute, celluloid was invented, followed by the rest of our plastics. Englishmen learned to use coal when trees became scarce in the sixteenth century. Satellites and fiber-optics (derived from sand) replace expensive copper for telephone transmission. And the new resources wind up cheaper than the old ones were. Such has been the entire course of civilization.

Extraordinary as it seems, natural-resource scarcity—that is, the cost of raw materials, which is the relevant economic measure of scarcity—has tended to decrease rather than to increase over the entire sweep of history. This trend is at least as reliable as any other trend observed in human history; the prices of all natural resources, measured in the wages necessary to pay for given quantities of them, have been falling as far back as data exist. A pound of copper—typical of all metals and other natural resources—now costs an American only a twentieth of what it cost in hourly wages two centuries ago, and perhaps a thousandth of what it cost three thousand years ago.... And the price of natural resources has fallen even relative to consumer goods....

The most extraordinary part of the resource-creation process is that temporary or expected shortages—whether due to population growth, income growth, or other causes—tend to leave us even better off than if the shortages had never arisen, because of the continuing benefit of the intellectual and physical capital created to meet the shortage. It has been true in the past, and therefore it is likely to be true in the future, that we not only need to solve our problems, but we need the problems imposed upon us by the growth of population and income.

The idea that scarcity is diminishing is mind-boggling because it defies the common-sense reasoning that when one starts with a fixed stock of resources and uses some up, there is less left. But for all practical purposes there are no resources until we find them, identify their possible uses, and develop ways to obtain and process them. We perform these tasks with increasing skill as technology develops. Hence, scarcity diminishes.

The general trend is toward natural resources becoming less and less important with economic development. Extractive industries are only a very small part of a modern economy, say a twentieth or less, whereas they constitute the lion's share of poor economies. Japan and Hong Kong are not at all troubled by the lack of natural resources, whereas such independence was impossible in earlier centuries.

And though agriculture is thought to be a very important part of the American economy, if all of our agricultural land passed out of our ownership tomorrow, we would be the poorer by only about a ninth of one year's Gross National Product. This is additional evidence that natural resources are less of a brake upon economic development with the passage of time, rather than an increasing constraint.

There is, however, one crucial "natural" resource which is becoming more scarce—human beings. Yes, there are more people on earth now than in the past. But if we measure the scarcity of people the same way we measure the scarcity of economic goods—by the market price—then people are indeed becoming more scarce, because the price of labor time has been rising almost everywhere in the world. Agricultural wages in Egypt have soared, for example, and people complain of a labor shortage because of the demand for labor in the Persian Gulf, just a few years after there was said to be a labor surplus in Egypt.

Nor does it make sense to reduce population growth because of the supposedly increasing pollution of our air and water. In fact, our air and water are becoming cleaner rather than dirtier,... wholly the opposite of conventional belief.

The most important and amazing demographic fact—the greatest human achievement in history, in my view—is the "recent" decrease in the world's death rate. It took *thousands of years* to increase life expectancy at birth from just over twenty years to the high twenties. Then in just the last *two centuries*, life expectancy at birth in the advanced countries jumped from *less than thirty years* to perhaps seventy-five years. What greater event has humanity witnessed?

Then starting well after World War II, life expectancy in the poor countries has leaped upwards by perhaps *fifteen or even twenty years* since the 1950s, caused by advances in agriculture, sanitation, and medicine. Is this not an astounding triumph for humankind? It is this decrease in the death rate that is the cause of their being a larger world population nowadays than in former times.

Let's put it differently. In the 19th century the planet Earth could sustain only one billion people. Ten thousand years ago, only four *million* could keep themselves alive. Now, *five billion* people are living longer and more healthily than ever before, on average. The increase in the world's population represents our victory over death.

One would expect lovers of humanity to jump with joy at this triumph of human mind and organization over the raw forces of nature. Instead, many lament that there are so many people alive to enjoy the gift of life because they worry that population growth creates difficulties for development. And it is this misplaced concern that leads them to approve the inhumane programs of coercion and denial of personal liberty in one of the most precious choices a family can make—the number of children that it wishes to bear and raise.

Then there is the war-and-violence bugaboo. A typical recent headline is "Excessive Population Growth a Security Threat to U.S.," invoking the fear of "wars that have their roots in the unrestrained growth of population." This is reminiscent of the Hitlerian cry for "lebensraum" ["living space"] and the Japanese belief before World War II that their population density demanded additional land.

There is little scientific literature on the relation of population to war. But to the extent that there has been systematic analysis—notably the great study of war through the ages by Quincy Wright (1968), the work on recent wars by Nazli Choucri (1974), and a study of Europe between 1870 and 1913 by Gary Zuk (1985)—the data do not show a connection between population growth and political instability due to the struggle for economic resources. The purported connection is another of those notions that everyone (especially the CIA and the Defense Department) "knows" is true, and that seems quite logical, but has no basis in factual evidence.

The most important benefit of population size and growth is the increase it brings to the stock of useful knowledge. Minds matter economically as much as, or more than, hands or mouths. Progress is limited largely by the availability of trained workers. The main fuel to speed the world's progress is the stock of human knowledge. And the ultimate resource is skilled, spirited, hopeful people, exerting their wills and imaginations to provide for themselves and their families, thereby inevitably contributing to the benefit of everyone.

Even the most skilled persons require, however, an appropriate social and economic framework that provides incentives for working hard and taking risks, enabling their talents to flower and come to fruition. The key elements of such a framework are respect for property, fair and sensible rules of the market that are enforced equally for all, and the personal liberty that is particularly compatible with economic freedom. There is justice in such an approach, and wisdom, and the promise of unlimited economic and human development.

Which should be our vision? The doomsayers of the population control movement offer a vision of limits, decreasing resources, a zero-sum game, conservation, deterioration, fear, and conflict, calling for more governmental intervention in markets and family affairs. Or should our vision be that of those who look optimistically upon people as a resource rather than as a burden—a vision of receding limits, increasing resources and possibilities, a game in which everyone can win, creation, building excitement, and the belief that persons and firms, acting spontaneously in the search of their individual welfare, regulated only by rules of a fair game, will produce enough to maintain and increase economic progress and promote liberty.

And what should our mood be? The population restrictionists say we should be sad and worry. I and many others believe that the trends suggest joy and celebration at our newfound capacity to support human life—healthily, and with fast-increasing access to education and opportunity all over the world. I believe that the population restrictionists' hand-wringing view leads to despair and resignation. Our view leads to hope and progress, in the reasonable expectation that the energetic efforts of humankind will prevail in the future, as they have in the past, to increase worldwide our numbers, our health, our wealth, and our opportunities.

POSTSCRIPT

Is There a World Population Crisis?

Is the world population growing rapidly? Yes. Is this a problem for less developed countries? Yes. Are population and poverty related? Yes. On these, Sadik, Simon, and other analysts agree.

Beyond these points of consensus, the population issues become much more controversial. Simon argues that population growth provides expanding human resources and that fears are unfounded. Population optimists, for example, can cite the high standards of living in densely populated countries such as Japan and the Netherlands as proof of this point. And they are correct that if the African country of Chad achieved an economic vitality equal to that of Japan, then many of its population problems would be ameliorated. The living conditions of Chad's people would certainly be better, and various socioeconomic factors would almost certainly lessen the fertility rate. There are some problems with this line of thought, however. One has to do with the prospects for development. At best, it will take a very long time, even under optimal conditions, for many LDCs to approach the development level of Japan or the Netherlands. In the meantime, the LDC population continues to rise steadily. It may even be that, given resource availability and other factors, some LDCs will never become fully developed. A second problem has to do with the use of resources. Many of the globe's resources—such as minerals, trees, and water—are being used at an increasing rate or even being destroyed and wasted as land is cleared for new living and agricultural areas. The increased use of energy also adds to the introduction of carbon dioxide into the atmosphere and, in general, increases all forms of biosphere pollution. The issue of whether or not economic development and environmental protection are mutually achievable is complicated by the expanding population. Technological optimists, such as Simon, believe that recycling, renewable energy, genetic engineering to increase crop production, and a host of other technological innovations will meet these environmental pressures. Population pessimists are equally certain that the world is on the road to calamity.

There are several sources to consult for recent information and views on the population issue. The most current source of statistics can be found in the annual edition of *The State of World Population, 1991* (United Nations Population Fund, 1991). Also, see such monthly journals as *Population Today,* which has some good summary data in its June 1991 edition, and also the entire edition of "World Population: Approaching the Year 2000," *The Annals of the American Academy of Political and Social Science* (July 1990).

ISSUE 20

Can Modern War Be Just?

YES: Robert L. Phillips, from *War and Justice* (University of Oklahoma Press, 1984)

NO: Robert L. Holmes, from *On War and Morality* (Princeton University Press, 1989)

ISSUE SUMMARY

YES: Philosophy professor Robert L. Phillips contends that the concept of a just war, and the rules for waging a just war, continue to apply in the modern era.

NO: Robert L. Holmes, also a professor of philosophy, argues that modern means of conducting war have made the concept of just war obsolete, and, therefore, have also rendered just causes for war meaningless.

War has been a virtually constant, calamitous companion of humankind as far back into history as we can see. And many philosophers, politicans, and statesmen have tried throughout history to distinguish between just and unjust wars. Just war theory falls into two categories. The first is designated by the Latin phrase *jus ad bellum,* which refers to the question of what are *just causes of war.* The second aspect of just war theory relates to *jus in bello,* or the standards that govern the *just conduct of war* once war has begun. Robert Phillips outlines the elements of both *jus ad bellum* and *jus in bello* in the first selection of this debate.

Is *any* war *ever* just? There are some people, called pacifists, who would argue that the phrase "just war" is an oxymoron. Pacifism is a complex idea, but those who are absolute pacifists would refuse to inflict death or physical injury on anyone for any reason, including immediate self-defense.

Most people, however, are not such complete pacifists. Therefore, anyone who is not sociopathic or absolutely amoral about war has implicit or explicit standards of just war. Even a *bellicist,* someone who thinks war is a healthy sociopolitical outlet, would not advocate war for any reason, using any means.

Another issue involved in deciding on just war is related to the fact that *jus ad bellum* and *jus in bello* are Latin phrases. A substantial part of just war theory, especially as detailed in the Phillips article, is a product of Western and Christian thought and tradition dating back to the great treatise *Politics* by Aristotle (384–322 B.C.). The writings of Saint Augustine (A.D. 353–430) and

Saint Thomas Aquinas (1226–1274) on the law of war are further examples. The Dutch thinker Hugo Grotius (1583–1645), whose study *De Jure Belli et Pacis* (On the Law of War and Peace) earned him the title "father of international law," is another example of the Western lineage of just war theory as it is usually discussed. Consequently, there are those who argue that concepts of right and wrong, of just war, are based on culture, not some universal and discoverable higher order.

A third conundrum of just war is whether or not states (countries) are governed by different standards of justice than are individuals. In virtually all societies it is considered immoral for an individual to attack or kill another individual except in immediate self-defense. If someone threatens your property (assuming you are not immediately threatened also), it is against the law in almost all jurisdictions to shoot the threatening person. In such a circumstance in a domestic political system, you can call the police, or you can sue in court to recover your property, or for damages. Countries take military action and kill others regularly, even when they are not immediately threatened. The U.S. invasion of Panama in 1989 is an example. But, it can be said, the domestic option of calling 911 or suing is not available in the international political system.

A fourth issue involved in the just war debate is whether or not changes in international norms and military technology have rendered the concept obsolete. In the following debate, Robert Phillips argues that the standards of just war can still be applied; Robert Holmes disagrees. He contends that since the means of war have become so horrific, modern war can no longer be discussed as just.

YES
Robert L. Phillips

WAR AND JUSTICE

This ... is a defense of the traditional position on the justified use of force by political states, a doctrine commonly labeled *bellum justum* and subdivided into questions having to do with grounds for initiating combats (*jus ad bellum*) and questions having to do with the correct behavior of combatants in wartime (*jus in bello*). ...

[S]ince war is probably inevitable it is advisable to attend seriously to the question of how to fight it morally. ...

I outline below, in point form, the doctrine of the just war, and in the following [text] I shall expand upon the points listed. ...

BELLUM JUSTUM

Jus ad Bellum

I. Last resort.
II. Declared by legitimate authority.
III. Morally justifiable:

   A. Defense against aggression.
   B. Correction of an injustice that has gone uncorrected by legitimate authority "in another place."
   C. Reestablishment of a social order which will distribute justice.
   D. Undertaken with the intention of bringing about peace.

Jus in Bello

I. Proportionality: The quantity of force employed or threatened must always be morally proportionate to the end being sought in war.
II. Discrimination: Force must never be applied in such a way as to make noncombatants and innocent persons the intentional objects of attack. The only appropriate targets in war are combatants.

   A. The Principle of Double Effect: In a situation where the use of force can be foreseen to have actual or probable multiple effects, some of which are evil, culpability does not attach to the agent if the following conditions are met:

1. The action must carry the intention to produce morally good consequences.
2. The evil effects are not *intended* as ends in themselves or as means to other ends, good or evil.
3. The permission of collateral evil must be justified by considerations of proportionate moral weight.

JUS AD BELLUM

The first thing to note is that the standard translation of *bellum justum* as "just war" may be misleading if it is supposed that war can somehow be itself endowed with moral substance. On the traditional view, war is always an evil insofar as it involves a physical attack upon another person. There may, however, be situations where fighting is the lesser of evils, but in such cases the use of force must be *justified*. Prima facie, attacking another person is evil and, indeed, can never be anything else qua attack. But we may upon occasion find that it is the only means of avoiding an even greater evil. Thus, it may be less misleading to speak of "justified war" instead of "just war."

I. Last Resort

The foregoing is relevant to the first consideration in the outline. Although war may be sometimes justified, it will always be morally correct to effect it only after it is clear that other means are not adequate to resolve the issue. It is a mistake to suppose that "last" necessarily designates the final move in a chronological series of actions. It *may* do so, as when a policeman pursuing a suspect goes through the steps of challenging the fleeing suspect verbally, then firing a warning shot if that fails, and finally firing at him as a last resort. There may also be cases, however, where time does not permit actually attempting less coercive means. If terrorists are holding some hostages and announce that they will kill them all in two minutes, we would certainly be justified in using force as our first act (Entebbe-style), though it would still be as a last resort....

II. Declared by Legitimate Authority

The claim that war must be declared by legitimate authority only is in some ways ambiguous....

The difficulty here is ... over the question: Who, or what, *is* legitimate authority? The claim that war may only be undertaken by legitimate authority, while perfectly correct, may involve question-begging where the issue which provoked fighting is precisely a dispute about who is the bearer of that authority....

The paradox is ... that war itself is most frequently the means whereby questions of legitimacy are decided in the eyes of the community of nations (though rival claimants may not accept this verdict). Thus in the context of a civil war the principle runs into problems. Here again we are faced with a situation where *bellum justum* ramifies into larger issues in political philosophy, particularly with those concerning de facto and de jure authority.... The claim that war may be undertaken only by legitimate authority reflects a political reality, namely, that factions at war *will* seek to establish their legitimacy. No matter how divided they may be on other issues, they both seek to be recognized as legitimate by their own people and by the community of nations. Thus they will both agree that the authority to use force is decided by legitimacy.... Our attention is thereby turned from questions of simple power to gain control and toward the issue of the right to govern.... [O]ne rarely (if ever) finds states basing their claims to use force on force *alone.*

III. Morally Justifiable

(A) The right to self-defense against an aggressor has always been regarded as fundamental by most just-war advocates.... [T]he bulk of just-war thinking suggests that, while the death of any person is an evil, an aggressor who refuses to stop what he is doing is responsible for his own death. What a person does not have a right to do is intend the death of the aggressor, in the sense that the purpose of his action should be to stop the aggressor from doing what he is doing. The aggressor's death may thus be accepted or justified as a collateral event if the only means of stopping him is killing....

A state, like an individual, also has the right of defense against aggression....

(B) The traditional version of *bellum justum* holds that a Christian prince has an obligation to intervene in the affairs of another state if there is an unjustice there that continues to be uncorrected by legitimate authority....

(C) If the purpose of political society is the distribution of justice, and if war is a permissible political act, then the purpose of war must ultimately be directed toward reestablishing a just order. This position is formal in the sense that it does not itself specify any particular ideology or social model but is dependent upon such things for its content.

(D) While war may sometimes be justified, it is always morally undesirable as a "state of affairs." Thus the decision to go to war must be accompanied with the intention to effect peace. This rules out various theories which recommend war as therapeutic or as desirable for the glory it brings the sovereign. Another provision which is sometimes attached to (D) holds that war should not be undertaken unless there is a reasonable prospect of winning. This reflects the fact that war is essentially an *agreement* between two states to settle a dispute by arbitrament of arms. A state is not morally justified in resorting to war and subjecting its citizens to death unless there is at least a chance of favorable outcome....

To summarize *jus ad bellum*: Wars of aggression are permitted under the traditional doctrine only if the cause is just; but all wars of aggression are prohibited under the modern interpretation, for no matter how serious the injury to a state, modern warfare is an immoral means for settling grievances and altering existing conditions. This amendment has been made for two reasons. First, the destructiveness of modern war makes it a wholly disproportionate means for the resolution of international disputes and for the redress of grievances, even where they are just. Second, to admit the right of states to initiate combats, even to correct injustice, would impede efforts of the world community to establish a judicial method of outlawing war altogether.

A war of defense against the injustice of aggression is morally permissible in both the traditional and the modern view. This is perceived as in no way a contradiction of the concern for peace, for peace may require defense....

JUS IN BELLO

The "other half" of *bellum justum* is *jus in bello*, or the doctrine of just behavior in combat. We return to the introductory outline:

I. Proportionality

The principle of proportionality holds that in cases where the use of force is justified it cannot be employed in absolutely any measure. Obviously, if the aim of war is the correction of injustice, then the level of force must not be such as to create new and greater injustices. . . .

II. Discrimination

What is true for proportionality is a fortiori true for the principle of discrimination. The notion that force ought to be morally justified only if it can be employed in a discriminate manner lies at the heart of *jus in bello*. The principle of double effect is, in turn, at the heart of discrimination.

(A) Put as simply as possible, by emphasizing intention as the defining feature of moral actions, the supporters of *bellum justum* attempt to mark a difference between killing in war and murder in two different cases. First, the killing of enemy combatants in a justified war may be morally acceptable under some circumstances. Second, the killing of noncombatants incidental to the prosecution of a necessary military operation in a justified war may also be morally acceptable under some circumstances. . . .

Double effect is derived from a quite general criterion of moral judgment enunciated succinctly but clearly by Aquinas: "now moral acts take their species according to what is intended and not according to what is beside the intention, since this is accidental" (*Summa* 2.2, q. 64, art. 7).

Aquinas, I take it, is arguing not that the consequences of actions are morally irrelevant but, rather, that when one

raises questions about the morality of a particular action (as opposed to its utility, its beauty, and so on) one is inevitably making reference to the agent's intentions. "Accidental" is used here not exclusively to mean the unforeseen but to include the foreseen but undesired consequences of the action. "Accidental" may be understood as "collateral."

Following this line, we may summarize the principle in the following way: In a situation where the use of force can be seen to have actual or probable multiple effects, some of which are evil, culpability does not attach to the agent if the following conditions are met: (1) the action is intended to produce morally good consequences; (2) the evil effects are not intended as ends in themselves or as means to other ends, good or evil; and (3) the permission of collateral evil must be justified by considerations of proportionate moral weight.

How do these considerations apply to the combat situation? . . .

If force is ever to be morally justified, its employment must be against a target other than a person as such. One must not be directly seeking the death of another human being either as such or as a means to some further end. Therefore, the intention or purpose of the act of force must be toward *restraint* of the aggressor. This is the beginning of an answer to the pacifist. For he and the defender of *bellum justum* are surely in agreement, and correctly so, that the death of another human being ought never to be directly willed if the target is the man himself in his humanity or the man who represents the values of the enemy in a particular historical situation (this prohibition must imply the intrinsic value of other persons). Yet, if force may be justified, then what is the target? The answer must be that the proper target of the discriminate use of force is not the man himself but the combatant *in the* man.

It may be objected that it is a logical impossibility to separate out the totality of actions plus the underlying rationale for such behavior which together constitute the combatant in the man.... A soldier going into combat with the intention of restraining or incapacitating combatants must know before he ever lifts a weapon that combat will result in the death of a great many persons.

A utilitarian might put the objection in the following way: Jones and Smith both go into combat armed with machine guns. Jones, a supporter of the traditional view, carries with him the intention to incapacitate or restrain the aggressor, whereas Smith intends merely to kill as many of the enemy as he can in order to avoid being killed himself. On meeting the enemy they both open fire, and they both kill one enemy each. What difference does "intention" make from the moral point of view? In both cases an act of extreme violence, the unleashing of a stream of bullets, has resulted in the death of a person. A corpse lies before both Smith and Jones—this is the brute, ultimate fact which no amount of "intentional" redescription can alter. Thus, there is only *one* action here, the killing (possibly murder) of a human being.

In trying to answer this there are two things that have to be said about intention. The first has to do with the way in which awareness of an agent's intentions is crucial in understanding the meaning of an action and consequently in knowing how correctly to describe it. If one were to universalize the utilitarian's position on the irrelevance of intention, the results would be quite disastrous for any attempt to understand human action. Setting the moral question entirely aside, we would be unable to make intelligible whole classes of human behavior if we supposed that such behavior could even be described as human action without making intention central. That is, there are cases where two quite different actions are identical with respect to result, observable behavior, and foreknowledge of the result; and the *only* way to distinguish the two is by reference to intention. As an example, take the case of self-killing. If we follow the critic's suggestion and consider as relevant only foreknowledge of result, behavior patterns, and end result (a corpse), then suicide would be effectively defined as *any* action which the agent knew would bring about his own death. This is clearly absurd, for it would not permit us to distinguish between an officer who shoots himself in order to avoid a court-martial and an officer of the same regiment who courageously fights a rear-guard action in such a way that he knows he will not survive. In both cases there is foreknowledge of one's own death, there are objective behavior patterns leading to that result, and there is the result itself. They differ importantly only with respect to intention. Intention is what makes them different actions. To put the point in a general way, failure to take account of intention means that we are unable to make the difference between doing x in order that y shall result and doing x knowing that y will result.[1]

Smith and Jones both have foreknowledge of the impending death of the enemy, they both take identical action, and the result is the same—the enemy soldier is dead. And yet there are two different actions here: Jones does x knowing that y will result; Smith does x in order that y shall result....

The crucial difference between Smith and Jones is that the latter is logically committed to behaving differently toward those enemy soldiers who have removed themselves from the role of combatant than is his companion Smith. The belief that force must be directed against the combatant and not against the man is the only presupposition which could provide a moral basis for taking prisoners.... To those who argue that there is no relevant difference between killing in war and murder in the case of one combatant killing another, we may reply that it is possible, given a well-thought-out doctrine for the justification of the use of force, to direct forceful actions in such a way that while the death of the enemy may be foreknown it is not willed. The purpose of combats as expressed in the actions of individual soldiers is the incapacitation or restraint of an enemy combatant from doing what he is doing as a soldier in a particular historical situation; it is not the killing of a man. This is the essence of the distinction between killing in war and murder in the case of combatants, and the moral relevance of the premise is exhibited in the obligation to acknowledge prisoner immunity, an obligation not incumbent upon someone who fails to observe the central distinction between the man and the combatant in the man.[2] ...

So far we have been discussing double effect exclusively in connection with the killing of enemy combatants in an attempt to deal with the criticism that all killing in war is murder. We must now tackle the "other half" of that criticism, namely, that the killing of noncombatants in war is murder....

The problem of noncombatant immunity is frequently thought to center upon the difficulty of distinguishing a separate class of noncombatants, particularly in modern warfare. This is, I think, a large mistake, and it arises in part from an excessively literal reading of war solidarity propaganda. In fact, it is relatively easy to distinguish, in any historical war, whole classes of people who cannot, save in the inflamed world of the propagandist, be said to be combatants in any sense which would make them the object of attack.... Generally speaking, classes of people engaged in occupations which they would perform whether or not a war were taking place, or services rendered to combatants both in war and out, are considered immune. This would exempt, for example, farmers and teachers (since education and food are necessities in and out of war) but not merchant sailors transporting war materiel or railway drivers in charge of munitions trains. In other words, the soldiers who are now eating and studying would have to do these things even if they were not soldiers, so that classes of people supplying those sorts of goods and services may be said to be immune from attack, whereas those who are engaged in the production and supply of goods used only in war are not immune. And, of course, certain classes of people may be said to be permanently noncombatant—young children, the mentally defective, and those who are in various ways physically incapacitated. Again, some "hard" or limiting cases will arise, particularly in guerrilla war, but they are less numerous than is sometimes supposed.

The *real* difficulty is not in delineating classes of individuals who merit immunity but in deciding what constitutes a direct attack upon them, for it is plausible to suppose that the deaths of noncombatants can be excused only if their deaths can be construed as collateral or beside the intention of the perpetrators....

Traditional just-war theory distinguishes persons qua persons and persons qua combatants, and it makes this distinction central to its justification of the use of force. Specifically, the death of no *person* should be willed. This maxim constitutes a moral precondition for soldiers fighting in a justified war.... [The soldier's] target is the combatant in the person and not the person qua person.... War is a morally justified arbitrament of arms aimed at resolving by means of discriminate and proportional force an injustice which is incapable of resolution by other means....

[I]n targeting the combatant and not the person,... our concern is to incapacitate the combatant, not to kill or punish the person. Recalling the distinction between doing x that y may result and doing x knowing that y will result, the killing of the enemy soldier may be accepted if that is the only means to remove him from the role of combatant. This is the distinction between killing in war and murder....

[I]f mankind is to survive, we must undertake the difficult intellectual work of thinking about how to *restrain* war.... [W]ar is not going to go away,... [and] the way of salvation in this matter is to achieve a nexus of morality and prudence. *Bellum justum* does precisely that.

NOTES

1. This is a modification of an example in A. MacIntyre, "The Idea of a Social Science," in *Against the Self-Images of the Age* (London: Duckworth, 1971), pp. 211–29.

2. There are many excellent discussions of the problem of prisoner immunity. The best is in M. Ramsey, *The Just War.*

NO

Robert L. Holmes

ON WAR AND MORALITY

My contention is that war in the modern world is not morally justified. I say "in the modern world" because my aim is not to try to assess wars that have been fought throughout past history, much less those that might be conceived in the imaginations of philosophers or writers of science fiction. The consideration of some of those is useful for purposes of illustration or the clarification of the finer points of theoretical analysis. But they are not the wars of vital concern to people. The wars that engage our moral sensibilities are those which nations are prepared to wage today, for whose preparation they gear their economies, and into whose waging they pour their wealth, their hopes, and their youth.

The argument is not that wars under all conceivable conditions are morally impermissible, an absolutist position that properly understood, is neither particularly interesting nor defensible. My position differs little in principle from that of the ordinary person. He does not believe that all wars under all conceivable circumstances are justified, but only that war under certain conditions is justified. The difference between his position and mine concerns what the conditions are. He believes that war is justified in circumstances calling for national defense, or to assist in the defense of other nations, and the like, whereas I maintain that the conditions that might theoretically justify war simply are not met in the actual world, hence that war is impermissible in the world as we know it....

When people talk about the morality of war, it is usually to proclaim that we all "know" that war is wrong. However, they usually continue with a "But..." and proceed to say that although we all hate war, nonetheless some wars are necessary to avoid greater evils. And in any event, there have always been wars and always will be, and you cannot change that unless you change human nature.

This combination of views—that war is immoral but nonetheless necessary—effectively removes the need to question the morality of war. Its wrongness has already been conceded in a way that allows for the continuation of war and even for a belief in its inevitability.

Those who take this line do not mean that war is wrong in the sense I mean it, however. What they mean is that war is bad, or unfortunate, or tragic, not that it is morally impermissible. And these are different modes of assessment. Plagues, pestilence, floods, and droughts are bad, but they are not immoral. The reason they are not is because they are not the acts of rational beings. Certain of them can be caused by the actions of such beings. But even then it is the act of bringing them about that is immoral, not the phenomenon itself. Everyone but the most fervent glorifier of war agrees that war is bad. That is not the issue. What is at issue is whether it is wrong. What I mean by saying that war is wrong is not only that it is bad but that it ought not to be waged, that governments ought not to declare and fight wars, societies ought not to provide them with the means by which to do so, and individuals ought not to sanction, support, and participate in wars....

* * *

My concern... is with the just war doctrine in the Western tradition, where it has been heavily influenced by Christianity, and in particular with some of its more recent formulations. I shall not present a history of the evolution of the tradition; that has been done by others and would be beside the point of our present concerns. My aim, rather, is to examine those aspects of the tradition that bear most directly upon my central argument concerning the morality of war and to assess the just war theory as an approach to the morality of war.

Two principal objections have been brought against the just war approach to war, neither of which, in my judgment, is successful, but one of which helps to focus a third objection that I think is decisive.

The first concerns alleged consequences of the prevalence of just war theorizing in certain historical periods. It is sometimes said that the most terrible wars in history occurred during the ascendancy of the just war theory and that the longest periods of relative tranquillity occurred when the theory was in eclipse....

But as tempting as it may be to dismiss the just war approach on these grounds, claims of the preceding sort are difficult to substantiate....

The second objection bears upon the changing character of war in the nuclear age. It holds that the nuclear age, with the threat of annihilation in the case of an all-out war between the superpowers, has rendered the just war theory obsolete. Michael Walzer, for example, speaks of the "monstrous immorality that our policy contemplates, an immorality we can never hope to square with our understanding of justice in war," adding that "nuclear weapons explode the theory of just war."[1] Various just war theorists, including James Turner Johnson, William V. O'Brien, and Robert L. Phillips,[2] defend the theory and argue that it is relevant to the contemporary age and, indeed, represents the only defensible way of thinking about the problem of morality and war....

* * *

Most modern theorists... devote little attention to the question of *whether* war is justified; they assume that it is and ask only under what conditions it is justified and how it is to be conducted justly. Their actual prescriptions, in fact, differ little from those of political realists, and apart from the underlying rationales they provide for them it would be difficult to tell them apart. If anything, the just war theorists may be more hardline than political realists, which suggests that adopting a moral perspective does not per se make it less likely that one will be militaristic. They tend to be strongly anticommunist, particularly anti-Soviet, to be pro-nuclear deterrence, and to feel that one is sometimes justified in initiating a war. All of them agree, however, that *jus in bello* requires that the conduct of war be limited....

If now we return to the second of the objections... concerning the relevance of the just war approach to the nuclear age, we may observe that [just war theorists] may ... be correct in saying in response to that objection that a limited use of nuclear weapons would not necessarily escalate into an all-out war. No one can know for certain. If *that* is what is meant by saying that the just war theory is relevant to the nuclear age, the point can be granted and the second objection considered met.

But there is another reply to the objection that is more telling. It is that even if [just war theorists] should be wrong about the possibility of keeping a limited nuclear war limited, all that would follow is that by just war criteria themselves an all-out war would be unjust. The fact that a certain type of war turns out to be unjust does not show that the just war theory is inapplicable to it; it shows only that it yields a certain outcome when applied to that type of war.[3] So if the question is whether the nuclear age has rendered the just war theory obsolete in the sense of showing that its criteria are no longer appropriate for the assessment of war, the answer is that it has not. Whether some, or all, or no nuclear wars turn out to be just by just war criteria is immaterial. That those assessments can be made shows the relevance of the theory to nuclear war in the sense its advocates intend.

The preceding discussion suggests a third and more serious objection to the just war doctrine.... [T]here are serious problems in reconciling the claims of *jus ad bellum* with those of *jus in bello* with regard to whether a just cause sometimes warrants, or at least excuses, violations of moral constraints in the conduct of war. A more fundamental question is whether even a war that is just according to both *jus ad bellum* and *jus in bello* criteria will still unavoidably involve the violation of moral constraints; whether, that is, there is something in the very nature of war that renders it wrong and that is not dealt with directly by the just war theory. The just war theory says that if certain conditions are met, it is permissible to go to war; and it says further that if certain other conditions are met, one's manner of conducting the war is moral. What it does not do is to ask whether there are things that one unavoidably does even when *all* of these conditions are met which cannot be justified morally. If there are, then the just war theory is defective in a far more serious way than suggested by either of the first two objections.

I believe that there are.... But the issue is complex and requires an examination of the relationship between *jus ad bellum* and *jus in bello*.

* * *

A war ... is justified if it is characterized by *jus ad bellum*: if, that is, the conditions constituting justice in the resort to war are met. These include but are not limited to a just cause. Traditionally ... one had to have legitimate authority and a right intention as well, with various other requirements often added, such as that the war be a last resort, have a likelihood of success, that the use of force be restrained, and that there be proportionality in the resultant good and evil.

A justified war, however, is not necessarily a just war. To be fully just a war must be characterized by both *jus ad bellum* and *jus in bello*. A war obviously cannot be just if one is unjustified in entering upon it in the first place, but neither can it be just, however just the cause and right the intention, if it utilizes indefensible means.[4] ...

Notice that I am concerned here with what is morally justified in the conduct of war, not with what is legally justified. There exist certain rules, known as the laws of war, generally accepted as governing the conduct of warfare on all sides.... This, however, is not my concern at the moment. My concern is with what is morally justified in warfare, whether or not it coincides with what is legally permissible....

Let us call the principle that one may do whatever is necessary to prosecute a just war a principle of just necessity....

According to this view,... whatever justifies resorting to war in the first place justifies the means necessary to winning it (or achieving one's objectives, if they fall short of victory). There are no independent moral constraints upon the conduct of war. This represents what may be called an internalist view of the relationship between *jus ad bellum* and *jus in bello*, in the sense that the standards for judging *jus in bello* are already, as it were, contained in the standards for judging *jus ad bellum*.

Distinguished from this, however, is an externalist view, which holds that there are independent standards for judging *jus in bello*—independent, that is, of *jus ad bellum*. Whatever the justice of one's resort to war, there are in this view limits to what one may do in conducting it.

The most prominent of these concerns the treatment of innocent persons, with writers like Ramsey, Phillips, and Anscombe maintaining that there is an absolute prohibition against the intentional killing of such persons.[5] ...

To justify the pursuit of victory in war requires showing that the necessary means to that end are justified. The permissibility of going to war provides no assurance they will be. One may not even know fully what those means are until the war has progressed, perhaps nearly to its conclusion. Yet, according to the usual thinking in just war theory, one may know in advance of going to war whether or not he is justified in so doing. If that is true, then the standards for *jus ad bellum* cannot by themselves, determine the standards for *jus in bello*.

This means that the internalist position, and with it the principle of just necessity, must be rejected. It is not the end that justifies the means but the means (among other things) that justify the end.[6]

This has even more far-reaching implications. Both the internalist and the externalist assume that war may be just; they differ only over the criteria for *jus in bello*. But if the impermissibility of the means necessary to win a war means that one may not justly pursue victory in that war, then the impermissibility of the acts necessary to the very *waging* of war mean that one may not justly wage war, whatever one's objectives. Waging war requires justifying the means of so doing as much as winning a war requires justifying the means to that end.[7]

To justify going to war, then, that is, to establish *jus ad bellum* in the first place, requires showing that what one would be doing by waging it is justified. If a war is justified, then the necessary means to waging it will indeed *be* justified—but not because they are legitimated by the justice of the war assessed independently of those means. They will be justified because to be justified in going to war requires establishing antecedently that those means are permissible. Again, it is not the end that justifies the means but the permissibility of the means (including the killing and destroying that are part of the nature of warfare) that, along with satisfaction of the other requirements of *jus ad bellum*, justifies the end.

The point is that killing and destruction are inherent in warfare, and unless they can be justified, war cannot be justified. It will by its very nature be wrong....

The relevant question... is whether all of what one does in the course of fighting a war can be morally justified (by which I mean, all of what one does that is associated with the nature of war; obviously one can do many gratuitously barbarous things that are unessential to the aims of war and that are morally prohibited).... [I]n addition to justifying the *means* of conducting war as part of justifying the resort to war, one must also justify those acts which are *constitutive* of the waging of war by whatever means. War by its nature is organized violence, the deliberate, systematic causing of death and destruction. This is true whether the means employed are nuclear bombs or bows and arrows. Often it is the doing of psychological violence as well. And... it is presumptively wrong to do violence to persons in these ways. So given that one can know to a virtual certainty that he commits himself to doing these things in going to war, fully to justify going to war requires justifying these acts as well. A necessary condition of the justifiable pursuit of *any objectives* in war, by *any means* whatever (hence a necessary condition of

the satisfaction of the criteria of both *jus ad bellum* and *jus in bello*), is that one be justified in engaging in such killing and violence in the first place....

[T]his means that most attempts to justify war from the early just war theorists to the present day are inadequate. For they do not meet this necessary condition....

Most just war theorists proceed... as though they assume that one can justify the resort to war independently of, and antecedently to, justifying both the necessary means of conducting it and the acts constitutive of waging it....

[A]ttention in *jus ad bellum* must be shifted away from the almost exclusive concern with the offenses and ancillary conditions commonly thought to justify war to a consideration of the precise nature of what one is doing in the waging of it; not, as in traditional accounts of *jus in bello*, starting from the assumption that war is justified and needs only to be waged humanely, but rather starting with an open mind about whether it is ever justified in the first place. *Unless one can justify the actions necessary to waging war, he cannot justify the conduct of war and the pursuit of its objectives; and if he cannot do this, he cannot justify going to war....*

* * *

If the means necessary to waging war cannot be justified, then war cannot be justified and no war can be just. Not only must there be moral constraints upon the *conduct* of war even if the war is in all other particulars justified; the possibility must be recognized that there are moral constraints upon the treatment of persons that prohibit the *waging* of war in the first place, that is, even engaging in the limited killing and destruction that otherwise just wars entail....

My concern [here] shall be with the killing of innocent persons. Nothing is more central to the moral assessment of war, and this issue is at the heart of the question whether the waging of war can be justified, whatever other limitations are imposed upon its conduct.... [T]here is no stronger moral presumption than that against the doing of violence to innocent persons. And knowingly killing them against their will is to do violence to them. This does not ... of itself mean that such killing is never justified; whether that is so is beyond my present concerns. But it does mean that the burden is upon those who would kill innocent persons to justify so doing, not upon those who believe it wrong to show that it is wrong....

* * *

Whether war, or at least modern war, which shall be our concern henceforth, inevitably entails the killing of innocent persons cannot be answered independently of a consideration of what constitutes innocence. Here one encounters disagreement. Some argue that virtually everyone in wars between states is noninnocent, others that nearly everyone in such wars is innocent. The most common strategy is to substitute the categories of noncombatancy and combatancy for innocence and noninnocence and to ignore the problems associated with the killing of innocents.[8] But I shall maintain that this will not do....

Modern warfare ... will inevitably kill innocent persons, most likely even on the side that acts unjustly in the initiation of the war. Not only the character of modern weaponry but also the principles on which most nations conduct war make this clear....

Given the presumption that killing innocent persons is wrong, the fact that war inevitably kills such persons means, in light of our argument that war can be neither just nor justified if the means necessary to waging it are not justified, that modern war is presumptively wrong....

* * *

Can the presumption of the wrongness of war be undercut by defeating the presumption that killing innocent persons in wartime is wrong? Most attempts to justify such killing maintain either that there are clear cases in which it is permissible or that there are circumstances, however ambiguous, in which overriding considerations allow it....

[Some just war theorists argue as follows.] Acts may sometimes have both good effects and bad, and what it important from a moral standpoint is to intend only the good. This by itself is usually not thought sufficient to make an act right, and other conditions are commonly incorporated into the notion of double effect, such as that the act itself be good or at least indifferent, the bad effect not be a means to the production of the good, and the good of the good effect be proportionate to the bad, in the sense of being greater than it or at least not less....

Writing in this tradition, Elizabeth Anscombe brings out the importance of this distinction for Christian ethics:

The distinction between the intended, and the merely foreseen, effects of a voluntary action is indeed absolutely essential to Christian ethics. For Christianity forbids a number of things as being bad in themselves. But if I am answerable for the foreseen consequences of an action or refusal, as much as for the action itself, then these prohibitions will break down. If someone innocent will die unless I do a wicked thing, then on this view I am his murderer in refusing: so all that is left to me is to weigh up evils. Here the theologian steps in with the principle of double effect and says: "No, you are no murderer, if the man's death was neither your aim nor your chosen means, and if you had to act in the way that led to it or else do something absolutely forbidden." Without understanding of this principle, anything can be—and is wont to be—justified, and the Christian teaching that in no circumstances may one commit murder, adultery, apostasy... goes by the board. These absolute prohibitions of Christianity by no means exhaust its ethic;... But the prohibitions are bedrock, and without them the Christian ethic goes to pieces. Hence the necessity of the notion of double effect.[9]

The point usually extracted from such reasoning, though Anscombe does not do so in this passage, is that one can prohibit the killing of innocent persons, even prohibit it *absolutely*, and yet proceed to kill such persons provided in so doing their deaths are merely foreseen and not intended....

Technically this is an externalist position. It does impose a restriction upon what one may do in the conduct of war. But in effect it is internalist, since it enables one to wage war in ways indistinguishable from those sanctioned by just necessity, which legitimizes all means necessary to the prosecution of a justified war.... [D]ouble effect legitimizes every action legitimized by just necessity, provided only that one not intend the harm that he does. In fact no action whatsoever is prohibited by the principle of double effect so long as one acts from a good intention....

[T]he principle of double effect... lends itself to the justification of virtually any action its user wants. On the assumption that we can "direct" or "aim" intentions as we please, any action whatever can be performed with a good intention or, at any rate, can be described as being performed with a good intention.... This is as true of pillage, rape, and torture as of killing. One suspects that defenders of the principle find that it invariably justifies just those actions they are antecedently disposed to believe are right....

If this is correct, then the particular externalist position we have been examining fails. If one prohibits the killing of innocents, he cannot then invoke good intentions to justify proceeding to kill them....

* * *

The killing of innocents by an aggressor is no worse *as such* than the killing of innocents by those who would oppose him by waging war. Human beings have as much right to be spared destruction by good people as by bad. If an aggressor poses a threat to innocent persons it is presumably because killing them will be a means to achieving certain ends, or because killing them is at least a byproduct of adopting those means. If I choose to kill innocent persons in order to prevent the deaths of others at the hands of an aggressor, I, no less than and perhaps even more than he (if his killing of innocents is only incidental to his attaining his ends) am using innocent persons as a means to an end. If this is correct, the presumption against killing innocents is not defeated by this reasoning.

* * *

Let me draw together our main conclusions at this point. I have argued that doing violence to persons is presumptively wrong, and that war by its nature does such violence. Because realist attempts to insulate war either wholly or partially from moral consideration do not succeed, this fact must be at the center of the assessment of war. It means, if I am correct, that attention needs to be focussed away from the standard conditions dealt with in the just war tradition and upon the nature of what one is doing in the very *waging* of war, however just one's cause and however carefully one otherwise abides by the standard rules for its conduct. This reveals, I maintain, that modern war inevitably kills innocent persons. And this, I contend, makes modern war presumptively wrong. What I consider the strongest arguments to defeat that presumption, by way of trying to defeat the presumption against the killing of innocent persons, also do not succeed. If that is the case, then war has not be shown to be justified, and if it has not been shown to be justified, then it is unjustified. This does not of itself mean that modern war *could* not be justified; to show that something has not been justified and that the main attempts to justify it are inadequate can never logically foreclose the possibility that a justification might someday be forthcoming. But that justification must be produced. And unless or until it is produced, war should cease to be in our repertoire of responses to world problems.

NOTES

1. *Just and Unjust Wars* (New York: Basic Books, 1977), p. 282.
2. See James Turner Johnson, *Can Modern War Be Just?* (New Haven, Conn.: Yale University Press, 1984); William V. O'Brien, *The Conduct of a Just and Limited War* (New York: Praeger, 1981); William V. O'Brien and John Langan, eds., *The Nuclear Dilemma and the Just War Tradition* (Lexington, Mass.: Lexington Books, 1986); and Robert L. Phillips, *War and Justice* (Norman: University of Oklahoma Press, 1984).
3. This point is well made by Phillips in *War and Justice*, p. xi.
4. On the issue of the relationship between *jus ad bellum* and *jus in bello*, see Melzer, *Concepts of Just War*, esp. chap. 2.
5. See Anscombe, "War and Murder," in Wasserstrom ed., *War and Morality*, pp. 42–53; Phillips, *War and Justice*, chap. 2; and Ramsey, *The Just War*, especially chap. 7.
6. One is justified in performing an act only if he is justified both in employing the means necessary to its performance and in performing any subsidiary acts constitutive of it. I cannot be justified in watering my garden unless I am justified in attaching the hose and turning on the water; or in mowing my lawn unless I am justified in cutting the grass. The justification of the act is not one thing and the justification of the means another. What one justifies in the first place *are* those means; to justify the act *is* to justify the means (and/or the constitutive acts). This is the truth in the saying that the end does not justify the means....
7. I am, for the sake of simplicity, speaking here as though what one must do in order to wage war constitutes the means to waging war. In actuality, those acts are constitutive of waging war. There are two related but distinguishable relationships here. One is that of means to end. It figures in the argument to show that the internalist position is incorrect. It involves showing that the means to victory in war must be justified in their own right; their permissibility does not follow automatically from the fact that the resort to war may be justified. The other is that of constituent to whole; it is central to the present argument regarding the justification of the resort to war, which involves pointing out that to be justified in resorting to war one must be justified in doing all those things that make up the waging of war.
8. Robert L. Phillips argues in his discussion of the just war that "I have refrained from making any reference to 'the innocent,' despite the fact that most of the current debate on the morality of war has been about treatment of innocent parties. This seems to me to represent a major confusion which has quite unnecessarily complicated the issue." See *War and Justice* (Norman: University of Oklahoma Press, 1984), p. 56. His reasons consist principally of the claim that "[it] is *combatants* who are the objects of attack in war, and, therefore, moral distinctions will center upon that notion rather than innocence. This is necessarily the case, since war is a contest of strength, an arbitrament of arms carried out under the direction of moral and political aims" (p. 58). It is unclear, however, why this particular characterization of war, even if it should be accepted as something approximating a definition, entails or even implies that noncombatancy is of sole moral importance. In wartime, innocent people are knowingly

and often deliberately killed. That fact establishes the relevance of innocence to the assessment of war. If... to kill innocent persons is to do violence to them, and to do violence is presumptively wrong, then that suffices to establish that killing innocent persons in wartime is presumptively wrong. And as it is with what is right and wrong in war that morality is concerned, such killing cannot fail to be of the first importance. Phillips contends that to focus upon innocence is to fail to distinguish between the whole person, to whom the notions of guilt and innocence are appropriate (p. 61), and the *role or function* of the person as combatant, to which they are not. But I hope to show that we can both recognize that distinction and see that the notion of innocence applies in each case.

9. "War and Murder," in Wasserstrom, ed., *War and Morality*, pp. 50–51.

POSTSCRIPT

Can Modern War Be Just?

The politics of war are changing because of evolving social norms regarding the horror of modern war and the related growth of international security arrangements. Today, the UN Charter, which all member countries have agreed to abide by, specifies that there are only two circumstances in which a country can legitimately use force: (1) in self-defense and (2) as part of peacekeeping or collective security operations under the auspices of the UN or a regional organization, such as the Organization of African Unity. The war crimes trials that prosecuted and, in some cases, resulted in the execution of German and Japanese war criminals after World War II established the precedent that aggressive war (violating *jus ad bellum*) and certain practices in war (violating *jus in bello*) were punishable under international law. There is currently an effort underway in the United Nations to bring war criminals in the Balkans to justice; a move to apprehend and try President Saddam Hussein of Iraq is also advocated by some. Still, issues of culture are troubling, since both just war theory and the structure and principles of the UN are largely the creation of Western thought and power. On one aspect of cultural differences on just war theory, read James T. Johnson and John Kelsay, eds., *Cross, Crescent, and Sword: The Justification and Limitation of War in Western and Islamic Tradition* (Greenwood Press, 1990).

Accusations of unjust war have also been leveled against Americans. Both the UN and the Organization of American States condemned the 1989 U.S. invasion of Panama (*jus ad bellum*). And the human rights monitoring group Americas Watch accused the United States of violating the Geneva Convention on warfare by violating the "ever-present duty to minimize harm to the civilian population" (*jus in bello*). The 1991 war in the Persian Gulf again brought criticism of the morality of the United States and coalition countries. This point of view is argued by Bernard D. Headley, "The 'New World Order' and the Persian Gulf War," *Humanity and Society* (Fall 1991). Some of the battle tactics, ranging from attacks on targets amid civilian concentrations to using bulldozers to bury entrenched (and resisting) Iraqi soldiers alive, also drew criticism.

For more reading on this intricate, critical issue, read Sheldon Cohen, *Arms and Judgment: Law, Morality and the Conduct of War in the Twentieth Century* (Westview Press, 1989) and Douglas P. Lackey, *The Ethics of War and Peace* (Prentice Hall, 1989).

CONTRIBUTORS
TO THIS VOLUME

EDITOR

JOHN T. ROURKE, Ph.D., is a professor of political science at the University of Connecticut. He has written numerous articles and papers, and he is the author of *Congress and the Presidency in U.S. Foreign Policymaking* (Westview, 1985); *The United States, the Soviet Union, and China: Comparative Foreign Policymaking and Implementation* (Brooks/Cole, 1989); and *International Politics on the World Stage*, 4th ed. (The Dushkin Publishing Group, 1991). He enjoys teaching introductory classes, and he does so each semester at the university's Storrs and Hartford campuses. Professor Rourke is involved in the university's internship program, advises one of its political clubs, has served as a staff member of Connecticut's legislature, and has been involved in political campaigns on the local, state, and national levels.

STAFF

Marguerite L. Egan   Program Manager
Brenda S. Filley   Production Manager
Whit Vye   Designer
Libra Ann Cusack   Typesetting Supervisor
Juliana Arbo   Typesetter
David Brackley   Copy Editor
David Dean   Administrative Editor
Diane Barker   Editorial Assistant
Shawn Callahan   Graphics
Richard Tietjen   Systems Manager

AUTHORS

ELLIOTT ABRAMS is a senior fellow of the Hudson Institute in Indianapolis, Indiana. He has held several positions in the U.S. government, including assistant secretary of state for inter-American affairs, assistant secretary of state for international organization affairs, and assistant secretary of state for human rights and humanitarian affairs.

PETER BAUER is a professor emeritus of economics and a fellow of Gonville and Caius College in Cambridge, England. His publications, whose controversial views on foreign aid are now becoming more widely accepted, include *Equality, the Third World and Economic Delusion* (Harvard University Press, 1983).

NINA BELYAEVA is the president of the Moscow-based Interlegal Research Institute and an adjunct fellow of the Center for Strategic and International Studies in Washington, D.C.

JACK R. BINNS is the vice president for TWI Trading Company, Inc., in Tucson, Arizona. He has also been a U.S. ambassador to Honduras and a political counselor to London and Costa Rica.

ROBERT BORK is the John M. Olin Scholar in Legal Studies at the American Enterprise Institute in Washington, D.C., and a former U.S. Court of Appeals judge for the District of Columbia Circuit.

BOUTROS BOUTROS-GHALI, a former foreign minister of Egypt, is the secretary general of the United Nations. He holds the distinction of being the first Arab and the first African to serve as secretary general of the United Nations.

He has also been a professor at Cairo University and a president of the Center of Political and Strategic Studies.

THEA BROWDER is a Washington, D.C.–based writer who has researched and written on a wide range of environmental topics for the Investor Responsibility Research Center.

ANGELO M. CODEVILLA, a former senior staff member of the U.S. Senate Select Committee on Intelligence, is a fellow of the Stanford University Hoover Institution on War, Revolution, and Peace in Stanford, California. He is the author of *While Others Build: The Common Sense Approach to the Strategic Defense Initiative* (Free Press, 1988).

HERMAN J. COHEN is the assistant secretary of state for African affairs.

RICHARD FALK is the Albert G. Milbank Professor of International Law and Practice in the Woodrow Wilson School of Public and International Affairs at Princeton University in Princeton, New Jersey. He is the author or editor of many books, including *Explorations at the Edge of Time: Prospects for World Order* (Temple University Press, 1992).

SHELDON FRIEDMAN is an economist in the Department of Economic Research of the AFL-CIO.

JEFFREY R. GERLACH is a foreign policy analyst at the Cato Institute in Washington, D.C.

WALTER GOLDSTEIN is a professor of international relations in Rockefeller College at State University of New York at Albany. He writes regularly for *Le Figaro* of Paris.

LEON T. HADAR is a professor in the School of International Service at American University in Washington, D.C., and an adjunct scholar in foreign policy studies at the Cato Institute, also in Washington, D.C.

WILLIAM D. HARTUNG is a senior research fellow of the World Policy Institute at the New School for Social Research in New York City. He is the author of *And Weapons for All: Arms Sales in U.S. Foreign Policy* (HarperCollins, 1994).

IVAN L. HEAD, who was a foreign policy adviser to the former prime minister of Canada Pierre Elliott Trudeau, is the president of the International Development Research Center in Canada.

ROBERT L. HOLMES is a professor of philosophy at the University of Rochester. He has published books and articles on ethics, war, and nonviolence.

DAVID HOROWITZ is a journalist and a coeditor of *Heterodoxy* magazine. He is the coauthor, with Peter Collier, of *Destructive Generation: Second Thoughts About the Sixties* (Summit Books, 1989).

RHODA E. HOWARD is a professor of sociology at McMaster University in Hamilton, Ontario, Canada.

SAMUEL S. KIM is a senior research scholar in the East Asian Institute at Columbia University in New York City. He has taught in the Woodrow Wilson School of Public and International Affairs at Princeton University, and he is the coauthor of *China's Quest for National Identity* (Cornell University Press, 1993), with Lowell Dittmer.

VINAY LAL is the William R. Kenan Fellow in the Society of Fellows in the Humanities at Columbia University in New York City.

WALTER LAQUEUR is the chairperson of the International Research Council at the Center for Strategic and International Studies in Washington, D.C.

JOHN F. McDONNELL is the chairperson and chief executive officer of McDonnell Douglas Corporation in St. Louis, Missouri.

JUDITH MILLER is a fellow of the Twentieth Century Fund in New York City and a writer for the *New York Times*.

PHILIP MORRISON is a professor at the Massachusetts Institute of Technology in Cambridge, Massachusetts. He was a physicist on the Manhattan Project, the United States' development effort to create an atomic bomb during World War II.

ROBERT L. PHILLIPS is a professor of philosophy and the director of the War and Ethics Program at the University of Connecticut in Hartford, Connecticut.

DIANE D. PIKCUNAS is a student of Asian affairs who serves as adjunct professor of education at the National Louis University in Lombard, Illinois. She is a coauthor, with Donald J. Senese, of *Can the Two Chinas Become One?* (Council for Social and Economic Studies, 1989).

JOHN PILGER is a British journalist and a frequent contributor to *New Statesman* magazine.

COLIN L. POWELL recently retired from his position as chairman of the Joint

Chiefs of Staff for the U.S. Department of Defense.

JAIME JOSE SERRA PUCHE is the secretary of commerce and industrial promotion for Mexico.

NAFIS SADIK is the executive director of the United Nations Population Fund (UNFPA) in New York City, which funds planning and population control projects in more than 120 countries.

JAMES M. SHEEHAN is a research associate at the Competitive Enterprise Institute in Washington, D.C.

GEORGE SHULTZ is a professor of economics at Stanford University in Stanford, California. He has held various positions in the U.S. government, including secretary of labor (1969–1970) and secretary of state (1982–1988).

JULIAN L. SIMON is a professor of economics and business administration at the University of Maryland at College Park. His publications include *Population Matters: People, Resources, Environment, and Immigration* (Transaction Publishers, 1990).

KOJI TAIRA is a professor of economics and industrial relations at the University of Illinois, Urbana-Champaign. He has served in the secretariat office of the International Labor Organization in Geneva, Switzerland, and his publications include *Economic Development and the Labor Market in Japan* (Studies of the East Asian Institute, 1970).

ALAN TONELSON is the research director of the Economic Strategy Institute in Washington, D.C. His essays on American politics and foreign policy have appeared in numerous publications, including *Foreign Policy* and the *Harvard Business Review*, and he is a coauthor of *Powernomics: Economics and Strategy After the Cold War* (Madison Books, 1991).

KOSTA TSIPIS is the director of the Program in Science and Technology for International Security at the Massachusetts Institute of Technology in Cambridge, Massachusetts. He is also a member of the board of directors for *The Bulletin of the Atomic Scientists*.

ROBERT W. TUCKER is a contributing editor to *The National Interest*.

SUE TUNNICLIFFE is a research associate for the Division of International Relations and Politics in the School of Social Sciences at Staffordshire University in Stoke-on-Trent, England.

CYRUS R. VANCE is a lawyer and a partner in the law firm of Thacher and Bartlett in New York City. He was the secretary of state under President Carter from 1977 to 1980.

JEROME B. WIESNER is a professor at the Massachusetts Institute of Technology in Cambridge, Massachusetts. He was a science advisor to Presidents Eisenhower, Kennedy, and Johnson, and he helped establish the Arms Control and Disarmament Agency.

ZHAO XIAOWEI is a prominent member of the Democratic Liberal Party, a Chinese mainland party in exile. He has written widely for Chinese publications.

INDEX